Computer Forensics

OTHER INFORMATION SECURITY BOOKS FROM AUERBACH

802.1X Port-Based Authentication
Edwin Lyle Brown
ISBN: 1-4200-4464-8

Audit and Trace Log Management:
Consolidation and Analysis
Phillip Q. Maier
ISBN: 0-8493-2725-3

The CISO Handbook: A Practical Guide to
Securing Your Company
Michael Gentile, Ron Collette and Tom August
ISBN: 0-8493-1952-8

Complete Guide to CISM Certification
Thomas R. Peltier and Justin Peltier
ISBN: 0-849-35356-4

Complete Guide to Security and Privacy
Metrics: Measuring Regulatory Compliance,
Operational Resilience, and ROI
Debra S. Herrmann
ISBN: 0-8493-5402-1

Computer Forensics: Evidence Collection
and Management
Robert C. Newman
ISBN: 0-8493-0561-6

Curing the Patch Management Headache
Felicia M. Nicastro
ISBN: 0-8493-2854-3

Cyber Crime Investigator's Field Guide,
Second Edition
Bruce Middleton
ISBN: 0-8493-2768-7

Database and Applications Security: Integrating
Information Security and Data Management
Bhavani Thuraisingham
ISBN: 0-8493-2224-3

Guide to Optimal Operational Risk and BASEL II
Ioannis S. Akkizidis and Vivianne Bouchereau
ISBN: 0-8493-3813-1

Information Security: Design, Implementation,
Measurement, and Compliance
Timothy P. Layton
ISBN: 0-8493-7087-6

Information Security Architecture: An Integrated
Approach to Security in the Organization,
Second Edition
Jan Killmeyer
ISBN: 0-8493-1549-2

Information Security Cost Management
Ioana V. Bazavan and Ian Lim
ISBN: 0-8493-9275-6

Information Security Fundamentals
Thomas R. Peltier, Justin Peltier and John A. Blackley
ISBN: 0-8493-1957-9

Information Security Management Handbook,
Sixth Edition
Harold F. Tipton and Micki Krause
ISBN: 0-8493-7495-2

Information Security Risk Analysis,
Second Edition
Thomas R. Peltier
ISBN: 0-8493-3346-6

Intelligence Support Systems: Technologies
for Lawful Intercepts
Paul Hoffmann and Kornel Terplan
ISBN: 0-8493-285-51

Investigations in the Workplace
Eugene F. Ferraro
ISBN: 0-8493-1648-0

Managing an Information Security and Privacy
Awareness and Training Program
Rebecca Herold
ISBN: 0-8493-2963-9

Network Security Technologies,
Second Edition
Kwok T. Fung
ISBN: 0-8493-3027-0

A Practical Guide to Security Assessments
Sudhanshu Kairab
ISBN: 0-8493-1706-1

Practical Hacking Techniques and
Countermeasures
Mark D. Spivey
ISBN: 0-8493-7057-4

Securing Converged IP Networks
Tyson Macaulay
ISBN: 0-8493-7580-0

Security Governance Guidebook with Security
Program Metrics on CD-ROM
Fred Cohen
ISBN: 0-8493-8435-4

The Security Risk Assessment Handbook:
A Complete Guide for Performing Security
Risk Assessments
Douglas J. Landoll
ISBN: 0-8493-2998-1

Wireless Crime and Forensic Investigation
Gregory Kipper
ISBN: 0-8493-3188-9

Computer Forensics

Evidence Collection and Management

Robert C. Newman

CRC Press
Taylor & Francis Group
Boca Raton London New York

CRC Press is an imprint of the
Taylor & Francis Group, an **informa** business
AN AUERBACH BOOK

CRC Press
Taylor & Francis Group
6000 Broken Sound Parkway NW, Suite 300
Boca Raton, FL 33487-2742

First issued in paperback 2019

ISBN-13: 978-0-8493-0561-0 (hbk)
ISBN-13: 978-0-367-38937-6 (pbk)

Library of Congress Cataloging-in-Publication Data

Newman, Robert C.
    Computer forensics : evidence, collection, and management / Robert C. Newman. -- 1st ed.
        p. cm.
    Includes bibliographical references and index.
    ISBN-13: 978-0-8493-0561-0 (alk. paper)
    ISBN-10: 0-8493-0561-6 (alk. paper)
    1. Evidence, Expert--United States. 2. Computer crimes--Investigation--United States. I. Title.

KF8961.N49 2007
345.73'0268--dc22   2006031576

Visit the Taylor & Francis Web site at
http://www.taylorandfrancis.com

and the CRC Press Web site at
http://www.crcpress.com

Preface

Why Is This Book Important?

Every day a new revelation concerning some Internet or cyber-crime is splashed across the television screen. Someone has compromised a corporation's database, threatening the security of the population's financial resources. Some corporate official has "cooked the books," causing employees and investors to lose millions of dollars. Someone has hacked into a computer system and stolen information that can be used in identity theft schemes. Millions of dollars are at stake—those of citizens, the government, and corporations.

On a larger scale, numerous scam and fraud schemes are being directed toward the public, specifically Internet users. A serious issue involves identity theft and identity fraud. Internet criminals are using personal information to steal personal assets from savings and checking accounts. These criminals are using phishing techniques to trick Web users into providing social security numbers, birth dates, and other information that is then used to commit some cyber-crime. Techniques called "dumpster diving," "phishing," and "shoulder surfing" are used to learn confidential personal information.

Numerous crimes are committed using the Internet, computers, and electronic devices. Of particular interest are those crimes relating to child predators and child pornography. Serious crimes such as murder, rape, kidnapping, stalking, drug trafficking, and numerous other felonies are committed using electronic devices. Criminals and cyber-terrorists are using these electronic resources as a tool. Everyone is aware of the use of computing devices and cell phones by terrorist cells to commit mayhem.

The current computer and networking market has been growing at an unbelievable rate and security preparedness has not kept pace with this growth. This is due in large part to the expansion of Internet access to almost all sectors of society. Everyone who has a computer can now have access to the Web. Nowadays, children are introduced to the Web at an early age at school and at home. Numerous electronic devices such as personal digital assistants (PDAs) and portable computers are saturating the network. The opportunity for expansion of services for the entire population is astronomical. This book is part of a program that is designed to provide a broad working knowledge of the security issues that permeate today's computer and network systems, and the forensic evidence that can be retrieved from these devices. It has been designed to provide corporate security personnel, educational organizations, government agencies, and members of law enforcement with a general understanding and working knowledge of the computer and electronic forensic environment.

This book is geared toward computer users in the business, government, and education communities, with the expectation that they can learn the basics of computer forensics. It is beneficial if the reader has some basic understanding of the telecommunications and computer topics; however, this is not necessary, as sufficient background is presented on all of the subjects. Two companion books by the author—*Broadband Communications* (ISBN 0-13-089321-8) and *Enterprise Security* (ISBN 0-13-047458-4)—provide a technical understanding of the current communications technologies and security issues. These books specifically cater to the business, government, and education markets and are more technical in nature.

This book provides a wide range of information relating to cyber-crime, E-commerce, and Internet activities that could exploit computer and electronic devices. Emphasis is placed on the numerous vulnerabilities and threats that are inherent in the Internet and networking environment. Efforts are made to present techniques and suggestions for corporate security personnel, first responders, investigators, and forensic examiners to successfully identify, retrieve, and protect valuable forensic evidence for litigation and prosecution.

In summary, this book is not highly technical. It provides just enough detail that allows the reader to apply the information provided and successfully address the numerous issues relating to computer and electronic evidence.

Organization of This Book

This book is divided into two major parts. Part 1 contains six chapters that provide basics relating to various crimes, laws, policies, forensic tools, and information needed to understand the underlying concepts of computer forensic investigations.

Chapter 1, Computer Forensic Investigation Basics, introduces the basic concepts that make up the field of computer forensics. The four-step process for computer forensic investigations is identified, as are the different types of evidence that are elements of computer forensics. The reader will become familiar with the various risks, threats, and incidents that relate to computer forensics. Differences between criminal and business policy investigations will be explored. This chapter sets the stage for the remainder of the book.

Chapter 2, Policies, Standards, Laws, and Legal Processes, introduces numerous laws and statutes that apply to computer-related crimes. It presents various techniques employed in court proceedings and acceptable electronic evidence. Security and computer-use policies and standards are related to security policy violations and criminal activities. The reader is exposed to numerous definitions of legal terms relating to electronic litigation. Expert witness requirements are presented.

Chapter 3, Electronic Forensic Examination Categories, identifies various crimes and incidents that are involved in electronic forensic investigations. This chapter shows how identity theft and fraud permeate all elements of the computer and electronics environment. It describes various types of evidence that can be gathered for each category of crime. The reader will become familiar with the various terms associated with these types of investigations and understand the importance of security and computer-use policies. Incidents that may be investigated by the corporate security department are described.

Chapter 4, Computer, Internet, and Electronic Crimes, explains to the reader what scams are and how scam artists work. The reader will become familiar with the crimes of identity theft and Internet fraud and their relationship to each other. The chapter identifies methods and techniques used to obtain evidence from Internet and Web resources. Resources for identifying evidence stored on business and personal computer assets, technical and legal terms relating to scams, fraud, and identity theft, and issues of child molestation and predators who are using the Web are described.

Chapter 5, Computers, Electronics, and Networking Environment, presents an overview of the E-commerce, networking environment, and the various hardware and software components and electronic devices that might contain forensic evidence. The chapter gives examples of forensic evidence that might be obtained from the crime/incident scenes and the types of evidence that can be recovered from computer and electronic devices. It lists the features available on network surveillance and management systems for the forensic investigator. The reader will learn about the hardware and software solutions that can provide investigative information addressing network security issues.

Chapter 6, Investigative Tools, Technical Training, and Forensic Equipment, identifies specialized tools and supplies required for electronic and computer forensic investigations. It describes various techniques employed for identifying and collecting electronic forensic evidence. It also discusses training requirements for electronic forensic investigators and examiners. It explains the use of software in computer network administration and surveillance and the equipment that provides for surveillance and capture of network traffic.

Part 2 contains eight chapters that provide information relating to crime scene investigations and management, disk and file structure, laboratory construction and functions, and legal testimony. Separate chapters are devoted to investigations involving computer systems, e-mail, and wireless devices.

Chapter 7, Managing the Crime/Incident Scene, makes the reader familiar with the responsibilities of the first responder at an incident site and helps the reader understand the requirements for managing the incident/crime scene. The reader will identify those steps necessary to make electronic evidence admissible in court, as well as the various players involved in an electronic/computer investigation. The chapter presents the issues relating to electronic and computer crime-scene investigations and shows how electronic forensics provides support in solving crimes. It presents a comparison of the investigative differences between corporate security and those of law enforcement. Information presented in this chapter can provide the investigator with the tools to make or break a case.

Chapter 8, Investigating Computer Center Incidents, helps the reader distinguish between white collar and blue collar crimes and corporate security violations and identify those processes taken when responding to security and policy violations. It explains how corporate incidents differ from law enforcement investigations and teaches specific steps to be taken when identifying, collecting, and protecting electronic evidence. The reader will be familiar with the requirements regarding the chain of custody for forensic evidence and will look at the possible areas where computer and electronic evidence resides.

Chapter 9, Computer Systems Disk and File Structures, identifies the various components of a hard drive and the structure of disk media. It explains the differences among the numerous disk drive interfaces and functions and stresses the importance of becoming familiar with the Windows, Macintosh, and Linux file structures. The chapter presents forensic tools used to identify and retrieve evidence from Windows, Macintosh, and Linux systems. The reader will learn the definitions of numerous terms relating to file and storage structures, and that most of the latent evidence that an examiner will recover will be located on the computer's hard drive.

Chapter 10, The Computer and Electronic Forensic Lab, exposes the reader to the functions of an electronic forensics laboratory and identifies the software, hardware, and infrastructure requirements of a forensics laboratory. The chapter discusses the processes required to identify and recover electronic evidence and the importance of documentation and chain of custody in the forensic process. The reader will see how evidence is recovered in the laboratory and learn the terms that are used in this environment.

Chapter 11, Extracting Computer and Electronic Evidence, teaches the functions that occur in a computer forensics lab and stresses the importance of the chain of custody and documentation. The reader will identify a process for deciding what evidence to collect, will look at the steps required to successfully process latent electronic evidence, and will understand the techniques required to image a hard drive.

Chapter 12, E-Mail and Internet Investigations, explains the basics of e-mail investigations oriented toward scams, spam, and other network activities. The reader will identify the various resources that can be utilized in these investigations and will look at the process for extracting investigative information from e-mail headers.

Chapter 13, Mobile Phone and PDA Investigations, identifies the components of mobile devices and how they can contain important investigative information. The chapter presents considerable information concerning the Subscriber Identity Module (SIM) component. The chapter provides a look at the different techniques and tools used on mobile phones and PDAs in a forensic investigation.

Chapter 14, Court Preparation, Presentations, and Testimony, helps the reader identify testimony requirements for electronic evidence presentations and learn how to be effective in technical courtroom presentations. The reader will also understand why examiners and investigators must be technically proficient, will learn the various legal terms associated with forensic testimony, and will become familiar with direct examination and cross-examination processes. Techniques will be presented to provide the forensic team with an edge in court testimony.

Appendices A through D provide a set of forensic investigation forms, exercises, answers to review questions, and other aids supporting the book.

How to Utilize This Book

More than 200 key terms are provided throughout the book (**bold type**) and the definitions of these can be found in the Glossary.

More than 100 review questions, which provide a fairly complete coverage of the material, are presented throughout the book. The answers to these questions can be found in Appendix C. Found in Appendix B are optional exercises and cases that emphasize the book's content. Users should practice safe Internet and computer use when working through the cases and exercises. Keep backup copies of everything!

Many Web resources were utilized in developing this book. The selected bibliography lists a number of resources that would be beneficial to the forensic professional. The information presented in this book is patterned after technical, legal, and managerial classes by computer forensic professionals from Cyber Crime Summits held at Kennesaw State University in Kennesaw, GA in 2005 and 2006.

About the Author

Robert C. Newman, CISSP, is currently an instructor of Information Systems in the College of information technology at Georgia Southern University. Before that, he was associate professor of telecommunications management at the Decatur, Georgia campus of DeVry Institute of Technology. He is a long-time student and practitioner of data processing, data communications, and networking technologies, having started his career at the University of South Carolina in 1969 in the computer science department, where he held a number of positions in a large computer operation, including operations manager. He has taught in the computer information technology departments in a number of institutions of higher learning. Professor Newman has an ongoing working relationship concerning technical networking, disaster contingency planning, and security issues with the Georgia Southern University IT Services' organization.

Newman has authored two college-level books, *Enterprise Security* and *Broadband Communications*. *Enterprise Security*, published in 2003, covers all aspects of security from a technical manager's viewpoint and is widely used both in undergraduate and graduate studies, in the United States and several foreign countries. *Broadband Communications*, published in 2002, covers all of the current broadband communications technologies from strategic, tactical, and operations points of view.

Newman earned degrees from the University of South Carolina, Columbia and Georgia State University in Atlanta. He has advanced degree work in computer science at the University of Alabama, Birmingham. In addition, he has completed many formal technical courses in computer technology and in telecommunications marketing and sales support environments. He is currently active in computer-forensic and enterprise information systems security education and has developed a security awareness program for the Georgia Southern campus.

Newman's professional experience includes many years in the telephone industry at BellSouth and AT&T. He accumulated a considerable amount of hands-on networking knowledge in software development, broadband operations, and network management and surveillance at BellSouth. Early in his career, he developed a solid background in IBM mainframe hardware and software.

Before his life in the computer industry, he was a member of federal, state, and county law enforcement agencies in Georgia, Alabama, and South Carolina. He is a graduate of the Northeast Georgia Police Academy and Georgia Post certified (GaPOST) and a Certified Information Systems Security Professional (CISSP). He is an active member of the Federal Bureau of Investigation's Coastal Empire Infragard organization. He has accumulated a wealth of knowledge on security and protection of data and computer resources and network administration. Security lectures are part of the network administration, management information systems, and data communications courses he currently teaches.

Professor Newman can be contacted at newmanrc@frontiernet.net or newmanrc@georgiasouthern.edu for comments and suggestions on the contents of this book.

Contents

SECTION II EVIDENCE COLLECTION AND MANAGEMENT

COMPUTER FORENSIC INVESTIGATION BASICS

I

Chapter 1

Computer Forensic Investigation Basics

Chapter Objectives

- Understand the basic concepts that make up the field of computer forensics
- Identify the four-step process for computer forensic investigations
- Identify the different types of evidence that are elements of computer forensics
- Become familiar with the various risks, threats, and incidents that relate to computer forensics
- Look at the differences between criminal and business policy investigations
- Set the stage for the remainder of the book

Introduction

A technological revolution in communications and information exchange is taking place within business, industry, government, and our homes. Americans use computer and networking facilities to bank and transfer money electronically, and are much more likely to receive e-mail than a letter. The worldwide Internet population is in the millions and growing every day. The Internet, computer networks, and automated data systems provide an enormous opportunity for illegal activities. This computer technology is being used to commit crimes against persons, organizations, governments, and property.

In this information technology age, the needs of law enforcement and corporate security are changing as well. Some traditional white-collar crimes in finance and commerce continue; however, paper trails have become electronic trails. Crimes associated with the theft and manipulations of data, such as identity theft, are detected daily. Crimes of violence are aided by technology. Terrorists are using the Internet to further their causes. Common criminals, drug cartels, and crime syndicates all use the network to conduct worldwide operations. Law enforcement and corporate security departments must step up to this challenge. New policies and procedures are required to effectively respond to these threats. Education and training in the field of computer forensics evidence is part of this solution.

The nature of computer and electronic evidence poses special challenges for its admissibility in court proceedings and corporate security investigations. Corporate security policies, corporate computer-use policies, and law enforcement procedures must address these challenges. Procedures concerning these forensic practices must include evidence collection, examination, analysis, protection, and reporting.

White-collar and blue-collar crimes are on the rise in the nation's businesses. Accounting fraud has impacted the stock market, retirement funds, and the earnings of major corporations. Accounting forensic specialists are using computer technology to gather evidence for criminal prosecution. The computer and network infrastructure provides an attractive target to individuals bent on creating mischief or committing some fraudulent or illegal activity. Software and hardware providers have developed numerous technical products that can be used by computer forensic investigators and examiners in responding to these incidents.

A. Forensics Defined

Forensics is formally defined as a study or practice relating to legal proceedings or augmentation. Most readers have viewed crime scene investigations, forensic investigations, cold case, and other forensic-related TV shows. While most of these episodes use deoxyribonucleic acid (DNA) evidence to identify suspects and victims to solve the cases, computer forensics uses computer digital technology to develop and provide investigative evidence to prove or disprove some allegation. **Computer forensics** is therefore described as those activities associated with the identification and preservation of computer or electronic evidence in support of some official or legal action. Additionally, analytical and investigative techniques are used to examine this evidence and data that is magnetically stored or encoded using the binary number system. There are basically four situations where a computer device is involved in some type of crime. The computer is:

The target of some illegal activity
The medium through which the illegal activity is committed

Incidental to the commission of the illegal activity

A combination of the previous three situations

1. Computer Forensic Science

Computer forensic science was created to address the specific requirements of law enforcement that would leverage this new form of electronic evidence. **Computer forensic science** is the science of acquiring, retrieving, preserving, and presenting data that has been processed electronically and stored on computer media.

Computer forensic science is different from most traditional forensic disciplines. The computer media and material that is examined and the techniques available to the examiner are products of a market-driven private sector. In contrast to traditional forensic analyses where examinations of evidence are performed in controlled laboratory settings, there is often a requirement to perform computer examinations at virtually any physical location. Rather than producing interpretative conclusions (such as DNA), as in many forensic disciplines, computer forensic science produces direct information and data that may have significance in a case. This type of direct data collection has far-reaching implications for the investigator and the forensic scientist and the results of the forensic computer examination.

Computer forensic examinations are conducted in forensic laboratories, data processing departments, and in some cases, the investigator's squad room. The assignment of personnel to conduct these examinations is based often on available expertise, as well as departmental policy. Regardless of where the examinations are conducted, a valid and reliable forensic examination is required. This requirement recognizes no bureaucratic, political, jurisdictional, or technological boundaries.

B. The Four-Step Process

Computer forensic investigations are very detailed and complex. Most important to the incident is the preservation of any evidence in its original form. Any modifications to date and time stamps or the data itself must be avoided; otherwise, the usefulness of the evidence may be deemed inadmissible. As a note, the defendant or defense attorney may use this as an argument to throw out such tainted evidence. There are four steps required in the computer forensics investigation: acquisition, identification, evaluation, and presentation. As Figure 1.1 depicts, the first two steps repeat until the investigation is completed. An overview will be presented here; however, considerable additional details will be provided in subsequent chapters.

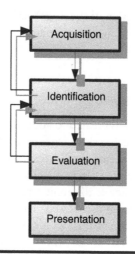

Figure 1.1 The four-step process.

1. Acquisition

There are basically two scenarios for acquiring computer evidence—the incident has already occurred or the incident is currently in progress. If the incident is ongoing, a different approach and different tools would be required in the investigation. It might be necessary to track a "live" intruder or capture electronic evidence as it occurs or in "real time." A tool such as a "sniffer" or "monitor" might be utilized to collect evidence as it occurs. Additional hardware and software tools will be discussed later in Chapter 6.

Evidence must be preserved for court or corporate use. Documentation suitable for federal, state, and local courts must be developed. The corporate security professional or law enforcement first responder must ensure that all evidence is protected and documented. The chain-of-custody or chain-of-evidence begins at this point in time. Briefly, **chain-of-custody** is the route the evidence takes from initial possession until final disposition. This documentation process is one of the most critical of the investigation and will be emphasized throughout this book.

2. Identification

Evidence is presented in both a physical and a logical context. Physical relates to the hardware or software components, such as a particular disk drive. The logical relationship might include the address or location of the evidence on a disk drive. It is essential that all information relating to the steps taken and the computer instructions issued be documented, as all steps must have the ability to be replicated repeatedly. A well-documented procedure is very important and could be thrown out of court if it cannot be duplicated consistently. A journal is usually the vehicle for recording all activities undertaken by the investigator.

3.   Evaluation

A determination must be made as to the relevance of the computer evidence to the case. A computer forensics investigator in concert with a computer forensics examiner must determine the relevance and validity of the evidence collected by the first responder. Of particular importance in this phase is to determine if the chain-of-custody has been maintained and also that the credibility of the evidence has not been tainted. Computer-related evidence is generally used in support of other evidence and is usually not used to identify a suspect or victim as in a DNA investigation. Considerable data might be recovered from a suspect computer system or electronic device and may well contain a considerable amount of irrelevant information. It is essential that the forensic team only collect information that is relevant to the case being investigated. Irrelevant information may confuse a jury and cause relevant information to be thrown out with the relevant evidence. More is not necessarily better; however, quality is better.

4.   Presentation

During a formal presentation, the forensic team must decide as to the worthiness of the various pieces of evidence. Some evidence may cloud the issue and should be discarded during the presentation. Both sides of an argument will be presenting their positions. Expert witnesses might be employed in these cases. Both the defense and the prosecution might provide an expert in computer forensic techniques. A lack of knowledge on the part of any forensic participant will degrade the presentation in the other's favor. The evaluator's handling and processing of the electronic or computer evidence will be subjected to scrutiny by the opposing side of the argument. The evaluator of evidence will be expected to defend the methods of evidence handling and processing. The chain-of-custody can be expected to be challenged; therefore, accurate and complete documentation must be maintained.

C.   What Is Electronic Evidence?

Electronic evidence is data and information of some investigative value that are stored on or transmitted by an electronic device, usually in digital form. Electronic evidence, therefore, is latent evidence in the same sense as fingerprints and DNA. (A latent fingerprint is difficult to view, but can be made visible for scrutiny). This evidence is not readily viewable and requires various hardware and software elements to make it "visible." The objective of the forensic team is to identify any evidence that might be found on the devices.

Several computer terms need to be explained further for readers who are not computer "techies." These terms include data, information, hardware, and software. **Data** is raw facts that can be processed by some computing device into accurate and relevant information. This could include the various items found on a fingerprint card or on a credit card statement. Items could include name, Social Security number, age, address, etc. Data is stored on magnetic media, usually in digital form of binary "1s" and "0s." **Information** might include a report that contains a list of all the credit cards recovered in an investigation along with any charges made on these cards, where the cards were used, the amount of the charges, and so forth. This information would be useful in a forensic investigation.

Generically, **hardware** is described as the physical equipment, media, and attached devices used in a computer system. This includes the computer, printers, and communication devices. **Software** is described as instructional coding that manipulates the hardware in a computer system. This could include programs such as JAVA, UNIX, and Linux. Chapter 5 will provide an overview of the various components of the computer and communication network and the potential evidence available from these electronic hardware and software components.

Electronic evidence is fragile as it can be altered, damaged, or destroyed by improper handling or examination. Therefore, it is essential that special precautions be taken to collect, document, examine, and preserve this type of evidence. Three types of evidence include circumstantial, physical, and hearsay. All of these types of evidence may be present in the investigation.

1.   Circumstantial

Circumstantial evidence is indirect evidence. Circumstantial evidence is the result of combining seemingly unrelated facts that, when considered together, can be used to infer a conclusion. Circumstantial evidence is usually a theory, supported by a significant quantity of corroborating evidence. Circumstantial evidence can include, in part, inferences about an event that was not seen. For example, if someone walked outside, found the ground was wet, and did not actually see it raining, then an inference could be made that it had actually rained while the individual was inside.

2.   Physical

Physical evidence is evidence that does not forget and is not confused by the excitement of the moment. It is not absent because human witnesses are—it is factual evidence. Physical evidence cannot be wrong and cannot perjure itself; however, its interpretation can be prone to error. This is direct, clear, and tangible evidence of something, requiring no assumptions or added logic to prove it to be true. It is the opposite of circumstantial evidence, and is often collected from an eyewitness.

3. Hearsay

Hearsay evidence consists of statements made out of court by someone who is not present to testify under oath at a trial. This is evidence based on what someone has told the witness and not on direct knowledge. Hearsay is generally not admissible in common law courts because it is of suspect value; however, there are exceptions to this prohibition, such as administrative-type hearings. One reason for the exclusion of hearsay is the practice of cross-examination of witnesses in open court by opposing lawyers; therefore, written or oral assertions made by a person not present cannot be subjected to cross-examination.

4. Repeatability and Reproducibility

The National Institute of Standards and Technology (NIST) requires that computer forensic test results be repeatable and reproducible. Under repeatability conditions, independent test results are obtained with the same method, on identical test items, in the same laboratory, by the same operator, using the same equipment within short intervals of time.

Under reproducibility conditions, test results are obtained with the same method, on identical test items, in different laboratories, with different operators, using different equipment.

As applied to computer forensic testing, **repeatability** is defined as the ability to get the same test results in the same testing environment (same computer, disk, mode of operation, etc.). **Reproducibility** is defined as the ability to get the same test results in a different testing environment (different computer, hard disk, operator, etc.).

Quality control and documentation of the testing process are essential to ensure repeatability and reproducibility of test results. Every step of the process must be documented at a level of detail that will provide enough information that the testing process, from setup to completion, could be repeated and analyzed. These records in addition to the forensic results regarding testing hardware and testing software must be controlled and protected to ensure the accuracy and integrity of the process.

Investigators must remember that the initial approach to an incident scene might be the only opportunity they have to recover evidence. Electronic evidence can be very fleeting and easily deleted, modified, or damaged. Search warrants must contain sufficient detail and be broad in scope to allow for the collection of all relevant latent evidence.

D. Who Is at Risk?

The reader might well become paranoid after reading this book. Crime is everywhere and the Internet is providing additional avenues for individuals to engage in illegal activities. The Internet is available to everyone. Criminals believe that they can remain anonymous and escape detection and prosecution; however, the field of electronic and computer forensics is rapidly responding to the threats. Those who are at risk include organizations and individual citizens. Internet chat rooms are providing an avenue for minors to be exploited by predators. E-mail systems provide an access to millions of potential victims. Victims often are trying to get something for nothing; however, there are no "free lunches." Scams appear every day, usually in e-mail, and there is a significant supply of potential victims. SPAM is another issue that impacts the business world. While this is not necessarily illegal, the possibility exists that it can contain code that could attack the network. Spyware is also a nemesis of all computer network users. SPAM and Spyware use up valuable corporate resources.

The Internet is also used for activities that are not necessarily "illegal." Use of the Internet at work may be a violation of corporate policies. Employees who surf the Internet can waste considerable corporate resources. Minor children may be exposed to situations that are not in their best interest. Predators look for victims in such places as chat rooms that are frequented by minors and school children. This book will address the issues relating to both corporate policy violations and criminal activities. Note that policy violations might well become criminal issues. Corporate accounting violations might well become criminal fraud cases. Electronic and computer evidence is usually available in criminal cases or corporate incidents and can be gathered by forensic investigators for civil or criminal action.

1. Incidents and Threats

A computer forensic investigation might be initiated for a number of reasons. Steps might be initiated for some suspected violation of company policies, some criminal incident, or an effort to recover lost data. Policy violations might include employee Internet abuse, unauthorized disclosure of confidential information, inappropriate e-mail use, use of company resources for personal use, and the list goes on. Corporate incidents can become criminal issues. Industrial espionage, criminal fraud, and theft are but a few issues that fit this category. Lastly, an incident might occur where data has been lost due to some unforeseen disaster or malicious activities. Computer forensic techniques might be employed in each of these instances. The latter situations fall under the category of disaster recovery techniques and will be discussed briefly in Chapter 10.

a. Incidents

Because all incidents and threats that occur are not criminal in nature, there is a requirement for organizations to conduct investigations to identify and correct these situations. Forensic techniques are being utilized to accomplish these tasks. A security department, an auditor, or a forensic firm might accomplish these forensic investigations. The same attention to forensic evidence must be applied to all investigations, whether policy or criminal. A partial list of incidents using electronic devices that could occur in a commercial, educational, or government organization includes:

User or customer errors
Intellectual property theft
Delays of processing data
Loss of data or information
Unauthorized disclosure of data
  or information
Data duplication
Corruption
Breach of contracts
Phone phreaking
Safety-related issues

Disloyal employees
E-mail abuse
Inappropriate network abuse
Computer break-ins
Pornography
Sexual harassment
Blackmail
Errors in billing
Disclosure of confidential
  information
Loss of operations

b. Threats

The Internet has become the vehicle for numerous threats against business enterprises, government, and private citizens. Many of these threats are originating in foreign countries. These threats may originate from criminals, terrorists, students, organizations, businesses, and the general population. The opportunities for illegal and suspect activities using the Internet are endless. Some of these attacks may be state sponsored. A short list of threats that might originate on the Internet includes:

Fraud against customers, suppliers,
  and employers
Repudiation of sales
False claims
Identity theft
Money laundering
Piracy
Child pornography

Child exploitation
Sabotage
Denial-of-service (DoS) attacks
Hacking
Trojan horses
Worms
Viruses

Many of the listed Internet activities may result in criminal prosecution and require sophisticated and lengthy electronic and computer forensic investigations.

Tools used in these investigations will be discussed in Chapter 6. A major difficulty investigating these incidents is finding out where the threats originated. Criminal elements with Internet access can reside anywhere in the world, and often are located in Third-World countries, where prosecution is difficult.

E.   Criminal versus Business Policy Investigations

The use of electronic and computer devices by the criminal element is increasing daily, as is the use of the Internet to commit a wide variety of crimes. These Internet crimes include numerous examples of fraud and theft and can be committed by individuals located anywhere in the world. Evidence recovered from these devices is being used to support convictions in numerous capital cases. Kidnappers, murderers, burglars, drug dealers, terrorists, and common criminals may use these devices in their illicit activities. The use of computer forensic evidence is of major significance for both corporate and criminal investigations. The forensic techniques discussed in this book will be the same for both situations.

1.   Criminal Activities

Common criminal activities involving major crimes that could be addressed using electronic and computer forensics in the investigations include:

Murder	Espionage
Kidnapping	Forgery
Theft	Drugs
Assault	Organized crime
Stalking	Prostitution
Burglary	Robbery

These investigations would be in direct support of the normal investigative processes and other supporting forensic categories, such as DNA identification. Many criminals use electronic and computer devices in their criminal activities. Evidence obtained from these sources supplement other law-enforcement activities.

Because computer and electronic devices are ubiquitous in today's society, it is no surprise that they could be used in illegal and improper ways. Violations of company policies and incidents involving federal, state, and local laws and ordinances are often committed with the aid of these devices. In most cases, company policy infractions will never reach the judicial system; however, one should not take this for granted. A simple violation of a company policy might well turn into a criminal issue.

A case of an employee accused of improper accounting practices might well turn into a fraud or theft issue. Investigations involving business policy and commercial activities may well require the assistance of subject matter experts (SMEs) who understand a specialized issue. These situations usually involve activities relating to financial records. A new field of forensic accounting is emerging as a source for financial system investigations. These forensic accountants must undergo an intense training program concentrating on the financial statements of business enterprises.

Forensic accounting focuses on the evidentiary nature of accounting data. Topics include the following:

Accounting fraud and fraud auditing
Compliance, due diligence, and risk assessment
Detection of financial statement misrepresentation and tax evasion
Bankruptcy and valuation studies
Generally Accepted Auditing Standards (GAAS), Generally Accepted Accounting Principles (GAAP), and Securities and Exchange Commission (SEC) violations
Nonstandard entries, structured transactions, and records and earnings tampering
Audit quality review and evaluation
Transaction tracing, reconstruction, and accountability
Litigation support and dispute avoidance
Money and information laundering
Underground economy

2. Network and Computer Center Threats

There are many opportunities for threats and miscellaneous incidents to occur in the computer and networking environment. This is particularly true in the internetworking environment, where attackers, crackers, and hackers abound. A threat from these individuals can have a potential adverse effect on the assets and resources of users and organizations. Threats can be listed in generic terms; however, they usually involve fraud, theft of data, destruction of data, blockage of access, and carelessness. Investigations of these incidents can be very difficult and usually require a forensic scientist's expertise.

Organizations must prepare for these possibilities and develop countermeasures. Security departments must plan and train their responders and investigators in preparation for these threats. Management must decide the appropriate responses based on dollar loss, embarrassment, monetary liability, or probability of occurrence. The most common networking threats to an organization include the following:

Virus, worm, Trojan horses   External hackers
Device failures   Natural disasters
Internal hackers   Industrial espionage
Equipment theft

The most common network security problem today is often communicated via e-mail. These transmissions could include viruses, worms, Trojan horses, SPAM, and phishes. Insiders (internal employees) initiate many of these attacks. The relative importance of a threat to the user or organization usually depends upon the type of transmission. For example, a financial institution or E-commerce site might be a frequent victim of an attack, whereas a fast-food Web restaurant might be spared. It should be noted, however, that an attacker might feel more secure in attacking a small network or an individual's laptop. The impact of a threat could have different ramifications between these two types of sites and the investigation complexity is considerably different.

Do not expect the Federal Bureau of Investigation (FBI) to respond every time someone reports a computer-related crime. As more crimes are committed with the aid of computer technology, more crimes are left to be handled by local law enforcement. Successful prosecution of cyber crime begins before the crime is committed. One must be prepared to react quickly and to understand the confines of the law to which the investigation is limited. This is important, not only for law enforcement, but also for managers, information technology (IT) personnel, and in-house counsel, to understand exactly what should be done or not done when a cyber crime happens.

Many companies try to handle cases internally due to fears that the public will lose confidence in them. Unfortunately, many times these actions, however well meant, preclude the prosecution of a case altogether. Issues of controlling publicity can be addressed, while allowing law enforcement to do its job.

Not all breaks in security are malicious; however, the results can be just as damaging. Some may stem from a purposeful interruption of a system's operation or may be accidental, such as a hardware failure or a software abnormality, sometimes called an undesirable feature. Security breaches must be minimized, whether they are malicious or accidental. The overall goal is to protect the network and computer system from any attack, and to prevent theft, destruction, and corruption of the resources of the individual user or organization. These situations, however, increase the caseload of the security department, as all must be investigated. Experience of the networking personnel and the corporate security investigators should help to quickly identify an incident versus an accident. Issues of this type are addressed with contingency planning and disaster recovery response initiatives. A **disaster recovery plan** outlines the procedures for an organization to return to normal operations following a disaster or incident.

3.   *Infrastructure Threat Targets*

There is information on the Internet that provides instructions on how to attack almost any type of protocol, operating system, or hardware environment. From the previous discussions it should be obvious that threats require a considerable amount of vigilance. After identifying the various threats, the next step is to identify the various computer and networking components that compose the threat environment. These include any hardware device or software component that might be assessable to the threats previously identified. Potential candidates include the following:

- Computers, servers, PCs, and administrative workstations
- Communication circuits
- Routers, gateways, and switches
- Hubs, media access units (MAUs), repeaters, and bridges
- Modems, data service units (DSUs), and network termination 1 (NT1s)
- Front-end processors, communication controllers, and multiplexers
- Network and operating system software
- Application software
- Power and air-conditioning systems

From this list, it should be obvious to the reader that opportunities abound for an attacker to wreak havoc on the individual user's computer or an organization's assets and resources. There are a number of hardware and software products that can be used to mitigate attacks to the computer and network resources. These tools are described in Chapter 6. These products also provide the computer forensic investigator with numerous tools in responding to these attacks and threats.

F.   Proactive versus Reactive Policies

Policies are plans or courses of action designed by organizations, both governmental and private, to influence and determine decisions and actions for some particular situation.

Numerous federal, state, and local laws identify criminal violations; however, company policies dictate and specify the actions expected by employees. It should be noted that a company-policy violation might easily become a criminal issue. This section will address the issue of company policies. Many organizations are requiring new employees to sign a policy statement regarding the proper use of company resources such as computers, supplies, space, and e-mail. These policies address issues such as sex, race, and age discrimination, porn surfing, theft of services, and indicate the penalty for violations. Many organizations are conducting background checks on prospective employees. The introduction of the policy statement into public and private organizations has become a tool for establishing expected behavior by employees. Often a warning banner specifying the security policy is displayed on the organization's Web page. Of particular importance is that the policies contain statements relating to the use of electronic, communication, and computer resources and devices. All of these devices might be used as evidence sources in some form of forensic investigations.

Policies can be either proactive or reactive. **Proactive policies** establish expected behavior in anticipation of some incident. **Reactive policies** happen after some incident occurs and are, therefore, too late to impact some situation. This is similar to locking the gate after the horses have escaped. Elements that might be included in a policy or standard are presented in Chapter 2.

1.   *White-Collar and Blue-Collar Crimes*

White-collar and blue-collar crimes are on the rise. Accounting fraud is becoming a nationwide issue. Numerous court cases involving corporate executives are currently ongoing. These cases involve millions of dollars of investor and corporate funds. Accounting forensic specialists are using computer technology to gather evidence for criminal prosecution. These subject matter experts must often work with computer forensics investigators and examiners to extract pertinent evidence from computing devices.

The disgruntled employee is the principal source of corporate computer crimes. Insiders possess the knowledge to gain unrestricted access to cause damage to the system or to steal system data. The insider threat also includes outsourcing vendors. Additional details concerning insider white-collar and blue-collar crimes will be presented in Chapter 8.

2.   *Legal Activity*

There are numerous federal and state laws and acts that have been enacted to counter Internet, computer, and electronic crimes. Additional efforts are under way to address illegal activities, such as identify theft, fraud, terrorism, and child pornography. Corporate security departments and law enforcement organizations must keep up with these changing legal environments. As an example, the Sarbanes-Oxley Act of 2002 provides penalties for destroying electronic records, sets record retention requirements, and makes electronic discovery stipulations. Chapter 2 will provide an overview of this colossal amount of legal code that will impact most computer investigations for civil, criminal, and corporate violations.

Chapter Summary

Computer forensics consists of numerous activities associated with the identification and preservation of computer or electronic evidence in support of some official or legal action in both civil and criminal matters. Training and educational programs are required to prepare law enforcement and corporate security in addressing these critical issues.

Corporate policies must be developed to counter illegal activities committed using technology resources. White-collar and blue-collar crimes are on the rise. Accounting fraud is becoming a nationwide issue. Numerous court cases involving corporate executives are currently ongoing. Security and computer-use policies that respond to these activities can be either reactive or proactive.

The four-step process of computer forensics investigations includes acquisition, identification, evaluation, and presentation. Chain-of-custody of evidence must be preserved in all computer forensics investigations, so that evidence will hold up in a court of law.

Evidence categories include circumstantial, physical, and hearsay. Different types of evidence might be recovered in numerous types of threats and incidents, including corporate illegal activities and crimes against persons and property. All of this evidence must be protected from modification and destruction.

There are a number of threats that can be directed toward computer systems and the network infrastructure. SPAM and e-mail frauds are increasing across the personal and corporate environments. Investigation of these incidents often requires specialized hardware and software products. These products can be used to identify vulnerabilities and provide investigative support.

Terms

Chain-of-custody — The route the evidence takes from initial possession until final disposition. It is also called the chain-of-evidence.

Circumstantial evidence — Indirect evidence, usually a theory, that is supported by a significant quantity of corroborating evidence.

Computer forensic science — The science of acquiring, preserving, retrieving, and presenting data that has been processed electronically and stored on computer media.

Computer forensics — Those activities associated with the identification and preservation of computer or electronic evidence in support of some official or legal action.

Data — Raw facts that can be processed by some computing device into accurate and relevant information.

Disaster recovery plan — Outlines the procedures for an organization to return to normal operations following a disaster or incident.

Electronic evidence — Data and information of some investigative value that is stored on or transmitted by an electronic device.

Forensics — Formally defined as a study or practice relating to legal proceedings or augmentation.

Hardware — Described as the physical equipment, media, and attached devices used in a computer system. This includes the computer, printers, and communication devices.

Hearsay evidence — Consists of statements made out of court by someone who is not present to testify under oath at a trial.

Latent — Is present or has potential, but is not evident or active.

Information — Processed data that enhance the recipient's knowledge. Raw facts, called data, are transformed into something meaningful and useful.

Physical evidence — Evidence that does not forget and is not confused by the excitement of the moment.

Policies — Plans or courses of actions designed by organizations, both governmental and private, to influence and determine decisions and actions for a particular situation.

Proactive policies — Establish expected behavior in anticipation of an incident.

Reactive policies — Response after an incident occurs, and is therefore too late to impact a situation.

Repeatability — Under repeatability conditions, independent test results are obtained with the same method, on identical test items, in the same laboratory, by the same operator, using the same equipment, within short intervals of time.

Reproducibility — Under reproducibility conditions, test results are obtained with the same method, on identical test items, in different laboratories, with different operators, using different equipment.

Software — Instructional coding that manipulates the hardware in a computer system.

Review Questions

1. The four-step process of computer forensics investigations includes_____, _____, _____, and _____.
2. T/F. Computer forensics investigations have the same requirements as those conducted using DNA evidence.
3. T/F. Chain of custody and chain of evidence are similar concepts.
4. T/F. Data and information are the same types of evidence.
5. Three types of evidence include _____, _____, and _____.
6. T/F. Sexual harassment, e-mail abuse, and errors in billing are examples of incidents that could occur when using electronic devices.
7. T/F. Common threats that might occur over the Internet include identify theft and child exploitation.
8. Common felony criminal activities that might use computer and electronic devices include _____, _____, _____, _____.
9. Policies that are established to avoid some type of unacceptable incident are _____.
10. Describe the difference between electronic evidence and latent evidence.

Chapter 2

Policies, Standards, Laws, and Legal Processes

Chapter Objectives

- Look at the numerous laws and statutes that apply to computer-related crimes
- Become familiar with acceptable electronic evidence
- Identify various techniques employed in court proceedings
- Determine expert witness requirements
- Look at sample security and computer-use policies and standards
- Differentiate between security policy violations and criminal activities
- Become familiar with numerous definitions of legal terms

Introduction

A computer crime involves the use of high-tech equipment to facilitate conventional crimes and permeates every aspect of society including the workplace. Computers and electronic devices can be vehicles for committing various crimes; therefore it follows that they may contain valuable evidence.

In criminal cases, the defendant is presumed innocent until the prosecution proves each element of the crime beyond a reasonable doubt. Criminal law requires the jury to acquit the defendant unless it is convinced of the defendant's guilt beyond a reasonable doubt; however, the law does not require absolute certainty.

A computer forensics specialist or subject matter expert (SME) is extremely valuable to assist in all stages of building a case; however, experts may be contracted to support either the prosecution or defense side of a case. These experts could include computer forensics specialists and others such as forensic accountants to support or challenge an argument before the court.

This chapter will also present information on policies and laws concerning issues relating to the use and misuse of computer and electronic devices. Issues that seem to be corporate policy issues might well evolve into civil and criminal cases. Forensic investigator teams must consider this possibility when conducting any electronic or computer investigation. Evidence recovered in these situations is easily compromised and can therefore be ruled as inadmissible in court proceedings. There are a number of laws and statutes that can impact the investigation.

Internal security organizations investigate incidents and violations of corporate policy violations. Many of these incidents may be minor; however, lately, numerous violations have been identified that impact the financial well-being of the organization. The talents of a forensic accountant could be required to investigate these financial issues.

A. Laws and Legal Issues

Laws can be categorized into civil, criminal, and tort. Civil law represents numerous laws recorded in volumes of legal code; criminal law addresses violations enforced through state prosecution; and tort law allows individuals to seek redress in the courts. This book will address criminal and civil law issues involving computer and electronic cases.

There are a variety of legal issues facing the computer-crime specialist. As technology progresses, laws are adapting to meet the changing environment. Understanding these issues is critical to the effective prosecution of criminals. It is essential that protective strategies be understood regarding avoiding potential litigation from individuals or corporations, which were the subject of a search and/or seizure operation involving computer equipment. A successful application of warrants and subpoenas is also required to hold up the relevance of evidence in legal proceedings. Several important laws and various issues that must be addressed include:

Electronic Communications Privacy Act (ECPA)
Cable Communications Privacy Act (CCPA)
Privacy Protection Act (PPA)
USA Patriot Act of 2001
Search and seizure requirements of the Fourth Amendment
Legal right to search the computer media
Legal right to remove the computer media from the scene
Availability of privileged material on the computer media for examination

Disclaimer: Information concerning the various laws and acts was obtained from the most recent documentation located on the Web and other sources; however, is subject to revision, and therefore may be dated. The reader should research and determine the most current version.

The **Electronic Communications Privacy Act (ECPA)** states that people have a reasonable expectation of privacy in their telephone use. It regulates the interception of electronic communications or wiretaps. It also regulates government access to stored electronic communications including e-mail and voice mail. Section 2510 of Title 18, Crimes and Criminal Procedure, describes numerous definitions relating to wire and oral electronic communications interception. There are basically three types of communications: oral (face to face), wire (voice) and electronic (e-mail, voice mail, etc.). Two parts of the ECPA address wiretaps and stored electronic communications.

1. Wiretaps

Wiretapping is the monitoring of telephone conversations by a third party, often by covert means. The telephone tap or wiretap received its name because, historically, the monitoring connection was applied to the wires of the telephone line of the person who was being monitored and drew off or tapped a small amount of the electrical signal carrying the conversation.

It is a felony to intercept any of the three types of protected communications absent a statutory exception. Examples of wiretapping include keystroking, sniffing, and cloned e-mail. Wiretap exceptions include a court order for intercept, consent, provider protection exception, and inadvertently obtained information. A consent document includes a signed user agreement or a banner. A **court order** is a document prepared and signed by a court, to give effect to a decision of a judge of that court. The provider protection exception allows interception and disclosure for the protection of the rights or property of the provider. Lastly, communications inadvertently obtained by an electronic communication service provider, which appears to pertain to the commission of a crime, may be disclosed to law enforcement.

2. Stored Electronic Communications

Stored electronic communications refers to e-mail while it resides on an e-mail server. This does not apply to e-mail that resides on an end user's computer. The e-mail server might reside at a service provider or a corporate data center. There are two categories of stored electronic communications: an electronic service provider and a remote computing service.

The electronic service provider provides users with the ability to send or receive wire or electronic communications. Examples include America Online, Earthlink, Frontiernet, and Bellsouth.net. A remote computing service utilizes a system that provides computer storage or processing services to the general public. An example would include an online file storage system. Note that service providers can be either public or private. A public provider would include an **Internet service provider (ISP)** and bulletin board system. An ISP is a company that provides user access to the Internet. A private provider would include corporate computer networks. Functions would include e-mail servers, Blackberry servers, and data storage facilities.

It is a misdemeanor for an electronic communications service or remote computing service to voluntarily disclose content of electronic or wire communications absent a statutory exception. Exceptions would include consent, provider protection exception, inadvertently obtained information, or required disclosure. A **misdemeanor** is described as any crime that is not a felony. Punishment for a misdemeanor is typically a fine or possibly jail time of less than one year. These are sometimes called "simple" misdemeanors. A **felony** is described as a crime of a graver or more atrocious nature than those designated as misdemeanors.

Information that might be available from electronic communications includes basic subscriber information, transactional records, and electronic content. Basic subscriber information might include:

Name
Address
Local and long-distance telephone connection records
Telephone number
Subscriber number or identity
Internet protocol (IP) address
Screen name
Account access and connection times
Subscriber length of service
Types of services utilized

The preceding information is generally available with a subpoena. Transactional records, however, generally require a court order. These could include:

Account activity   Internet activity
Payment history   Web site user logs

The last information component that might be available is the electronic content. A search warrant is required if e-mail is unopened and in storage for less than 180 days. There is no requirement for the suspect to be notified. If e-mail is opened or in storage for more than 180 days, a search warrant or subpoena with notice to the subscriber is required. Notice can be delayed for 90 days to prevent flight, witness tampering, destruction of evidence, or jeopardizing the investigation. If a search warrant is used, no such notice is required. There are additional requirements to preserve evidence. These time frames may be different in some jurisdictions and the investigator must determine the warrant requirements.

3. Privacy Protection Act

The **Privacy Protection Act (PPA)** was designed to protect people involved in first amendment activities from searches when they themselves are not involved in criminal activity. It primarily protects work product and documentary materials. The PPA prohibits government officials from searching or seizing any work product or documentary materials held by a "person reasonably believed to have a purpose to disseminate to the public a newspaper, book, broadcast, or other similar form of public communication." There are exceptions to the act. These include:

Probable cause that the person possessing material has committed or is committing a criminal offense

Items are contraband or fruits of a crime and immediate seizure is needed to prevent death or serious bodily injury to a human being

There is reason to believe that notice would result in the destruction of material

This act only applies to search warrants and court orders—subpoenas are not affected

4. Cable Communications Privacy Act

The **Cable Communications Privacy Act (CCPA)** prevents a cable company from releasing personally identifiable information about a subscriber unless the government offers clear and convincing evidence that the subscriber is a suspect and the subscriber is given an opportunity to contest the issue at an adversarial hearing. Data collection is limited to that which the system regards as necessary to maintain daily operations, such as billing records, maintenance and repair orders, premium service subscription information, and subscriber complaints. Access to this information is restricted to system personnel, businesses that provide services for the system (accountants), program and program guide providers, service auditors, and franchising representatives. It has been amended by the USA Patriot Act.

5. USA Patriot Act

The USA Patriot Act was a response to the 9/11 attacks. It amends portions of both ECPA and CCPA. The act deters and punishes terrorist activities in the United States and around the world, and enhances law enforcement investigation tools. It expands federal agencies' powers in intercepting, sharing, and using private telecommunications, especially electronic communications, focusing on criminal investigations by updating the rules that govern computer-crime investigations. It also sets out procedures and limitations to seek redress for individuals who feel their rights have been violated, including against the U.S. government. It is also used to detect and prosecute other alleged potential crimes such as providing false information on terrorism. The act was renewed on March 2, 2006.

6.   *The Fourth Amendment*

The Fourth Amendment can be broken down into two distinct parts. The first part provides protection against unreasonable searches and seizures; the second part of the amendment provides for the proper issue of warrants. When warrants are issued, there must be probable cause. A warrant is not necessary for a search or seizure under certain circumstances. Officers may search and seize objects that are in "plain view." Before the search and seizure, however, the officers must have probable cause to believe that the objects are contraband. There are Fourth Amendment implications for searching and retrieving data from computer and electronic devices. These include the legal right to search the computer media and to remove it from the scene. There are also issues concerning the availability of privileged material on the computer media for examination. The legal community must get involved to sort out these issues.

B.   Witnesses

A **witness** is described as someone who testifies to what he or she has seen, heard, or otherwise observed and who is not a party to the action. Except for the accused party, all persons can be compelled to be witnesses in a trial, but not every question asked must be answered. Facts that need not be disclosed on demand are known as privileged information. Information may be privileged even when the response would serve the cause of truth and justice.

A **subpoena** is a process to cause a witness to appear and give testimony, commanding an appearance before a court therein named at a time therein mentioned to testify for the party named under a penalty therein mentioned.

Only powerful social interests, however, can justify refusal to answer questions, so privileges are few. Among those established is the need of the nation to protect military and diplomatic secrets, often called executive privilege. No person has to provide information that is self-incriminating, either as a witness in a trial or in response to police questioning. This protection is guaranteed by the Fifth Amendment of the U.S. Constitution. Although technically not a privilege, a related rule is that evidence obtained by unlawful search or seizure by police is inadmissible in court; it is considered more important to maintain legal protection for all than to convict guilty parties.

In addition, some disclosures made in confidence need not be revealed. Attorneys cannot repeat what their clients have told them privately. One spouse can neither be forced nor permitted to reveal the secrets of the other spouse; indeed, some states excuse one spouse from testifying at all when the other is being prosecuted or sued. These historic protections have generally been expanded to include a few special relationships; in some jurisdictions, attorneys, physicians, and members of the clergy are not permitted to testify on confidential communications they received by them in their professional capacity.

Nearly all persons with knowledge relevant to a case can testify; only those persons limited by extreme youth or mental incapacity are precluded. Ordinary witnesses may state only their own knowledge and are required to express facts rather than opinions. A special category called expert witnesses also exists. Experts sometimes utilize hearsay and routinely express opinions. Computer forensic scientists, for example, can testify as to the validity of electronic data and the methods of obtaining that evidence. A forensics accountant can describe illegal financial activities and show how a criminal activity occurred.

Legal codes declare that evidence is relevant when it has a tendency "in reason" to prove or disprove disputed facts. Direct testimony of an eyewitness is relevant because it can show that an event occurred. A document found on a computer may or may not show that its owner created the document. Another person could have created it if the computer was left powered on and unattended. Its probative force is weak when viewed alone, but coupled with other equally weak evidence it may suffice to prove a fact. This indirect or circumstantial evidence can be effective in a court case, which is often the case of computer-generated evidence. **Indirect testimony** is evidence providing only a basis for inference about the fact in dispute.

Direct testimony includes statements made under oath by a party or the party's witness. After a party or witness testifies, the other party has the right to ask questions on cross-examination. After that, the administrative law judge might ask if there is any "redirect," which means if there is any more direct testimony in light of questions asked on cross-examination.

C.   Evidence

Evidence provides the means by which disputed facts are proved to be true or untrue in any trial before a court of law or an agency that functions like a court. Because American law is committed to a rational rather than a formalistic system of evidence, no value is assigned to the form or the quantity of evidence offered. Effectiveness is generally determined by how persuasive the evidence seems, especially to a jury. Some transactions, such as wills, transfers of land, and the sale of very valuable goods, must be evidenced by written documents. The following are some of the detailed rules that must be addressed in a legal action.

Evidence must be produced on given points by one side or the other in a court trial. This evidence is used to persuade the judge or jury of its truth and is assigned by law. Best known is the rigorous requirement that the prosecution in a criminal case must prove the defendant's guilt beyond a reasonable doubt. Lesser burdens placed on other litigants typically involve proving their case by a preponderance of the evidence. A person may be found not guilty of fraud when guilt is not proved beyond a reasonable doubt; however, he or she may still be held liable for damages in a civil action for the same violation and the same evidence. This occurs because negligence can be shown by a preponderance of the evidence.

Rules of admissibility determine which items of evidence judges or juries may be permitted to hear, see, or read. Modern codes declare that all "relevant" evidence should be admitted for consideration unless specifically excluded by law. Certain facts, however, may not be admissible because of their supposed tendency to confuse and mislead the jury, even though they are legal.

Relevant circumstantial evidence may be excluded, however, when it can be misused. For example, a defendant's prior criminal record of fraud cannot be admitted as evidence to prove that the person is guilty of a present crime. In a lawsuit, the fact that the defendant is insured is excluded because it diverts attention from the problem of legal fault to the improper question of ability to pay damages.

Hearsay evidence consists of statements made out of court by someone who is not present to testify under oath at a trial. Even if relevant, hearsay evidence generally is excluded unless some exception can be found. One reason for the exclusion of hearsay is the practice of cross-examination of witnesses in open court by opposing lawyers; written or oral assertions made by a person not present cannot be subjected to cross-examination.

Various exceptions are made, however, to the exclusion of hearsay evidence. Not everything that a witness "heard said" is considered hearsay, for sometimes the very speaking of words is important apart from their truth. Moreover, not all hearsay is excluded from consideration. The fact that an accused person has confessed guilt may support a conviction despite denials or silence at a trial. A confession is an admission by a person to the action in question—a classic hearsay exception. A confession is not admissible, however, when obtained by threats or promises of favor.

The recognized exceptions usually invoke either or both of two principles: (1) The statement was made by a speaker who had reason to be truthful, and (2) the speaker is now unavailable to testify. The classic example is a "dying declaration" that may prove the cause of death of a speaker who knew that death was imminent, because the deceased had little reason to lie and cannot now testify.

Legal evidence is not limited to the sworn testimony of witnesses. Specific objects, when identified by oral testimony, may often be introduced in evidence when their existence or appearance tends to prove or disprove an alleged fact. Thus, electronic devices, computer components, media storage, printouts, and manuals may be introduced as evidence.

The evidence presented by the prosecution or by the defense may consist of the oral testimony of witnesses, documentary evidence, and physical evidence, such as a cell phone or a mouse with the defendant's fingerprints on it. During direct examination, the party (prosecution or defense) who called the witness first presents the oral testimony of witnesses. The witness is then subjected to a cross-examination in which the opposing party attempts to discredit the testimony or demonstrate that it is incomplete. Following cross-examination, the original party may conduct a redirect examination of the witness in order to discredit matters brought out during cross-examination. The opposing party may then cross-examine the witness again.

The prosecution must not knowingly use perjured (false) testimony against the defendant or suppress evidence favorable to the defendant. Generally speaking, the prosecution may not use evidence obtained in violation of the defendant's constitutional rights. For example, evidence collected during an unreasonable police search or confessions obtained illegally are inadmissible at the trial to prove the defendant's guilt.

D. Search Warrants

A **search warrant**, in criminal law, is an order of a court, usually of a magistrate, issued to an officer of the law. This order authorizes a search of the premises named in the warrant for stolen articles, property possessed in violation of the law, or the instruments or evidence of a crime. The warrant authorizes the officer to seize particularly described items and to bring them before the court that issued the warrant. In common law, search warrants were used mainly to discover stolen property. By modern law, their use has been extended to a variety of items, including obscene literature, and any other items that may be used in evidence.

Under the Fourth Amendment of the U.S. Constitution a search warrant can be issued only on oath of a complainant showing probable cause for its issuance. The warrant must specify definitely the place in which the search is to be made and the property to be seized. An officer who, in executing the warrant, does not comply with or exceeds its terms is liable civilly for all acts not authorized by it; an action to recover damages may be instituted against the officer for trespass or assault, or both. In addition, items seized under an illegally issued or executed warrant may not be used as evidence in a criminal trial.

1. Discovery

Modern civil litigation is based upon the idea that the parties should not be subject to surprises at trial. **Discovery** is the process whereby civil litigants seek to obtain information both from other parties and from nonparties or third parties. Parties can obtain information with a series of tools. These tools include document requests, interrogatories, requests for admissions, and dispositions.

Document requests: A party can seek documents and other real objects from parties and non parties

Interrogatories: A party can require other parties to answer questions

Requests for admissions: A party can require other parties to admit or deny the truth of certain statements

Depositions: A party can require individuals or representatives of organizations to make themselves available for questioning

Federal procedure also requires parties to divulge certain information without a formal discovery request, in contrast to many state courts where most discoveries can only be had by request.

2. *Interrogatories and Requests for Production*

Requests for interrogatories and production of documents must be in accordance with applicable civil and local rules of the court where the matter is filed. Details are available at the Discoveryresources.org Web site. There are a number of terms and definitions that apply in the interrogatory and production process.

Application software: A set of electronic instructions, also known as a program, which instructs a computer to perform a specific set of processes.

Archive: A copy of data on a computer drive, or on a portion of a drive, maintained for historical reference.

Backup: A copy of active data, intended for use in restoration of data.

Computer: Includes but is not limited to network servers, desktops, laptops, notebook computers, employees' home computers, mainframes, the Personal Digital Assistants such as PalmPilot, Cassiopeia, HP Jornada and other such handheld computing devices), digital cell phones, and pagers.

Data: Any and all information stored on media that may be accessed by a computer.

Digital camera: A camera that stores still or moving pictures in a digital format (TIFF, GIF, etc.).

Document: Includes but is not limited to any electronically stored data on magnetic or optical storage media as an "active" file or files (readily readable by one or more computer applications or forensics software); any "deleted" but recoverable electronic files on said media; any electronic file fragments (files that have been deleted and partially overwritten with new data); and slack (data fragments stored randomly from random access memory (RAM) on a hard drive during the normal operation of a computer (RAM slack) or residual data left on the hard drive after new data has overwritten some but not all of previously stored data).

Hard drive: The primary hardware that a computer uses to store information, typically magnetized media on rotating disks.

Help features/documentation: Instructions that assist a user on how to set up and use a product including but not limited to software, manuals, and instruction files.

Imaged copy: A bit-by-bit (mirror image) copy of a hard drive.

Input device: Any object that allows a user to communicate with a computer by entering information or issuing commands (e.g., keyboard, mouse, or joystick).

Magnetic or optical storage media: Include but are not limited to hard drives (also known as "hard disks"), backup tapes, CD-ROMs, DVD-ROMs, USBs, JAZ and Zip drives, and floppy disks.

Network: A group of connected computers that allow people to share information and equipment (e.g., local area network (LAN), wide area network (WAN), metropolitan area network (MAN), storage area network (SAN), peer-to-peer network, client-server network).

Operating system: Software that directs the overall activity of a computer (e.g., MS-DOS, Windows, Linux, Macintosh).

Network operating system: Software that directs the overall activity of networked computers.

Software: Any set of instructions stored on computer-readable media that tells a computer what to do. This includes operating systems and applications.

Storage devices: Any device that a computer uses to store information.

Storage media: Storage media are any removable devices that store data.

There are several requests that might be required pertaining to the preservation of evidence. These include:

Written policies on preservation of records
Destruction of documents
Persons in charge of maintaining document retention and destruction policies
Preservation of evidence
Storage of documents

Interrogatories could include the identification of the data universe and information personnel.

Specific requests would apply to the following information resources:

Backup and archive media   Other sources of electronic evidence
Computer hardware   Data security measures

Computer software   Network details
Operating systems   E-mail
Telephony

3.   *Electronic Discovery*

Electronic discovery (E-discovery) refers to any process in which electronic data is sought, located, secured, and searched with the intent of using it as evidence in a civil or criminal legal case. E-discovery can be carried out offline or via a network access. Court-ordered hacking for the purpose of obtaining critical evidence is also a type of E-discovery. **Hacking** involves advanced computer skills for breaking into computers and networks.

The nature of digital data makes it extremely well suited to investigation. Digital data can be electronically searched with ease, whereas paper documents must be scrutinized manually. Digital data is difficult or impossible to completely destroy, particularly if it gets into a network. This is because the data often appears on multiple hard drives, and digital files, even if it is deleted, it can be undeleted.

In the process of electronic discovery, data of all types can serve as evidence. This can include text, images, calendar files, databases, spreadsheets, audio files, animation, Web sites, and computer programs. Electronic mail can be an especially valuable source of evidence in corporate issues, civil litigation, or criminal cases, because people are often less careful in these exchanges than in hard-copy correspondence, such as written memos and postal letters.

Computer forensics is a specialized form of E-discovery in which an investigation is carried out on the contents of the hard drive of a specific computer. After physically isolating the computer, investigators make a digital copy of the hard drive. Then the original computer is locked in a secure facility to maintain its pristine condition. All investigation is done on the digital copy.

E-discovery is an evolving field that goes far beyond mere technology. It gives rise to multiple legal, constitutional, political, security, and personal privacy issues, many of which have yet to be resolved.

E.   Laws Relating to Computer Crimes

This section describes various laws, statutes, acts, and **standard operating procedures (SOPs)** that can play a role in the computer-crime environment. Security and privacy is often mentioned in the press. **Security** is defined as freedom from risk or danger, and freedom from doubt, anxiety, or fear. **Privacy**, however, is defined as being secluded from the sight, presence, or intrusion of others. These terms must not be confused with each other.

Individuals and organizations must be aware of various laws that have been enacted to protect the privacy of electronic data. These include:

Health Insurance Portability and Accountability Act (HIPPA)
Sarbanes-Oxley Act of 2002 (Sarbox)
Children's Online Privacy Protection Act of 1998 (COPPA)
California Database Security Breach Act of 2003
The Computer Security Act
The Privacy Act of 1974
Uniform Electronic Transactions Act
Electronic Signatures in Global and National Commerce Act
Uniform Computer Information Transactions Act

1.   Health Insurance Portability and Accountability Act

The Health Insurance Portability and Accountability Act (HIPAA) was enacted by the U.S. Congress in 1996. The administrative simplification provision requires the establishment of national standards for electronic health care transactions and national identifiers for providers, health insurance plans, and employers.It requires the Department of Health and Human Services (HHS) to establish national standards for electronic health care transactions and national identifiers for providers, health plans, and employers. It also addresses the security and privacy of health data. Adopting these standards is alleged to improve the efficiency and effectiveness of the nation's health care system by encouraging the widespread use of electronic data interchange in health care.

2.   Sarbanes-Oxley Act

On July 30, 2002, the Sarbanes-Oxley (Sarbox) Act (Public Law 104-204) went into effect, and changed the corporate landscape in the United States in regard to financial reporting and auditing for publicly traded companies. The law establishes stringent financial reporting requirements for companies doing business in the United States. It defines the type of records that must be recorded and for how long. It also deals with falsification of data.

Sarbox was passed in response to a number of major corporate and accounting scandals involving prominent companies in the United States. These scandals resulted in a decline of public trust in accounting and reporting practices. The legislation is wide ranging and establishes new or enhanced standards for all U.S. public company boards, management, and public accounting firms. The act covers issues such as establishing a public company accounting oversight board, auditor independence, corporate responsibility, and enhanced financial disclosure. It was designed to review the dated legislative audit requirements, and is considered one of the most significant changes to the laws of U.S. securities since the 1930s. Titles VIII and IX have been included as they are especially relevant to electronic investigations.

a.   Title VIII: Corporate and Criminal Fraud Accountability Act of 2002

It is a felony to "knowingly" destroy or create documents to "impede, obstruct or influence" any existing or contemplated federal investigation. Auditors are required to maintain "all audit or review work papers" for five years. The statute of limitations on securities fraud claims is extended to the earlier of five years from the fraud, or two years after the fraud was discovered, from three years and one year, respectively. Employees of issuers and accounting firms are extended "whistle-blower protection" that would prohibit the employer from taking certain actions against employees who lawfully disclose private employer information to, among others, parties in a judicial proceeding involving a fraud claim. Whistle-blowers are also granted a remedy of special damages and attorney fees. A new crime for securities fraud with penalties of fines and up to ten years imprisonment has been enacted.

b.   Title IX: White-Collar Crime Penalty Enhancements

The maximum penalty for mail and wire fraud increased from five to ten years. This act creates a crime for tampering with a record or otherwise impeding any official proceeding. The Securities and Exchange Commission (SEC) is given authority to seek court freeze of extraordinary payments to directors, offices, partners, controlling persons, and agents of employees. The U.S. Sentencing Commission reviews sentencing guidelines for securities and accounting fraud. The SEC may prohibit anyone convicted of securities fraud from being an officer or director of any publicly traded company.

Financial statements filed with the SEC must be certified by the Chief Executive Officer (CEO) and Chief Financial Officer (CFO). The certification must state that the financial statements and disclosures fully comply with provisions of the Securities Exchange Act and that they fairly present, in all material respects, the operations and financial condition of the issuer. Maximum penalties for willful and knowing violations of this section are a fine of not more than $500,000 and/or imprisonment of up to five years.

3.   Children's Online Privacy Protection Act of 1998

The United States Children's Online Privacy Protection Act, effective April 21, 2000, applies to the online collection of personal information by persons or entities under U.S. jurisdiction from children under age 13. It spells out what a Web site operator must include in a privacy policy, when and how to seek verifiable consent from a parent and what responsibilities an operator has to protect children's privacy and safety online. Section 1303 contains information on the regulation of unfair and deceptive acts and practices in connection with the collection and use of personal information from and about children on the Internet. The entire act can be reviewed on the Web at www.ftc.gov/ogc/coppa1.htm.

4.   California Database Security Breach Act of 2003

The law requires that any agency, person, or business that owns or licenses computerized data that includes personal information must disclose any breach of the security of its computer system following discovery or notification of the breach. Residents of California whose unencrypted personal information was reasonably believed to have been acquired by an unauthorized person must be notified. According to the U.S. Attorney General, victims of identity theft must act quickly to minimize the damage; therefore, expeditious notification of possible misuse of a person's personal information is imperative. Personal information includes the following data items:

- An individual's first name or first initial and last name in combination with any one or more of the following data elements, when either the name or the data elements are not encrypted:
  - Social Security number
  - Driver's license number or California Identification Card number
  - Account number, credit or debit card number, in combination with any required security code, access code, or password that would permit access to an individual's financial account

It is essential that efforts be made to keep electronic data secure from criminals, thereby ensuring compliance with these laws and avoiding serious legal consequences. A number of miscellaneous acts and practices have been enacted for security, privacy, and financial compliance.

5.   The Computer Security Act

The **Computer Security Act of 1987** provides for improving the security and privacy of sensitive information in federal computer systems. The security measures in any system are what enable it to operate fully, including maintaining privacy. The act defines "sensitive information" to include any unclassified information that, if lost, misused, or accessed or modified without authorization, could adversely affect the national interest, conduct of federal programs, or the privacy to which individuals are entitled under the Privacy Act. The Computer Security Act requires federal agencies to identify their computer systems that contain sensitive information, establish training programs to increase security awareness and knowledge of security practices, and establish a plan for the security and privacy of each computer system with sensitive information.

The term "computer system" means any equipment or interconnected system or subsystem of equipment that is used in the automatic acquisition, storage, manipulation, management, movement, control, display, switching, interchange, transmission, or reception of data or information; and includes computers, ancillary equipment, software, firmware, and similar procedures, services, including support services, and related resources.

6. The Privacy Act of 1974

Because governments are the most voracious consumers and often abusers of personal information, it is important to have meaningful protection for citizens. The purpose of the Privacy Act is to balance the government's need to maintain information about individuals with the rights of individuals to be protected against unwarranted invasions of their privacy stemming from federal agencies' collection, maintenance, use, and disclosure of personal information about them.

The historical context of the act is important to an understanding of its remedial purposes. In 1974, Congress was concerned with curbing the illegal surveillance and investigation of individuals by federal agencies that had been exposed during the Watergate scandal; it was also concerned with potential abuses presented by the government's increasing use of computers to store and retrieve personal data by means of a universal identifier, such as an individual's Social Security number.

The **Privacy Act of 1974** (5 U.S.C. 552a) is intended to provide individuals with broad protection from the unauthorized use of records that federal agencies maintain about them. It requires agencies to account for disclosures of records that they maintain, and to take steps to minimize and protect the accuracy of records. It also requires agencies to reveal the purposes for which they are collecting information, and it gives individuals a right to gain access to records about them. Individuals may sue in federal district court if their rights under the Privacy Act are violated, and there are criminal penalties for knowing and willful violation of the act.

7. Uniform Electronic Transactions Act

The **Uniform Electronic Transactions Act (UETA)** provides a legal framework for electronic transactions. It gives electronic signatures and records the same validity and enforceability as manual signatures and paper-based transactions. This model act was adopted by the National Conference of Commissioners on Uniform State Laws (NCCUSL) in 1999. As of June 2, 2004, 46 states had enacted UETA.

8.   *Electronic Signatures in Global and National Commerce Act*

Congress enacted the **Electronic Signatures in Global and National Commerce Act (E-SIGN)** that establishes the validity of electronic records and signatures. It governs in the absence of a state law or where states have made modifications to UETA that are inconsistent with E-SIGN. By adopting the official version of UETA, states have the authority to modify, limit, or supersede some E-SIGN provisions, including its consumer protection provisions.

9.   *Uniform Computer Information Transactions Act*

The software industry was the initial focus of this model law and software companies have been a driving force in shaping the **Uniform Computer Information Transactions Act (UCITA)**. However, many other industries will be affected as the scope of UCITA extends to nearly all "transactions in information." For example, UCITA will impact the music industry, the information technology industry, public and private libraries, data processing service providers, publishers of statistical data, traditional print publishers, online database providers, and the consumer of information. As the scope of UCITA has expanded so has the political nature of the debate.

F.   E-Mail Laws

There are several laws that apply specifically to electronic mail. E-mail can be sent over both personal- and employer-based computer systems. There are different rules for these situations. Two Title 18 USC laws that address these issues include Sections 2511 and Sections 2701–2711. Note that United States Code or USC is a multivolume publication of the text of statutes enacted by Congress.

1.   *Title 18 USC Section 2511—Interception of Communication (Interception in Transit)*

Subject to this act, no person may intentionally intercept or attempt to intercept, or authorize or procure any other person to intercept or attempt to intercept, at any place in the Republic, any communication in the course of its occurrence or transmission.

2.   *Title 18 USC Section 2701–2711—Electronic*
      Communications Privacy Act (ECPA)
      (Unlawful Access to Stored Communications)

ECPA prohibits unlawful access and certain disclosures of communication contents. Additionally, the law prevents government entities from requiring disclosure of electronic communications from a provider without proper procedure.

G.   Computer Crime and Intellectual Property Section (CCIPS)

The United States Department of Justice's CCIPS provides information on two categories of laws that are relevant to both security and law-enforcement organizations. These involve Criminal Intellectual Property Laws and Federal Computer Intrusion Laws. Specific details are available on the Web at www.cybercrime.gov. Many of these laws can be found in various sections of Title 18 USC. Additional laws are being enacted each year, requiring considerable legal research to ascertain the proper procedures for computer and electronic forensic investigations. Both corporate legal offices and government legal departments must keep up to provide guidance to the various investigative personnel. Cases can be thrown out due to improper procedures undertaken during the various stages of a forensic investigation. Relevant laws include:

- 18 USC § 1362—Communication Lines, Stations, or Systems
- 18 USC § 2510—Wire and Electronic Communications Interception and Interception of Oral Communications
- 18 USC § 2701—Stored Wire and Electronic Communications and Transactional Records Access
- 18 USC § 3121—Recording of Dialing, Routing, Addressing, and Signaling Information

H.   Policies and Standards

The Federal Accounting Standards Advisory Board (FASAB) is the body that establishes accounting principles for federal entities. The Office of Management and Budget (OMB) adopts Statements of Federal Financial Accounting Standards (SFFAS). These interpretations are recommended by the FASAB and adopted in their entirety by OMB. The primary rules for accounting principles are included in the GAAP.

1.   *Generally Accepted Accounting Principles (GAAP)*

Generally Accepted Accounting Principles (GAAP) are the accounting rules used to prepare financial statements for publicly traded companies and many private companies in the United States. The GAPP for local and state governments operate under a different set of assumptions, principles, and constraints, as determined by the Governmental Accounting Standards Board (GASB). In the United States, as well as other countries practicing English common law system, the government does not set accounting standards, in the belief that the private sector has better knowledge and resources. The GAAP are not written in law, although the SEC requires that it be followed in financial reporting by publicly traded companies.

2.   *ISO 17799 Code of Practice for Security Management*

ISO/IEC 17799 provides best practice recommendations on information security management for use by those who are responsible for initiating, implementing or maintaining information security management systems. Information security is defined within the standard as "the preservation of confidentiality (ensuring that information is accessible only to those authorized to have access), integrity (safeguarding the accuracy and completeness of information and processing methods) and availability (ensuring that authorized users have access to information and associated assets when required)."

The 2005 version of the standard contains the following eleven main sections:

Security policy
Organization of information security
Asset management
Human resources security
Physical and environmental security
Communications and operations management
Access control
Information systems acquisition, development, and maintenance
Information security incident management
Business continuity management
Compliance

3.   *Information Technology Evidence Standards*

Information presented in this section will provide an overview of three information technology (IT) evidence standards. The documentation for each standard is available on the Web. These standards are quite lengthy and complex; however, IT forensic practitioners have a need to know this information.

- Guidelines for evidence collection and archiving
- Guidelines for best practice in the forensic examination of digital technology
- Best practices for computer forensics

RFC3227 defines guidelines for evidence collection and archiving. The purpose of this document is to provide security departments with guidelines on the collection and archiving of evidence relevant to some security incident. If evidence collection is performed correctly, it is more useful in apprehending an attacker, and stands a greater chance of being admissible in the event of a prosecution.

The **Scientific Working Group on Digital Evidence (SWGDE)** has published a document entitled "Best Practices for Computer Forensics." The purpose of the document is to describe the best practices for computer forensics. The document is not all inclusive and does not contain information relative to specific operating systems or forensic tools.

The **International Organization on Computer Evidence (IOCE)** has published the document titled "Guidelines for Best Practice in the Forensic Examination of Digital Technology." The scope of the document covers procedures, equipment, systems, personnel, and accommodation requirements involved in the entire forensic process of digital evidence.

I. Policies

Organizations can avoid litigation and unnecessary grief by publishing and maintaining policies that employees and other interested parties find easy to read and observe. These policies would set forth the rules concerning the use of the organization's computer, electronic, and network resources. Well-defined policies are necessary to give investigators and examiners the authority to conduct electronic and computer forensic investigations. These policies would set forth the procedures and processes involved and demonstrate, in objective terms, due process in all investigations. Without defined policies, organizations risk exposure to litigation by both current and former associates. There are several categories of policy statements that could comprise the organizations policy. These might include computer resource policies, computer user requirements and restrictions, and organizational security policies. Some of these policies are communicated by placing a warning banner on the organization's home page.

1. Computer Resource Policies

A number of sources are available that provide lists of technology-use policies. Policy statements are usually approved by an organization's officers and legal staff. A short policy list follows:

Use of any computing resource is restricted to those having proper authorization to use that particular resource.

No one shall knowingly endanger the security of any computing resource, nor willfully interfere with authorized computer usage by circumventing or attempting to circumvent normal resource limits, logon procedures, or security regulations.

No technologies shall be connected to the unit's computing resources that interfere with authorized usage of those resources.

The unit's computing resources shall not be used to attempt unauthorized use, or to interfere with another person's legitimate use, of any computer or network facility anywhere.

Computing resources and network facilities shall not be used for commercial purposes without specific authorization from a duly authorized designee.

Passwords to any computing resource shall only be issued to authorized users.

Only those persons with proper authorization shall modify or reconfigure any computing resource or network facility.

Users of the unit's computing resources shall have no expectation of privacy of materials stored on those resources.

Authorized computer users shall take full responsibility for messages that they transmit through the unit's computing resources.

2.   *Computer-Use Requirements and Restrictions*

Acceptable computer-use policies are usually specific to the organization. Computer-use policies are usually established by IT management. Sample policies follow:

Misrepresenting a person's identity or relationship to the unit when obtaining or using computer or network privileges is prohibited.

Accessing, reading, altering, or deleting any other person's computer files or electronic mail, without specific authorization, is prohibited.

Copying, installing, distributing, infringing, or otherwise using any software, data files, images, text, or other materials in violation of copyrights, trademarks, service marks, patents, other intellectual property rights, contracts, or license agreements is prohibited.

Creating, installing, or knowingly distributing a computer virus, worm, Trojan horse, or other surreptitiously destructive program on any computer or network facility, regardless of whether any demonstrable harm results, is prohibited.

3.   *Organizational Security Policies*

A **security policy** is a generic document that outlines rules for computer network access, determines how policies are enforced, and sets forth the basic architecture of the organization's security environment. This document establishes the framework within which an organization establishes needed levels of information security to achieve the desired confidentiality goals. It contains a policy statement of information values, protection responsibilities, and organization commitment for a system. These security policies should apply to all employees, staff members, volunteers, students, faculty, independent contractors, maintenance personnel, and agents that have an association with the organization. The organization's security department would be responsible for monitoring and investigating violations.

A **security architecture** is a detailed description of all aspects of the system that relate to security, along with a set of principles to guide the design. A security architecture describes how the system is put together to satisfy the security requirements. This architecture includes the following components:

Security audit—A process of searching a computer system and database for the purpose of identifying security problems and vulnerabilities.

Security countermeasures—Countermeasures established that are aimed at specific threats and vulnerabilities or involve more active techniques as well as activities traditionally perceived as security.

Security features—The security-relevant functions, mechanisms, and characteristics of hardware and software systems.

Security perimeter—The boundary where security controls are in effect to protect assets.

Security requirements—Types and levels of protection necessary for equipment, data, information, applications, and facilities.

Audits and investigations might be directed at a security violation or a security incident. A **security violation** is an instance in which a user or other person circumvents or defeats the controls of a system to obtain unauthorized access to information contained therein or to system resources. A **security incident**, however, is any act or circumstance that involves classified information that deviates from the requirements of governing security publications. This could include compromise, possible compromise, deviation, and inadvertent disclosure.

J.   Internal investigations

Before security resources are allocated to investigating some internal complaint or incident, a determination must be made as to the credibility of the complaint. There may be political and adverse organizational consequences, including significant costs of conducting an overt investigation. There are a number of questions that might be asked before an internal investigation is initiated.

- Is there a credible reason to conduct or not to conduct the investigation?
- What are the potential adverse consequences if the allegation is true or false?
- What are the financial, logistical, and practical costs associated with conducting an internal investigation?
- Can an informed decision be made without an official investigation?

Consideration must be given to the possibility of leaks by employees, shareholders, government agencies, and the media. A cover-up might be as devastating as a proactive investigation.

1.   *Civil and Criminal Computer Incidents*

There are endless opportunities for computer users to create havoc on the network. Often these users do not realize the turmoil that they are causing. This situation is akin to "joy riding." Many computer users, including juveniles and students, will try anything to see if they can do it. These individuals are often called "script kiddies." Examples of such acts include but are not limited to the following:

Excessive game playing
Sending excessive messages either locally or within the unit (including but not limited to electronic chain letters)
Initiating denial-of-service (DoS) attacks
Printing excessive copies of documents, files, data, or programs
Modifying system facilities, operating systems, or disk partitions
Attempting to crash or tie up a computer; damaging or vandalizing computing facilities, equipment, software, or computer files
Causing an inordinately large number of requests for files
Spamming
Sniffing
Running scans
Reconfiguring
Using an inordinately high percentage of bandwidth

Do not be concerned if these terms look like a foreign language. They will be explained later in the book. It is important that computer forensic investigators speak the language of computer and electronic technology. This will become obvious when the defense attorney asks an investigator to explain some computer or electronic term and the witness is clueless.

2.   *Security Departments*

Most large corporations, government offices, and educational entities have an internal department that is charged with protecting the organization's capital resources.

These functions include the protection of physical facilities, various assets, and information system and technology resources. The U.S. Government also has a number of organizations that provide some type and level of security.

The United States Department of Homeland Security (DHS) is a cabinet department of the Federal Government of the United States with the responsibility of protecting the territory of the United States from terrorist attacks and responding to natural disasters. The department was created from 22 existing federal agencies in response to the terrorist attacks of September 11, 2001.

DHS is the third largest cabinet department in the U.S. federal government, after the Department of Defense and Department of Veterans Affairs. It has approximately 180,000 employees. Other agencies with significant homeland security responsibilities include the Department of Health and Human Services and the Energy Department.

3. Civil Litigation

The majority of civil law jurisdictions follow an inquisitorial system of adjudication, in which judges undertake an active investigation of the claims by examining the evidence and preparing reports. Civil litigation begins when a plaintiff requests access to a computer hard drive, via a court order or agreement. Generally the forensic expert makes a forensic copy of the drive for analysis. Often the defendant is required to provide the drive for a lengthy time period.

The plaintiff requests the forensic expert to identify, locate, and isolate specific information contained on the hard drive. This is the data identification phase of the litigation. The defendant may claim the drive contains proprietary, privileged, or protected information. The court must acknowledge this and make provisions to recover relevant data. If protected or proprietary information is to be identified, the expert advises the defendant as to what is to be delivered to the plaintiff. The defendant will then review the identified information and notifies the expert which items are indeed protected or privileged. A negotiation may occur at this time as to which information can be used. After the deliverable items are identified, the expert extracts and/or copies those items from the original media and includes the results in a formal report.

The discovery phase follows the data identification phase. After the items are identified and extracted, the expert will provide the information to the plaintiff. Prior to the trial, the defendant then requests, through discovery, the information the expert has identified and placed in the report. After the plaintiff has the data, the defendant may request a copy of all data retrieved. The plaintiff then provides a copy of the report and data to the defendant. The following is a summary list of the discovery process:

Defendant turns over computer for analysis
Expert performs analysis and identifies and extracts data

Defendant may be allowed to influence the data analysis claiming privileged and/or protected data

Data that is identified is turned over to plaintiff

Note that anything written down or in the report is subject to the discovery process. The normal civil legal processes proceed at this point with attorneys arguing their case and presenting evidence. There is, however, the possibility that either the plaintiff or defendant will request that specific data be redacted. **Redaction** is the process of altering, adapting, or refining to suit a particular purpose and will usually require the expertise of a forensic examiner or scientist. This process is discussed in Chapter 11.

An issue that arises in both civil and criminal cases that involve electronic evidence is the expertise of counsel. A common recurring problem is the defense counsel's lack of knowledge (clueless) about electronic discovery. Remember that discovery is the compulsory pretrial disclosure of documents relevant to a case, which enables one side in a litigation to elicit information from the other side concerning the facts in the case. Counsel often has a tenuous grasp of computer systems and does not understand the client's devices or data, which means that sound guidance about preserving digital evidence cannot be provided. The end result in this short-sighted view is the computer-illiterate counsel does not seek the computer forensic expert required. This lack of computer forensic expertise is so pervasive it may take years and several high-profile E-discovery debacles before lawyers fully appreciate how much their lack of knowledge hurts their clients.

4. *Criminal Prosecution*

Currently criminal procedure puts the burden of proof on the prosecution. It is up to the prosecution to prove that the defendant is guilty, as opposed to having the defendant prove any innocence; thus any doubt is resolved in favor of the defendant. This provision is known as the presumption of innocence, which may operate somewhat differently in different countries.

All jurisdictions allow the defendant the right of counsel and provide defendants with their own lawyer, at the public expense, if they cannot afford one. This is expressed in the **Miranda warning**, which is part of an arrest procedure. Again, the efficiency of this system depends greatly on the jurisdictions. In some jurisdictions, the lawyers provided to indigent defendants are often overworked or incompetent, or may not take much interest in the cases they have to defend. In cases involving computer forensics, many lawyers and the courts will not be familiar with the technology.

In a criminal case, the government generally brings charges in one of two ways: either by accusing a suspect directly in a "bill of information" or other similar document, or by bringing evidence before a grand jury to allow that body to determine whether the case should proceed. If there is, then the defendant is indicted. In the federal system, a case must be brought before a grand jury for indictment if it is to proceed. Some states, however, do not require indictment. Once charges have been brought, the case is then brought before a **petit jury**, or is tried by a judge if the defense requests it. The jury hearing the case is selected from a pool by the prosecution and defense.

The burden of proof is on the prosecution in a criminal trial, who must prove beyond a reasonable doubt that the defendant is guilty of the crime charged. The prosecution presents its case first, and may call witnesses and present other evidence against the defendant. After the prosecution rests, the defense may move to dismiss the case if there is insufficient evidence, or present its case and call witnesses. All witnesses may be cross-examined by the opposing side. The defendant is not required to testify under the Fifth Amendment to the United States Constitution, but must answer the prosecution's questions if there is an election to take the stand. After both sides have presented their cases and made closing arguments, the judge gives the jury legal instructions and they adjourn to deliberate in private. The jury must unanimously agree on a verdict of guilty or not guilty.

If a defendant is found guilty, then sentencing follows. Sentencing often occurs at a separate hearing after the prosecution, defense, and court have developed information based on which the judge will craft a sentence. In capital cases, a separate "penalty phase" occurs, in which the jury determines whether to recommend that the death penalty should be imposed. As with the guilt phase, the burden is on the prosecution to prove its case, and the defendant is entitled to take the stand and may call witnesses and present evidence.

After sentencing, the defendant may appeal the ruling to a higher court. American appellate courts do not retry the case; they only examine the record of the proceedings in the lower court to determine if errors were made that require a new trial, resentencing, or a complete discharge of the defendant, as is mandated by the circumstances. The prosecution may not appeal after an acquittal, although it may appeal under limited circumstances before verdict is rendered, and may also appeal from the sentence itself.

5. Law Enforcement Involvement

The following is a list of government offices and watchdog groups that address various aspects of computer forensics and other law enforcement initiatives.

FBI: Federal Bureau of Investigations—A federal law enforcement agency that investigates alleged violations of federal criminal laws governing banking, gambling, white collar fraud, public corruption, civil rights, interstate transportation of stolen property, and elections. The FBI is part of the Justice Department.

SEARCH: The National Consortium for Justice Information and Statistics—Provides the tools for justice system organizations to work together to solve communication problems and to implement standard practices.

HTCIA: High Technology Crime Investigation Association—Designed to encourage, promote, aid, and affect the voluntary interchange of data, information, experience, ideas and knowledge about methods, processes, and techniques relating to investigations and security in advanced technologies among its membership.

FACT: Forensic Association of Computer Technologists—A not-for-profit association for the purpose of training law enforcement in the scientific techniques of examining computers.

NWC3: National White Collar Crime Center—Provides a nationwide support system for agencies involved in the prevention, investigation, and prosecution of economic and high-tech crimes. It supports and partners with other appropriate entities in addressing homeland security initiatives, as they relate to economic and high-tech crimes.

USPIS: U.S. Postal Inspection Service—The mission of the United States Postal Inspection Service is to protect the U.S. Postal Service, its employees and its customers from criminal attack, and protect the nation's mail system from criminal misuse.

K. Expert Witnesses and Computer Forensic Experts

Evidence resulting from a computer forensics investigation can mean the difference between winning and losing a case. Often the only evidence that exists, aside from circumstantial, is the evidence found as the result of a computer forensics investigation. Paper files can be shredded, lost, tossed, or altered. Witnesses can forget the facts as they occurred or use "selective memory" on the stand. Computer and electronic forensics evidence cannot be refuted, as it is the result of a scientific process and exists in an obviously tangible form.

Computer forensics specialists and examiners are trained in specific techniques applicable to the field. It is important to remember that experts in other computer-related fields are not generally trained in forensics. For example, experts in computer hardware, software, or data recovery will not have the expertise necessary to successfully retrieve, analyze, and report accurate findings from electronic media without specific forensics training.

A new category of subject matter expert is the forensic accountant. This individual is trained in the fundamentals of accounting and financial management and uses computer technology resources to identify questionable or illegal financial activities. With the proliferation of white-collar crime in business, this individual becomes a valuable witness for both the organization and the prosecution. A forensic accountant, when paired with a computer forensic examiner, provides a formidable team in financial fraud investigations.

Locating a capable professional is not a difficult task. Time available to the investigator, however, will be a major consideration. Depending upon the number of computers potentially involved in the case, the work may be very time consuming. The specialist selected must have ample time to conduct a thorough investigation and write an accurate report. The professional must also provide all the related support services required, such as responding to interrogatories, providing court reports, and providing expert testimony.

Qualified professionals and experts can be found on Internet sites created specifically for this purpose. Numerous listings can be identified by surfing "computer forensics" organizations. When interviewing prospective professionals, the following criteria will help accomplish this task:

- Search for a computer forensics specialist who is an experienced expert witness. It is preferable for the expert witness to be able to explain and discuss how the investigation was conducted, who came to various conclusions, and determined their findings, rather than relying on another expert witness to interpret your specialist's investigation.
- Have the expert explain the process of computer forensics. Can the expert explain the process in a language that a jury can understand, or is it described using scientific jargon that will sound like gibberish to the court? If the case is heard in a small town, consider the makeup of the jury.
- Discuss the preparation of court reports. The expert chosen should have ample experience in the generation of court reports, and should be knowledgeable of the intricacies that should be contained in this documentation.
- Consider how an individual's voice will sound in court. The expert chosen should be articulate and self-assured without sounding pretentious or arrogant. Remember the audience.
- Explore the expert's knowledge concerning the federal rules of evidence, admissibility of expert testimony, the hearsay rule and its exceptions, chain of custody, and suitable documentation.
- Be sure that the lines of communication remain open and that the expert is informed of every twist and turn in the case that might impact the expert's role in the matter.

The earlier a forensics specialist, forensics investigator, or forensics examiner is involved in the matter, the greater the chance that usable evidence will result from the investigation. It is essential that nonforensic professionals, including IT professionals, not have access to the electronics and media. If someone has accessed the device, even turned it on or off, since the time the computer or electronic device became suspect, evidence can be contaminated. *(Note: internal personnel instigate 80 percent of security policy violations.)*

A computer forensics specialist or subject matter expert (SME) will be extremely valuable to assist in all stages of building a case, including:

Ascertaining whether the device(s) in question may contain information relevant to the subject of concern

Assisting in preparing and responding to interrogatories (written questions)

Planning and providing expert testimony

Retrieving and examining information that is accessible only through the use of forensics techniques, software, hardware, and methods

Developing court reports

Note that subject matter experts may be contracted to support either the prosecution or defense side of a case. These experts could include computer forensics specialists and others such as forensic accountants to support or challenge some argument before the court. There is a growing list of subject matter experts and specialists for every conceivable subject. This type of case involves a number of "minefields." It is especially easy to make a computer or electronic witness look ignorant or incompetent. A relevant axiom is "a little knowledge is a dangerous thing."

1.   *National Institute of Justice Methods*

The National Institute of Justice (NIJ) has developed methods for electronic investigations and forensic analysis. NIJ works with the National Institute of Standards and Training (NIST) and other federal partners to develop methods to test commercial computer forensic software and establish minimum performance standards. NIJ provides publications specific to electronic crimes. The Web site is located at www.ojp.usdoj.gov/nij. Topics include:

Electronic Crime Scene Investigation: A Guide for First Responders
Using best practices when seizing electronic evidence
Forensic Examination of Digital Evidence: A Guide for Law Enforcement
Searching and Seizing Computers and Obtaining Electronic Evidence in Criminal Investigations
Security Threats to the 802.11 Wireless Networks

Additional websites include www.nij.ncjrs.gov/publications/pub-search.asp and www.nij.ncjrs.gov/publications/searchform.asp.

Chapter Summary

There are a variety of legal issues facing the cybercrime expert. As technology progresses, laws, and statutes are adapting to meet the changing environment.

Understanding these issues is critical to the effective prosecution of criminals. The primary acts addressing these issues include the Electronic Communication Privacy Act, Cable Communications Privacy Act, Privacy Protection Act, and the Fourth Amendment.

It is essential that participants understand the various legal processes and activities that occur when prosecuting a cybercrime. Numerous legal terms concerning electronic evidence and witness presentations must also be understood to be successful in a criminal trial. The technical witness must also be knowledgeable and competent in topics concerning the electronic and computer environment.

Often it will be necessary to solicit assistance from computer forensics specialists and examiners who are trained in specific techniques applicable to the field. Both the defense and the prosecution teams may employ these professionals. It is important to remember that experts in other computer-related fields are not generally trained in forensics. For example, experts in computer hardware, software, or data recovery will often not have the expertise necessary to successfully retrieve, analyze, and report accurate findings from electronic media without specific forensics training.

There are a number of organizations that are charged with addressing incidents involving cyber crimes. These include the FBI, USPIS, HTCIA, NWC3, SEARCH, FACT, and state law enforcement agencies.

The National Institute of Justice has developed methods for electronic investigations and forensic analysis. Numerous publications specific to electronic crimes and investigations are available on the Web. A number of state and private organizations are also active in the areas of forensic education for law enforcement and corporate security personnel.

Most large corporations, government offices, and educational entities have an internal security department that is charged with protection of the organization's computer and information resources. These organizations establish a security policy document that outlines rules for computer network access, determines how policies are enforced, and sets forth the basic architecture of the organization's security environment.

Terms

Application software — A set of electronic instructions, also known as a program that instructs a computer to perform a specific set of processes.

Archive — A copy of data on a computer drive, or on a portion of a drive, maintained for historical reference.

Backup — A copy of active data, intended for use in restoration of data.

CCIPS — Computer Crime and Intellectual Property Section.

CCPA — Cable Communications Privacy Act.

Court order — A document prepared and signed by a court, to give effect to a decision of a judge of that court.

Deposition — A testimony made under oath can be a written statement by a witness for use in court in his absence.

Direct testimony — Includes statements made under oath by a party or the party's witness.

Discovery — The process whereby civil litigants seek to obtain information both from other parties and from nonparties or third parties.

Document — Includes but is not limited to any electronically stored data on magnetic or optical storage media as an "active" file or files (readily readable by one or more computer applications or forensics software); any "deleted" but recoverable electronic files on said media; any electronic file fragments (files that have been deleted and partially overwritten with new data); and slack (data fragments stored randomly from random access memory on a hard drive during the normal operation of a computer [RAM slack] or residual data left on the hard drive after new data has overwritten some but not all of the previously stored data).

ECPA — Electronic Communications Privacy Act.

Electronic discovery (E-discovery) — Refers to any process in which electronic data is sought, located, secured, and searched with the intent of using it as evidence in a civil or criminal legal case.

E-SIGN — Congress enacted the Electronic Signatures in Global and National Commerce Act, which establishes the validity of electronic records and signatures.

Evidence — Provides the means by which disputed facts are proved to be true or untrue in any trial before a court of law or an agency that functions like a court. Evidence includes testimony, records, documents, material objects, or other things presented at a trial to prove the existence or nonexistence of a fact.

Felony — Described as a crime of a graver or more atrocious nature than those designated as misdemeanors.

First Amendment — The First Amendment to the United States Constitution contained in the Bill of Rights. It provides for freedom of speech, press, religion, peaceable assembly, and to petition the government.

Fourth Amendment — The Fourth Amendment to the United States Constitution contained in the Bill of Rights. It dictates probable cause for search and seizure.

Generally Accepted Accounting Principles (GAAP) — The accounting rules used to prepare financial statements for publicly traded companies and many private companies in the United States.

Hacking — *Involves advanced computer skills for breaking into computers and networks.*

Hearsay evidence — Consists of statements made out of court by someone who is not present to testify under oath at a trial.

Help features/documentation — Instructions that assist a user on how to set up and use a product including but not limited to software, manuals, and instruction files.

Indirect testimony — Providing only a basis for inference about the fact in dispute.

Internet service provider (ISP) — A company that provides access to the Internet.

Interrogatory — A written question, as to a witness, usually answered under oath.

IOCE — International Organization on Computer Evidence.

ISO 17799 — Code of Practice for Security Management.

Keylogger — A computer program that captures the keystrokes of a computer user and stores them.

Miranda warning — Based on a U.S. Supreme Court decision, is a person's legal rights under U.S. law (the right to remain silent, etc.), and, except on Indian reservations, is supposed to be read to persons being arrested.

Misdemeanor — Any crime that is not a felony. Punishment for a misdemeanor is typically a fine or possibly jail time of less than one year. These are sometimes called "simple" misdemeanors.

Petit jury — Lesser; minor jury.

Privacy — Being secluded from the sight, presence, or intrusion of others.

Privacy Protection Act — Designed to protect people involved in First Amendment activities from searches when they themselves are not involved in criminal activity.

Redaction — The process of altering, adapting, or refining a result to suit a particular purpose.

RFC3227 — Defines guidelines for evidence collection and archiving.

Script kiddies — Younger and less sophisticated users who break into a network or computer system with malicious intent.

Search warrant — In criminal law, is an order of a court, usually of a magistrate, issued to an officer of the law.

Security — Freedom from risk or danger, and freedom from doubt, anxiety, or fear.

Security audit — A process of searching a computer system and database for the purpose of identifying security problems and vulnerabilities.

Security incident — Any act or circumstance that involves classified information that deviates from the requirements of governing security publications.

Security policy — A generic document that outlines rules for computer network access, determines how policies are enforced, and sets forth the basic architecture of the organization's security environment.

Security violation — An instance in which a user or other person circumvents or defeats the controls of a system to obtain unauthorized access to information contained therein or to system resources.

Sniffer/sniffing — A program to capture data across a computer network. Hackers use it to capture user ID names and passwords. A sniffer is a software tool that audits and identifies network traffic packets. It is also used legitimately by network operations and maintenance personnel to troubleshoot network problems.

Standard operating procedure (SOP) — Prescribed procedure to be followed routinely.

Stored electronic communications — Refers to e-mail while it resides on the e-mail server.

Subject matter expert (SME) — An individual possessing expertise and experience in some topic.

Subpoena — A process to cause a witness to appear and give testimony, commanding him or her to appear before a court therein named at a time therein mentioned to testify for the party named under a penalty therein mentioned.

SWGDE — Scientific Working Group on Digital Evidence.

UCITA — Uniform Computer Information Transactions Act.

UETA — Uniform Electronic Transactions Act.

Wiretapping — The monitoring of telephone conversations by a third party, often by covert means.

Witness — Described as someone who testifies to what he has seen, heard, or otherwise observed and who is not a party to the action.

Review Questions

1. The accounting rules used to prepare financial statements for publicly traded companies and many private companies in the United States are _____.
2. Describe the differences between a warrant and a subpoena.
3. Describe the difference between a felony and a misdemeanor.
4. A _____ is a software tool that audits and identifies network traffic packets. Hackers use it to capture user ID names and passwords.
5. The monitoring of telephone conversations by a third party, often by covert means is called _____.
6. Develop a list of agencies that are responsible for electronic forensic investigations.
7. Describe the stored electronics communications environment.
8. Describe the activities that might be expected from a computer forensics expert.
9. Identify acts of vandalism that might occur on electronic networks such as the Internet.
10. The _____is designed to protect people involved in First Amendment activities from searches when they themselves are not involved in criminal activity.

Chapter 3

Computer Forensic Examination Categories

Chapter Objectives

- Identify the various crimes and incidents that are involved in electronic forensic investigations
- See how identity theft and fraud permeates all elements of the computer and electronics environment
- Look at the various types of evidence that can be gathered for each category of crime
- Become familiar with the various terms associated with these types of investigations
- Understand the importance of security and computer-use policies
- Look at the various incidents that may be investigated by the corporate security department

Introduction

It should not be a surprise that computer and electronic crimes are on the rise. The economic impact of such crimes must be significant; however, it is difficult to know the cost of such incidents. Because these crimes and incidents occur worldwide, statistics are no doubt understated, if at all.

It has been estimated that computer crimes result in billions of dollars in losses worldwide. This number consists of actual loss plus loss of productivity. There are generally two categories of computer crimes—those that use a computer or some electronic device to commit a crime or incident and those that are used against these devices. Here is a compilation of some of the most prominent computer-style crimes and incidents:

Network intrusions	Illegal material content
Destruction of data and information	Spoofing of Internet protocol (IP)
Modification of data or data-diddling	addresses
Denial-of-service (DoS) and	Fraud
distributed DoS (DDoS)	Embezzlement
Eavesdropping	Espionage
Software piracy	Information warfare
Music piracy	Cyber-terrorism
Theft of logins and passwords	Social engineering
Malicious code and programs	Dumpster diving
Masquerading	Child molestation

Some of these items listed are techniques that are used to commit an actual crime. It should be noted that these illicit activities might also be used to commit some other crime, such as a felony or capital offense. It is quite plausible for an individual to use social engineering and dumpster-diving techniques to commit fraud by stealing someone's entire bank balance.

A. Common Law Overview

The main categories of common law include criminal law, civil law, and regulatory law.

Criminal law is concerned with individual conduct that violates governmental laws that were enacted for public protection. **Civil law** is concerned with wrongs inflicted upon an organization or individual that result in some damage or loss. **Regulatory law** sets standards of performance and conduct expected by various entities. There are additional special laws that address privacy and intellectual property.

This book categorizes electronic forensics investigations as those involving petty crimes, serious crimes, civil actions, and corporate security issues. Most criminal computer and electronic investigations will be in support of some other major case category. A kidnapping might be solved by digital evidence found in an e-mail, cell phone records, or on a suspect's computer system. The electronic forensics investigators and examiners would be part of the primary case team.

The next sections will provide an overview of the categories of both criminal and corporate illegal activities that might benefit from a forensic investigation. Also presented are lists of evidence types that might be useful when pursuing these investigations. There are a number of common types of evidence that should be gathered for most electronic investigations. E-mail transmissions, address books, and Internet activity logs are all potential sources of evidence. Information is presented in three categories—financial crimes, computer crimes, and common law crimes.

B.   Financial Crime Categories

Crimes discussed in this section include auction fraud, economic fraud, property theft, and identity theft. A fraud is defined as a fraudulent conversion and obtaining money or property by false pretenses. Included are confidence games and bad checks, except forgeries and counterfeiting. Theft is generally defined as the act of stealing or larceny.

1.   Auction Fraud

Online frauds have become an issue with the advent of electronic business and electronic commerce activities on the Internet. These activities are known as business-to-consumer (B2C), consumer-to-consumer (C2C), and business-to-business (B2B). Amazon.com is primarily a B2C Web site, whereas EBay is primarily a C2C Web site. **Auction frauds** occur on Internet sites that offer consumer items for sale to the general public. Often the items offered for sale over these sites are not by individuals, but business enterprises. There are groups of people who offer to sell and buy items over these Internet sites, but have no intention of fulfilling the contract. Unsuspecting buyers send payment for items that are never shipped or the item sent is not as advertised.

   Both search warrants and subpoenas will probably be required to collect forensic evidence. Evidence might be found in these areas:

Account data regarding online auction sites	Internet activity logs
	Internet browser history
Accounting software and associated data	Online financial institution records
	Telephone records
Customer information	Databases
Credit card data	Testimonial documents
E-mail transmissions	Chat logs
Image files and printouts	

2.   Economic Fraud and Property Theft

A number of crimes are categorized under economic fraud and property theft. Many of these incidents could occur in the corporate environment. Illegal activities might involve theft of resources from an organization or manipulating financial records for personal gain. Computer system software can be modified and manipulated by unscrupulous employees for personal gain or as part of a conspiracy involving other insiders. These offenses could also involve online fraud and other crimes, such as counterfeiting, check laundering, money laundering, and identity-theft activities.

Some of the evidence findings are similar to those for auction and online fraud. These include:

Address books	False identification
Calendar	Financial records
Check, currency, and money orders	Signature images
Credit card skimmers	Internet activity logs
Customer information	Online financial institution software
Credit card data	Financial audit reports
Databases	Software maintenance logs
E-mail transmissions	
False financial transaction forms and screen shots	

3. Identity Theft

Identity theft is defined as the deliberate assumption of another person's identity, usually to gain access to the person's finances. Identity theft is big business for the criminal community and is a worldwide epidemic. Numerous scams are perpetuated daily on the general public and specifically on Internet and e-mail users. Many of these scams are caused via e-mail phishing and poor Internet practices. Considerable resources are devoted to countering these threats by commercial organizations and law enforcement. Commercial organizations, educational institutions, governmental agencies, and the general public spend millions on hardware and software products for protection of their resources. Identity theft can involve social engineering activities, dumpster diving, mail theft, ATM ID theft, and numerous scams.

Evidence is similar to that of online fraud, economic fraud, and property theft. Tools employed by the criminal might include hardware and software, negotiable instruments, suspicious Internet activity, and identification templates. A brief review of the following tool lists provides some indication of the magnitude of identity theft crimes.

Hardware and software devices include:

Credit card generators	Scanners
Credit card reader/writer	Skimmers
Cameras	

Forged identification and identification templates include:

Check-cashing cards
Driver's license
Social Security cards
Electronic signatures

Birth certificates
Vehicle registrations
Proof of auto insurance
Scanned signatures

Internet activities related to identity theft include:

E-mails and newsgroups postings
Erased documents
Online orders
Online trading info

System files
File slack and unallocated space
Web activity at suspect sites

Negotiable instruments include:

Business checks
Cashier's checks
Counterfeit money
Credit card numbers
Fictitious court documents
Fictitious gift certificates

Fictitious loan documents
Money orders
Personal checks
Stock transfer documents
Vehicle transfer documents

C. Computer Crime Categories

Crimes discussed in this section include software and video piracy, computer threats and intrusions, telecommunications fraud, and e-mail issues. **Piracy** is defined as the unauthorized duplication of goods protected by intellectual property law (e.g., copying software unlawfully).

1. Software and video piracy

The Internet provides an available conduit for both computer software and video piracy activities. Proprietary products are stolen and often copied, cloned, and offered for resale at reduced prices, thereby denying revenue to legitimate businesses. When investigating these crime scenes, look for duplication, recording media, and packaging materials. Evidence might be uncovered from the following:

Software cracking items
E-mail transmissions
Chat logs
Internet activity logs

Product serial numbers
Image files of software certificates
Copyrighted software, videos, and
 music

2. Computer threats and intrusions

Major issues concerning computer users are threats involving the proliferation of viruses, worms, and Trojan horses. Most computer center managers spend considerable manpower and funding to block intrusions and threats that could impact the organization's resources. Considerable hardware and software in the form of firewalls and routers are deployed across the organization's computer facilities. As studies show, incidents involving computer intrusions often originate within the organization and insiders account for approximately 80 percent of illegal computer activities. This is true mainly because insiders know the information, such as log-ons and passwords, which allows access into the various systems.

Large computer centers often maintain a security function that monitors both inside and outside threats to the information technology resource. Violations of the organization's security policies and computer-use policies are investigated by this function. Financial organizations and other high-profile businesses might want to suppress public knowledge of any security breach. For this reason, management might elect to avoid a criminal complaint and handle the issue internally.

There are a number of hardware and software tools that can be employed to monitor the computer system resources. These include sniffers and monitors. Evidence might be found in the following:

Address books   IP addresses and usernames
Configuration files   Internet chat logs
E-mail transmissions   Source program code
Executable programs   Text files
Internet activity logs   Printouts
System logs

D. Telecommunications Fraud

Both criminal activities and malicious acts can be performed in the telecommunications and networking area. The telecommunications environment includes wired networks, wireless networks, the broadband network, and local telephone service. Most local exchange carriers maintain a security staff for investigating theft of services, sabotage, and incidents involving company personnel. Telecommunications companies operate vary large mainframe computer centers that process every conceivable type of application system. The corporate databases contain all subscriber records for the covered area of service. There are, however, new rules concerning the access to these subscriber records by law enforcement and the government. Criminal activities identified by corporate security would be referred to the appropriate law enforcement agency for prosecution. Useful evidence would include the following:

Cloning software	**Phreaking** manuals
Subscriber database records	Internet activity records
Electronic IDs	Telephone records
E-mail transmissions	Cell phone records
Financial records	Blue-box device

1.   E-Mail Issues

A number of issues can be associated with the e-mail system. These consist of threats, stalking, harassment, fraud, phishing, spam, etc. Corporate e-mail can be the vehicle for sexual harassment, pornography, violations of company policies, and the list is also endless. E-mail is an effective method of message transmission for terrorist organizations. Corporate computer centers usually operate an e-mail server that maintains traffic information and log files on all transmissions. This history might be backed up offline on storage media. A subpoena would most likely be required to view the data. Chapter 12 is devoted to the issues of e-mail forensics. Evidence types would include:

Address books	Internet activity
Diaries	Legal documents
E-mail transmissions	Telephone and cell phone records
Financial records	E-mail system logs
Graphic Images/photos	Victim research data

E.   Personal Crime Categories

This section describes crimes of domestic violence, extortion, gambling, controlled substances, prostitution, death, assault, and child exploitation. Computers and electronic devices usually do not play a prominent role in these crimes; however, circumstantial evidence obtained from electronic devices can play a major part in investigating these types of crimes.

1.   Domestic Violence

Domestic violence is defined as physical and/or emotional harm suffered by a person who is a family member of, or residing in the same home as, the offender who caused the harm or injury. The parties involved in domestic violence are often reluctant to prosecute their attackers. As most first responders already know, this is usually a difficult and dangerous situation. Considerable supporting evidence might be found on computers, e-mail, cell phones, and personal digital assistants (PDAs) that are located at the crime scene. Other evidence might be available on databases at medical and financial institutions. Evidence sources could include the following:

Address books	Medical records
Diaries	Telephone and cell phone records
E-mail transmissions	Police report history
Financial records	Neighbors and relatives

2.   Extortion

Extortion is used to obtain property or money by the use of violence, threats, or intimidation. Extortion can be related to other crimes, such as kidnapping and threats. E-mail transmissions and Web traffic can be subpoenaed from Internet service providers (ISPs). Cell phone traffic could be a source to establish time, date, and location information. Evidence sources could include the following:

Date and time stamps	History logs
E-mail transmissions	Temporary Internet files
Internet activity logs	User names

3.   Gambling

Gambling is the unlawful engaging in playing, operating, or assisting in operating a game of chance for money or some other stake. Gambling can be related to organized crime. Investigative techniques include following the money through financial organizations and looking at e-mail and telephone records to identify participants. Evidence sources could include the following:

Address books	E-mail transmissions
Calendar	Financial records
Customer database	Internet activity logs
Play records	Online financial institutions
Electronic cash	Sports-betting statistics

4.   Controlled Substances

Drugs and certain other chemicals, both narcotic and non-narcotic, which come under the jurisdiction of federal and state laws regulating their manufacture, sale, distribution, use, and disposal are designated **controlled substances**. Drug trafficking activities occur in all law enforcement jurisdictions worldwide and activities could be related to organized crime and terrorist organizations. Customer databases can often be located on laptop computers. Cell phone data may contain contact numbers for customers, suppliers, and runners and cell phone records can show time, date, and called numbers. E-mail servers could contain evidence of activities. Evidence sources could include the following:

Address books
Calendar
Database
Drug recipes
E-mail transmissions

False identification
Financial records
Internet activity logs
Prescription form images

5.   Prostitution

Prostitution includes sex offenses, including attempts, of a commercialized nature.

Prostitution can be related to the drug trade or organized crime. Customer lists can be maintained on a computer. Data could include customer names, costs, addresses, and phone numbers. Medical records could establish patterns. Evidence sources could include the following:

Address books
Biographies
Calendar
Customer database
E-mail transmissions

False identification
Financial records
Internet activity logs
Medical records
Web ads

6.   Death and Assault Investigation

Assault is the crime of violence against another person. In some jurisdictions, assault is used to refer to the actual violence, while in other jurisdictions assault refers only to the threat of violence, while the actual violence is battery. Computer forensic investigations would be in support of the primary incident of assault or death. E-mail, cell phone, and Internet records can all contain valuable leads in these investigations. Evidence sources could include the following:

Address books
Diaries
E-mail transmissions
Financial records
Images

Internet activity log
Legal documents and wills
Medical records
Telephone and cell phone records

7.   Child Exploitation

Child exploitation could include trafficking, prostitution, molestation, abuse, and pornography. The Internet is the primary vehicle for transmission of pornographic images. Child exploitation crimes can be investigated using a variety of sources. Pornography evidence might be found on a number of Web sites and can also be attachments to e-mail transmissions. A sexual predator Web site is located at the National Sex Offender Registry, www.familywatchdog.us. Evidence sources include the following:

Chat logs	Graphic images
Date and time stamps	Photographs
Cameras	Internet activity logs
E-mail transmissions	Movies
Graphic edits and viewing software	File directories

F.   Cyber-Terrorism and Information Warfare

Cyberspace is defined as the global network of interconnected computers and communication systems. **Cyber-terrorism** is the convergence of terrorism and cyberspace. As the Internet becomes more pervasive in all areas of human endeavor, individuals or groups can use the anonymity afforded by cyberspace to threaten citizens, specific groups, communities, and entire countries, without the inherent chance of capture, injury, or death to the attacker. As the Internet continues to expand, and computer systems continue to be assigned more responsibility while becoming more and more complex and interdependent, sabotage or terrorism via cyberspace may become a more serious threat.

1.   Cyber-Terrorism

According to the Federal Bureau of Investigation (FBI), cyber-terrorism is any "premeditated, politically motivated attack against information, computer systems, computer programs, and data which results in violence against non-combatant targets by sub-national groups or clandestine agents." Cyberspace is constantly under assault since cyber-spies, thieves, saboteurs, and thrill-seekers break into computer and networking systems. These individuals steal personal data and trade secrets, vandalize Web sites, disrupt service, sabotage data and systems, launch computer viruses and worms, conduct fraudulent transactions, and harass individuals and organizations.

These attacks are facilitated with increasingly powerful and easy-to-use software tools, readily available on the Internet. Cyber-terrorism also includes attacks that result in violence against persons, property, and infrastructures, and often leads to death or bodily injury, explosions, plane crashes, water contamination, or severe economic damage.

Terrorists are using sophisticated techniques to communicate over the Internet. These techniques involve steganography, embedded messages, encryption, and hidden messages. Web sites have been constructed that are oriented toward the overthrow of civilized societies.

The federal government is responsible for addressing the terrorist issues. Anyone who uncovers subversive messages should contact the local FBI office. Screen shots could be saved as evidence.

2.   *Information Warfare*

Information warfare is a kind of warfare where information and attacks on information and its system are used as a tool of warfare. Information warfare may include transmitting propaganda to enemies to convince them to give up, and denying them information that might lead to their resistance. Information warfare may also include feeding propaganda or even disinformation to one's own population, either to build support for the war effort or to counter enemy propaganda. This is similar to "brainwashing." This technology might also be used during a time of crisis or conflict to achieve or promote specific objectives over a specific adversary or adversaries.

Many nations seek to acquire, exploit, and protect information in support of their objectives. This exploitation and protection can occur in the economic, political, or military arenas. Knowledge of the adversary's information is a means to enhance his or her capabilities, degrade or counteract enemy capabilities, and protect assets, including information.

Information warfare consists of targeting the enemy's information and information functions, while protecting the atacker's own, with the intent of degrading the will or capability to fight.

Information warfare, proactive and reactive, could include the following activities:

Bombing a telephone switching facility
Destroying the telephone switching facility's software
Hardening and defending the switching facility against air attack
Using an antivirus program to protect the facility's software

G.   Forensic Accounting

Forensic accounting is accounting that is suitable for legal review by including data that has been arrived at in a scientific fashion. Forensic accounting is also sufficiently thorough and complete so that an accountant, in an independent and professional judgment, can deliver a finding. The quality must be sustainable in legal proceedings, or within judicial or administrative review.

Forensic accounting techniques include auditing, auditing for fraud, investigative techniques, court and legal proceedings, rules of evidence, legal processes, money tracing, valuation methods, and investigating mergers and acquisitions. These techniques can also provide evidence in divorce cases, general litigation support, dispute resolution, and are applicable to tracking and building cases against terrorists and organized crime individuals. Remember Al Capone and the tax evasion conviction.

Findings of a forensic accountant are based upon the scientific detection and interpretation of the evidence introduced into the books and records of an accounting system. If there is no impact on the accounting system, there is no accounting evidence. Forensic accounting is explanatory analysis, cause and effect including the discovery of deception. The primary method employed by forensic accountants is objective verification.

Forensic accounting is focused on both the evidence centered on economic transactions and also reporting what is contained within the accounting system. A legal framework surrounds the evidence so that it will be suitable for establishing accountability and/or valuation.

1. *Forensic Accountant*

Forensic accounting incidents fall into one of four categories: (1) economic damages, (2) fraud and other forms of economic crime, (3) business valuation, and (4) family law. Forensic accountants utilize an understanding of business information and financial reporting systems, accounting and auditing standards and procedures, evidence gathering and investigative techniques, and litigation processes and procedures to perform their work.

Forensic accounting investigative specialists work with financial information for the purpose of conveying complicated issues in a manner that others, such as juries, can easily understand. While some forensic accountants and forensic accounting specialists are engaged in the public practice of forensic examination, others work in private industry for such entities as banks and insurance companies or governmental entities such as local law enforcement departments, the FBI, and Internal Revenue Service (IRS).

H. Corporate Security and Computer-Use Policies

Most violations that occur in the corporate environment do not require law enforcement intervention. Most incidents involve a violation of a corporate security policy or an official computer-use policy. A **policy** designates a required process or procedure within an organization. Corporate security department investigators handle these incidents, usually without any fanfare. There are, however, incidents that occur in the corporate world that evolve into serious criminal charges. This section's focus is on those infractions that remain in the realm of the corporate security department.

E-mail and Internet users are particularly tempted to download malicious code from e-mail attachments and hostile Web pages. Users also tend to download and install applications including freeware, shareware, beta or demo tryouts, and instant messaging off the Internet, which could involve licensing and security issues. Information obtained from visited Web sites may be inaccurate, misleading, or hateful, leading to the need for quality control, copyright awareness, and/ or filtering of Web sites. Not only does the receiving of e-mail and Web pages create problems, but outgoing e-mail and posting of Web pages by employees are additional problem areas. Organizations could be at risk because of employees' use of the network.

E-mail and Web monitoring should address policy violations in the following areas:

Software downloading	Viruses, worms, and Trojan horses
SPAM control	Malicious intruders
Inappropriate material	DoS and DDoS
Intellectual property	

1. *Corporate Security Investigations*

Members of the organization's security team could be responsible for investigations that involve violation detection and evidence collection. They may also be responsible for restoring systems to a production status with the assistance of information technology (IT) services. Team members must be thoroughly trained in the proper steps required for a successful computer forensic investigation.

The organization must post a statement that cyber crimes are prosecuted to the fullest extent of the law. *Note that cyber crimes can be categorized as premeditated or inadvertent.* There must be standard procedures for reporting incidents to outside authorities and when internal action is taken. Incident management must include standard procedures for collecting evidence, logging evidence, and breaching confidentiality. Care should be taken to not compromise the investigation.

Evidence collection, logging, and security must be in accordance with the standard law enforcement type of investigation because the corporate incident could become a criminal matter. Sloppy corporate security work could preclude any criminal action.

The security department might issue bulletins concerning the status of the organization's internal IT systems during an investigation. These would include attacks, hoaxes, SPAM, scams, and incidents relating to viruses, worms, and Trojan horses.

2. Computer-Abuse Investigations

Internal computer-abuse investigations usually involve several phases. Corporate policy would dictate those departments or individuals who would be notified of an incident. This could involve human resources and/or senior management. The scope of the investigation would be determined by management and the security department. A determination would be made whether an investigation was appropriate or required. If warranted, an investigation is initiated that could include the following steps:

> Define the scope of the investigation
> Document and maintain a log of investigation activities
> Secure computer and electronic devices
> Document hardware and software configurations of a system
> Collect and print any results that show misconduct
> Isolate or move evidence to secure location
> Preserve data and time stamps
> Use a write blocker
> Image hard drive
> Authenticate data using cyclic redundancy check (CRC), secure hash algorithm 1 (SHA1), or message digest 5 (MD5)

Four examination steps would be appropriate, usually based on the specific type of allegation. These would include examining Web browsers, e-mail, UseNet, and specific searches of directories and logs.

Step 1: Examine Web browser. Look at subject lines and addresses to identify trivial or minimal, non-work related Web activity. This evidence might be located in the following areas:

> Cookies   History
> Cache   Windows swap files
> Bookmarks   Web mail

Step 2: Examine e-mail. Look at trivial, minimal non-work related e-mail on various clients. Evidence may be found in folder indexes, attachments, or message content.

Step 3: Examine UseNet. Search trivial, minimal non-work-related UseNet activity. Check both UseNet Client and UseNet Activity.

Step 4: Additional review options. There are a number of additional search options available to the investigator. A good place to start is to examine all relevant log files. Examine directories for installed programs and executables to identify pirated code. Look at directories to identify non-work related data files. More sophisticated efforts could include the following:

Evaluate unallocated space for erased files

Examine the registry for leftover entries from program uninstalls

Search for other network applications such as Internet Relay Chat or Instant Messaging (IM)

Upon completing the investigation and examinations, a report would be completed and provided to human resources and corporate management or those specified in the organization's security policies. A decision could be made after this preliminary investigation to report to law enforcement for prosecution.

I.   Compliance Analysis Investigations

Computer forensics involves preserving digital evidence for a criminal trial. Examiners must prove that there have been no changes to the data on the seized system. To do this, they must use various software and hardware products to make a bit-by-bit copy of a seized hard drive and properly examine the contents without altering the data. This requires thousands of dollars worth of equipment and properly trained, full-time examiners.

Compliance analysis, on the other hand, is a simpler and faster process that involves viewing a defendant/offender's files at "arm's length" (i.e., pornographic images, Word documents relating to identity theft, and temporary Internet files relating to credit card fraud). To do this, the investigator does not have to make a copy of the hard drive.

A computer forensic examination is usually conducted after a full investigation by a law enforcement agency and after a search or arrest warrant has been executed. Compliance analysis is more appropriate for probation and pretrial service officers, as they are not conducting a full-blown investigation.

Compliance analysis is done in the field prior to installation of monitoring software, during a random inspection, or when there is a suspicion of violation of the conditions of supervision.

Investigators or compliance officers performing compliance analysis should keep accurate notes on what was done, and should be prepared to articulate why it was done. Officers should be trained to properly shut down and seize the system immediately if evidence of new criminal activity is detected. The system, along with the officer's notes, can then be turned over to the proper law enforcement agency or a local electronic crimes task force that will most likely have an extensive computer forensic laboratory available.

A compliance analysis "field kit" can be composed of the following items:

Analysis application: An application designed to scan files for images, keywords, etc., that can be launched from a CD-ROM or other removable medium. It allows the compliance officer to easily examine contents of files.

Universal serial bus (USB) flash drive: A small, portable means of mass storage.

Various freeware/shareware/software tools: Small applications that can perform various tasks such as generating MD5 hash values, and gathering PC system information.

Blank floppy disks and compact diskrecordable/rewritable (CDR/W).

Labels, twist ties, and small evidence bags.

Notebook or journal.

Because there are a tremendous number of individuals on probation, this compliance analysis can consume a lot of resources, particularly those involving child pornography and pedophiles.

Chapter Summary

Cyber crime involves illegal activities that use a computer or an electronic device to commit a crime or incident and those that are used against these devices. These crimes could involve identify theft and fraud, computer and network intrusions, property crimes, personal attacks, and cyber-terrorism.

Common law categories include criminal law, civil law, and regulatory law. Electronic forensic investigations could involve petty crimes, serious crimes, civil actions, and corporate security issues. Identity theft and fraud is widespread throughout the world's population. E-mail is the primary vehicle to perpetuate these crimes.

Computer and electronic evidence might be used as evidence in a number of criminal investigations. These include extortion, gambling, child exploitation, assault, death, domestic violence, prostitution, and drug-trafficking cases. The various items of data and information available are significant and usually can be recovered when using the correct techniques.

Forensic accounting is suitable for legal review by including data that has been arrived at in a scientific fashion. Forensic accounting techniques include investigative techniques, court and legal proceedings, rules of evidence, legal processes, valuation methods, and investigating mergers and acquisitions. In today's corporate environment, the function of a forensic accountant is frequently employed in fraud and money laundering investigations.

Terms

Assault — The crime of violence against another person.

Auction fraud — Fraud that occurs on Internet sites offering consumer items for sale to the general public.

Backdrop — A computer desktop background that could be a sprite (small icon) or just a pattern.

Child exploitation — Includes child pornography, trafficking, obscenity, and child prostitution.

Civil laws — Concerned with wrongs inflicted upon an organization or individual that result in damage or loss.

Controlled substances — Drugs and certain other chemicals, both narcotic and nonnarcotic, that come under the jurisdiction of federal and state laws regulating their manufacture, sale, distribution, use, and disposal.

Criminal law — Concerned with individual conduct that violates governmental laws that were enacted for public protection.

Cyberspace — Defined as the global network of interconnected computers and communication systems.

Cyber-terrorism — Includes the convergence of terrorism and cyberspace.

Domestic violence — Physical and/or emotional harm suffered by a person who is a family member of, or residing in the same home as, the offender who caused the harm or injury.

Extortion — Obtaining property or money by the use of violence, threats or intimidation.

Forensic accounting — Accounting that is suitable for legal review by including data that has been arrived at in a scientific fashion.

Fraud — Intentional perversion of truth; deceitful practice or device resorted to with intent to deprive another of property or other right.

Gambling — The unlawful engaging in playing, operating, or assisting in operating a game of chance for money or some other stake.

Identify theft — The deliberate assumption of another person's identity, usually to gain access to the person's finances or frame them for a crime.

Information warfare — A new kind of warfare where information and attacks on information and its system are used as a tool of warfare.

Intrusion — Any set of actions that attempt to compromise the integrity, confidentiality, or availability of a resource.

Phreaking — The art of exploiting bugs and glitches in the telephone system.

Piracy — The unauthorized duplication of goods protected by intellectual property law (e.g., copying software unlawfully).

Policy — An established course of action that must be followed.

Prostitution — Includes sex offenses, including attempts, of a commercialized nature.

Regulatory law — Law that sets standards of performance and conduct expected by various entities.

SPAM — The practice of sending massive amounts of e-mail promotions or advertisements (and scams) to people that have not asked for it.

Review Questions

1. What are the differences between criminal, civil, and regulatory law?
2. Identify ten of the most prominent computer-style crimes and incidents.
3. Identify evidence findings that might be available for auction and online fraud.
4. What tools might be employed by the criminal element to commit an identify theft?
5. A computer intrusion might provide the attacker with what information sources?
6. Describe forensic accounting techniques.
7. Identify E-Mail and Web monitoring activities that address policy violations.
8. Describe the function of a security policy.
9. Provide an overview of cyber-terrorism.
10. Define SPAM and give an example.

Chapter 4

Computer, Internet, and Electronic Crimes

Chapter Objectives

- Understand scams and how scam artists work
- Become familiar with the crime of identity theft
- Look at the issue of Internet fraud
- See how scams and identity theft are closely related
- Identify methods and techniques to obtain evidence from Internet and Web resources
- Look at issues of child molestation and predators who are using the Web
- Recognize the resources for identifying evidence stored on business and personal computer assets
- Learn the technical and legal terms relating to scams, fraud, and identity theft

Introduction

The computer forensic investigator must understand the environment where crimes are committed. The Internet and the computer-networking environment are a complex subject. The investigators must understand the complex issues relating to personal computer-user safety and security. There are many possibilities of predators, who pose both financial and personal risks, waiting for some unsuspecting victim.

Broad spectrums of network-oriented threats are prevalent today. These include criminal groups, foreign intelligence services, terrorists, hackers, phishers, spammers, and malware authors. Ongoing efforts are devoted to countering and neutralizing these threats.

One of the most prevalent security issues today is identity theft. Identify theft can occur from a number of sources, with the Internet being the fastest and easiest vehicle for gathering information about an individual. The most likely source of these intrusions is e-mail. This chapter will address identity theft, fraud, and other threats to network users and provide some guidance to successfully prosecute these situations.

A pervasive threat to network users is the scam artist. These Internet predators are using techniques to steal the identities of Web users to commit fraud. There is a close relationship between fraud, identity theft, and scams. Techniques and activities will be discussed that can be used to identify evidence.

Another issue concerns children and their ability to access Internet network sites that could impact the family's safety. Child molestation and child pornography cases are on the rise. Computer forensic examiners must learn the tactics of these predators and identify techniques to develop evidence.

A. Scams and Scam Artists

Information presented in this section concerns a number of approaches that a scammer or con artist might take to attempt to steal a user's identity with the intent of committing fraud. These attempts usually look legitimate and can fool many network users into responding with compromising information.

Scam artists use Dumpster diving, mail theft, and lost/stolen wallets to commit their crimes. These criminals are also using other techniques to defraud the general public. Information is gathered by overhearing conversations made on cell phones, from faxes and e-mails, by hacking into computers, from telephone and e-mail scams, and even from careless online shopping and banking. This technique is called "social engineering." Scam artists are good at putting together legitimate-sounding scripts, Web sites, and e-mails. Some techniques that can be used to defraud Internet users include promises of free credit reports; get-rich-quick techniques, pyramid schemes, and prizes. A number of techniques include direct questions requesting personal information.

Two groups of individuals that pose serious threats to network users are phishers and spammers. **Phishers** execute phishing scams in an attempt to steal identities or information for monetary gain. They may also use spam and malware to accomplish their objectives. **Spammers** distribute unsolicited e-mail with hidden or false information in order to sell products, conduct phishing scams, distribute malware, or attack organizations.

The forensic investigator must get into the mind of the scammer. One technique of doing this is to understand the standard operating procedures (SOPs) of these criminals. The following sections provide samples of potential scammer "tools."

1. Free Credit Reports

Many of the "free credit report" e-mails received are scams. Either the scammer is trying to identify Social Security numbers or will be billing later with a service charge. If there is some suspicion, check out the company via the Better Business Bureau, U.S. Attorney, and Federal Trade Commission (FTC). Companies are not in business to provide a "free" service without any strings attached.

2. Free Prizes

Users often receive either a phone call or e-mail offering a free gift or prize and asking to just send credit card information to take care of shipping and handling. Watch out! Free means free, which means there should be no charge. Also, consider this sham might be a group sending out a cheap gift in exchange for finding a "live" phone number or e-mail address. Responding may result in hundreds of spams or telemarketing calls.

3. Pyramid Schemes and Chain Letters

There are many e-mail chain letters/pyramid schemes. One says, "Bill Gates is testing a new e-mail-tracking program and wants your help. Forward the e-mail to friends and Microsoft will pay $__ for each person that receives it." Others say, "You will get a gift or money from each person who comes after you." Another says to "Follow the simple instructions below and your financial dreams will come true." Do not respond or forward these e-mails. As ScamBusters (www.scambusters.org) — an Internet Web site offering information on the latest Internet scams—says, "Any e-mail that asks a user to forward it to friends is a possible scam. Look for the letters 'fw' at the beginning of the addressee."

4. Questionnaires

Questionnaires seem to arrive daily in the mail. These include questions that help the person sending it find out birth dates, passwords, and even blatantly may ask for a Social Security number. Do not answer these, even with false information. Answering lets the other parties know that they have reached a "live" person and may eventually give away compromising information. These people are slick and can easily convince unsuspecting users to divulge unintended information. That is why they are called con artists. *Note: providing incorrect information may actually be someone else's real information.*

5. Job Advertisements

Another opportunity to get scammed involves answering job advertisements. Do not place a Social Security number or date of birth on resumes sent out for jobs. Recently there have been scams involving Internet job Web sites (for instance, Monster.com) and newspaper want ads. Under no circumstances should an applicant provide a Social Security number to a human resources person found through a newspaper ad or an Internet ad prior to an actual interview or prior to authenticating both the company and the person asking for the information. If there are any doubts, contact the company directly using a phone number found on the company Web site or telephone book. Anyone can set up a Web site. Check the company out with the Better Business Bureau for that area as well as the state attorney general to make sure that this is a legitimate company. Typical tip-offs include e-mail addresses that do not include a company name in the domain section and mailing addresses or fax numbers in cities that differ from corporate headquarters.

6. Work-at-Home

Advertisements on television and the Web show people making millions working at home. An application would be required to start this work-at-home job. As one probably suspects by now, the application will ask for many personal details including a Social Security number, bank account number, and date of birth. This is good information to initiate an identity theft and the intent is probably fraud. The components of this fraud include freight forwarding and overpayment for services. Products are shipped to the work-at-home location. These products, say cameras, are then shipped to other locations. The scammer provides a financial incentive, say $1,000, to the work-at-home person, using a worthless check. The work-at-home person is asked to provide money, say $500, in the form of a kickback. The problem is that the credit cards or checks used by the scammer to pay for the cameras are worthless. The incentive check is worthless. The producer of the cameras is demanding payment from the work-at-home victim. The work-at-home victim is out $500, the cost of the cameras, and the shipping cost.

7. Charities

Telephone scams can involve solicitations from various charities. Do not provide credit card information over the telephone. The millions of dollars donated by individuals to relief efforts in Southeast Asia, following the tsunami in 2004, brought criminals and scammers out of the woodwork. Scammers may take advantage of the new "do not call lists" being compiled by state governments. No one from the state will be calling consumers asking if they want to be included on the "do not call list," nor will these lists require a consumer to provide a Social Security number via telephone. People who do contribute to charities should determine the percentage of the funds that actually go to "legitimate" charities. Sometimes it is a very small amount, with most of the money going to "administration," which is a new Porsche.

8.   *Credit Information Requests*

Do not respond to e-mails from E-Bay or PayPal that ask for credit information, Social Security number, and other personal data. These scams are called "phishing" exercises and they are looking to catch a "fish." Many of these scams are from financial organizations and the country has been blanketed with them. The e-mail may even threaten that an account or service will be discontinued. Prior to responding, contact the company directly via phone or e-mail to verify that the e-mail was legitimate. Do not be fooled by logos and even the TRUSTe seal. Internet users may also get an e-mail stating that a certain amount of money has been credited to their accounts. Clearly this is a money-laundering scam. They will ask for a "yes" or "no" to indicate if the service was ordered. Do not respond, but rather forward to the Identity Theft Resource Center (ITRC) so that it can be sent to the federal authorities for possible investigation.

9.   *Check Cashing*

There are a number of schemes involving check cashing from "firms" based in foreign countries. These scammers advise that "due to delays in clearing checks and money orders in Europe, they need 'financial agents' to process payments for their U.S. orders." Basically, checks are received from scammers. These checks would be deposited in the personal accounts of work-at-home victims. These victims would then write checks from these accounts. The original checks received from the scammers would be worthless. Additional details on this can be found at www.ic3.gov.

Tips: Scammer Tools for the Unwary

Credit information requests
Check cashing
Charities
Free prizes
Job advertisements
Free credit reports
Pyramid schemes and chain letters
Questionnaires
Work-at-home

10. Scam Baiting

Scam baiting is the practice of eliciting attention from the perpetrator of a scam by feigning interest in whatever bogus deal is offered. The scam baiter pretends to be duped, with the intention of making the perpetrators waste time and/or money, and exposing them to public ridicule. Scam baiters may involve the scammers in a long correspondence or encourage them to travel seeking a payoff. This activity will require someone with a high level of technical expertise and experience. Entrapment must be avoided if prosecution is the objective.

11. Resources

The ScamBusters Web site is an excellent resource to get information on the latest Internet scams. Most scams, by phone or e-mail, ask the user to provide either credit card account information or a Social Security number. The ITRC recommends that users never give out this information unless they initiate the call and know that they are speaking to a legitimate company representative. A list of current scams can be obtained by accessing the ITRC Web site. If a scam is suspected, forward the entire e-mail to ITRC at itrc@idtheftcenter.org.

Internet users can also contact the FBI Internet Crime Complaint Center at www.ic3.gov, the local State Attorney General's office, or the Federal Trade Commission at 877-FTC HELP or send the complaint via e-mail to spam@uce.gov. Computer forensic investigators must keep current on the latest scams and frauds. Scammers have the advantage and are usually one step ahead of the authorities; however, investigators can take advantage of the situation by proactively surfing Web sites for new scams.

B. Activities That Initiate Personal Asset Crimes

The best way to avoid scams, fraud, theft, and identity theft is to exercise caution and guard personal information that applies to personal financial assets. Awareness and education are the key. There are a number of specific suggestions and action items that can assist the investigator in identifying and locating evidence relating to these types of crimes. The following questions relate to protecting personal information and can be used to prompt a victim to provide an answer of some investigative value. The victim will also benefit from these questions, and hopefully, will not commit the same mistake again.

Has the victim provided a Social Security number, birth date, bank account number, driver's license number, or credit card number to anyone recently?
Buyers should only provide credit card or bank account numbers when actually paying for a purchase. They must keep Social Security numbers confidential. It is the key that unlocks an identity, so do not give it to any unidentified person. Find

out why it is necessary to provide it. Ask health insurers and other companies that may use Social Security number as an ID number to provide a substitute number. If the state department of motor vehicles uses it as a driver's license number, ask for an alternate number.

Has the victim received any telephone calls or e-mail asking for personal information? Beware of imposters. Crooks pretending to be from companies where consumers conduct business may call or send an e-mail, claiming they need to verify personal information. Be especially suspicious when contacted by someone asking for information they should already have. Record auto-ID telephone numbers on suspect calls. Before responding, contact the company directly to confirm that the call or e-mail is indeed from them.

Does the victim use a mailbox for paying bills? Keep personal mail safe. Mail often contains account numbers and other personal information. Collect it promptly from mailboxes and ask the post office to hold it while away. Send bill payments from the post office or a public mailbox, not from home. Rural mailboxes are susceptible to mail theft. Criminals look for the telltale red flag to steal mail that might contain bill payments.

Has the victim received applications for credit cards, catalogs, contests, work-at-home, or moneymaking opportunities? Remove names from credit marketing lists. Credit bureaus compile marketing lists for pre-approved offers of credit. These mailings are a gold mine for identity thieves, who may steal them and apply for credit in a victim's name. Get off these mailing lists by calling 888-567-8688 (Social Security number and date of birth will be required to verify an identity). Removing entries from these lists does not hurt chances of applying for or getting credit. Unsolicited applications for credit cards should be disposed of properly. Use a shredder for documents that might contain personal information. A dumpster diver may be looking through personal trash and use the application to commit fraud. Fax machines are usually not secure and electronic traffic might be intercepted.

Does the victim post logins and passwords in a conspicuous location? Memorize computer passwords and personal identification numbers (PINs). Do not leave them in a wallet or on a desk where someone else could find them. Secure personal data. Keep personal information locked up at home, at work, at school, in a vehicle, and other places where easy access is restricted.

Has the victim responded to any requests for information over the Internet? Practice safe Internet usage. Do not send sensitive information such as credit card numbers by e-mail, since it is not secure. Look for clues about security on Web sites. When asked to provide financial or other sensitive information, on a Web page, the letters at the beginning of the address bar at the top of the screen should change from "http" to "https" or "shttp." The browser may also show that the information is being encrypted, or scrambled, so that no one who might intercept it can read it. But while personal information may be safe in transmission, there is no guarantee that the company will store it securely. See what Web sites say about how personal information is safeguarded in storage.

Tips: Protection Techniques

Beware of imposters
Do not provide a credit card number unless you are actually purchasing
  something
Keep Social Security numbers confidential
Keep personal mail safe
Memorize computer passwords and PIN numbers
Practice safe Internet usage
Remove entries from credit marketing lists
Secure personal data

The forensic investigator might contact one of the three major credit bureaus to gather reports on an individual's credit record. Investigative leads might be gleaned from the entries in the reports. Note that a subpoena will probably be required.

C. Identity Theft

Identity theft and identity fraud are terms used to refer to all types of crime in which someone wrongfully obtains and uses another person's personal data in some way that involves fraud or deception, typically for economic gain. Identity theft is the fastest growing crime in the United States today. Besides mail theft, dumpster diving, and lost/stolen wallets, criminals are stealing information by overhearing conversations made on cell phones, from faxes and e-mails, by hacking into computers, from telephone and e-mail scams, and even from careless online shopping and banking. The FTC has estimated that more than 20 percent of all cases involve telecommunications and the Internet. It is essential that investigators understand how thieves steal information via telephone and computer systems. Scammers, previously discussed, use scamming techniques to succeed in stealing someone's identity.

An individual's fingerprints, which are unique, cannot be given to someone else for their use. However, personal data, especially a Social Security number, bank account or credit card number, telephone calling card number, and other valuable identifying data can be used by unscrupulous individuals for fraudulent activities. In the United States and Canada, for example, many people have reported that unauthorized persons have taken funds out of their bank or financial accounts, taken over their identities altogether, running up vast debts and committing crimes while using the victims' names. In many cases, a victim's losses may include not only out-of-pocket financial losses, but substantial additional financial costs associated with trying to restore the individual's reputation in the community and correcting erroneous information for which the criminal is responsible.

Many individuals do not realize how easily criminals can obtain personal data without having to break into their personal space. Criminals may engage in "shoulder surfing" in public places such as telephones and automatic teller machines (ATMs). Criminals may be watching from a nearby location as the victim enters telephone calling card numbers or credit card numbers or listen in on conversations as credit card numbers are provided over the telephone when conducting personal transactions. ATM users should not leave their transaction receipts in the device's printer.

Even the areas near home or office settings may not be secure. Some criminals engage in "dumpster diving," going through garbage cans or a communal dumpster or trash bin. This is a good location to obtain copies of checks, credit card or bank statements, or other records that typically bear personal information such as name, address, and telephone number. These types of records make it easier for criminals to get control over personal accounts and assume an identity.

Everyone receives applications for "pre-approved" credit cards in the mail, but discards them without tearing up the enclosed materials. Criminals may retrieve them and try to activate the cards for their use without the owner's knowledge. Some credit card companies, when sending credit cards, have adopted security measures that allow a card recipient to activate the card only from a personal home telephone number, but this is not yet a universal practice. Also, if personal mail is delivered to a place where others have ready access, criminals may simply intercept and redirect this mail to another location. There are numerous stories of thieves stealing Social Security checks and other government checks out of mailboxes. Government agencies are encouraging program recipients to use direct deposit for their benefit payments.

In recent years, the Internet has become an appealing place for criminals to obtain identifying data, such as passwords or even banking information. Network users frequently respond to "SPAM." SPAM is unsolicited e-mail that promises some benefit, generally not forthcoming. Personal identifying data might be requested from the user. In some cases, criminals reportedly have used computer technology to obtain large amounts of personal data.

With enough identifying information about an individual, a criminal can take over that individual's identity to conduct a wide range of crimes. For example, false applications for loans and credit cards, fraudulent withdrawals from bank accounts, fraudulent use of telephone calling cards, or obtaining other goods or privileges that the criminal might be denied if a real name was used. The criminal might take steps to ensure that bills for the falsely obtained credit cards, or bank statements showing the unauthorized withdrawals, are sent to an address other than the victim's. The victim may not become aware of what is happening until the criminal has already inflicted substantial damage on the victim's assets, credit, and reputation.

Victims of identity theft and fraud may find the task of correcting incorrect information about their financial or personal status, and trying to restore their good names and reputations extremely daunting. Unfortunately, the damage that criminals do in stealing another person's identity and using it to commit fraud often takes far longer to undo than it took the criminal to commit the crimes.

1.   *Avoid Becoming a Victim of Identity Theft*

This section provides suggestions for avoiding becoming a victim of identity theft. However, if a crime has already been committed, these can prompt the investigator to ask leading questions that might prompt valuable information.

To reduce or minimize the risk of becoming a victim of identity theft or fraud, there are some basic steps an individual can take. Be careful about giving out personal information to others unless there is a reason to trust them, regardless of location. Many organizations are now requiring a number of identifications before a user is authenticated. These might be the last four digits of a Social Security number, date of birth, and mother's maiden name. Always be suspicious if someone wants to know any of these identifiers.

Start by adopting a "need to know" approach to personal data. Credit card companies may need to know the mother's maiden name so that they can verify an identity when someone calls to inquire about an account. A person who calls purporting to represent a user's bank, however, doesn't need to know that information if it is already on file with the bank. The only purpose for such a call is to acquire confidential information for that caller's personal benefit. Individuals should restrict the amount of information printed on personal bank checks. Revealing information such as a Social Security number or home telephone number on personal checks is not a good idea.

Do not routinely provide personal data to people who may not need that information. If a stranger calls and offers a chance to receive a prize or other valuable item, be suspicious. Citizens should not respond over the phone to a caller's requests for personal data such as a Social Security number, credit card number and expiration date, or mother's maiden name. Request a formal document via mail and then review the application carefully when received and make sure it is going to a company or financial institution that is well known and reputable. The Better Business Bureau can provide information about businesses that have been the subject of complaints.

When traveling, have personal mail held at the local post office, or ask someone you know well and trust, such as a family member, friend, or neighbor, to collect and hold your mail while you are away. When you call someone while traveling and need to pass on personal financial information, do not do it at an open telephone booth where passersby can listen in on your conversation. Use a telephone booth where the door can be closed, or use a less public location to call.

Check financial information regularly, and look for what should and what should not be there. Holders of bank or credit card accounts should be receiving monthly statements that list transactions for the most recent month or reporting period. If these monthly statements are not being received, call the financial institution or credit card company immediately and ask about it. If you are told that statements are being mailed to another unauthorized address, advise the financial institution or credit card representative immediately that a change of address was not authorized and that someone may be improperly using the accounts. In that situation, ask for copies of all statements and debit or charge transactions that have occurred since the last statement received. Obtaining those copies will help individuals work with the financial institution or credit card companies in determining whether some or all of those debit or charge transactions were fraudulent. Note that some companies may cover charge card fraud charges of less than $50.

Unauthorized debits or charges against financial accounts can occur if someone has gotten personal financial data. Checking monthly statements carefully may be the quickest way to become aware of fraudulent activities. Bank and credit card statements should be verified against transaction receipts to avoid unauthorized withdrawals or charges. This means that consumers must keep all receipts. Criminals will take advantage of sloppy personal financial administration.

It is possible for a skimmer to be used on an ATM to capture confidential information. Be wary of odd-looking ATM card readers, as they might be skimmer devices. The machines dispense the correct amount of money to unsuspecting victims while their card details are being recorded onto the suspect device. The captured data is downloaded to the criminal's computer to make new cards, which will be used after some months. There are many ways in which the culprits get card data from ATM machines. One way involves installing an unusual-looking device over the card slots of the machine for skimming. Another modus operandi involves installing tiny hidden cameras embedded among brochures near the machine and which are focused on where ATM users enter their PINs. Unnoticeably, thieves also use transparent overlays on ATM keypads that record PINs or tamper with the other machines in a multiple-ATM location to make a skimming-device-installed ATM machine the only one available for use.

If someone has managed to get access to personal mail or other data, it will be necessary to take immediate action. Credit cards may have been opened in the victim's name or funds taken from a bank account. Customers should contact the financial institution or credit card company immediately to report those transactions and to request further action. The credit reports should list all bank and financial accounts under the account name, and will provide other indications of whether someone has wrongfully opened or used any accounts in a consumer's name.

Maintain careful records of personal banking and financial accounts. Even though financial institutions are required to maintain copies of checks, debit transactions, and similar transactions for five years, individuals should retain monthly statements and checks until satisfied that their records are correct. Note that the Internal Revenue Service (IRS) requires supporting documentation for seven years. If the need arises to dispute particular transactions, original records will be more immediately accessible and useful to the institutions that have been contacted.

Even if users take all of these suggestions, it is still possible to become a victim of identity theft and fraud. Paper copies of transactions containing personal data, such as credit card receipts, ATM transactions, gas pump receipts, or car rental agreements, may be found by or shared with someone who decides to use this data for fraudulent purposes. Do not throw these receipts into receptacles where they can be retrieved by those dumpster divers looking for an easy victim.

The latest technique used by cyber-thieves is to use the wireless network to steal information from personal computers. Techniques used include war driving and war chalking. Internet users frequently purchase laptops for wireless access and do not take the necessary precautions to protect against these criminal activities. Wireless users must change the default logon/password and initiate the security protection attributes of the laptop and personal digital assistant (PDA).

Generally not associated with Internet fraud and identity theft is the transmission of documents over fax machines. There is a possibility that transmissions from fax machines could be intercepted by some technique and copied without the user's knowledge. If fax transmissions are not encrypted or sent over secure communication links, the possibility exists for an interception. If this were to occur, the objective is more likely to be corporate espionage and not identity theft.

D.　Victims of Identity Theft

Victims of identity theft or fraud should act immediately to minimize the damage and impact on personal funds and financial accounts, as well as personal reputation. There are a number of contact addresses and Web sites that are useful resources for victims of identity theft. Obviously, an official report must be filed with the local law enforcement agency. The possibility exists that there are other victims of this type of fraud in the same geographic area. The reports can help the investigator establish a pattern of criminal activities.

1.　Contacts

Contact all creditors where name or other identifying data has been fraudulently used. For example, customers may need to contact a long-distance telephone company if a long-distance calling card has been stolen or fraudulent charges are discovered on a bill. Contact all financial institutions where an identity thief has taken over a personal account or accounts that have been created in someone's name but without his or her knowledge. Customers may need to cancel or block those accounts, place stop-payment orders on any outstanding checks that may not have cleared, and change ATM card, account, and PIN.

The FTC, under the Identity Theft and Assumption Deterrence Act, is responsible for receiving and processing complaints from people who believe they may be victims of identity theft. This agency can provide informational materials and refer complaints to appropriate entities, including the major credit reporting agencies and law enforcement agencies. Contact the FTC to report the situation at www.consumer.gov/idtheft/. A complaint can be filed at https://rn.ftc.gov/pls/dod/. Additional information is available on the FTC's identity theft Web pages. Complainants can also call the local FBI or Secret Service office to report crimes relating to identity theft and fraud.

If someone suspects that an identity thief has submitted a change-of-address form with the post office to redirect mail, or has used the mail to commit frauds involving an identity, contact the local office of the Postal Inspection Service. If someone suspects a Social Security number is being fraudulently used, contact the Social Security Administration at www.ssa.gov/. The IRS can be contacted at www.irs.gov for suspected improper use of identification information in connection with tax violations.

2. *Credit Reporting Agencies*

Consumers suspecting a crime can call the fraud units of the three principal credit reporting companies. Check the local telephone directory under headings such as "Credit Reporting Agencies" for names of similar companies. The major credit reporting agencies are:

Equifax
P.O. Box 740241
Atlanta, GA 30374-0241
1-800-685-1111   http://www.equifax.com/

Experian
P.O. Box 2104
Allen, TX 75013-0949
1-888-EXPERIAN   http://www.experian.com/

Trans Union
P.O. Box 1000
Chester, PA 19022
1-800-916-8800   http://www.tuc.com/

3. *Federal Deposit Insurance Corporation (FDIC)*

The FDIC's Consumer Response Center has responsibility for investigating all types of consumer complaints about FDIC-supervised institutions and for responding to consumer inquiries about consumer laws and regulations and banking practices. The FDIC staff can provide an avenue for efficient and effective resolution of consumer complaints or inquiries. The contact address is:

> Federal Deposit Insurance Corporation
> Consumer Response Center
> 2345 Grand Avenue, Suite 100
> Kansas City, MO 64108-2638

The FDIC has created a Web page to inform consumers about the new Fair and Accurate Credit Transactions Act's (FACTA) consumer provisions, which gives new rights to free credit reports. FACTA also provides new rights to obtain credit scores. FACTA became law in December 2003. Consumer Alerts—Fair and Accurate Credit Transactions Act (FACT Act) are available at www.ftc.gov/opa/2004/06/factaidt.htm.

4.   Check-Verification Companies

If clients have checks stolen or bank accounts set up by an identity thief, contact the major **check-verification** services. In particular, where a particular merchant has received a stolen check, contact the merchant's verification company. These might include:

> Check Rite: www.checkrite.com
> CrossCheck: www.crosscheck.com
> Equifax: www.equifax.com
> National Processing Co. (NPC): www.npc.net
> TeleCheck: www.telecheck.com

Others can be identified by typing "check verification" in the search field in Yahoo or Google. These check-cashing services could provide the investigator with information concerning locations and time frames that could be significant evidence in a court case.

E.   Internet Fraud

Fraud is a deception deliberately practiced in order to secure unfair or unlawful gain. How can the Web user discern whether the offer is valid or a fraud? First, if the offer smells fishy and sounds too good to be true, it probably is a fraud. It is usually not possible to get something for nothing. Human nature, however, sometimes overrules common sense. Fraud is covered under a number of current U.S. statutes. Information concerning Internet fraud and tips to avoid Internet fraud can be viewed at www.fraud.org/internet/intset.htm.

The Internet offers a global marketplace for consumers and businesses. But the criminal element also recognizes the potentials of cyberspace. The same scams that have been conducted by mail and telephone can now be found on the World Wide Web and in e-mail, and new cyber-scams are emerging. It is often difficult to discern the difference between reputable online sellers and criminals who use the Internet to defraud network users. Network users must learn how to protect themselves by learning how to recognize the danger signs of fraud. It is essential that victims or attempted victims of Internet fraud report scams quickly so law enforcement agencies can shut down fraudulent operations.

1.   *Internet Fraud Tips*

The investigator can research the dealer or vendor. If the seller or charity is unfamiliar, check with the state or local consumer protection agency and the Better Business Bureau. Also check with the Secretary of State for incorporations. Some Web sites have feedback forums, which can provide useful information about other consumer experiences with particular sellers. Get the physical address and phone number in case there is a problem later. Look for information about how complaints are handled. It can be difficult to resolve complaints, especially if the seller or charity is located in another country. Check the Web site for information about programs the company or organization participates in that require adherence to standards for reliability and help to handle disputes. Be aware that absence of complaints is not a guarantee. Fraudulent operators open and close quickly, so the fact that no one has made a complaint yet does not mean that the seller or charity is legitimate. Consumers still need to look for other danger signs of fraud.

Look for promises of easy money. If someone advertises claims to earn money with little or no work, get a loan or credit card even with bad credit, or make money on an investment with little or no risk, it is probably a scam. Get-rich-quick schemes are not new. A legitimate seller will provide all the details about the products or services, the total price, the delivery time, the refund and cancellation policies, and the terms of any warranty. For more information about shopping safely online, go to www.nclnet.org/shoppingonline.

Beware of pressure tactics for a quick answer. Legitimate companies and charities will be happy to provide time to make a decision. It is probably a scam if they demand an immediate response or will not take "No" for an answer. Be suspicious of contests operated by unfamiliar companies. Fraudulent marketers sometimes use contest entry forms to identify potential victims.

Be cautious about unsolicited e-mails. They are often fraudulent. When you are familiar with the company or charity that sent the e-mail and do not want to receive further messages, send a reply asking to be removed from the e-mail list. However, responding to unknown senders may simply verify a working e-mail address and result in even more unwanted messages from strangers. The best approach may simply be to delete the e-mail. These e-mails might also contain computer viruses.

Beware of imposters. Someone might send an e-mail pretending to be connected with a business or charity, or create a Web site that looks just like that of a well-known company or charitable organization. When not sure of the legitimacy of the organization, find another way to contact the legitimate business or charity and inquire.

Guard personal information. Do not provide a credit card or bank account number unless you are actually paying for something. A Social Security number should not be necessary unless applying for credit. Be especially suspicious when someone claiming to be from a personally known company asks for information that the business already possesses.

Beware of "dangerous" downloads. In downloading programs to see pictures, hear music, play games, etc., users could download a virus that wipes out computer files or connects the computer's modem to a foreign telephone number, resulting in expensive phone charges. Only download programs from known and trusted Web sites.

Credit cards are the safest way to pay for online purchases because consumers can dispute the charges if they never get the goods or services or the offer was misrepresented. Federal law limits consumer liability to $50 if someone makes unauthorized charges to cardholder accounts, and most credit card issuers will remove them completely when the problem is reported promptly. There are new technologies, such as "substitute" credit card numbers and password programs that can offer extra measures of protection from a thief attempting to use a stolen or cloned credit card.

Tips: Avoiding Fraud

Be suspicious of contests
Beware of imposters
Beware of suspicious downloads
Do not respond to unsolicited e-mails
Guard personal information
Look for complaints and complaint processes
Pay the safest way
Remember that easy money does not exist
Research the dealer or vendor
Resist pressure
Understand the offer

2.   New Solutions

Bank of America's online customers in North Carolina, South Carolina, and Georgia have a new way to help prevent fraud and identity theft with the launch of an industry-leading protection service with its online banking. A new free service, called SiteKey™, allows customers to pick one of thousands of images, write a brief phrase, and select three challenge questions. The customer and the bank can pass that information securely back and forth to confirm each other's identity.

Using SiteKey is like getting a safe deposit box that takes two keys to open. Before the customer and the bank agree to open the box together, they confirm each other's identity. Bank of America, which has the most online banking customers in the country, is the first major financial services company to provide this added level of security.

3. Internet Fraud Statistics

Statistics have been developed that show the percentage of frauds for various scams initiated over the Internet. The top ten frauds identified by the National Fraud Information Center are as follows:

Type of Fraud	Percent
Online auctions	51
General merchandise	19
Nigerian money offers	9
Phishing	5
Information/adult services	3
Lotteries/lottery clubs	2
Fake check scams	2
Computer equipment/software	1
Fake escrow services	1
Internet access services	1

Note that the top two scams are oriented toward merchandise purchases where goods were never delivered or misrepresented. In the number three rank, is a "get-rich-quick" scam where false promises of riches were made. The initial contacts for these frauds were the Web (77 percent) and e-mail (22 percent). The average loss to fraud victims totaled $895.

F. Combating Identity Theft and Fraud

A number of government and private organizations have information about various aspects of identity theft and fraud: how it can occur, what can be done about it, and how to guard personal privacy. To help learn more about the problem and its solutions, users might find the attached list of Web sites on identity theft and related topics interesting and informative. Considerable information is available at http://www.usdoj.gov/criminal/fraud/idtheft.html.

1. Government Contacts

Consumer.gov	www.consumer.gov
Federal Bureau of Investigation	www.fbi.gov
Federal Deposit Insurance Corporation	www.fdic.gov
Federal Trade Commission	www.ftc.gov
United States Postal Inspection Service	www.usps.com/postalinspector
United States Secret Service	www.secretservice.gov/index.shtml

2. Nongovernment Contacts

American Association of Retired Persons (AARP)	www.aarp.org
Better Business Bureau	www.bbb.org
Center for Democracy and Technology	www.cdt.org
National Association of Attorneys General (NAAG)	www.naag.org
National Consumers League	www.nclnet.org
National Fraud Information Center	www.fraud.org/
Privacy Rights Clearinghouse	www.privacyrights.org/
Chamber of Commerce	www.uschamber.com/default

3. Awareness and Education

Identify theft and fraud can be avoided or minimized if the population becomes aware of the enormity of the problem. Education and awareness are must-have attributes. It is obvious criminals are just waiting to take advantage of anyone who lets his or her guard down. After an individual has become a victim of identify theft or fraud, it is too late.

There are community forums concerning identify theft and fraud offered in many cities. Many of these are free. Check with the local Better Business Bureau and Chamber of Commerce for possible schedules. Local law enforcement departments should be involved in this education process. The local board of education should be involved in actively presenting educational programs in all public school systems.

4. *Using the Internet for Investigations*

The Internet provides a valuable tool for the forensic investigator. Learning the technique for "surfing" can provide a surprising amount of leads during an investigation. Remember that the criminals have perfected this method for their illegal activities. Cyber-thieves can use information provided over chat rooms, blogs, and e-mail to compromise the security of naïve network users. There is no reason that the law enforcement community cannot benefit from the same resources. Look at the reasons that the average citizen is defrauded and reverse the logic. Do not forget to keep an accurate journal.

Law enforcement departments investigating predator and child molestation cases might use the Internet to identify child pornography suspects. The Internet has a national predator database (www.familywatchdogs.us) that can be useful in these investigations. Computer forensic scientists can also assist in tracking and identifying these illegal activities.

G. Exploiting Children on the Web

A survey by the National Center for Missing and Exploited Children and Cox Communications revealed that 42 percent of parents do not review the content of what their teenagers read or type in chat rooms or via instant messaging. Parents also did not know the lingo used by teenagers to communicate over the Web and 28 percent did not know if their teens talked to strangers online. Parents are encouraged to become more involved in their children's online habits and behaviors.

Studies reveal that many parents are not involved in their children's Internet habits and behaviors. Children may impact the security and safety of the entire family due to their inexperience and naïveté. The same scammers and con men who compromise adults might use children to gain access to personal and confidential information relating to their parents' accounts and assets. Because there are many "latchkey kids," there are many opportunities for individuals to "use" children in their criminal pursuits.

Forensic investigators have initiated a number of trial searches on the Web to show how easy it is to identify minor victims. Using tools available to anyone, it has been shown that profiles for minors can be identified after 20 minutes of Web research. These searches can be used to develop information about schools, neighborhoods, hobbies, and parents' work habits and schedules.

1. Child Predators

Child molestation, trafficking, abuse, and child pornography cases are on the rise. Computer forensic investigators and examiners must learn the tactics of these predators and identify techniques to develop evidence that will hold up in court. A **pedophile** is an adult whose primary sexual interest is in children.

It was once believed that the stereotypical pedophile was a raincoat-clad "dirty old man" lurking near the neighborhood elementary school. As awareness has grown, the facts have revealed that a pedophile can come from any walk of life, any economic background, religion, or race. A pedophile could be as close as the guy next door or the "grandfatherly" man down the street. Investigators must realize that there really is no stereotypical type when it relates to child predators.

There are a number of attributes and objectives that are common to child sexual predators:

- Prey on the innocence of a child
- Feed on the thrill of violating a child's trust
- Find the perfect game and capture their victim
- Spend time watching children, talking to them, evaluating their mind frame
- Dig deep into the psyche of a child
- Watch a child's every move and observe his or her feelings
- Play the game slowly
- Befriend the child, play with him or her, and get to know him or her
- See a chance to advance the game, and take each calculated move as it comes
- Gain the child's trust, reinforce it, and then eventually violate it

In an undercover surveillance operation, one child predator bragged how easy it is to gain a child's trust while talking on the Internet. This predator said he could spot a lonely child, who makes the easiest target.

2. Child Predators on the Internet

While the computer age has opened a whole new world for children to explore and learn from, the information superhighway also has a dark side. Just as they prey on land, pedophiles lurk on the Internet waiting to lure innocent children into their web of deviance, as they look for their next victim.

These deviates meet others who claim children for their victims; they share stories pictures, and encourage each other along the way. The tricks they use on the Internet are a little different. They can hide behind the screen and no one can tell their age. They know how to relate to children and find it easy to communicate on that level. They present themselves in areas children frequent and pose as children and get to know the child they are communicating with and pass themselves off as a friend. Often, they will use smoking cigarettes, using drugs, talking about sex, or some activity they should not be involved with as an incitement to lure the child to meet them without anyone knowing.

The trap is then laid. An adult will lure the child out to meet with them. Thinking it is another child, they set off to meet their friend. What happens next depends on the plan of the predator. For some, this would be enough. The fact that they won their trust enough to get them to meet them may be all the ground rules they need to molest the child. Some may attempt a closer relationship by playing the con a little longer.

Child predators are cons and their goals are as varied as their egos. The limits for one may just be the beginning point for another and there is no way to predict how any given predator will react, as their personalities differ. Their needs are not the same in many ways and there is only one thing they have completely in common: that is the fact that they find their thrill in luring a child into their well-concocted plan.

Investigating child-predator crimes is difficult for law enforcement since everyone has a computer at his or her residence, school, church, fast-food store, book store, and often children are unsupervised when they are using these computers. Children do not realize the danger and exposure they are creating for themselves, friends, and families. Law enforcement agencies are developing programs for presentations to educate school children. There are a set of rules to reduce a child's risk of exploitation:

- NEVER allow children to give out any personal information such as last name, address, telephone number, parent's first or last names, work phone numbers, name of employer's or business names, or the school name or location.
- NEVER let a child send anyone a photograph or any other items via the Internet without obtaining the parent's permission.
- NEVER let children respond to any messages that make them uncomfortable. Do not allow someone to say mean or naughty things.
- NEVER let the child get together or meet with anyone met online.

There are a number of child predator registers available on the Internet. The National Alert Registry site is located at www.registeredoffenderlist.org/. A Web site devoted to child predation is us.geocities.com/CapitolHill/7836/predator.html.

3.   *Child Predator and Privacy Laws*

Megan's Law, the federal version, was enacted on May 17, 1996. Megan's Law mandates that every state develop a procedure for notifying residents of sex offenders residing there. The act requires the states to register sex offenders convicted of sex crimes against children. Megan's Law allows the states discretion to establish criteria for disclosure, but compels them to make private and personal information on registered sex offenders available to the public.

The United States **Children's Online Privacy Protection Act of 1998 (COPPA)**, effective April 21, 2000, applies to the online collection of personal information by persons or entities under U.S. jurisdiction from children under 13. It spells out what a Web site operator must include in a privacy policy, when and how to seek verifiable consent from a parent and what responsibilities an operator has to protect children's privacy and safety online.

4. *Child Predator Investigations*

NetSmartz and the **Internet Crimes Against Children (ICAC)** Task Force Program have developed age-appropriate presentations for grades K–2, 3–6, middle and high school, law enforcement, parents, and communities. Parents, guardians, educators, and law enforcement also have access to resources for learning and teaching about the dangers children may face online. NetSmartz was created by the **National Center for Missing & Exploited Children®️ (NCMEC)** and the Boys & Girls Clubs of America (BGCA). A source for law enforcement child sexual-exploitation investigation assistance is provided by the NCMEC and is located at www.cybertipline.com/. Other Web sites include www.fbi.gov/publications/pguide/pguidee.htm; and www.ftc.gov/bcp/conline/edcams/kidzprivacy/adults.htm.

Since 1984 the NCMEC has served as the congressionally mandated national clearinghouse for child protection in the United States. In 1996 the U.S. Congress established the Exploited Child Unit (ECU) within NCMEC. The ECU serves as a resource center for the public, parents, law enforcement, and others on the issues of the sexual exploitation of children.

In addition to handling reports received via the CyberTipline, the ECU serves as a technical and informational resource for law enforcement. Investigating child sexual-exploitation cases may require specialized technical skills outside the scope of usual investigation methods. Analysts are available to assist in any child sexual-exploitation case, not just those originating from the CyberTipline. The technical assistance services available from the ECU are listed below.

> Child Victim-Identification Project
> CyberTipline historical searches
> Internet searches
> Internet service provider (ISP) contacts
> Law-enforcement contacts
> Public-record database searches
> Technical expertise

The ECU can be contacted at 1-800-843-5678 for further assistance.

A recent report concerning children 10 to 17 years old stated that 1 in 4 had an unwanted exposure to sexually explicit pictures, 1 in 5 received a sexual solicitation, 1 in 17 was threatened or harassed, and 1 in 33 received an aggressive sexual solicitation (meeting, telephone calls, money, gifts, or mail). It has been estimated that in 2005, 77 million children were accessing the Internet. With so many youths online and vulnerable to predators, it is extremely important for parents, law enforcement officials, prosecutors, and victim service providers to know as much as possible about Internet crimes against children so they can prevent victimization and prosecute offenders.

Chapter Summary

Identity theft is the fastest growing crime today. Scam artists use a number of techniques including dumpster diving, mail theft, and lost/stolen wallets to commit their crimes. There are a number of techniques that the investigator can use to collect evidence involving identify theft and fraud cases.

The Internet offers a global marketplace for both consumers and businesses. The criminal element also recognizes the potentials of cyberspace. The same fraud and scams that have been conducted by mail and telephone can now be found on the World Wide Web and in e-mail. New cyber-scams directed at the unwary are being initiated every day. Forensic investigators can use the Internet resources to gather evidence.

Credit reports are available from the credit-reporting agencies. Credit card statements and bank statements can be reviewed for criminal activity.

Victims of identity theft and fraud have a number of contacts where reports can be filed. These include the FTC, FDIC, FBI, Secret Service, IRS, and the U.S. Post Office.

The Internet can assist the investigator and the general public with identifying predators and child molesters. Evidence can also be retrieved from e-mail transmissions and from a suspect's computer files. Photographs involving child pornography are often transmitted over the Internet and stored on a user's laptop computer. There are many Web sites devoted to the subjects of child predators and sex crimes that include laws, registries, reporting, and awareness groups.

Terms

Chain letter — A typical chain letter consists of a message that attempts to induce the recipient to make a number of copies of the letter and then pass them on to two or more new recipients.

COPPA — A U.S. law that took effect on April 21, 2000, and requires parental consent for certain Web sites to knowingly collect personally identifiable information on children under the age of 13.

Dumpster diving — The practice of rummaging through trash, whether commercial or residential, to find items of use that have been discarded.

Fraud — A deception deliberately practiced in order to secure unfair or unlawful gain.

Identity theft — The act of impersonating another, by means of using the person's information, such as birth date, Social Security number, address, name, and bank account information.

ITRC — Identity Theft Resource Center.

Malware — Short for malicious software, software designed specifically to damage or disrupt a system, such as a virus or a Trojan horse.

Megan's Law — Enacted in 1996, this federal law requires local law enforcement agencies in all 50 states to notify schools, day care centers, and parents about the presence of certain sex offenders in their area.

NCMEC — National Center for Missing & Exploited Children.

Pedophile — An adult whose primary sexual interest is in children.

Phishers — Execute phishing scams in an attempt to steal identities or information for monetary gain.

Pyramid scheme — A fraudulent scheme in which people are recruited to make payments to the person who recruited them while expecting to receive payments from the persons they recruit.

Scam — A confidence trick, confidence game, or con is an attempt to intentionally mislead a person usually with the goal of financial or other gain. The confidence trickster, con man, scam artist, or con artist often works with an accomplice called the shill, who tries to encourage the mark by pretending to believe the trickster.

Scam baiting — The practice of eliciting attention from the perpetrator of a scam by feigning interest in whatever bogus deal is offered.

Social engineering — Includes the practice of obtaining confidential information by manipulation of legitimate users. A social engineer will commonly use the telephone or Internet to trick people into revealing sensitive information.

SPAM — Unsolicited, unwanted, irrelevant, or inappropriate messages, especially commercial advertising in mass quantities.

Spammers — Distribute unsolicited e-mail with hidden or false information in order to sell products, conduct phishing scams, distribute malware, or attack organizations.

Spyware — Spyware is similar to a Trojan horse in that users unwittingly install the product when they install something else.

Review Questions

1. Identify techniques and tools that a scammer might use to commit illegal activities.
2. _____ is the practice of eliciting attention from the perpetrator of a scam by feigning interest in whatever bogus deal is offered.
3. List three sources where an investigator might collect information concerning scammers and scam activities.
4. Identify the three credit-reporting agencies.

5. _____ is the act of impersonating another, by means of using the person's information, such as birth date, Social Security number, address, name, and bank account information.

6. _____ is a deception deliberately practiced in order to secure unfair or unlawful gain.

7. The top two frauds identified by the National Fraud Information Center involve merchandising: _____ and _____.

8. The practice of rummaging through trash, whether commercial or residential, to find items of use that have been discarded is called _____.

9. _____ includes the practice of obtaining confidential information by manipulation of legitimate users.

10. _____ is unsolicited, unwanted, irrelevant, or inappropriate messages, especially commercial advertising in mass quantities.

Chapter 5

Computers, Electronics, and Networking Environment

Chapter Objectives

- Understand the E-commerce networking environment and identify the various hardware and software components
- Identify computer and electronic devices that might contain forensic evidence
- Provide examples of forensic evidence that might be obtained from the crime/incident scenes
- Identify the types of evidence that can be recovered from computer and electronic devices
- Understand the hardware and software solutions that address network security issues
- See how telephone management software can provide investigative information

Introduction

This chapter provides an overview of computer, electronic, and communication devices used in the world's Internet and telecommunications network. All members of the computer forensics team must understand how the computer or electronic components work and how they relate to an investigation. Considerable data and information is stored on or transmitted by electronic devices. Security and forensic issues relating to hardware and software components used in these systems are discussed in this chapter.

Computer system and networking components comprise a significant portion of a major organization's physical assets. These devices, along with their respective operating systems and application software, present an enormous opportunity for security breaches and illegal activities. This chapter describes the major hardware components that are part of an organization's computer and networking operations. Also offered are policy suggestions designed to provide a standardized approach to the investigative tasks for corporate security departments.

The aim of proactive computer networking security measures and counter-measures is to limit damage to an organization's assets. Enhancement to security efforts includes the deployment of hardware devices such as firewalls, gateways, and routers. Sophisticated software products control these hardware devices. These devices are candidates to effect a successful forensic investigation in response to some incident.

A number of system vendors such as IBM, Cisco, Sun Microsystems, Syman-tec, Network Associates, and Hewlett-Packard provide hardware and software solutions oriented toward enterprise security and surveillance. Hardware, software, and management solutions for the detection and recording of surveillance data will be presented in this chapter. **Intrusion detection** and **intrusion prevention** information could be critical in computer networking investigations.

The advent of the **client/server** environment increases the need for security measures to protect these computer resources. These devices provide the processor and storage capabilities for a number of network systems such as E-commerce, E-business, and distributed computing. Securing and tracking of mechanized trans-actions has become a number one priority. Banking and other financial transactions leave an audit trail and therefore are very important in fraud investigations.

Voice communications systems play a major role in the network. These sys-tems provide access to a number of sensitive resources that must be protected from both internal and external attacks and intrusions. Telephone calls and cell-phone calls are recorded by the various carriers and may provide a wealth of supporting evidence in both corporate and criminal investigations. Commercial call-track-ing systems keep track of all telephone calls and can produce a number of reports including traffic patterns, telephone numbers called, and time/date stamps.

A. E-Commerce and E-Business Issues

Computer forensics investigators must understand the infrastructure and com-ponents, both hardware and software, that are part of the twenty-first century computer and electronic environment. This is because many violations and illegal activities occur in this environment, which is primarily a commercial computer, business-oriented playing field. Because of this business slant, the computer forensic investigator must often call upon the services of an expert in the business community to assist in an investigation. There are often requirements for a forensics accountant to testify using evidence obtained from a computer that is strictly accounting in nature. **E-business (electronic business)** is defined as business that is conducted electronically involving the processes necessary to support the day-to-day activities, whereas **E-commerce (electronic commerce)** refers to a set of technologies, applications, and activities that relate to the sales and marketing functions of an organization. Organizations, individuals, and businesses are linked through computer networking systems for the purpose of providing electronic transactions allowing for the exchange of goods, services, information, and capital. The forensics accountant might be more concerned with the activities concerning financial accounting and issues such as generally accepted accounting practices (GAAPs), whereas the computer forensics personnel would be adept at working in the computer, electronic, and networking environment.

Individuals across the world use personal computers and electronic devices to communicate, work, learn, entertain, and plan. Everyone has come to view these devices as extensions of the personal psyche. For this reason, computers and other devices often contain important information, which can be used as evidence in legal proceedings, even if the information is not directly related to computers. This computer-based evidence can be anything from e-mail, to photographs, to confidential data and documents. Most importantly, the data frequently can be retrieved from a suspect device, even if the user has deleted the information.

Computing devices can be used as tools in illegal activities, may contain evidence of some wrongdoing, or may be a target of some unscrupulous activity. Investigators need to realize that evidence can also be recovered from a multiple of electronic devices in addition to computer systems. Categories of devices include network devices, telephone systems, image devices, and personal communication devices. Most of these devices are highly technical in nature and require an expert to speak to evidence that might be obtained from such components. A computer scientist might be required who can explain the technical aspects and capabilities of a computer or electronic device.

B.   Computers and Computer Devices

This section will provide an overview of most computer, network, and electronic devices that are used in the industry. The graphics presented have been drawn to reflect physical connectivity rather than a logical view. Computer forensics examiners are usually interested in the physical connectivity of these devices. Cable connectivity between the various devices must be preserved when obtaining and securing electronic and computer evidence.

Computer and electronic evidence consists of data and information with some potential investigative value. This evidence is either stored or transmitted by various computer and communication devices. It is essential that investigators realize that special precautions must be taken in the collection, preservation, and examination of this evidence. Electronic evidence can easily be altered, damaged, or destroyed on these electronic and computing devices.

Computers are generally classified as **mainframes** or **personal computers (PCs)**. **Mainframes** are large, complex computers that are exceptionally fast and contain considerable amounts of data storage and processing power. These expensive computers are generally deployed in large organizations and governments. Figure 5.1 depicts the mainframe environment. PCs, including desktops and laptops, are portable and fairly inexpensive, and provide the individual user with sufficient computing power to exist in the electronic age. These devices are generally used to access e-mail, chat rooms, the Internet, and personal software. Another class of computing configuration is called the **client/server** model. Many organizations use this model today. It is defined as a network that uses a computer called a server, which provides the client or user with a computer service. The server may be used as a remote computer that is connected via a network to a mainframe computer. Figure 5.2 depicts a client/server environment.

All of these computing devices maintain both the system and application software that is used to provide some solution to some problem. Mainframes and servers use massive hard-disk drives for media storage, whereas PCs use random access memory (RAM), compact disks (CDs), floppy disks, flash drives, and Zip drives. The forensic examiner will be primarily concerned with the evidence contained on the PC drives. Generally speaking, forensic investigations on a mainframe system will require the services of a computer scientist or a computer systems programmer. Each category discussed in this chapter will include a section concerning potential evidence that might be identified and retrieved from the various devices.

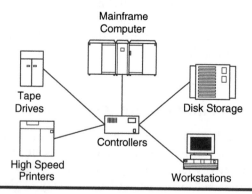

Mainframe
Computer

Tape
Drives

Disk Storage

Controllers

High Speed
Printers

Workstations

Figure 5.1   Mainframe configuration.

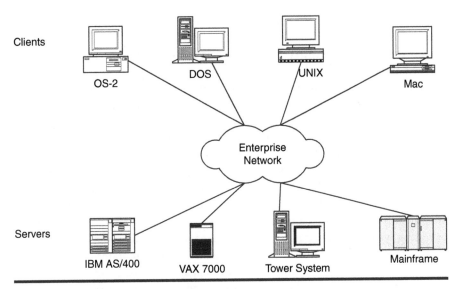

Clients

OS-2

DOS

UNIX

Mac

Enterprise
Network

Servers

IBM AS/400

VAX 7000

Tower System

Mainframe

Figure 5.2   Client/server environment.

1.   Computer Systems

This section identifies a wide variety of the types of computer system components commonly encountered in crime scenes, provides a general description of each type of device, and describes its common uses. In addition, it presents the potential evidence that may be found in each type of hardware. A computer system typically consists of a central processing unit (CPU), memory, data storage devices, monitor, keyboard, and mouse. The computer might be a stand-alone device or it may be connected to a network. Additional components can include printers, scanners, external storage devices, and network communication devices. The four categories of computer systems discussed include mainframes, client/servers, laptops, and personal computing devices.

Caution: Many computing devices contain memory that requires continuous power to maintain the information. Unplugging the power source or allowing the battery to discharge can cause a loss of data and information stored on these devices. An uninterruptible power supply (UPS) is often used with computing and networking devices.

a.   Mainframes

A mainframe is a large, high-speed, multiuser, multiprocessing computer, supporting many users concurrently. Its configurations include a large memory storage capacity and numerous high-speed peripherals. Figure 5.1 depicts a mainframe computer with a controller that connects to various high-speed peripherals. It is most often used as a "number cruncher" that is accessible over high-capacity communication networks.

Governments, universities, and large corporations use these expensive computers for a multitude of applications. Applications include finance and accounting, human resources, sales and marketing, military and space, law enforcement, logistics, and education. Activities include all types of computing functions and information storage, word processing, calculations, communications, and graphics.

Evidence is most commonly found in databases and files that are stored on hard drives and storage devices. A **database** is a collection of files serving as a data resource. A file is a group of data with some form of commonality. A **database management system (DBMS)** is software that manages and provides access to the database. A database administrator usually administers the DBMS, whereas files are generally created and maintained by the general computer user. The mainframe operating system and the database system manage and maintain information concerning the activities against these components. Utility programs can be used to retrieve information concerning the activities against databases and files. Specific data is also available via utilities and customized application programs. Information retrieved might include time and date of activities as well as content—basically an audit trail. As a note, systems programmers do not like to share or cooperate with internal users or anyone else. A subpoena might be required to obtain information from these databases.

Important and relevant evidence may be found in individual files and files located on the database. Evidence found might reveal illegal or criminal activities such as gambling, pornography, pedophilia, fraud, espionage, or even terrorism. A short list of potential evidence targets created by the individual user includes:

E-mail files	Internet bookmarks/favorites
Documents/text files	Spreadsheet files
Address books	Database files
Mailing lists	Audio/video files
Calendars	Image/graphics files

Specific information can be retrieved from these systems by using software utility programs or having a programmer create a special application for retrieval. This avenue is not cheap!

The computer's operating system creates and maintains a number of files for managing the system. In most cases the individual user is not aware that this data is being accumulated. Passwords, Internet activity, and temporary files are examples of data that can be recovered and examined. Data that can be extracted includes date/time stamps of creation, modification, and deletion, file attributes, and user identification. Computer-generated files include:

History files	Configuration files
System logs	Print spool files
Temporary files	Cookies
Hidden files	

Evidence can also be collected from memory relating to data devices and components. Most of this information is related to computer system functions; however, it might contain latent evidence. Most of this potential evidence is not available to the casual user and will require the services of a computer professional. Examples include:

Deleted files	Reserved areas
Free space	Slack space
Unallocated space	Metadata
Bad clusters	Software registration information
Hidden partitions	System areas
Lost clusters	Computer date/time

Computer users can make it difficult for anyone to track their activities. Passwords might be required to access files and they might be encrypted or compressed. There are numerous opportunities for the cyber-criminal to hide illegal activities. User IDs can be faked, file names can be camouflaged, and files can be hidden in other files. Steganography techniques can be employed to hide data in a number of storage areas. Computer forensic examiners and computer professionals would need to be involved in identifying this type of evidence. Again, this is not cheap! There are commercial organizations that will contract to perform these types of investigative functions.

b.   Client Servers/PCs/Laptops

Client/server is a type of distributed computer architecture where end users of PCs (clients) request services from designated processors or peripherals (servers). This configuration is depicted in Figure 5.2. Usually some type of network is required to provide a connection between the client and the server and they can be located anywhere in the world. The servers are usually a much smaller version of the mainframe computer; however, they contain many of the features and functions found in the larger processor. The server is usually not accessible by the general computer user; however, application programs and user databases might well be located on the server.

Most computer forensic investigations will be conducted on the personal computer devices located in business surroundings and in the residences of suspects. Most employees will have access to a desktop computer, which can hold a considerable amount of latent forensic evidence. Often a user will have a docking device to attach a laptop computer and use it as a desktop. With the advent of wireless communications, laptop PCs, personal digital assistants (PDAs), and even cell phones can access these computer systems from anywhere in the world, given the proper access.

Forensic evidence might be located on the user's desktop and on the organization's server. It is more likely that evidence can be recovered from the user's desktop. The server might not be available as evidence because it might be essential to the organization. E-mail, calendar files, and system database files will probably be located on the organization's server. E-mail servers could contain valuable evidence for the investigator. These techniques will be discussed in Chapter 12. Most of the evidence available on the mainframe system is also available on the desktop and server. It should be easy to obtain a seizure warrant for the user's desktop computer; however, a subpoena will probably be required to secure any evidence from other devices. A short list of potential evidence includes:

Documents or text files	Image/graphics files
Database files	Audio/video files
Spreadsheet files	Internet bookmarks/favorites

Desktop computer users can also use logons, passwords, compression, hidden files, and encryption of their files. Most evidence can be recovered from the desktop hard drive or from one of the removable storage devices. External disk drives, floppy disks, zip drives, and thumb drives may all contain forensic evidence.

2.   *Personal Computing and Wireless Devices*

Many people are using laptop computers, PDAs, and other portable electronic devices to access corporate networks and the Internet. Many of these devices also utilize wireless connectivity to access mainframe and client/server systems. These personal, portable computers are excellent candidates for forensic evidence. Laptops have the same features as desktop computers and often contain more RAM and hard drive storage. It is common for a laptop to contain one megabyte of RAM and 80 gigabytes of disk storage. Most new versions have **universal serial bus (USB)** connections and firewire ports for storage devices and other peripherals. USB ports allow for the connection of a mouse, keyboard, floppy disk drive, thumb drive, **dongle**, and other devices. New versions of hard drives contain in excess of 200 gigabytes of storage.

a.   *Personal Digital Assistants (PDAs) and Organizers*

A PDA is a small electronic handheld device that can include computing, telephone/fax, paging, and networking features. This device approaches the full functionality of a desktop computer, but usually does not have disk drives. PDAs might possess card slots or ports that could interface with a modem, hard drive, or other device. They can synchronize their data with other computer systems by connecting to a cradle. A **BlackBerry** is a handheld device that competes with another popular handheld, the Palm, and is marketed primarily for its wireless e-mail handling capability.

These devices are used for handheld computing, information storage, and communication. Because a PDA is a portable device requiring batteries, data will be lost if the batteries fail. Charging devices must be collected with the device.

Significant and varied information and data can be retrieved from PDAs. Potential evidence could include the following items:

Address book   Logon and password
Calendars   Telephone book
Documents   Text messages
E-mail   Voice messages
Handwriting

The PDA can function as a cell phone and personal organizer and can provide access to the Internet. It is taking the place of pagers. A downside is that it is often lost and stolen and can be cloned.

Employees and employers are using these portable devices as extensions to the workplace's computer resources. These devices are taken home at night and on business trips. Students leave their laptops in automobiles, libraries, coffee shops, and restaurants; therefore, opportunity for theft occurs frequently as owners fail to provide security. Laptops often contain confidential business and personal information. A stolen laptop could allow a criminal to access confidential databases. Laptops can also be used to perpetuate various criminal activities. Theft of services, corporate espionage, child pornography, and fraud are examples of illegal activities that can be identified through forensic examination of laptop disk and storage devices. The depth of the forensic investigation increases because storage media might be located at the suspect's workplace, home, automobile, camper, friends' home, vacation home, relatives' home, and so forth.

Evidence potential is similar to that of the client/server desktop computer. A short list includes:

Documents or text files   Image/graphics files
Database files   Audio/video files
Spreadsheet files   Internet bookmarks/favorites

b.   Pagers

A pager is a handheld, portable electronic device that provides a remote, electronic paging function. These devices are being replaced by cell phones and PDAs. A pager is used for sending and receiving short electronic messages or signals. These can include numeric values such as telephone numbers and codes such as 911. These numeric values are often used by criminals as codes for some illegal activity. Some have the capability of receiving alphanumeric text including e-mail. A note is in order—once the pager is no longer in proximity to a suspect, turn it off. Continued access to electronic communication over a pager without proper authorization can be construed as unlawful interception of electronic communication.

Evidence retrieved might include voice and text messages, telephone numbers, e-mail, and address information. Pagers depend on batteries for power; therefore, they cannot be stored for long time periods before the memory erases. Numeric pagers can be used to transmit numbers and codes. Alphanumeric pagers can receive numbers and letters and can carry full text. Voice pagers can transmit voice communications in addition to alphanumeric text. Two-way pagers might contain both incoming and outgoing messages.

3.   *Telephone Systems and Communication Devices*

Voice communication systems include **private branch exchanges (PBXs)**, **automatic call distributors (ACDs)**, key systems, and hybrid systems. These systems are computer-based and are controlled by an operating system and a collection of voice system applications. They have similar vulnerabilities as client/server and mainframe installations.

The PBX is usually a centrally located specialized computer that allows employees and other users to communicate within some specified area such as a building or a campus. The computer telephony integration (CTI) application provides an interface between the PBX and a computer system. The PBX can accommodate fast data transmission over T-1 circuits to the central office, which is a component in the public switched telephone network (PSTN). Figure 5.3 depicts computer systems that have CTI software capabilities. There is a database located at each of the CTI-enabled computers. The operators located at the CTI computers know who is calling because the system matches the incoming telephone number with the local database information. There could be significant evidence located on these database records.

An ACD is a specialized telephone system designed originally for processing many incoming calls, now increasingly used for outgoing calls. An ACD can be integrated into a PBX for multifunctionality support. ACDs are historically used for processing many calls in industries such as airlines, rental car agencies, and mail-order houses.

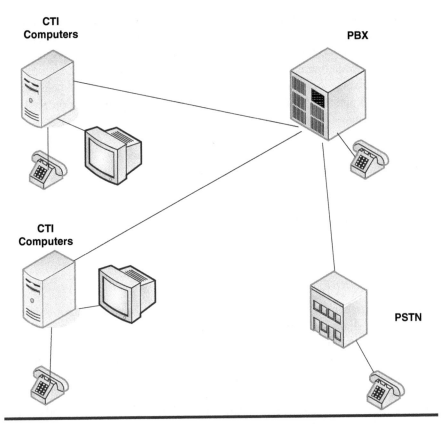

Figure 5.3   Computer telephony integration (CTI) components.

E-commerce transactions can be completed over the telephone system. Agents working in an ACD call center process many of these voice-oriented transactions. The database records are accessed and modified from both sources; therefore, security issues relating to computer systems must also apply to voice systems.

Many key systems are designated by the capacity in central office lines and stations. For example, an 824 system could accommodate a maximum of 8 lines to the central office and 24 stations in the user location. In a key system, each line is terminated via a button on a telephone instrument. A hybrid, in which the attendant transfers calls and the user dials an outgoing call access code, is usually required. Many key systems require proprietary telephone sets, and may not use the standard 2500 telephone set. Because key system attendants must announce each call to the called party, most modern systems have an internal paging feature that allows the attendant to hold a two-way conversation over a speaker/microphone that is built into the telephone set.

Thieves and hackers use telephone and computer networks to commit fraud by stealing telephone services. Employees, historically, committed this theft by making long-distance calls during business hours. With the increased sophistication of PBXs and the external access afforded to users, intruding into a PBX system is easier and has also become a security and integrity issue. Phone hackers use computers with auto-dialing modems to break security passwords and gain access into PBX systems, where they can use or sell long-distance services at the expense of the PBX owner. A subpoena will probably be required for any information retrieved from these systems. Information might include:

Telephone numbers	Demographics
Time and date of calls	Schedules
Call initiator and receiver numbers	Messages

Telephone and network companies often use their security departments to investigate incidents and crimes that involve their systems.

a.   *Telephones and Cell Phones*

A telephone can consist of a handset, cordless, or direct-connected communication device. It can draw power from the telephone network, AC converter, or battery. Cell phones are rapidly becoming the personal transmission device of choice. Many users are electing the cell phone over the conventional type of telephone. Chargers must be collected with any portable device that is seized.

These devices provide two-way communication from one device to another, using a number of network transmission facilities including land lines, radio, and cellular systems. Cell phones are capable of storing an enormous amount of information.

Many of the communication devices can store names, phone number lists, and caller IDs. Some devices can also store calendars, appointments, receive e-mail, and record messages. Potential evidence includes:

Appointment calendars	Phone book
Caller ID	Text messages
Electronic serial number	Voice mail – Instant messages
E-mail	Voice mail password
Memos	Web browsers
PIN numbers	Calling card numbers
Password	Debit card numbers

The portable devices rely on battery power and will lose data stored in the memory if the battery power is not maintained. The on-screen image may contain valuable information. Note that evidence on the devices can be compromised or deleted if they are not stored in Faraday evidence bags. The investigator must determine if the cell phone operates with GSM, TDMA, CDMA, 3G, 4G, or GPRS networks.

There are devices available for looking at the **subscriber identification module (SIM)**, which is the smart card necessary for the operation of GSM phones.

b.   Answering Machines

The ubiquitous answering machine might be overlooked as a source of forensic evidence. Answering machines are usually associated with some type of telephone and contain tape, disk, and memory storage.

These devices can be used to screen calls and record messages when the owner is not available. Messages can be recorded for greeting a caller. Most of these devices are digital and possess the ability to display the calling telephone number. These devices depend upon local electrical power and battery backup to operate. This is opposed to the normal telephone that receives its power from the local telephone central office. Any investigator should be aware that evidence stored in memory will be lost if the batteries fail, so precautions must be taken when seizing these devices for forensic examination.

Answering machines possess many features in addition to storing telephone-call messages. Information might include date and time stamps and other voice recordings. These might include:

Caller ID	Memos
Deleted messages	Phone numbers and names
Last number dialed	Tapes

4.   Network Devices

There are many devices in the telecommunication and broadband networks that contain potential electronic evidence. Network devices might include modems, data service unit (DSUs), multiplexers, routers, firewalls, switches, wiring hubs, and the list goes on. These devices, however, are technical in nature and require an experienced technician to reveal their contents.

The functions of these devices are generally related to the transmission and reception of some type of analog or digital communication signal. These devices are almost always transparent or invisible to the general user. The transmission of voice and data, however, would not happen without these devices.

Various network surveillance hardware and software are utilized to monitor and track network activities. Hardware devices such as monitors, protocol analyzers, and sniffers are employed in the surveillance systems. These specialized and complex devices can identify and capture numerous items of data and information from the network. Any and all network traffic is susceptible to surveillance. These transmissions might be protected, compressed, encapsulated, and encrypted. Some items of evidence may include:

IP addresses	Date and time stamps
Logons and passwords	Messages
Data files	

A number of system vendors such as IBM, Cisco, Sun Microsystems, Symantec, Network Associates, and Hewlett-Packard provide hardware and software solutions oriented toward enterprise security and surveillance. Intrusion detection and prevention information could be critical in computer networking investigations. **Intrusion detection (ID)** is a type of security management system for computers and networks. An ID system gathers and analyzes information from various areas within a computer or network to identify possible security breaches, which include both intrusions (attacks from outside the organization) and misuse (attacks from within the organization). An **ID** system is any device that exercises access control to protect computers from exploitation. These systems are either host-based or network-based.

Data collection methods require significant storage and the need for occasional erasing of old data to make room for new. Many networking devices may possess a limited amount of data storage. The open source programs *tcpdump* and *windump* as well as a number of commercial programs can be used for data capture and analysis. Network forensics and network management are discussed in Chapter 6.

5.   *Imaging Devices*

Imaging is the digital capture, storage, manipulation, and delivery of copies of analog originals, which may be texts, manuscripts, pictures, or other information types. Categories discussed include printers, scanners, and fax machines. Evidence might be recovered in the proximity of the device or in the print hopper.

a.   *Printers*

Categories of printing devices include thermal, laser, inkjet, and impact. They can be connected to computing devices and the network via various cabling arrangements including serial, parallel, USB, firewire, and modem. Some printers contain a memory buffer, allowing them to receive and store multiple pages while they are printing. Some models incorporate a hard drive storage device. The devices are used to print text and images from some computing device, either locally or remotely over some network. Check the proximity of the device for printouts or look in the stacker.

Printers often maintain usage logs with time and date information and may store network information. Evidence may be obtained from the following items:

Documents   Superimposed images on a roller
Hard drive   Time and date stamp
Ink cartridges   User usage log
Network ID

b.   Scanners

A scanner is an optical device connected to a computing device that scans a document and converts it to a computer-readable document. Scanners are available as flatbeds, sheet fed, and handheld devices. This device converts documents, photographs, and graphics to an electronic file that can be viewed, manipulated, and transmitted over a network such as the Internet.

The device might possess a memory capacity that could reveal significant evidence. The mere presence of the device at a crime scene might be evidence. Crimes such as counterfeiting, identity theft, check fraud, and child pornography might be identified by evidence obtained from a scanner.

c.   Fax Machines

Facsimile (fax) machines are used to scan documents and transmit to some remote fax machine via the network. They are often used to transmit documents that require a signature.

Fax machines can store preprogrammed telephone numbers and a history of transmitted and received documents. Some machines contain sufficient memory allowing multipage faxes to be scanned in and sent at a later time and also allowing incoming faxes to be held in memory for printing later. Some faxes have the capacity of storing hundreds of pages of incoming and outgoing messages.

Evidence is generally limited to send/receive log, telephone numbers, and the print cartridge. Both originals and copies may be present in the fax machine hoppers. Specific information available could include:

Speed dial lists
Stored faxes—incoming and outgoing
Fax transmission logs—incoming and outgoing
Header line
Clock setting

Evidence could be identified in images, sound, and video. Additional information could include date and time stamps and data on removable cartridges. Memory cards containing photographs need to be uploaded to a computer device. Criminals like to take photographs of incidents and sometimes take photos and movies during the commission of a crime. An arsonist might take photos of fires being set; a rapist might take photos of his victims. As a note, a camera phone can also provide photographic evidence, even though it may be of poor quality.

6. *Storage Devices*

Storage devices come in all shapes, sizes, and capacities. Hard drives are used in mainframes, servers, PCs, and laptops. Memory cards are present in many electronic devices. Three categories of storage drives include floppy disk, hard disk, and removable cartridge.

Floppy disk: A typical 5¼-inch floppy disk can hold 360 K or 1.2 MB (megabytes). 3½-inch floppies normally store 720 K, 1.2 MB or 1.44 MB of data.

Hard disk: Can store anywhere from 20 MB to more than 200 GB. Hard disks are also from 10 to 100 times faster than floppy disks.

Removable cartridge: Are hard disks encased in a metal or plastic cartridge, so they can be removed just like a floppy disk. Removable cartridges are very fast, though usually not as fast as fixed hard disks.

Removable electronic storage devices consist of those that do not lose information when power is removed. RAM, however, will lose data when the power is removed. The following is a partial list of media storage devices:

SCSI RAID 0, 1, 5	Multimedia card
Fiber Channel RAID	eXtreme Digital
IDE/SCSI	Computer hard disk drives
Serial ATA	Laptop hard disk drives
USB/Firewire drives	Server hard disk drives
CDs/DVDs	External hard disk drives
4 mm, 8 mm tapes	Mobile phone SIM cards
Zip disk	Tape
Floppies	PCMCIA hard disk drives
Compact flash	Solid state storage
IBM MicroDrive	Camera memory cards
Flash drive	Storage farms
Smart Media	LaCie hard drives
Secure Digital	LaCie external enclosures

Memory cards and storage devices can store hundreds of images in a credit card-size module. Thousands of images can be stored on the larger devices. These storage cards and devices are used in a variety of electronic devices, including computers, digital cameras, cell phones, and PDAs. These storage devices provide additional, removable methods of storing and transporting data and information.

Potential evidence is similar to that of a computer system. Evidence categories include user-created files, computer-created files, and other data areas. User-created files may contain important evidence of criminal activity such as address books and database files that may prove criminal association. Both still and video photographs may show evidence of pedophile and child pornography activity. Gambling, organized crime, and drug deal lists might be found in spreadsheets. Users have the opportunity to hide evidence in a variety of ways, such as hiding files within other files on a hard disk or under an assumed name.

Disk files include evidentiary data such as date and time of creation, modification, deletion, and access. This data also shows user name or identification and file attributes. Computer-created files could include the following:

Backup files	Log files
Configuration files	Printer spool files
Cookies	Swap files
Hidden files	System files
History files	Temporary files

The disk system also possesses information concerning data areas that are used in the course of the normal computer system processes. Searching disk systems for evidence is a time-consuming and expensive effort. Software and hardware tools will be presented in Chapter 6.

7. Miscellaneous Electronic Devices

There are a number of miscellaneous electronic devices that might be of interest in a forensic investigation. Access control devices fit in this category and include smart cards, dongles, and biometric scanners.

A smart card is a small handheld device that contains a microprocessor capable of storing various items of information. It is capable of storing a monetary value, password, digital certificate, and other information. A dongle is a device that looks like a USB flash drive; however, it contains information such as software license codes. The dongle is used primarily for access control to a computer or program and can function as an encryption key. A biometric scanner is a device that is usually implemented as an access device, which recognizes physical characteristics of a person, such as a fingerprint.

These devices provide access control to computer systems, secure areas, and software products. Potential evidence might include identification and authentication information of the card and the card user. They might also provide level of access, configurations, identification, and authentication for the device user, permissions of the user, level of access permitted, and permissions of the device itself.

A smart card can provide the investigator with another avenue to pursue. There are a number of circumstances that might raise suspicions with smart cards. Multiple cards should raise a red flag, as they might be counterfeit, altered, or stolen.

a.   Cameras

Digital cameras, video cameras, cell phones, PDAs, and film cameras can contain forensic photographic evidence. Digital cameras can record images for both images and video. They provide storage media and conversion hardware capable of transferring digital feeds to computer media.

Digital cameras capture images and video in a digital format that is easily transferred to computer storage media for viewing and editing. Resolution is a significant issue when selecting a digital camera. Batteries are required to maintain the memory in the camera. Some of these devices require a charger.

C.   The Next Steps

It should be obvious from the information presented in this chapter that latent evidence exists in many different types of electronic and computing devices. It should also be obvious that special techniques, hardware, software, and support are required for extracting and preserving this evidence. Technical and legal training is also an important element for forensic examiners, first responders, and investigators. Chapter 6 provides an in-depth look into the various investigative tools that are required for forensic investigative teams to accomplish their missions.

Chapter Summary

Computing and electronic devices can be used as tools in illegal activities and may contain evidence of some criminal activity or some violation of a corporate policy. Considerable evidence can be recovered from media storage devices such as computer hard drives. Investigators need to realize that evidence can also be recovered from a multiple of electronic devices in addition to computer systems. These categories of devices include telephone systems, image devices, and personal communication devices.

Data and information is often stored on mainframe and client/server computer systems. Evidence may be available on a database or via a DBMS. Evidence recoverable might be contained in documents, address books, mailing lists, calendars, graphics, and spreadsheets. Evidence gathered might support cases alleging illegal civil and criminal activities. Evidence would also be useful when investigating corporate policy violations.

Forensic evidence might be contained in many electronic devices that possess a memory storage capacity. These devices include film and video cameras, fax machines, scanners, printers, answering machines, and pagers. Specialized equipment might be required to capture this evidence. All portable devices will probably require some charging device that must be collected with the seized evidence.

Terms

Automatic Call Distributor (ACD) — A telephone facility that manages incoming calls and handles them based on the number called and an associated database of handling instructions.

BlackBerry — A handheld device made by RIM (Research In Motion) that competes with another popular handheld, the Palm, and is marketed primarily for its wireless e-mail handling capability.

Private branch exchange (PBX) — A telephone system within an enterprise that switches calls between enterprise users on local lines while allowing all users to share a certain number of external phone lines.

CD-R (Compact Disk-Recordable) — A disk to which data can be written but not erased.

CD-RW (Compact Disk-Rewritable) — A disk to which data can be written and erased.

Client/server — Describes the relationship between two computer programs in which one program, the client, makes a service request from another program, the server, which fulfills the request.

Clik!™ — Portable disk drive.

Database Management System (DBMS) — Manages the data files in the database and may provide independence of programs and data.

Dongle — A hardware key.

DVD (Digital Versatile Disk) — Similar in appearance to a compact disk, but can store larger amounts of data.

E-business (electronic business) — The use of Internet and digital technology to execute all the business processes in the enterprise.

E-commerce (electronic commerce) — The process of buying and selling goods and services electronically involving the Internet and networks.

Intrusion detection (ID) — A type of security management system for computers and networks.

Intrusion prevention — Any device that exercises access control to protect computers from exploitation.

Jaz® — A high-capacity removable hard disk system.

LS-120 (Laser Servo-120) — A floppy disk technology that holds 120 MB of data.

Magnetic media — Disk, tape, cartridge, diskette, or cassette device used to store data magnetically.

Mainframe — An industry term for a large computer, typically manufactured by a large company such as IBM for the commercial applications of Fortune 1000 businesses and other large-scale computing purposes.

ORB — High-capacity removable hard-disk drive.

Personal computer (PC) — A computer designed for use by one person at a time.

Subscriber identification module (SIM) — The smart card necessary for the operation of GSM phones.

Universal serial bus (USB) — A hardware interface.

Zip® — A 3.5 inch removable disk drive.

Review Questions

1. _____ is defined as business that is conducted electronically involving the processes necessary to support the day-to-day activities.

2. Describe the differences between intrusion detection and intrusion prevention systems.

3. _____ are large, complex computers that are exceptionally fast and contain considerable amounts of data storage and processing power.

4. Define client/server.

5. What is the relationship between a database and a DBMS?

6. Identify five important and relevant items of evidence that may be found in individual files and files located on a database.

7. Identify five computer-created files where forensic evidence that might be found.

8. Identify five types of evidence that can be collected from memory contained in data devices and components.

9. Provide a list of ten different types of media storage devices.

10. Identify the types of evidence that might be collected from telephone and cellular calling devices.

## Chapter 6

Investigative Tools, Technical Training, and Forensic Equipment

Chapter Objectives

- Identify the specialized tools and supplies required for electronic and computer forensic investigations
- Describe the various techniques employed for identifying and collecting electronic forensic evidence
- Identify training requirements for electronic forensic investigators and examiners
- Explain the use of software in computer network administration and surveillance
- Look at resources that provide for surveillance and capture of network traffic

Introduction

Special tools, equipment, and software are required to collect computer and electronic evidence. Advances in technology have increased the complexity of forensic investigations involving the latest devices. Different types of packaging are required for media storage devices and wireless communication devices to preserve the evidence.

New tools and techniques for identifying, collecting, preserving, transporting, and storing computer and electronic evidence are required. Additionally, new advanced training methods are also required to function in this new high-technology environment.

Advanced computer hardware and software tools must be procured and investigators trained in their usage. Disk drive imaging kits are required for seizing evidence from computer hard drives. Specialized software is required for searching media storage for critical forensic evidence.

Hardware and software solutions are available for the identification and capture of potential electronic forensic evidence. Devices such as monitors, sensors, analyzers, and sniffers contain programmable software that aids in these investigations. Network surveillance tools provide for online evidence collection.

First responders, computer forensic examiners, and investigators must receive training involving the use of the new forensic tools and must also become adept at technology testimony in the courtroom environment.

Corporate security departments are being challenged with new requirements to investigate activities relating to violations of security policies and white-collar crime. These organizations must also become proficient in the use of the new computer and electronic forensic tools. The corporate security personnel must learn new investigative techniques and requirements for both proactive and reactive incidents.

A.   Forensic Investigation Requirements

A wide variety of tools, including specialized equipment, computer hardware and software, are required in investigations that involve evidence retrieved from incident scenes where electronic devices are present. These investigative tools are in addition to those that are required for any incident scene investigation. Some law enforcement agencies use a vehicle that is especially equipped and supplied for these investigations. Valuable evidence can be lost forever because storage containers or other supplies are not available at the scene.

A number of commercial vendors provide tools that can be used in computer and electronic investigations and examinations. Product and service categories include the following:

Disk manipulation, formatting, partitioning
Data recovery specialists
Disk/text/hex editing
General purpose software: a variety of uses
Graphic viewers and processing
Hashing—CRC, SHA, MD calculations

Linux (*UX tools)
Windows administrative tools

Common crime-scene supplies must also be included in any first-responder kit. These include a supply of forms normally used in investigations and crime-scene protection articles. Common items would include crime-scene barricade tape, flashlight, chalk, etc. A kit that contains supplies specifically required for electronic evidence collection, documentation, and transport would be a necessity for the forensic investigator. The contents of both a fly-away kit and a computer forensic kit are described in Chapter 10.

Corporate security personnel and investigators have varied requirements when investigating policy and computer-use violations. Many of the crime-scene investigation requirements, however, also apply to the corporate incident scene. Some types of corporate violations can easily become criminal issues and require law enforcement intervention. This makes it incumbent on security personnel to follow procedures that are congruent with law enforcement practices and procedures.

1. Tool kits

Specialty tool kits will be required for the forensic examiner to successfully investigate a computer or electronics case. Investigations might occur at the incident scene, at a remote location, or in a forensic laboratory. Crime-scene responders and examiners usually possess kits for collection, storage, and transportation of evidence; however, they do not fulfill the requirements for computer and electronic evidence. Specialty tool kits might contain instruments to open a computer case to retrieve a hard drive including screwdrivers, pliers, and a flashlight. The Paraben forensic tool kit (Figure 6.1) might contain documentation aids, disassembly and removal tools, package and transport supplies, and miscellaneous items. The Black Box tool kits contain also every conceivable tool for accessing computer and electronic devices. Documentation aids would include cable tags, indelible felt-tip markers, and stick-on labels.

A kit for disassembly and removal of evidence would contain the following nonmagnetic tools:

Flat blade and Phillips screwdrivers	Specialized computer case screwdrivers
Torque drivers	Standard pliers
Hex-nut drivers	Star-nut drivers
Needle-nose pliers	Wire cutters
Secure-bit drivers	Bolt cutters
Small tweezers	Hammer

Figure 6.1   Paraben forensic tool kit and black box tool kits.

Obtaining the evidence is only the first step in the evidence procurement cycle. If the evidence is not protected, it will be useless in court proceedings. Computer and electronic components can be rendered useless by faulty handling. Packaging and transportation supplies include the following items:

Antistatic bags   Crime-scene tape
Faraday bags   Packaging material such as Styrofoam
Antistatic bubble wrap   and Styrofoam peanuts

Figure 6.2   Paraben first responder kit.

Evidence bags   Packing tape
Evidence boxes   Sturdy boxes of various sizes
Evidence tape/seals

A collection of items that support the evidence collection effort include the following:

Antistatic gloves   Floppy disks
Large rubber bands   Printer paper
Magnifying glass   Hand truck
Seizure disks of various capacities   Power strip
Flashlight   Extension cord

Experience will indicate the types of tools that the forensic examiner will require at the crime scene or incident site. Each investigation team would also possess a laptop computer and a camera. Additional tools are available from Paraben Corp. (Figure 6.2).

2.   Forensic Workstations

Desktop and laptop computers can be utilized as forensic workstations. If any electronic forensic examinations are to be conducted at the incident scenes, the laptop solution will probably be required, unless the organization has a mobile forensic lab. Desktop computers will be the most appropriate solution for a forensic lab setting. Configurations for these workstations are almost endless and usually depend upon the budget of the department. These devices must function properly with the software and hardware products that are selected for both computer and electronic forensic investigations. Several vendors offer software products that have been used successfully in computer forensic investigations. Additionally, a number of special interface cables are required for attaching to hard drives and other computer media storage devices. Software forensic tools must comply with industry and court standards, so that evidence obtained is admissible in court. Details concerning the requirements for a computer forensic laboratory, including a desktop forensic workstation, are provided in Chapter 10.

B. Forensic Software

Numerous software products are available for the forensic examiner. These products would usually be loaded on a laptop computer specifically dedicated to computer forensic investigations. A number of vendors provide software products that have proven successful in electronic cases. Often these software products are used in conjunction with a hardware device specifically designed for electronic investigations. A sniffer device might use an expert system software package to capture network traffic and identify relevant digital forensic evidence.

Numerous software products and systems provide for network administration, surveillance, imaging, analyses, carving, pattern matching, and other forensic evidence management. Specific products include X-Ways Forensics, Encase, Access Data FTK, Digital Intelligence, and ILook. Some of these software packages are specifically for law enforcement use. In addition to these packages, there are a number of applications that perform specialized forensic functions. This section describes product suites, utilities, and specialized programs that might be used by a forensic examiner.

1. *Computer Forensic Products*

A brief description is provided for a number of acceptable forensic software products. These include X-Ways Forensics, Encase, Forensic Toolkit (FTK), and ILook. Other products may be acceptable; however, the investigator must ascertain those that are acceptable to the court where the issue is to be decided.

X-Ways Forensics, by X-Ways Software, is an advanced computer examination and data recovery software product that is used by computer investigative specialists in private enterprise and law enforcement.

Encase, by Guidance Software, offers an industry standard in computer forensic investigation technology. This product provides investigators with a single tool, capable of conducting large-scale and complex investigations from beginning to end. Law enforcement officers, government/corporate investigators, and consultants around the world utilize this software product in their electronic investigations.

The **Forensic Toolkit (FTK)**, by Access Data, provides a tool for complete and thorough forensic examinations. FTK has full text indexing, advanced searching, deleted file recovery, data-carving, e-mail and graphics analysis, and other advanced features.

ILook is an all-in-one computer forensics suite currently maintained by the Internal Revenue Service (IRS). It is available free of charge to law enforcement agencies and certain U.S. government agencies. ILook is not available to the general public. The suite consists of the ILook External Imager, an analysis program, and a few utilities. IXimager is a Linux-based custom boot CD that produces forensic-grade compressed output.

2. Computer and Electronic Forensic Utilities and Programs

Digital intelligence has created several forensic software tools in-house specifically for forensic use. These tools include **DriveSpy**, **PDBlock**, and **PDWipe**.

DriveSpy uses familiar DOS commands (CD, DIR, etc) to navigate the system under investigation, extends the capabilities of the associated DOS commands, or adds new commands as necessary, and provides a familiar DOS-like prompt during system navigation. DriveSpy processes operate on the following components:

Large hard drives (greater than 8.4 gigabytes)
Floppy disks and removable media
FAT12/16/16x/32/32x partitions
Hard drives without partitions (removable media)
Hidden DOS partitions (full functionality)
Non-DOS partitions (physically)
Long file names (fully decoded and listed)
File creation (Win95/98), modification (DOS), and access dates (Win95/98)
Erased files (with their companion long file name, if one exists)
Slack space
Unallocated space

With operating systems becoming more and more complex, it is increasingly difficult to protect fragile computer evidence. PDBlock is a stand-alone utility designed to prevent unexpected writes to a physical disk drive. When PDBlock is executed on a computer, its job is to prevent all writes to the physical drives.

PDWipe is based on the wiping technology found in DriveSpy. PDWipe advertises the capability of wiping large hard drives (in excess of 8.4 gigabytes) in just under 11 minutes.

C. Computer Media Recovery

Computer data recovery requires knowledge of the Microsoft **file allocation table (FAT)** file system. FAT consists of a table an operating system maintains on a hard disk. It provides a map of the clusters (the basic units of logical storage on a hard disk) where a file has been stored. Technical details are provided in Chapter 9. Issues concerning the FAT file system could include:

Events that occur when a file is deleted
Long file name or short file name usage
Time stamp (time and date) issues when a file is moved or copied

Differences in file properties when it is moved from one directory on a logical volume to another on the same volume versus moving it from one logical volume on a physical disk to a different logical volume on the same physical disk

Physical versus logical volume details

File creation information and properties

Data that can be recovered after a file has been deleted

Microsoft Windows "recycle bin" usage

1. MD5 Algorithm

Message digest-5 (MD5) is a hashing algorithm that is used to verify data integrity through the creation of a 128-bit message digest from data input. This message may be of any length and is claimed to be as unique to that specific data as a fingerprint is to the specific individual. MD5, which was developed by Professor Ronald L. Rivest of the Massachusetts Institute of Technology (MIT), is intended for use with digital signature applications, which require that large files be compressed by a secure method before being encrypted with a secret key, under a public key cryptosystem. MD5 is currently an Internet Engineering Task Force (IETF) Request for Comments (RFC) 1321 standard. According to the standard, it is "computationally infeasible" that any two messages that have been input to the MD5 algorithm could have as the output the same message digest, or that a false message could be created through apprehension of the message digest. The repeatability requirement of digital evidence relies on the MD5 algorithm to prove the integrity of imaged hard-disk drives.

2. SHA Algorithm

The **secure hash algorithm (SHA)** family is a set of related cryptographic hash functions. The most commonly used function in the family, SHA-1, is employed in a large variety of popular security applications and protocols, including TLS, SSL, PGP, SSH, S/MIME, and IPSec. SHA-1 is considered to be the successor to MD5, an earlier, widely used hash function. The SHA algorithms were designed by the National Security Agency (NSA) and published as a U.S. government standard. SHA-1 creates a 256-bit message digest versus the 128-bit message digest of MD5.

3. CRC Algorithm

The **cyclic redundancy check (CRC)** is a mathematical algorithm that translates a file into a unique hexadecimal code value. A CRC is a type of checksum. A checksum algorithm takes a file (or other string of bytes) and calculates from it a few bytes (the checksum) that depend on the entire file. The idea is that, if anything in the file changes, the checksum will change. CRC checksums are usually used to detect random, uncorrelated changes in files; therefore, they are useful in ensuring reproducibility when imaging hard-disk drives.

D. Forensic Hardware Devices

A number of hardware devices are available that are specifically designed for both proactive and reactive electronic investigations. These devices might include the ability to copy an image from a computer hard drive or collect data and information via some electronic surveillance monitor. Additionally, probes and sniffers that can capture network traffic and data collection devices that can be attached to computing and network devices and systems are also available.

1. Imaging

Ghost imaging is the copying of the contents of a computer's hard disk into a single compressed file or set of files (referred to as an image). This allows the contents of the hard disk, including configuration information and applications, to be copied to the hard disk of other computers or onto an optical disk for temporary storage. Examinations must not be conducted on original disk media because the data could be compromised and are therefore not useful in legal proceedings.

Using an imaging product, the examiner can clone (copy) the entire contents of a hard disk to a portable medium such as a writable CD or to a server. The portable image can then be used to set up each hard disk in other computers, automatically formatting and partitioning each target disk. Ghost imaging is useful where one system is to be replicated on a number of computers in a classroom or for a team of notebook computer users who all need the same system and applications. On personal computers, ghost imaging is used to back up everything on the hard disk, often while reinstalling an operating system. The forensic usage of imaging is to preserve the original disk contents without making any modifications. Figure 6.3 depicts three devices that can be used for imaging hard-disk drives.

E. Surveillance Equipment

Investigators often require surveillance or eavesdropping devices for collecting evidence to identify criminal activities or violations of corporate security policies. Three primary techniques employed include snooping, sniffing, and probing. An additional practice employed in some investigations is the use of wiretaps.

Figure 6.3   Disk imaging devices.

1.   Snooping

Snooping, in a security context, is unauthorized access to another person's or company's data. The practice is similar to eavesdropping, but is not necessarily limited to gaining access to data during its transmission. Snooping can include casual observance of an e-mail that appears on another's computer screen or watching what someone else is typing. More sophisticated snooping uses software programs to remotely monitor activity on a computer or network device.

Malicious hackers (crackers) frequently use snooping techniques and equipment such as keyloggers to monitor keystrokes, capture passwords and login information, and to intercept e-mail and other private communications and data transmissions. Corporations sometimes snoop on employees legitimately to monitor their use of business computers and track Internet usage; governments may snoop on individuals to collect information and avert crime and terrorism.

Although snooping has a negative connotation in general, in computer technology snooping can refer to any program or utility that performs a monitoring function.

2.   Sniffing

In common industry usage, a **sniffer** (with a lowercase "s") is a program that monitors and analyzes network traffic, detecting bottlenecks and problems. Using this information, a network manager can keep traffic flowing efficiently. A sniffer can also be used legitimately or illegitimately to capture data being transmitted on a network. A network router also reads every packet of data passed to it, determining whether it is intended for a destination within the router's own network or whether it should be passed further along the Internet. The term "sniffer" is occasionally used for a program that analyzes data other than network traffic. Sniffer (with a capital "S") is a trademark owned by Network General. The generic term may have originated from Sniffer®, which is said to be the first packet capture and decode software that was offered for the purpose of network analysis and troubleshooting.

3.   Probing

In telecommunications generally, a probe is an action taken or an object used for the purpose of learning something about the state of the network. For example, an empty message can be sent simply to see whether the destination actually exists. Ping is a common utility for sending such a probe. A **probe** is a program or other device inserted at a key juncture in a network for the purpose of monitoring or collecting data about network activity. Probes can be used in conjunction with network surveillance systems to capture digital data. Hackers use various techniques to constantly probe networks for vulnerabilities.

F.   Network Security Management

A basic knowledge of computer networks is a prerequisite to understanding the principles of network security. Primarily the network configurations would include the Internet, a local area network (LAN), an intranet, and/or an extranet. There are a number of threats that managers and administrators of computer networks will need to confront. A number of specialized tools are available that can be used to reduce the exposure to the risks of network computing. Many of these tools are implemented as software and can be an important source of data and information in computer forensic investigations.

Computer network investigations usually occur in the realm of corporate network security administrators. Most of these incidents will involve improper use of corporate network facilities and resources, violations of computer-use policies, or violation of a corporate security policy. Many of these issues and incidents are resolved by internal security personnel; however, some issues must be escalated to law enforcement agencies.

With the advent of the Internet and Web-based E-commerce, the network has become a vehicle for numerous illegal activities. The primary malicious network threats involve viruses, worms, and Trojan horses. Identity theft and fraud occurs primarily via e-mail transmissions, direct mail, and telephone solicitations. Another issue with e-mail systems is the enormous amount of SPAM being transmitted daily. There are numerous hardware and software systems and tools that can be deployed against these network-oriented threats.

Network management and surveillance can be accomplished by utilizing dedicated devices, by host computers on the network, by people, or by some combination of all of these. No matter how network management is performed, it usually includes several key functions. The network functions in order are:

- Monitoring
- Control
- Troubleshooting
- Statistical reporting

These functions assume the role of network watchdog, boss, diagnostician, and statistician. All of these functions are closely interrelated, and often, many of them are performed on the same device. An examiner can initiate these functions manually or they can be initiated automatically by the network management system.

G. Network Management Tools

The primary network management surveillance systems and network management products and services available include NetView, OpenView, SunNet Manager, and RMON. Most network management systems use a protocol called Simple Network Management Protocol (SNMP), which is the standardized software package for supporting network management. Technical programming staff members often use software languages such as Perl, Linux, and UNIX to create scripts (programming code) for data pattern searches. Most computer center operations employ technical support personnel who can provide this service.

1.   NetView

IBM Tivoli **NetView** ensures the availability of critical business systems and provides rapid resolution of problems. It discovers TCP/IP networks, displays network topologies, correlates and manages events and SNMP traps, monitors network health, and gathers performance data.

Functions provided by NetView allow the user to quickly identify the root cause of network failures. It also:

Builds collections for management of critical business systems
Integrates with leading networking vendors
Maintains device inventory for asset management
Measures availability and provides fault isolation for problem control and management
Reports on network trends and analysis

2.   OpenView

HP **OpenView** is a suite of business computer management or "E-services" programs from Hewlett-Packard (HP), which states that the suite is "among the world's 20 largest software businesses." The OpenView programs are frequently sold to HP 9000 and e3000 business server customers. An HP customer's IT professionals can use OpenView to manage applications, device availability, network conditions and status, system performance, service and program maintenance, and storage resources.

3. SunNet Manager

Solstice **SunNet Manager** is a comprehensive set of tools and services that is used to perform fundamental tasks in managing a network. SunNet Manager is also an extensible platform that allows for the development of network management applications.

SunNet Manager provides additional tools for viewing and analyzing returned data: the Results Browser allows the user to analyze data that has been stored to a disk file, while the software allows for a graphical representation of either incoming data or stored data.

4. RMON

RMON (Remote Network Monitoring) provides standard information that a network administrator can use to monitor, analyze, and troubleshoot a group of distributed LANs and interconnecting network circuits from a central site. RMON specifically defines the information that any network monitoring system will be able to provide.

RMON can be supported by hardware monitoring devices, called "probes" or through software or some combination. A software agent can gather the information for presentation to the network administrator with a graphical user interface. A number of vendors provide products with various kinds of RMON support.

RMON collects nine kinds of information, including packets sent, bytes sent, packets dropped, statistics by host, by conversations between two sets of addresses, and certain kinds of events that have occurred. A network administrator can find out how much bandwidth or traffic each user is imposing on the network and what Web sites are being accessed. Alarms can be set in order to be aware of impending problems.

H. Network Forensics

Network forensics is the capture, recording, and analysis of network events in order to discover the source of security attacks or other problem incidents. Network forensics systems consist of active and passive systems.

Online systems include those in which all packets passing through a network traffic point are captured and written to storage with analysis being done subsequently in batch mode. Since all traffic is recorded, much of it may be irrelevant to the investigation. This approach requires large amounts of storage, usually involving a RAID system. A RAID consists of a collection of disk drives that offers increased performance and fault tolerance.

Real-time systems involve those in which each packet is analyzed in a rudimentary way in memory and only certain information is saved for future analysis. This approach requires less storage but may require a faster processor to keep up with incoming traffic. Network traffic may be flowing at 100 Mbps or greater. The downside to this technique is the possibility that legitimate traffic could be discarded.

Both approaches require significant storage and the need for occasional erasing of old data to make room for new. The open source programs *tcpdump* and *windump* as well as a number of commercial programs can be used for data capture and analysis.

One concern with the passive approach is one of privacy because all packet information (including user data) is captured. Internet service providers (ISPs) are expressly forbidden by the Electronic Communications Privacy Act (ECPA) from eavesdropping or disclosing intercepted contents except with user permission, for limited operations monitoring, or under a court order. ECPA was discussed in Chapter 2. Network forensics products are sometimes known as Network Forensic Analysis Tools (NFATs).

Network forensics applications include the capturing and analyzing of network communications using the following techniques:

Capturing and analyzing wireless communications
Building low-cost wireless forensics platforms utilizing high-powered wireless cards and open-source software
Determining whether volatile data on live systems may be of interest and how to extract that data in a forensically sound manner
Dumping the contents of RAM
Exporting metadata regarding running processes and network connections
Working with encrypted storage volumes
Creating effective, interactive reports that educate and impress
Importing data into litigation management software

The U.S. Federal Bureau of Investigation's **Carnivore** is a controversial example of a network forensics tool. It monitors e-mail and other traffic through ISPs.

I. Computer Forensic Training

The investigator must be trained in the proper use of various imaging utilities available to the computer examiner. Knowledge of verification methodologies and the testing of forensic tools is required. With the size of media increasing daily to almost unthinkable amounts, the fast, secure, and validated method of creating a forensically sound image, backup, or working copy is a daunting task for any skill level of computer forensic examiner. Hard-disk drive capacities are exceeding 200 gigabytes. The variety of media storage devices is skyrocketing, as most electronic communication devices possess some type of storage.

In many cases, investigators are limited by media size, purpose, scope of warrant, or consent, and cannot remove the media from the scene. It is also possible and likely that they are not allowed to shut the device down and remove it from service. There are many examples where this will be true, such as a server in a hospital, an ATM network, or some other vital operation. It is essential that policies and procedures in this area stand up in court and in the commercial realm. These inhibitors must be overcome by advanced training methods. Training is expensive and takes the investigator out of the field; however, the alternative is lost cases.

1. *Training Requirements*

Forensic investigators and examiners must understand the concepts, techniques, and tools providing a solid foundation in concepts related to the investigation, preservation, and processing of computer-based evidence. Corporate security departments must decide if technical support is to be outsourced or provided in-house. Specific technical training can be divided into three categories, namely hardware, software, and procedural:

Hardware

    PC hardware
    Processors
    Memory
    Motherboards
    Hard/floppy/removable drives
    Physical and logical characteristics of hard and floppy drives
    IDE and SCSI channel configuration guidelines

Software

    Computer data
    Bits and bytes
    Hexadecimal and binary
    ASCII
    Norton's DiskEdit and DriveSpy
    Master boot record
    Partitions and file systems
    Partition tables
    Boot records
    Boot-up sequence of a DOS-based computer
    Operating systems
    FAT-12/FAT-16/FAT-32
    Time and date stamps (access, modification, creation)
    Long/short file names

MS-DOS command line review
Understanding file types and files headers

Procedural

Computer and electronic crime fundamentals
Evidence collection, packaging, and storage considerations
Media imaging—copying hard drives, disks, multimedia cards, etc.
Cell phone evidence
Recovering deleted files
Keyword searching
Data compression
Data encryption
Potential evidence in MS Windows
"Hidden" media
Creating a forensic boot floppy

Knowledgeable people must be employed to conduct computer forensic investigations. All the hardware and software in the world will be useless if the examiner does not know how to use these tools successfully. The use of these tools will also be in vain if the evidence is not preserved properly and the chain of evidence maintained. On-the-job training is an acceptable alternative if there is an experienced professional available to provide this knowledge. The state-of-the-art of computer and electronic technology is changing so fast that experienced forensic examiners must also train on an ongoing basis to keep up. Departmental and unit budgets must contain funds for a training program. The old saying "pay me now or pay me later" rings true. This section will provide an overview of the organizations that offer training programs and classes in the computer forensic environment.

2. *Training Providers*

Training and educational programs are available for various levels and categories of criminal justice. These are presented both online and in a classroom setting. Many providers offer a general program directed at criminal justice; however, some are specific to forensic investigations. These programs include:

Associate's degree in Criminal Justice
Bachelor's degree in Criminal Justice
Master's degree in Criminal Justice
Certificate in Criminal Justice
Court Reporting
Forensic Science/Crime Scene Investigation

Homeland Security
Law Enforcement
Private/Criminal Detective

Some providers of forensic tools also provide for computer forensic training. Both Access Data and Guidance Software provide this type of training packages. Various high-technology organizations also offer training academies and computer forensic boot camps. Formal training classes might include the following topics:

Data Recovery   Password Recovery
On-Site Acquisition   Litigation Support
Electronic Risk Control   Expert Testimony
Document Discovery

3.   Specialized Training

First responders and investigators require special skills to successfully process any evidence that might be present at an incident scene. This is particularly true to incidents where computer and electronic devices are present. Incidents might be solved with evidence that is contained on these devices, but can be easily overlooked by the untrained and unaware.

The duties, assignments, and procedures vary from departments and agencies regarding the investigators or technicians; therefore, the job description may vary depending on geographic locations. For example, if the employee resides in an area with a large population where it consistently ranks in the top 10 nationally in violent crime occurrences, then the evidence documentation and collection portion of a crime-scene response can be a full-time job. Whereas a geographic location with a much smaller population and fewer criminal acts might necessitate a combination of required job skills. Some law enforcement departments have a policy of sworn versus nonsworn personnel preferences. Local jurisdictions might have special requirements concerning the legal status of forensic examiners and investigators.

Most departments today prefer, if not require, some type of college degree. The departments or agencies in the various geographic areas post their particular requirements and duties. Education requirements for security professionals in business operations may be entirely different. This could become a significant issue as a corporate policy violation could escalate into a criminal investigation. Untrained or undertrained corporate security personnel could destroy critical evidence.

Regardless of whether the investigator's major education is in general studies, criminal justice, or forensics, a suggestion is to augment those studies with minor courses in basic computer training, document drafting, and photography. Any curriculum designed for crime-scene investigations in criminal justice classes will probably be presented in a general studies department.

Most of the experience to become proficient will be gained in an on-the-job phase of employment. Most departments also offer their employees an opportunity for peace officers standards and training (POST) employment or in-service training to further the employee's development. Most of the POST employee educational classes for the crime-scene investigator would be specific classes geared to crime-scene response, evidence collection, forensic photography, fingerprint technology, homicide, and death scene investigation.

If the student wishes to search, there are a few colleges today that are offering programs for POST graduation classes in various forensic disciplines and crime-scene response.

If someone is interested in seeking a job in computer evidence recovery, it would be helpful to spend a weekend at some computer-service shop where cases are being opened and various maintenance procedures are being performed.

4. *Forensic Investigations Training*

The rate of identity theft, fraud, abuse, and criminal activity on computer systems is reaching alarming rates. Violations of corporate security policies and computer-use policies are commonplace. Corporate security, law enforcement, and information security professionals are often required to perform computer forensics duties on their jobs. Training programs are available to address most of these requirements. Specific subjects relating to computer and electronic forensic investigations include:

Overview of computer crime
Computer forensics training with open-source tools
Preparing sterile examination media
Acquisition, collection, and seizure of magnetic media
Issues when presenting data in court
Documenting a "chain of custody"
The marking, storage, and transmittal of evidence
Investigating data streams
File storage dates and times
File deletion/recovery
Preservation and safe handling of original media
Recovering deleted data from a cell phone
Digital camera evidence
PDA evidence
Recovering Internet usage data
Recovering swap files/temporary files/cache files
Making bit-stream copies of original media
Common data hiding techniques
Examining CD-ROM media

Carving out files "hidden" in unallocated disk space
Word document forensics and password cracking
Understanding Microsoft Windows from a forensics point of view
Working with NT file system
Combing partition table and boot record
Investigating the master file table (MFT)
Linux/UNIX computer forensics

Specialized training is offered by vendors who offer forensic tool kits. These include Encase Forensic Edition, X-Ways Forensics Addition, Forensic Toolkit (FTK), and Linux dd.

J. Support Organizations

Organizations engaged in forensics investigations can find support from a number of agencies. These include the National White Collar Crime organization (NW3C) and Computer Crime and Intellectual Property Section (CCIPS).

The mission of NW3C is to provide a nationwide support system for agencies involved in the prevention, investigation, and prosecution of economic and high-tech crimes and to support and partner with other appropriate entities in addressing homeland security initiatives, as they relate to economic and high-tech crimes. They are a congressionally funded, nonprofit corporation whose membership primarily comprises law enforcement agencies, state regulatory bodies with criminal investigative authority, and state and local prosecution offices. While NW3C has no investigative authority itself, its job is to help law enforcement agencies better understand and utilize tools to combat economic and high-tech crime.

The Department of Justice (DOJ) and other agencies are continually working to better prevent computer crimes and enforce existing laws concerning computer crime. Information is available on legislation, high-profile computer crimes, and cyber crime summits. The DOJ continually provides informal guidance to prosecutors and investigators as they work through complex substantive, procedural, and practical elements of computer-crime cases. While this guidance does not provide any legal rights or obligations, it is helpful to law enforcement as they address challenging questions of law, policy, or practice. Numerous links are available on the CCIPS Web site. The Web site concerning searching and seizing computers and obtaining electronic evidence in criminal investigations is of particular interest. It is located at www.usdoj.gov/criminal/cybercrime/.

Chapter Summary

Specialized tool kits will be required for computer and electronic forensic investigations. Investigations and examinations might occur at an incident scene, at some remote location, or in a forensic laboratory. First responders and examiners must be equipped with kits that provide for collection, storage, protection, and transportation of forensic evidence.

All members of the electronics team must be trained in the proper use of various forensic tools to successfully accomplish their investigations. Knowledge of hardware and software tools and investigative methodologies using these tools is required. Common forensic tools include FTK, Encase, X-Ways, ILook, and Linux dd.

The Internet and Web-based E-commerce, along with local area networks and their derivatives of intranets and extranets, are providing an avenue for numerous illegal activities. Organizations must be concerned about malicious network threats that involve viruses, worms, and Trojan horses. In addition, identity theft and fraud is initiated worldwide via e-mail transmissions and other network transmissions. A number of hardware and software tools are available for network security and integrity management of these network resources. These include NetView, OpenView, SunNet Manager, and RMON products.

Two support organizations providing information concerning cyber crime and other computer investigations include the NW3C and CCIPS. Numerous links on their Web sites provide a wealth of information for computer forensic examiners and investigators.

Terms

Cyclic redundancy check (CRC) — A mathematical algorithm that translates a file into a unique hexadecimal code value.

Digital intelligence — Has created several forensic software tools in-house specifically for forensic use.

Encase — By Guidance Software, offers an industry standard in computer forensic investigation technology.

File allocation table (FAT) — A table that an operating system maintains on a hard disk that provides a map of the clusters (the basic units of logical storage on a hard disk) where a file has been stored.

Forensic Toolkit (FTK) — By Access Data, provides a tool for complete and thorough forensic examination.

Ghost imaging — The copying of the contents of a computer's hard disk into single compressed files or set of files.

ILook — An all-in-one computer forensics suite currently maintained by the Internal Revenue Service (IRS).

Message digest-5 (MD5) — A hashing algorithm that is used to verify data integrity through the creation of a 128-bit message digest from data input.

NetView — Functions provided by NetView allow the user to quickly identify the root cause of network failures.

Network forensics — The capture, recording, and analysis of network events in order to discover the source of security attacks or other problem incidents.

OpenView — Manages applications, device availability, network conditions and status, system performance, service and program maintenance, and storage resources.

Probe — An action taken or an object used for the purpose of learning something about the state of the network.

RMON (remote network monitoring) — Provides standard information that a network administrator can use to monitor, analyze, and troubleshoot a group of distributed local area networks (LANs) and interconnecting network circuits from a central site.

Secure hash algorithm (SHA) — A set of related cryptographic hash functions. SHA-1 creates a 256-bit message digest.

Sniffer (with a lowercase "s") — A program and/or hardware that monitors and analyzes network traffic, detecting bottlenecks and problems. Note: Sniffer with an uppercase S is a registered product name.

Snooping — In a security context, is unauthorized access to another person's data or company's data.

SunNet Manager — A comprehensive set of tools and services used to perform fundamental tasks in managing a network.

X-Ways Forensics — An advanced computer-examination and data recovery software product.

Review Questions

1. Identify ten generalized tools that might be part of the electronic tool kit.
2. Identify ten specialized supplies that should be included in the forensic identification and packaging kit.
3. Identify eight items that will be included in the investigator's tool kit for incident scene examinations and evidence collection.
4. What is the purpose of imaging?
5. Discuss the use of a sniffer for evidence collection activities.
6. A _____ is a program or other device inserted at a key juncture in a network for the purpose of monitoring or collecting data about network activity.
7. What is the difference between MD5 and SHA algorithms?
8. Training for forensic investigators can be divided into three categories, namely _____ _____, _____, and _____.
9. T/F. Network forensics includes proactive activities to discover the source of security attacks or other problem incidents.
10. Identify three network systems that can be utilized for network security, monitoring, and forensic investigations.

EVIDENCE COLLECTION AND MANAGEMENT

Chapter 7

Managing the Crime/ Incident Scene

Chapter Objectives

- Understand the requirements for managing the incident/crime scene
- Become familiar with the responsibilities of the first responder at an incident site
- Identify those steps necessary to make electronic evidence admissible in court
- Look at the issues relating to electronic and computer crime-scene investigations
- Identify the various players involved in an electronic/computer investigation
- See how electronic forensics provides support in solving crimes
- Look at the investigative differences between corporate security and those of law enforcement

Introduction

The initial response to an incident involving computers or electronic evidence can originate from a variety of sources. A complaint can be received at a corporate security hotline or a surveillance activity can provide an indication of a policy violation or a possible criminal activity. A law enforcement agency might request assistance in an investigation that has uncovered electronic evidence.

Specific responsibilities include protecting the incident scene, preserving evidence, collecting evidence, and submitting the evidence for further analysis. There is a possibility that a considerable amount of physical evidence will be present. This physical electronic evidence will play a critical role in the overall investigation and resolution of some suspected violation.

First responders and computer forensic experts have to conform with many rules and regulations if the evidence they uncover is to be acceptable to the courts. The first step in obtaining computer forensic evidence is getting a search warrant to seize the suspect system. This warrant must include wording that allows the investigators to seize not only the computer, but also any media and hardware thought to be connected with the crime. A warrant also needs to be clear about the search of network and file servers, whether backup media is included, and if hardware, software, and peripheral devices can be removed to another location to conduct the search.

If it is thought that evidence is contained in e-mails, this also should be specifically mentioned in the search warrant. E-mail is a sensitive area as it can be considered personal, so solid justification is needed before a suspect's e-mail is to be searched.

In all circumstances, data not connected to the crime must not be touched. Doctors, lawyers, and clergy store documents on their PCs and much of this information is confidential. While the computer forensic expert needs to uncover evidence, care must be exercised to protect the personal information of any innocent third parties.

A.   Scope of the Problem

Criminal activities are proliferating in our society with the help of computers and related electronic devices. Technology is employed by criminals as a means of communication, a tool for theft or extortion, and a repository to hide incriminating evidence or contraband materials. Members of law enforcement must possess current knowledge, resources, and equipment to effectively investigate today's criminal activity. The law enforcement community is, therefore, challenged to identify, investigate, and prosecute individuals and organizations that use these emerging technologies to support illegal activities.

Illegal activities and violations of corporate security and computer-use policies are escalating. It has been estimated that 80 percent of these violations are committed by internal personnel. Most investigations concerning these incidents are conducted by internal security personnel; however, some are serious enough to warrant law enforcement intervention.

Computers, electronic devices, and digital media are increasingly used in unlawful activities. These devices may be contraband, fruits of the crime, a tool of the offense, or a storage container holding evidence of the offense. Investigation of any criminal activity has the potential of producing electronic evidence. Electronic components might include a pocket-sized personal data assistant, a floppy diskette, a compact disk (CD), or the smallest electronic chip device. Images, audio, text, and other data on these media are easily altered or destroyed. It is imperative that law enforcement personnel identify, seize, and protect such devices in accordance with applicable statutes, policies and best practices and guidelines.

1. The Incident Scene

The first responders to an incident/crime scene have the responsibility of protecting any and all computer and electronic evidence that might be useful in future civil and criminal actions. The steps and requirements are the same whether the incident is a corporate incident or a violent crime scene. Evidence is where the investigator finds it. Evidence from personal and property crimes might be in plain view or require a DNA analysis. Computer and electronic evidence is more subtle and might not be evident or obvious at the incident scene. The first responders can destroy critical latent evidence if they have not been trained in the proper identification, collection, and packaging procedures for electronic investigations.

Most incident and crime scenes are unique; however, some are similar, particularly those that involve computer systems. Investigators must take a broader view of the incident scene to include other possibilities such as computer forensic evidence. This means that both corporate security departments and law enforcement agencies must train their personnel in computer and electronic investigation techniques. Much of this potential evidence might be circumstantial, but it could possibly be used to support the primary physical and direct evidence that has been developed. A list of drug users and sales on a laptop computer found at a crime scene could be persuasive to a jury if it has been properly obtained.

2. The Initial Response

An incident involving computers or electronic evidence can originate from a variety of sources. A law enforcement agency investigating a crime scene could identify a number of computers and other electronic devices that might contain electronic evidence relevant to the current criminal investigation. The crime-scene investigators must be trained in the procedures required when this type of potential evidence is encountered. Valuable evidence can be lost by careless and improper handling by untrained personnel.

Corporate security audits or a surveillance activity could have provided an indication of a policy violation or a possible criminal activity. Anonymous complaints to a corporate hotline might have provided information concerning possible security violations. A prompt assessment of the situation must be made, usually with limited information. The security personnel must decide if an investigation is appropriate or if a referral must be made to law enforcement authorities. Answers to the following questions will better prepare the first responder in determining the role of the computer or electronic device in some potential illegal activity.

- Are any of the hardware or software components stolen?
- Did the suspect use the system to commit some offense? For example, preparation of fake IDs or other counterfeit documents were created on a scanner or printer.
- Is the computer used to store evidence of some offense? Are lists of drug users on the hard drive?
- Did a computer intruder use the computing device to attack other systems and to store stolen credit card information?
- Was the device used in violation of a corporate security policy?

This is not an all-inclusive set of questions that need answering, as the list changes frequently. The investigator will have to take a "best shot." After the computer or electronic device's role is understood, the investigator must decide if there is probable cause to seize hardware, software, media, or data.

Procedures for initiating the **documentation** and audit trail are similar for all investigations. The investigator receiving the initial complaint must record the incident in some type of log or **journal**. A sample journal is included in Appendix A. Minimum information collected should consist of the date and time, address and location, type of complaint, and the individuals involved. Any other information volunteered should be recorded.

When arriving at the incident scene, the responder should be aware of anyone leaving or in close proximity to the area. Journal entries should be made identifying these individuals. It is important for the responding person to be observant when approaching, entering, and exiting an incident scene. If this is a crime scene, contact must be made with the crime scene team leader before entering the area. If this is a corporate incident, policy procedures will dictate the appropriate steps taken by the security employee. Corporate security policies are discussed in subsequent sections.

Investigators must decide what, if any, evidence can be collected from the incident scene. Materials and documents present at an incident scene might be confidential. Doctors, lawyers, and clergy store documents on their PCs and much of this information is privileged. While the computer forensic expert needs to uncover evidence, care must be exercised to protect the personal information of any innocent third parties. A sample form entitled "First Responder Seizure Record" is included in Appendix A.

B. Crime Scene Investigation

The purpose of a crime scene investigation is to establish events that occurred and to identify those responsible. This is done by carefully documenting the conditions at a crime scene and recognizing all relevant physical evidence. The ability to recognize and properly collect physical evidence is often critical to both solving and prosecuting crimes. In a majority of cases, the first responder who protects and searches a crime or incident scene plays a critical role in determining whether physical evidence will be acceptable in solving or prosecuting criminal activities.

A crime scene investigation is a difficult and time-consuming job. There is no substitute for a careful and thoughtful approach. An investigator must not leap to conclusions as to what happened based upon limited information, but must keep an open mind regarding evidence collected at the scene. Tunnel vision might cause the investigator to overlook an important piece of evidence. Reasonable inferences about what occurred are also produced from the scene appearance and information is obtained from witnesses. Observations will help guide the investigator to document specific conditions and recognize valuable evidence. A broad understanding of crime scene investigations is often only achieved by on-the-job activities. It is essential that someone, such as a team leader, keep track of all activities ongoing in the investigation. An "Investigation Progress Checklist" is included in Appendix A.

C.   Electronic and Computer Investigations

Most police investigations begin at the scene of a crime. This is usually not true with computer system investigations. A computer or cell phone might be the target of a corporate policy violation, where an employee is suspected of violating a policy, causing corporate security personnel to investigate. It is possible, however, that the corporate security investigator might uncover a potential crime that could involve the law enforcement authorities.

The scene is simply defined as the actual site or location in which the incident took place. It is important that the first investigator on the scene properly protect the evidence. The entire investigation hinges on that first person properly identifying, isolating, and securing the scene. The scene should be secured by establishing a restricted perimeter. This might be accomplished by using some type of rope or barrier, usually crime-scene tape, or simply locking a door to a server room. The purpose of securing the scene is to restrict access and prevent evidence destruction.

Once the scene is secured, the restrictions should apply to all nonessential personnel, including law enforcement personnel. An investigation may involve a primary scene as well as several secondary scenes at other locations. Other incident scenes could include vehicles, work locations, vacation sites, or a living space. On major scenes, a safe and secure space and/or comfort area should be designated at the incident scene to brief investigators, store required equipment, or use it as a break area. A space might need to be identified for marking, packing, and inventorying evidence.

The protocol for critical incident management being taught today identifies a three-layer or three-tier perimeter. The outer perimeter is established as a border larger than the actual scene, to keep onlookers and nonessential personnel safe and away from the scene, an inner perimeter allowing for a command post and comfort area just outside of the scene, and the core or scene itself. An extreme advantage will be realized by taking the time to properly teach first responders and investigators to evaluate and secure the scene.

D. Physical Evidence at a Crime Scene

Evidence used to resolve an issue can be categorized as **testimonial evidence** and physical evidence. The testimonial evidence would be any witnessed accounts of an incident. The **physical evidence** would refer to any material items that would be present on the crime scene. These items would be presented in legal proceedings or corporate investigations to prove or disprove the facts of an issue. The investigators might use evidence collected at an incident scene to:

Prove that a crime has been committed or a policy violation exists
Link a suspect with a scene or a victim
Establish any key elements of a crime or incident
Establish the identity of a victim or suspect
Corroborate verbal witness testimony
Exclude those not involved

The evidence located and recovered at a scene, as well as the intelligence gathered, might determine the direction the investigators take in the case.

E. Types of Evidence

Evidence identified and collected will fall into two general categories—those involving petty crimes and felonies and those involving computer and electronic crimes concerning corporate policy violations. There are special and unique collection, handling, and packing procedures for most of this evidence.

Evidence from misdemeanor and felony crimes might include impressions from fingerprints, tool marks, footwear, fabrics, tire marks, and bite marks. Human matter might include blood, semen, body fluids, hair, nail scrapings, and bloodstain patterns. Weapon evidence might include gunshot residues, weapons, gunpowder patterns, casings, projectiles, fragments, pellets, wadding, and cartridges. Miscellaneous evidence might include arson accelerant, paint, glass, and fibers.

Evidence from computer and electronic investigations could include desktop computers, laptops, printers, copiers, cell phones, personal digital assistants (PDAs), CDs, floppy disks, USB memory sticks, digital cameras, Zip disks, hard drives, and any other device that has a storage capacity. Obviously all of this evidence consists of high-technology devices that will require a different type of investigation and investigator.

F. Processing the Crime Scene

In an organized approach to crime scene investigations there are three basic and simple stages in properly processing the crime scene: scene recognition, scene documentation, and evidence collection. An organized approach is a sequence of established and accepted duties and protocols. An organized approach ensures the following activities:

Conducting thorough and legal search
Expeditious processing of evidence without compromise
Complete scene documentation
Utilization of standard methods and techniques for evidence recovery
Understanding use and knowledge of resources and equipment
Ensuring all pertinent evidence is recovered
Proper handling and packaging of evidence
Distributing evidence to labs for analysis
Following safety precautions

1. Evidence Recognition and Identification

The recognition or identification of evidence begins with the initial search of the scene. The search can be defined as the organized and legal examination of the crime scene to locate items of evidence to the incident or crime under investigation. There are several search methods or patterns applied in an organized search. Factors such as the number of searchers, the size of the area to be searched, type of evidence, etc. are used to determine the method or pattern to be employed in the crime scene search. The initial response to an incident must be expeditious and methodical.

Because most investigations start with very limited information, care and common sense are necessary to minimize the chances of destroying evidence. A plan of operation can be developed and initiated from an initial **walk-through** of the scene. The plan is to decide what evidence may be present and if it may be fragile and should be collected as soon as possible. The incident scene must be preserved with minimal contamination and disturbance of physical evidence. A determination must be made concerning resources, equipment, and assistance necessary for processing.

2. Scene Documentation

In the documentation stage of an organized approach for processing the crime scene all functions have to correspond and be consistent in depicting the crime scene. The final result of a properly documented incident or crime allows others to take the finished work and reconstruct the events that occurred at the scene. An incident scene **sketch** will be useful later in the investigation.

Consideration of hazards or safety conditions may also need to be addressed. If the incident scene is a high-traffic business area, personnel and possibly customer control might be required. Contractors, sales representatives, maintenance personnel, and business partners might occupy the general incident area. Make a note of these people in the case journal.

3. Evidence Collection

The evidence collection or recovery step in crime scene processing includes the methods, techniques, and procedures used in retrieving evidence. Patience and care are very important at the crime scene. The investigator should take the proper time and care in processing the scene. The work is tedious and time consuming.

Teamwork in crime scene investigations is essential. The entire investigation may involve many people from different organizations. Each individual has a vital role in the investigation process. Continual communication among all parties involved is paramount.

The work done at a crime scene is very challenging and time consuming. If hard-drive images are to be recovered on site, computer cases have to be opened, cables connected, and possibly a lengthy imaging technique initiated. Searches of media might be done at the incident scene. The investigator's imagination will determine the process of retrieving the evidence and the time frame involved.

Documenting computer crime scene conditions can include immediately recording transient details. Certain evidence is fragile and if not collected immediately can easily be destroyed or lost. The scope of the investigation also extends to considerations of arguments which might be generated in this case and documenting conditions which would support or refute these arguments.

In addition, it is important to be able to recognize what should be present at a scene, but is not, and objects that appear to be out of place. If storage media such as CDs and floppy disks are scattered around the area, someone might have been in a hurry to leave or to destroy evidence. It is also important to determine the full extent of a crime scene. A crime scene is not merely the immediate area where a suspect concentrated his or her activities, but is also adjacent areas, off-site areas, and vehicles. Evidence might be located anywhere in the world with crimes involving the Internet or corporate networks.

Although there are common items frequently collected as evidence, literally any object can be physical evidence. Anything that can be used to connect a victim to a suspect or a suspect to a victim or crime scene is relevant physical evidence. A suspect will often disavow any connection to the electronic evidence seized; therefore, supporting evidence that connects the suspect to the electronic devices must be collected. Fingerprints might be lifted from a computer mouse, CRT screen, device surface, or even DNA from a coffee cup.

G. Issues and Warnings when Seizing Evidence

Only evidence relevant to a case can be seized by investigators. Knowing the role of the computer will indicate what should be taken. For instance, if it is thought that the computer was used to store evidence, then all storage media should also be seized for the computer forensic inspection. This would include floppy disks, CDs, USB storage, and any other device that might contain evidence. If the computer was running programs to collect and analyze information, any relevant books or manuals found at the scene should be seized to help computer forensic experts understand the programs.

Any suspects present must be prevented from touching the computing devices. A computer that is running at the time of seizure should not be allowed to shut down, as this sequence might delete valuable evidence. Pulling the plug out of the wall might prevent programs on some computers from wiping incriminating information during the shutdown sequence. Note different computers and operating systems function differently. The computer forensic expert can test the shutdown sequence later, to see if it includes any destructive programs that could be activated to erase evidence on the device.

When a computer and its peripherals are removed from a crime scene, a great deal of care has to be taken while dismantling the equipment to prevent any malicious programs from being activated should the computer power system be booby-trapped. One has to ensure that all cables are labeled so they can be reassembled later. Figure 7.1 depicts a sample chain of custody checklist.

Figure 7.2 depicts an evidence receipt checklist. The investigative team can use these two forms as a memory jogger. These forms are also available in Appendix A.

The entire setup should be photographed or a video taken before starting disassembly; notes should be taken at every step; and every cable should be labeled stating where it was attached. There are several ways to set up a computer and its peripherals. When it arrives in the computer forensics lab, the suspect device will need to be set up exactly as it was at the crime scene. Static bags must be utilized for storing electronic components. Investigators must wear a static ground protection device to reduce the chance of a static discharge damaging critical evidence. Figure 7.3 shows a static-ground device.

A number of issues are unique to investigating and prosecuting computer and electronics criminal cases. First, the investigation may interfere with the normal conduct of the organization's business. Evidence associated with the investigation may be located on this same production computer system. This evidence might be commingled with other data that is used in the normal course of business. This might make the gathering of evidence very difficult.

Computer and Electronics Chain of Custody Checklist	
☐	Created unique case and evidence number
☐	Documented some asset tag or serial number that uniquely identifies the evidence
☐	Document make and model of system the data was taken from
☐	Documented BIOS time
☐	Documented location the evidence was found in (inside case, inside drawer of desk, inside briefcase)
☐	Documented physical description of evidence
☐	Annotated notes for any accesses to the evidence before you arrived
☐	Annotated notes for any step that occurs outside of your normal process
☐	Filled in history annotating when you received the drive and from whom
☐	Updated chain of custody for each action taken with the original evidence

Figure 7.1   Computer and electronics chain-of-custody checklist.

Several additional considerations that must be addressed include:

There is a compressed time frame for the investigation
Experts might be required and might not be available
Some jurisdictions define electronic evidence differently
Locations of the crime are geographically dispersed

The crime scene investigation consists of many steps requiring considerable documentation efforts. Logs and journals addressing the chain-of-custody are absolutely required for any electronic evidence to be admissible in court.

H.   Steps for a Crime/Incident Scene Search

Education and preparation are major components of a successful crime scene search for electronic evidence. Investigators who usually perform criminal crime scene

Computer and Electronics Evidence Receipt Checklist

	☐	Took evidence with authorization
	☐	Created unique case and evidence number
	☐	Documented some asset tag or serial number that uniquely identifies the evidence
	☐	Received signature from owner or manager
	☐	Noted date and time of seizure
	☐	Completed receipt for all evidence taken
	☐	Provided copies to owner or manager

Figure 7.2   **Computer and electronics evidence receipt checklist.**

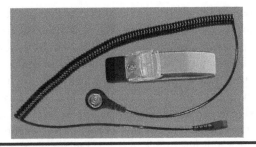

Figure 7.3   **Static-ground devices.**

searches are usually not qualified for computer crime scene searches. Proper search warrants are a must when processing a computer site. Special skills and knowledge are also required in these types of investigations. Personnel skill sets will be discussed in subsequent sections. Search warrants and subpoenas were discussed in Chapter 2.

The basic steps involved in a computer site search include the following:

Secure and protect scene
Initiate preliminary survey

Evaluate physical evidence possibilities
Prepare narrative description
Take photographs of scene
Prepare diagram/sketch of scene
Conduct detailed search/record and collect physical evidence
Conduct final survey
Release incident/crime scene

Note that many of the steps also apply to crime scene searches for crimes involving misdemeanors and felonies; however, the orientation is one that is more technical in nature. A computer or some electronic device might be a tool that was used in commiting a crime, which means that normal evidence-gathering techniques for forensics processing should be followed. The steps for processing evidence on computer and electronic devices are presented in Chapter 8.

It does not matter whether the incident site is involved in a corporate security issue, a civil, or a criminal investigation. The steps will be the same in all cases. It is certainly possible and likely that a corporate or civil matter will become a criminal investigation. If the proper procedures were not followed by the investigators, evidence can be excluded in future court proceedings.

1.   Secure and Protect Scene

It is essential to secure and protect the area comprising the computer system in question. Crime scene tape is a good first step. It is also essential that the organization's computer personnel be excluded from the area. Most computer specialists are not familiar with computer forensics techniques and could also be part of the investigation. Security must be provided for the area while the investigation is proceeding. Determinations of any employees or visitors who may have entered the computer site need to be identified. Document anyone who has access to the site or anyone who might have a reason to be involved with the computer site. Do not rely on your memory, as it will not suffice in court! Documentation requirements will be discussed in detail in subsequent sections.

2.   Initiate Preliminary Survey

Computer and electronic evidence usually takes on the same form: computers, peripherals, cell phones, PDAs, various storage media, digital cameras, etc. The investigator will have a general knowledge of the types of evidence that can be collected; however, new devices might show up at a crime scene. A cautious walkthrough is a good first step to get a feel for the complexity of the site. Several rooms and buildings might become part of the investigation. Due to the networking capabilities of computer systems, even remote sites or vehicles might become involved in the investigation. The investigator must maintain control of the situation and the physical site. An inventory log and chain-of-custody form must be completed and photographs made of all relevant devices and related electronic evidence. Specific activities that might be included in this phase of the investigation include:

Determine all the locations that might need to be searched
Look for any specifics that must be addressed relating to hardware and software
Identify possible personnel and equipment needs for the investigation
Determine which devices can be physically removed from the site
Identify all individuals who had access to the computer or electronic resources

3. *Evaluate Physical Evidence Possibilities*

This step is a continuation of the preliminary survey and may not be perceived as a separate step. After the site is thoroughly photographed, a more detailed search can begin. Before any devices are handled, remember that fingerprint evidence might become evidence in establishing who used these devices. The smallest, most insignificant piece of evidence might solve a case.

Any network capability and connections to the computer site must be identified. Networking will broaden the investigation considerably. If there is an Internet connection, it can become a worldwide investigation involving various Internet service providers and subpoenas. Cell-phone evidence will involve various telephone network carriers and subpoenas. Current identity fraud and scam cases originate in foreign countries.

Prioritize the evidence collection process to prevent loss, destruction, or modification. Focus first on items easily identifiable and accessible and proceed to out-of-view evidence. Look for the obvious first—the suspect might have been sloppy.

4. *Prepare Narrative Description*

A journal or narrative must be prepared concerning the investigation and the crime scene search. Anything and everything is important when conducting the site investigation. Remember that the defense attorney is going to query any witnesses on the most obscure item possible. A technique suggested is to represent crime scenes in a "general to specific" scheme. Describe the site in broad terms and then get very specific with details. A good idea is to cross-reference the journal with the photographic evidence and the chain-of-custody form.

The narrative effort should not degenerate into a sporadic and unorganized attempt to recover physical evidence. Under most circumstances, evidence should not be collected while developing the narrative. The narrative process can be accomplished by using audio, video, and/or text. Remember the axiom "haste makes waste."

5.   *Take Photographs of Scene*

Developing a photographic profile of the crime scene is a requirement for computer forensic investigations. Photographs should be taken as soon as the incident scene is secured and before any computers or electronic devices are moved. Photographs should be taken from all angles of the physical site. Closeups of cable connections for all devices should be included. Note these cables will need to be tagged in another step. Any video screens being displayed would be photographed. The photographic effort would need to be recorded on a photographic log. A sample log is depicted in Appendix A. Specifics for identifying and capturing photographic evidence are as follows:

Capture overall, medium, and closeup views of various items of computer and electronic evidence
Use a scale device such as a ruler for size determination
Take a photograph of the item with and without the scale device
Photograph the item in place before its collection and packaging
Photograph any item or place that might corroborate the statements of a suspect or witness
Take crime area photographs from eye level
More is better—film is cheap; consider digital
Prior to lifting latent fingerprints, photograph should be a 1:1 ratio

Consideration should be given to the type of camera used in the photographic evidence gathering effort. Look at the benefits of a digital camera versus a standard film camera. A macro lens will be required for quality closeup shots. Also required will be some light source such as a flash unit. Remember the photographic evidence could be presented to a jury.

If the investigative unit has the budget, an alternative to the digital or film camera is the motion picture or video camera. An advantage to this approach is that an audio explanation can accompany the video and might play well in the courtroom.

a.   *Photographs*

Photographs should be taken as soon as possible to depict the scene as it is observed before anything is handled, moved, or initiated into the scene. Photographs allow a visual permanent record of the crime scene and items of evidence collected from the crime scene. There are three positions or views that the crime scene investigator needs to achieve with the photographs: (1) overall scene photographs showing the most possible view of the scene, (2) mid-range photographs showing the relationships of items, and (3) a close-up of the item of evidence. A closeup should be taken of items that have serial numbers, tags, and universal product codes (UPCs).

Software products and other electronic devices often have a radio frequency identifier (RFID) sensor attached. All stationary evidence where the photograph will be used to assist in the analytical process should be taken using a tripod with the proper lighting techniques for creating any needed shadows. This usually means a second, remotely located flash unit. A second photograph adding a measuring device should be taken of items where the photo will assist in the analytical process.

A photographic log must be maintained for all evidence photographed. A sample form is included in Appendix A. An entry is required for every photo taken. Items of information that should appear on this form include:

Investigator name
Agency name and case number
Camera brand and lens type
Film type, speed, and brand
Digital camera information
Photo number
Time and date for each image
Description and location of item being photographed

These photos must correlate with the investigator's journal and any other document that refers to this evidence.

6.   *Prepare Diagram/Sketch of Scene*

A diagram or sketch establishes a permanent record of items, conditions, and distance/size relationships. They also supplement the photograph record. Usually a rough sketch is drawn at the crime scene and is used as a model for a complete, formal document that would be completed later. The sketch can be coordinated with any logs or journals via a numbering scheme.

Sketches are used along with the reports and photographs to document the scene. A crime scene sketch is simply a drawing that accurately shows the appearance of a crime scene.

A general progression of developing a sketch includes the following steps:

Lay out the general perimeter of the computer or evidence site
Fill in fixed objects such as computer desks, computer systems, and peripherals
Record the position or location of any evidence
Record any relevant measurements or distances
Provide a key or legend and some orientation

Items of information that should appear on the sketch include the following:

Specific location	Compass orientation
Date and time	Evidence depictions
Case identifier	Measurements
Sketch preparer	Key or legend
Sketch scale	

A sketch is simply drawn to show items and the position and relationship of items. It does not have to be an architectural drawing made to a scale; however, it must include exact measurements where needed. The advantage of a sketch is that it can cover a large area and can be drawn to leave out clutter that would appear in photographs. Remember that the sketch and photographic log must be consistent with each other.

7. Conduct Detailed Search, Record, and Collect Physical Evidence

The search, record, and collect phases for computer and electronic evidence will be different from the normal criminal investigation. The computer investigator will usually have a general idea as to the types of evidence that will be present at the incident scene. A checklist can be developed that will identify most types of computer and electronic evidence that might be at a crime scene. The major difference between investigations will probably be the size of the computer system and the amount of disk storage that will need to be secured or imaged. Seizure of electronic devices, such as cell phones and PDAs, should not pose any special problems due to their small size. These small communication devices, however, must be stored in Faraday bags to mask out any signals.

It might be necessary to determine the amount of disk storage records that need to be copied or imaged for later forensic analysis. On large databases it will be next to impossible to copy or image the entire storage device. In this case, a forensic examination might have to occur at the crime scene. Note that hard disk drives currently on the market can store more than 200 gigabytes of data.

All electronic devices seized must be protected using antistatic bags. Any cell phone seized must be placed in a Faraday bag. All disk media must be bagged and tagged. All cables must be tagged and the identifiers must correspond to the evidence collection logs and photographic evidence logs. Conflicts in documentation will cause considerable grief in a court of law. Also, if a computer system is to be reconstructed later, cable connections and maps must be precise.

There are four basic premises to the search, record, and collect phase of the investigation. These steps are as follows:

The best search options are typically the most difficult and time consuming
The physical evidence cannot be overdocumented
There is only one chance to properly perform the task
Two basic search approaches include cautious search of visible areas and vigorous search of hidden areas

8.   Conduct Final Survey

After the investigative team has completed all tasks relating to the search, record, and collect phases at the crime scene, a critical review should be conducted to ensure that nothing has been missed. This is the last chance to cover all the bases and ensure nothing has been overlooked. The investigators must ensure that they have gone far enough in the search for evidence, documented all essential things, and made no assumptions that may prove to be incorrect later. A short list will provide assistance to the investigative team:

Double-check documentation to detect inadvertent errors
Check to ensure all evidence is accounted for before leaving the crime scene
Ensure all forensic hardware and software used in the search is gathered
Ensure possible hiding places of difficult access areas have not been overlooked

An incident scene debriefing is the best opportunity for personnel and participants to ensure the investigation is complete.

9.   Release Incident/Crime Scene

The last step in the evidence investigation phase is to release the incident scene back to the owners. The release is accomplished only after completion of the final survey. The investigation team should provide an inventory of the items seized to the owner/manager of the incident site. A receipt for electronic evidence must be completed for any devices seized. A sample receipt form is available in Appendix A. A formal document should be provided that specifies the time and date of the release, to whom released, and by whom released. Note that as soon as the incident scene has been released, a warrant might be required to reenter.

I.   Documentation Procedures

Reports and other documentation pertaining to an incident must be compiled into a **case file** by the lead investigator or team leader. This case file is the official record of actions taken and evidence collected at the scene. This documentation allows for independent review of the work conducted.

Law enforcement departments and corporate security organizations use a variety of preprinted documents or forms that are designed to record certain aspects of various incident investigations. These documents normally have resulted from a trial-and-error approach based on actual case experiences. Despite variations in the design of these documents, the purpose and goals behind their use are usually identical from one organization to another.

Often, there is a tendency to regard forms as a means to cover every possibility that personnel may confront. These documents normally serve only as reminders of the minimum pertinent information needed to perform a task. Each incident scene will require some deviation from the norm, based on the complexities at hand. Forms are not substitutes for thinking; they are merely tools to assist personnel to fully exercise training and experience to meet the needs of a given situation.

Since computer and electronic crime scenes are fairly predictable in the types of situations that arise and the evidence to be recovered is also basically the same, forms can be developed that are specific in nature. Log forms and chain-of-custody forms can be developed that are specific to these electronic and computer investigations. Other types of forms that are general in nature to most incident investigations can be generic in nature.

A common thread that runs through all steps of a forensic investigation is documentation. Every step in the process requires a form to be completed. There are normally six important categories of documentation that are considered applicable to any search:

Journal or narrative description
Diagram/sketch
Chain-of-custody
Photographic log
Evidence recovery and receipt
Latent print-lift log

The primary focus in the incident might be oriented toward a computer or electronic investigation and might not include any aspects of a misdemeanor or felony crime; however, a simple corporate computer policy violation might lead to something more significant. Keeping this in mind, the investigator must develop general documentation for all incidents. A brief description of these generic forms follows.

J.   Administrative Audit Worksheet

The **administrative audit worksheet** provides for documentation of major events, times, and movements relating to the search efforts. It also includes documentation of initial and continuing management and administrative steps taken to ensure that an organized search was accomplished. Information might include a chain-of-command for the organization where the incident occurred. The team leader might complete this worksheet to ensure all steps and documentation have been successfully completed. The computer and electronic investigation checklist provides a checklist for the team leader. This administrative audit must be performed by someone who has overall authority in the investigation. The major benefit from conducting this audit is to ensure all the bases are covered and there are no holes in the investigation. Do not wait until testimony is in progress to discover an important step was overlooked. There are additional spaces on the checklist for activities the team leader might include in the audit. Components include the following:

1.   Narrative Description

The narrative description describes the general appearance of the incident scene as first observed. Generally this would describe an employee's work area (cubicle), a server room, a computer room, or some network equipment closet.

2.   Photographic Log

The photographic log provides specific documentation of the process of scene photography that records the overall, medium, and close-up views of the incident scene. The log produced would represent the technical and descriptive information concerning the photographic task. Of particular importance are the photographs of cabling arrangements.

3.   Diagram/Sketch

The diagram or sketch would provide documentation of physical evidence locations, as well as measurements showing pertinent size and distance relationships in the crime scene area. This document would include a scale, compass orientation, and a legend.

4.   Evidence Recovery Log

The evidence recovery log would include documentation of the recognition, collection, marking, and packaging of physical evidence for administrative and chain-of-custody purposes. This form will be the major document prepared by the investigator for computer and electronic incidents. Because this document will usually be presented in court, make some effort to write legibly. Also accuracy counts—an incorrect device serial number on the log will be a problem.

5.   Latent Print-Lift Log

The fingerprint log provides documentation of the recognition, collection, marking, and packaging of lifts made of latent prints discovered at the scene. Generally overlooked in a computer investigation, a print on a mouse or computer screen might be useful in establishing who was using the device.

K.   Personnel Duties and Responsibilities

The following sections will discuss how crime scene duties can be divided among personnel. Also identified are various job categories, and evidence-gathering functions.

The number and qualifications of personnel responding to an incident will depend on the size of the security organization or investigative department. Often a single individual might perform all of the functions. Someone must be a team leader or the primary person responsible for the investigation. This investigator in charge must identify specific responsibilities and develop investigative plans in accordance with departmental policy and jurisdictional laws. Large departments might field a team that includes the following personnel:

Team leader
Photographer and photographic log recorder
Sketch preparer
Evidence recorder/evidence recovery personnel
Specialists

This section will provide a list of activities and responsibilities for each of these job titles. In all of these investigations, someone must have overall responsibility for incident management. The team leader might also be the chief investigator. The same individual could conceivably handle all of the evidence identification, collection, and packaging. This arrangement would be feasible for small investigations.

1.   Team Leader

The team leader assumes control of the incident scene and ensures the safety of personnel and security of the scene. This function is important for both corporate security incidents and law enforcement criminal investigations. In computer and electronic investigations personnel must use appropriate protective equipment and follow standard recommendations to protect them and the evidence from any electrical hazard. Note: static discharges can render electronic evidence useless. Additional responsibilities include:

Conduct initial walk-through for purposes of making a preliminary survey, evaluating potential evidence, and preparing a narrative description.

Determine search patterns, and make appropriate assignments for team members.

Designate command-post location and ensure exchange of information between search and investigative personnel.

Coordinate with other law enforcement agencies or corporate security organizations.

Ensure that sufficient supplies and equipment are available for personnel.

Control access to the scene and designate an individual to log everyone into the scene.

Continuously reevaluate efficiency of search during the entire course of operation.

Release the scene after a final survey and inventory of the evidence has been done.

Access forensic needs and call forensic specialists to the scene.

The Computer Forensic Investigation Checklist (Appendix A) is a valuable tool to ensure no steps in the investigation are missed. Dates and signatures for each task will ensure the investigation is complete. The various tasks include the following:

Get a case assignment
Secure and protect the scene
Initiate preliminary survey
Evaluate physical evidence options
Photograph scene
Prepare diagram or sketch
Prepare narrative description
Record and collect physical evidence
Retrieve hard drives and other storage devices
Retrieve media
Do an evidence inventory
Label and tag evidence
Pack evidence
Transport evidence
Take evidence to storage or lab
Do a preliminary report
Create image of hard drives
Carve disks or match pattern
Retrieve cell phone evidence
Search electronic media
Do final walk-through
Release incident/crime scene

2. *Photographer and Photographic Log Recorder*

The photographer's primary responsibility is to record evidence and to prepare a photographic log. Major evidence items must be photographed before they are moved. The photographer must also coordinate these activities with those who are developing the evidence log and scene sketch. Specific activities include:

Photograph entire area before it is entered. This would include office areas, resident computer-work areas, automobiles, computer rooms, server rooms, and network closets.

Photograph all electronic devices, media, and computer components.

Photograph all cabling arrangements.

Photograph entire scene with overall, medium, and close-up coverage, using measurement scale when appropriate.

Photograph all latent fingerprints and other impression evidence before lifting and casting are accomplished. Use a 1:1 macro-camera lens for closeup shots.

3. *Sketch Developer*

The primary function of the sketch developer is to diagram the immediate area of the incident scene and orient the diagram with the sketch. This team member identifies major items of evidence on the sketch and designates and labels areas to be searched. This individual also advises the team leader and all other search members of the nomenclature for designated areas. Determinations are made for taking measurements, orientations are identified, a scale is developed, and this information is double-checked. In most cases, headcount for this position will not be funded. The team leader or photographer could perform these tasks.

4. *Evidence Recorder/Custodian*

The evidence collector, recorder, and custodian are responsible for the evidence integrity and chain-of-custody. Note that evidence must be photographed before collection. A primary function is to maintain the evidence log. This includes describing evidence and its location on appropriate bags, containers, or envelopes. This person must sign and date evidence containers and maintain the chain-of-custody. It is important to remember computers and electronic devices require special handling to avoid static discharges and destruction of evidence. Sufficient collection containers must be available for the various types of evidence that might need to be seized.

5.   *Forensic Scientist or Evidence Recovery Technician*

In the scientific community, the forensic scientist or evidence recovery technician is accepted as a forensic specialist. This specialty function provides a professional, organized step-by-step approach to the processing of a crime scene. Extensive study, training, and experience in crime scene investigations are needed for the investigator to be proficient in the field.

They must be well versed in all areas of recognition, documentation, and recovery of physical evidence that may be deposited at the scene. A general knowledge of what analysis may be performed in the lab as well as proper procedures in handling, collecting, and packaging of items of evidence is needed to ensure those recovered items will safely arrive at the lab.

6.   *Specialists and Consultants*

It is sometimes necessary to bring in computer forensic science expertise from an outside agency or organization. Typically, specialists are brought in from industry, the academic community, private scientific laboratories, and forensic consultant agencies. In high-technology crime cases, both the prosecution and the defense will probably employ a computer scientist. There are several important issues that should be considered when contracting for computer forensic specialists:

Look at the competence and reliability of the specialist.
Ensure the specialist will work at a crime scene within law enforcement guidelines.
Identify the role of the specialist in presenting expert testimony in court.
Determine the cost in advance when contracting forensic consultants.

Specialists should be identified before they are needed in an actual case. A current list should be maintained, if possible. The agency should meet with these individuals to determine the best manner to jointly conduct search planning, operations, and follow-up activity.

Chapter Summary

The initial response to an incident scene will set the stage for the rest of the investigation. The first responder or investigator must be especially observant of the incident scene and the adjacent areas. Access to the scene must be controlled and all potential electronic evidence protected from damage or modifications.

Evidence identification, collection, and packaging at the incident scene must be handled according to strict procedures. The chain-of-custody must be preserved. Electronic evidence must be protected from modification, damage, or destruction.

Electronic devices must be packaged in antistatic bags. Cell phones must be packaged in Faraday bags.

There are different motivations for corporate security departments and law enforcement agencies. The types of incidents might involve corporate policies and are not necessarily criminal in nature. Corporations may not want the general public to know of internal issues and problems. Corporate security violations, however, can become law enforcement issues; therefore, evidence must be protected.

Documentation is a critical function that must be addressed in all electronic and computer investigations. A team leader must monitor the investigative process and ensure all critical functions have been performed. Appendix A provides a checklist for those activities that should occur in the investigation. Numerous forms are available for documenting all forensic activities and processes. An administrative audit will ensure all steps of the investigation have been successfully completed.

Terms

Administrative audit worksheet — Provides for documentation of major events, times and movements relating to the search efforts.

Case file — The official record of actions taken and evidence collected at the scene.

Documentation — Written notes, printed forms, sketches, photographs, evidence recovered, and actions taken during an investigation.

Evidence custodian — A collector, recorder, and custodian who is responsible for the evidence integrity and chain-of-custody.

First responder — The initial person arriving at an incident scene prior to the arrival of the investigator in charge.

Journal — A notebook that is used by first responders and investigators when working a crime scene. All investigative activities that take place are recorded in the journal.

Search — The organized and legal examination of the crime scene to locate items of evidence to the incident or crime under investigation.

Sketch — Establishes a permanent record of items, conditions, and distance/size relationships. It also supplements the photograph record.

Testimonial evidence — Any witnessed accounts of an incident.

Physical evidence — Any material items that would be present on the crime scene.

Walk-through — An initial assessment conducted by carefully walking through an incident scene to evaluate the situation, recognize potential evidence, and determine resources.

Review Questions

1. What is the difference between testimonial evidence and physical evidence?
2. What is the purpose of a case file?
3. What is the purpose of a sketch?
4. What categories of information would be contained in an Administrative Audit Worksheet?
5. What is the purpose of collecting evidence at an incident scene?
6. Identify the three basic stages in properly processing crime scene investigations.
7. The evidence collection or recovery step in crime scene processing includes the ____ ____, _____, and _____ used in retrieving evidence.
8. Identify the basic steps involved in a computer site search.
9. Describe five issues that are unique to investigating and prosecuting computer and electronics criminal cases.
10. Provide a list of all job categories that might make up an electronic forensics team.

Chapter 8

Investigating Computer Center Incidents

Chapter Objectives

- Distinguish between white-collar and blue-collar crimes and corporate security violations
- Identify those processes taken when responding to security and policy violations
- See how corporate incidents differ from law enforcement investigations
- Learn specific steps taken when identifying, collecting, and protecting electronic evidence
- Become familiar with the requirements regarding the chain-of-custody for forensic evidence
- Look at the possible areas where computer and electronic evidence resides

Introduction

Computer and electronic evidence consists of data and information that is stored on or transmitted by some device. It is fragile and can be easily damaged, modified, or destroyed. Any corporate security investigator or law enforcement investigator arriving at an incident scene must exercise due diligence. Evidence may be present on cell phones, electronic organizers, personal digital assistants (PDAs), and can be compromised by remote electronic transmissions.

All activities at an incident scene must be in compliance with official departmental or corporate policies and procedures. Corporate incident investigations often occur because of some violation of a security or computer-use policy violation. Security department investigators still must adhere to any federal, state, or local laws. Security personnel should have proper training in the identification, collection, and protection of electronic evidence.

First responders must visually identify potential evidence, whether conventional physical evidence or electronic evidence. The scene must be controlled and all persons must be removed from the immediate area. The first responder must evaluate the scene and formulate a search plan. Steps must be taken to ensure the safety of all persons at the incident scene.

Network and telephone connections must be identified. Wiring closets must be located and transmission equipment identified. Local area network (LAN), intranet, and extranet configurations may be part of the investigation scene. Specialists may be required for these LAN investigations and could be provided by an internal information technology (IT) department. The investigation scope, however, could extend to areas outside the borders of the United States.

The objective of an electronic forensic investigation is usually to provide digital evidence of a specific or general activity. The forensic investigation can be initiated for a variety of reasons. These may involve a criminal investigation, a civil litigation, a corporate incident, or some disaster recovery incident. Forensic techniques are useful for a wide variety of situations, including steps to reveal a trail of lost or misplaced data.

Rigid recovery procedures are required when conducting computer and electronic forensic investigations. Sloppy work at the initial stage of an investigation can cause a loss of evidence or make the evidence useless for any prosecution or litigation activities.

There are numerous situations involving corporate security issues and criminal activities that might profit from an electronic forensic investigation. Corporate policy violations can often become criminal matters; therefore, investigations should always proceed as if forensic evidence will be presented in a legal environment.

The physical environment of the incident scene in a business setting can be quite different from a normal crime scene. Computer centers can be intimidating to the unprepared and uninformed individuals. Corporate security department investigators will usually respond to incidents involving internal policy violations. These investigators, however, will be out of their element if a crime is associated with the corporate incident. Law enforcement departments must be prepared to respond to incidents that can involve or occur on business premises.

A.   Corporate Criminal Activities

Illegal business activities are divided into **white-collar crime** and **blue-collar crime**. White-collar crime overlaps with corporate crime because the opportunity for fraud, bribery, insider trading, embezzlement, computer crime, and forgery is more available to white-collar employees. Some crime is only possible because of the identity of the offender, e.g., transnational money laundering requires the participation of senior officers employed in banks. White-collar crime can be further defined as those illegal acts that are characterized by deceit, concealment, or violation of trust and that are not dependent on the application or threat of physical force or violence. Occupational crime occurs when crimes are committed to promote personal interests, say, by altering records and overcharging, or by the cheating of clients by professionals. Organizational or corporate crime occurs when corporate executives commit criminal acts to benefit their company by overcharging, price-fixing, false advertising, etc.

The types of crime committed are a function of the opportunities available to the potential offender. If the individual is employed in a low or unskilled job and lives in an inner-city environment, stealing inventory from the workplace may not produce value and not many neighbors may have valuable property to steal. This has significance both for the type of crime likely to be committed and for law enforcement. Because there are fewer opportunities to use a skill, more blue-collar crime may involve the use of force and, because more people are injured, there is a greater chance that the victim will report the crime. In criminology, blue-collar crime is any crime committed by an individual from a lower social class as opposed to white-collar crime, which is associated with crimes committed by individuals of a higher social class. The Federal Bureau of Investigation has previously defined white-collar crime as those illegal acts that are characterized by deceit, concealment, or violation of trust and that are not dependent on the application or threat of physical force or violence.

Blue-collar crimes tend to be more obvious and attract more active police attention (e.g., for crimes such as vandalism or shoplifting, which protect property interests), whereas white-collar crimes can intermingle legitimate and criminal behavior and those who commit them can be less obvious. Thus, blue-collar crime will more often use physical force, whereas white-collar crime will tend to be more technical in nature, e.g., in the manipulation of accountancy or inventory records. It is estimated that a great deal of white-collar crime is undetected or, if detected, it is not reported.

Categories of white-collar crimes include corporate crime, state crime, and state-corporate crime. The distinction is that a white-collar crime is likely to be a crime against the corporation, whereas a corporate crime is a crime committed by the corporation. The distinction blurs, however, when the given crime promotes the interests of the corporation and its senior employees because a business entity can only act through the agency of the natural persons that it employs. These issues have been highlighted in ongoing legal cases involving large corporations.

In terms of social class and status, those employed by the state, whether directly or indirectly, are more likely to be white-collar; therefore, more state crime will be committed through the agency of white-collar employees. Because the negotiation of agreements between a state and a corporation will be at a relatively senior level on both sides, this is almost exclusively a white-collar "situation" that offers the opportunity for crime.

B.   Preparation

Different categories of circumstances will require a different type of response and investigation. If there is an allegation of internal financial fraud or theft of trade secrets, the approach will be very different than an obvious violation of a security or computer-use policy. Employees could be hacking the corporate databases, making illegal modifications to operating systems, copying unlicensed software, surfing pornography, and the list goes on. Suspicion of financial fraud might require a forensic accountant or computer forensic scientist to investigate the issue.

Before any overt investigative action, the activities must be coordinated with the security department, the employee's management, personnel, and possibly law enforcement. The nature of the complaint must be determined before any action is undertaken. If the complaint is a violation of a security or computer-use policy, the investigator should have already collected evidence to support the allegation. These activities can be conducted surreptitiously via key loggers, monitors, and sniffer devices. False accusations by management can result in employment lawsuits and cause embarrassment to the organization; therefore, facts must support any action.

If a criminal activity is revealed, such as child pornography or drug trafficking, a search warrant might be required. Up-front preparation will pay off in the long run. If a criminal activity is identified, the steps required for a law-enforcement forensic investigation will be initiated and the security organization and the corporation will lose control of the situation. Note: a preliminary investigation by the security department might not find any criminal evidence; however, it might be uncovered during a forensic investigation of the suspect's computer system. With this in mind, documenting the incident scene is an important step.

C.   Case Categories

Many different categories of corporate policy violations can benefit from the introduction of forensic investigations. Often these violations involve a computer-use issue or a security policy violation. The most common scenarios are wide and varied. Common examples might include the following:

Corporate espionage
Discrimination issues
Employee Internet or e-mail abuse
Improper accounting practices
Misuse of company resources
Pornography
Security and computer policy violations
Sexual harassment
Theft of company property
Unauthorized disclosure of corporate information and data

Electronic forensic techniques have been utilized to assist in solving a number of petty and felony crimes. The use of DNA as evidence to identify a subject or eliminate a suspect pool is commonplace; however, computer forensic techniques can also supplement the activities of the criminal investigative team. Examples of criminal activity where electronic evidence might assist the investigators include:

Capital crimes where information and data is stored electronically
Crimes against the state
Criminal fraud and deception
Cyber crimes
Cyber-terrorism
Industrial and governmental espionage
Damage assessment following an incident
Information warfare
Petty crimes where information and data is stored electronically
Unauthorized disclosure of government data or information

D.   Preliminary Investigation and Fact Finding

There are a number of important issues that must be considered when corporate security is investigating an incident or crime involving computer and electronic devices. Two basic rules are: change nothing and record everything. Investigators, hopefully, will make every effort to get the system back in operation as quickly as possible. A preliminary goal is to determine whether the incident is a true crime, failure, or an accident. Office personnel and technical support staff must be prepared to explain what has happened and the scope of damage or depth of the problem. Efforts must be made to preserve all potential evidence and recover from the incident. Steps must then be taken to prevent it from happening again. Law enforcement does not need to be involved if criminal activity has not been indicated. Once law enforcement is involved, the security department loses control of the investigation.

Other considerations that might be viable are:

Did the incident originate from an internal or external source?
Is it currently an ongoing, active issue?
Is it an intrusion, incident, or attack that has already occurred?
Is it an intrusion, incident, or attack that has already occurred and is likely to occur again in the near future?

Corporate administrators will know when a system cannot be brought down. They can help the security staff make a backup of the entire system after an intrusion or attack and be prepared to testify to what processes occurred. This means recording every keystroke and step. Hopefully, the administrators already have a backup of the system made before the intrusion, incident, or criminal act occurred. This backup copy will also have to be provided as evidence. Investigators must make a copy of all logs along with user-ID data and other data related to the operation of the system. This data is the audit trial, without it there is no case. Be prepared to testify to how the logs were created, what they mean, and how the system operates.

If the investigation involves the Web, there are several preliminary items of information that would be critical in the investigation. Any addressing information, such as the Internet protocol (IP) address or uniform resource locator (URL) would be important. This could read "www.name.type" or could be a number such as 127.242.64.8. The time and date of the Web contact and a printed copy of the screen image, if available, can be provided. Was a copy of the Web site saved on the computer (favorites) or computer media? All activities involved in this evidence identification must be noted in the investigator's journal. The next several sections provide instructions for documentation that must be completed for every incident and investigation.

E. Documenting the Corporate Incident Scene

Documentation of an incident scene creates a permanent historical record that must stand up to intense scrutiny. Formal procedures and processes must be followed for each incident scene investigation. Documentation is an ongoing requirement throughout any incident scene investigation. It is very important to accurately record specific details concerning the location and placement of electronic devices, computers, storage media, and any other conventional evidence. Departmental policies, and various federal, state, and local laws must be observed. Often corporate entities have specific security and computer-use policies that must be followed in their investigations. Remember that corporate policy violations can become criminal matters.

The incident scene search must be a planned, coordinated, and executed effort by corporate security personnel to locate physical evidence in support of some policy violation or complaint. Two search approaches can be taken. These can include a cautious search of visible areas, avoiding evidence loss or contamination, and a vigorous search of concealed areas. In either case, the best search options are usually the most difficult and time consuming. It should be noted that physical evidence must be well documented.

Corporate security and computer-use policies will dictate the type of investigation initiated. Wasting time surfing the Web or using a cell phone during business hours for personal business would be handled differently than surfing pornography or conducting personal business over the Internet. Some security and computer-use policies are included later in this chapter.

When a formal violation is investigated, a decision must be made about whether to confront. It may not be necessary for the suspected violator to be present at the scene. This location is, after all, a corporate location, and the devices belong to the organization. There are a number of basic documentation steps taken during the initial walk-through of the incident scene that will ensure relevant evidence is captured. These include the following:

Document the condition, location, and power status of any computing devices. Note the locations of peripherals, such as printers, external hard drives, mouse and keyboard devices, and monitors. Check the computing devices for power-on status; however, do not turn any device on or off, as evidence can be destroyed or modified by this action.

Identify any storage media that might be visible around the work areas or in disk storage trays. Check for storage in desk drawers. Do not remove any disks from the computing devices.

Develop an inventory of any electronic devices including cell phones and PDAs at the incident scene. Do not change the power on/off status of these devices.

Identify and document any devices or components that will not be collected as evidence. Items perceived as not useful at the onset may be useful later in the investigation.

Produce a 360-degree photographic journal of the incident scene. Take close-up photographs of any monitor displays that are visible. Photograph cable connections. A video camera scan of the incident scene could prove to be beneficial. A video could be made of any active monitor displays. A photographic evidence log must be maintained.

Collect printouts from the work area or the printer tray. Collect software documentation, such as user manuals. Screen shots from the video monitors or plasma screens might be of use, particularly if pirated or illegal software is being used.

Information concerning the development of photographic and evidence logs is described later in the chapter. A chain-of-custody must be maintained because of the potential for legal action. As previously stated, the chain-of-custody is the route evidence takes from initial possession until final disposition.

F.   Conducting Interviews

Investigators may wish to conduct preliminary interviews at the incident scene. Witnesses, potential suspects, and others present at the scene must be identified and separated. Those involved must not be given an opportunity to coordinate their stories. If a search warrant or subpoena is involved, ensure it is inclusive of all potential evidence that should be collected.

Consistent with law enforcement, security departmental, or corporate policies and procedures obtain the following information and details:

Chain-of-command list with corresponding responsibilities
Documentation of any hardware and software installed on the systems
Location of any off-site media storage
Owners and/or users of any computers or electronic devices found at the incident scene
Passwords, logons, usernames for PCs, laptops, etc.
Physical map of the incident scene layout
System passwords and log-ons for applications
System usage and purposes
Unique security schemes or destructive processes

If the investigation involves the Internet, network service providers and Internet service providers (ISPs) must be identified.

G.   Identifying and Collecting Evidence

The first person responding to an incident can make or break a case. Without developing advance, sound, validated, ethical and legal processes and procedures, the security team may very well lose evidence recovered while on site. Worse yet, if equipment is damaged, individuals may be responsible for the financial loss to the department or owners of the equipment. Organizations must feel secure regarding policies and procedures for first responders working an incident scene. Other issues that must be addressed include packaging, transportation, and storage of evidence.

It is essential that first responders be trained in good forensic practices as it relates to the search and seizure of electronic and computer media. Also, the responder must know the processes of identification and acquisition of electronic evidence. A special note: if the device is powered off, leave it off; if it is on, leave it on. Let the forensic specialist decide the proper course of action for disconnecting the device.

Large departments may employ personnel who can image hard-disk drives. A number of activities must occur after copies or images have been made of the electronic evidence. A forensic examiner may perform these responsibilities. These include the following:

Investigate data and settings from installed applications and programs
Look at the general system structures
Identify factors relating to the user's activities
Identify and recover all files including those deleted
Access and copy hidden and protected files
Access and copy temporary files
Use forensic techniques to recover residue from previously deleted files

A full and detailed report must be created from these investigations. It is also very important to maintain an audit log of any activities associated with the electronic components, data, and information. These steps must be repeatable and reproduced to be considered viable forensic evidence. A forensic investigator might be the team leader for the entire investigation. However, in small security organizations the same individual may perform all forensic functions. Sample forms for logging details of the incident and documenting the chain-of-custody for corporate security investigations are provided in Appendix A.

Processes must be initiated for investigating data storage devices and/or data processing equipment consisting of a home computer, laptop, server, office workstation, or removable media such as compact disks (CDs), to determine if the equipment has been used for illegal, unauthorized, or unusual activities. It can also include monitoring a network for the same purpose. Remember computer forensics experts must:

Identify sources of documentary or other digital evidence
Preserve the evidence
Analyze the evidence
Present the findings

They must do so in a fashion that adheres to the standards of evidence admissible in a court of law. Considerations, in the following order, include:

Gathering electronic evidence
Understanding the suspects
Securing the machine and the data

Examining the machine's surroundings
Recording open applications
Powering down carefully
Inspecting for traps
Fully documenting hardware configuration
Duplicating the hard drives

This section has provided a simplified description of the most elementary facts surrounding computer forensics. Previous chapters have presented detailed explanations of processes and procedures required by forensic investigators and examiners. It is not feasible to cite a complete account of the scenarios that computer forensics specialists and examiners might encounter, as the possibilities are virtually unlimited. However, the facts presented here represent minimum activities and requirements. For example, every investigation requires a noninvasive acquisition of a bit-by-bit image of the original disks, a noninvasive examination of the image, verifiable chain-of-custody, and assurance of the integrity of the data.

H. Stand-Alone and Networked Computers

Most desktop and laptop computers operate in a stand-alone mode and are connected to the Internet via a communication device such as a modem (Figure 8.1). Stand-alone mode means the computing device is not connected to a network, such as a LAN or another computing device. This will usually be the situation when these devices are located at a suspect's residence or in a vehicle. A search warrant, if required, will not be very complex in these situations because the crime scene is fairly easy to define. Evidence, however, could be located at the ISP location.

Laptop configurations usually consist of the chassis with an integral plasma display, keyboard, mouse, and hard drive. It is possible to add on a number of devices using a Personal Computer Memory Card International Association (PCMCIA) card or using multiple universal serial bus (USB) ports. Wireless access can also be integral in the chassis or added via a PCMCIA card. Laptop computers are powered

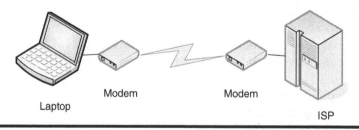

Figure 8.1   Stand-alone laptop computer.

by an internal battery, which requires a charging device. Latent evidence can be lost if the battery discharges.

Computers located at a business location will usually be networked. Multiple computers at a nonbusiness location might also indicate a networked environment. Networked systems such as a LAN will require someone who possesses specialized knowledge in the evidence-seizure phase of the investigation. Most law enforcement agencies and corporate security departments will not possess this expertise. A number of computer forensic consultant agencies can provide this expertise. A note of caution: this expertise is not cheap.

Computer systems located at business, education, and government locations are usually interconnected with each other over some type of network. Securing and processing an incident scene of this type poses special problems. Improper shutdowns can destroy or modify data and could result in some civil liability. Advance planning should occur before attempting to recover evidence from these networked computer configurations. Figure 8.2 depicts a simple LAN with three workstations, a hub/switch device, a server, and a printer. Evidence could be located on any of these devices, depending upon their sophistication.

The computer network might include access to a mainframe system, servers, or just computer-to-computer connectivity. Multiple operating systems, complex hardware configurations, and various wiring arrangements can all add complexity to the identification and recovery of evidence at these incident scenes. Be suspicious if an employee seeks to assist the investigators because this person might be involved in a cover-up of vital evidence. Chapter 5 provides detailed information concerning the various computer and electronic device configurations.

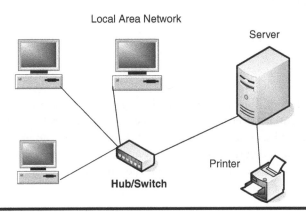

Figure 8.2   Local area network (LAN).

I.   Miscellaneous Devices

A number of miscellaneous electronic devices might be present at an incident scene. Today's technology allows almost any device to contain electronic or forensic evidence. A simple wristwatch can contain a USB port for uploading data. Never overlook any potential candidate. When seizing these devices, never attempt to operate them; let the forensic examiner handle the tasks later in the forensic lab. Many of the devices listed below might provide evidence associated with some illegal activity or some violation of corporate policies. Data present on these devices can be lost if not handled properly. Seizure of removable storage media, such as Zip, CD, floppy, and Jaz devices, requires the seizure of the equipment that created them. *Note additional latent evidence such as fingerprints and fluids (DNA) might be present on any of these devices.*

Examples of other electronic devices that might provide latent evidence include the following:

Answering machines
Caller-ID devices
Cell phones
Copy machines
Digital cameras
Dongles
External disk drives
Fax machines
USB flash drives
GPS devices
Pagers
PDAs
Printers
Removable media (floppies, CDs, Zips)
Scanners
Telephones with features
VCRs
Wireless access points

The investigator must determine if the organization has taken due diligence, including precautions to ensure that all of the hardware and software that is reasonably available, and is an industry standard, has been installed to prevent unauthorized intrusions or use of the system. The amount of loss might be based on damage the intrusion caused, not the cost to repair the damage.

J.   Disclaimers That Aid Investigators

Often information technology (IT) management is derelict in notifying users of security policies and data access security levels. This lapse can result in a case being thrown out of court, because the user can claim there were not any rules or policies on the use of the network, computer, or electronic device. Each computer network and terminal should have a disclaimer that the material contained in the computer is proprietary and only for official use. A **disclaimer** is a statement denying responsibility for a particular action. It should state that unless the user has been granted permission to be in an area or has permission to change a site, file, or database it will be considered a criminal act to intrude or make changes. It should further state that it is a crime to disseminate any information contained in the system, except that which has been expressly approved by the computer owner.

The computer user should be notified as to who owns it. This notice should state that the device is to be used expressly for business and that the owner has the right to search and look at anything stored on or created by the device at anytime. Does the system display a banner warning stating that only authorized users are permitted in the system or within certain areas of the system? Have employees and other authorized users of the system signed a user agreement or memorandum of understanding outlining their responsibility and areas of access. This agreement should include language that explains the repercussions of accessing unauthorized security levels and the possibility of committing a crime by doing so. Two sample disclaimers follow:

> Use of this website and its contents are at the user's risk. The website assumes no responsibility for consequences from the use of the information contained in this site, or in any respect for the accuracy, adequacy or completeness of such information. The website is not responsible for, and expressly disclaims all liability for, damages of any kind arising out of use, reference or reliance on such information.

> The links provided by this website are intended to provide a wide range of information. The links from this website could be directed to access other Internet resources, information, or procedures that are unrelated to it. The presence of a link does not imply any endorsement of the material on the websites or any association with the website's operators.

Investigators should determine if the incident organization has a disclaimer for computer and resource usage. This effort could save a lot of wasted time for an internal incident investigation.

K. E-Mail Investigations

E-mail abuse is a problem in many corporate organizations. Abuses can consist of inappropriate and offensive message content to various forms of harassment and threats. It is also a major issue caused by **SPAM**, which is defined as unsolicited e-mail messages. Many productive personnel hours are wasted responding to and deleting SPAM from the various e-mail servers. Official computer-use policies can address many internal situations; however, SPAM requires another approach that involves the security and network department.

Investigating policy violations and crimes that include e-mail is similar to investigating other types of incidents that relate to computer abuse. The objective of the investigator is to identify those individuals involved, collect evidence, and build a case. Forensic investigators must determine if SPAM is illegal in the locality of the abuse. In multiple-state and multiple-country organizations, this effort could become difficult and tedious. Often, a crime is affected by using an e-mail facility. Criminals and terrorists are using e-mail to commit other crimes and acts of violence. Because e-mail is a major communications medium, any crime can involve it. These incidents might involve extortion, espionage, stalking, abduction, pornography, and many other major and minor crimes.

If the e-mail incident involves individuals that are part of the organization's internal network, the approach of the security personnel will be different from one that involves external parties. E-mail can be accessed from the victim's workstation and is also accessible on the e-mail server. The victim can be expected to cooperate in the investigation and the e-mails can be easily recovered and printed as evidence. Official security policies and computer-use policies will usually dictate whether there is a violation. If it is determined that the e-mail is part of a criminal activity, then the security department must follow the guidelines of the organization for reporting the incident to authorities. These may require a subpoena for the files located on the e-mail server or a search warrant for the suspect's workspace and devices.

The investigator should take a preliminary look at evidence that might indicate a possible e-mail-related crime or corporate e-mail policy violation. Minimum information should include the following:

The name of the ISP
The offender's name and address
Copy of the e-mail exists
ISP has the e-mail in the computer mailbox

Two considerations closely related to e-mail are newsgroup and chat room investigations. Items of information required are similar to that for e-mail. These include the following for a newsgroup:

The name of the ISP
The name of the newsgroup
The name of the posting
Printed copy of the screen image
Copy of the posting saved on the computer or computer media

Considerations for a chat room investigation include the following items of information:

Name of the chat room
Name of the server where the chat room is located
Identity of a nickname or screen name used
IP address used during the chat
Copy of the chat dialog window or user's list
Information saved to a computer or disk

E-mail forensic examinations are discussed in Chapter 12 and sample exercises are included in Appendix B. Forensic investigators and examiners can expect to spend considerable time working with e-mail evidence on a wide variety of cases.

L.   Types of Evidence

Not all items at an incident scene will consist of electronic evidence. Printouts, handwritten notes, and photographs might be in the space surrounding the computer area. These items might contain all the information available if evidence cannot be retrieved from the computers or electronic devices.

It is, therefore, essential that proper care be taken to ensure that such evidence is recovered and preserved. Items relevant to subsequent examination of electronic evidence may exist in written passwords, calendars, mail, literature, and blank pads of paper with indented writing. Hardware and software manuals might prove useful to the forensic examiner. Most of these items will be in close proximity to the computer devices. The contents of the search warrant will dictate the areas where evidence can be seized. Documentation is one of the most important steps in the investigation. A journal must be maintained that keeps a running record of all activities that occur during the investigation.

M.   Evidence Handling

There are a number of issues relating to electronic and computer evidence that must be addressed to ensure proper evidence handing. Categories that ensure that evidence will be useful and valid include:

Forms and documentation
Labeling and tagging
Protecting and packaging
Transportation of evidence
Storage requirements

Someone in a decision-making position must decide if the incident is to be treated as a criminal act, civil liability act, or an accident. This decision will determine the next steps in the investigation.

1. Forms and Documentation

As noted in previous chapters, the name of the game is documentation and more documentation; however, it must be relevant to the investigation. Extraneous notes on nonrelated subjects can cause evidence to be tossed out in court cases. Two forms that are presented for corporate security investigations include a journal and chain-of-custody. If other forms are required, the issue will probably be criminal, and law enforcement personnel will have their own forms. These forms, however, are available in Appendix A and could be easily adapted for corporate security use.

2. Labeling and Tagging

Computer and electronic devices and media that are collected as evidence must be thoroughly labeled or tagged and an inventory log maintained as part of the chain-of-custody. Any cables removed must be labeled, describing their connectivity. Media must be secured in evidence bags and labeled as to their contents and location when removed. The task of retrieving evidence is usually the function of the forensic investigative team, who is experienced in the process required to ensure evidence is admissible in legal proceedings. This task can involve the taking of photos and videos, along with creating drawings of the crime scene and sketches of the locations of various pieces of evidence.

3. Protecting and Packaging

Most corporate security departments are not prepared to follow chain-of-custody requirements. Special training programs are required that address the necessity of preserving the chain-of-custody through various types of documentation. Law enforcement departments have special forensic teams whose responsibility is to ensure a viable and legal chain-of-custody.

Employees of IT departments are generally not qualified to collect computer forensic evidence. It is not a good idea to use IT personnel in these functions because they might be part of the problem. Internal personnel account for approximately 80 percent of corporate security violations.

Simply starting a computer changes files and many of those changes affect significant dates and time stamps. Remember any access to the disk risks overwriting pertinent information and destroying potential evidence. Security first responders must ensure that computing devices remain untouched until a qualified forensics specialist can create a certified, bit-by-bit copy of a drive. A write blocker is used to protect the evidence on the hard drive. The image can then be examined without jeopardizing the investigation. Suppose someone has already tried looking at the drive. The best course of action is to leave the machine exactly as it is, whether it is on or off and explain the situation to the forensics professional. This professional should be trained to manage the circumstances. A job title used in some security organizations is a Certified Electronic Evidence Collection Specialist (CEECS) who might collect electronic and computer evidence. This job description is called "bag & tag" and "first responder."

After all the evidence has been collected, logged, and properly labeled and tagged, it must be packaged in acceptable containers. Special precautions must be taken when handling electronic evidence or the distinct possibility exists that it will be rendered useless. Computing and electronic devices are fragile instruments that are sensitive to temperature, humidity, static electricity, magnetism, and physical shock. Proactive actions must be undertaken by the investigators to ensure that nothing will contribute to the modification, addition, deletion, or destruction of their evidence. Figure 8.3 shows various tools for protecting electronic evidence.

To preserve the integrity of the chain-of-custody, documentation should provide an audit trail of the packaging process. When multiple computers are collected, efforts should be made to package the components for each computer together or at least mark the packages as part of a unit. (For example: Computer A—box 1 of 5—keyboard SN#). Serial numbers should have been noted on the log form; however, it will be easier to reconstruct the computer configurations if the SN# is also on the package. Also, if the device is entered into the court record as evidence, the chain-of-custody can be supported.

Figure 8.3   Paraben tools for protecting forensic evidence.

There are five basic steps for packaging computer and electronic devices. These include the following:

1. Ensure all collected evidence is properly documented, labeled, and inventoried *before* the packaging process.
2. Pay particular attention to latent or trace evidence and take the necessary actions to preserve it. Fingerprints might be on the screen or mouse.
3. Pack magnetic media in antistatic packages (Figure 8.3). Avoid standard plastic bags. *Note: Cell phones and other handheld wireless devices collected at the scene must be immediately placed in Faraday bags to avoid corruption of evidence contained in the device.*
4. Avoid folding, bending, or scratching computer media, such as floppies and CDs. These components must not be exposed to magnetic fields or excessive heat.
5. Ensure all containers used to hold evidence are properly labeled.

4.   Transportation

After all the steps have been taken in the packaging phase, the next step is to safely transport all the evidence to the storage area or directly to the forensic lab. Of particular importance is the chain-of-custody. The transporting personnel must ensure that all packages on the evidence log have been transported to the appropriate location. This location could be at a corporate site or a forensic lab. The transportation phase has four steps:

Keep electronic evidence from electromagnetic sources. These could include radio transmitters and speaker magnets.

Avoid storing evidence in vehicles for prolonged time periods because circuit boards and storage media could warp. Conditions of excessive heat, cold, or humidity can manage electronic components.

Ensure that any computers or other devices too large or bulky to box are secured in the vehicle against shock or excessive vibrations.

Maintain the chain-of-custody on all evidence transported.

5.   Storage

The last step is to store the evidence in an approved storage area. This must be a locked, controlled area. Someone must be responsible for controlling access to this area. Logs must be maintained of anyone who enters this area. Logs must be maintained of any devices that are removed for examination or for court activity. The chain-of-custody must be preserved. There cannot be any violations that negatively impact the chain-of-custody. There are two broad steps and one specific activity in the storage procedure. These are:

Ensure all evidence is inventoried in accordance with departmental policies and legal requirements.

Store evidence in a secure area away from any foreign source that might reduce the importance and content of the evidence. Evidence must be protected from electromagnetic sources, moisture, dust, and any harmful contaminants.

Appropriate personnel must ensure that devices requiring ongoing power are connected to a reliable power source. Date, time, and configurations are preserved on computer systems via an internal battery. Portable devices powered by battery and a battery charger must also be connected to a power source.

If the incident has evolved into a criminal issue, storage will probably not be an issue for the security department. Law enforcement investigators will probably transport the evidence directly to a forensic lab for examination. If the evidence is to be transported directly to a law enforcement or commercial forensic lab, then the receiving lab personnel must prepare receipts for all devices, media, and paraphernalia. A sample receipt is depicted in Appendix A. If this is the process, then the receiving lab personnel must be involved in the packaging and transportation function.

N.   Forensic Investigation Documents

All of the steps in the forensic investigation require some type of documentation. Most have already been briefly mentioned. Documentation and forms that can be used in security incidents and investigations are similar to those used by law enforcement. Official policies must be in place, which describe the investigative activities for these incidents. Checklists are very helpful to ensure that security personnel have successfully completed all steps. The checklist provides the team leader with a method for comparing, scheduling, verifying, and identifying all items that must be addressed in the investigation.

A number of forms can be developed to assist in these steps. The following section provides examples of such forms that can be used in these corporate security incidents. These forms and checklists are also provided in Appendix A. These forms would be utilized by security personnel in internal investigations. If the incidents were to become criminal in nature or involve civil litigation, this documentation would be invaluable. These forms could be provided to law enforcement as a starting point for any future investigation activities. Evidence forms available in Appendix A include:

Investigation journal
Chain-of-custody form
Evidence detail log
Photographic log
Evidence receipt

Checklists exist for most evidence forms. These forms help the investigators and examiners keep track of the details in a case. Checklists available in Appendix A include:

Chain-of-custody checklist
Evidence receipt checklist
Investigation checklist

O. Law Enforcement Involvement

If the organization has any intention of prosecuting someone connected to a security incident, considerations concerning law enforcement involvement must be made early in the investigation. Security-related incidents often do not result in convictions because law enforcement departments were not properly contacted. There are a number of law enforcement levels that are available to respond to investigate incidents. These include federal, state, military, and local authorities, in addition to district attorneys, Inspector General offices; and so forth. The incident response team must be acquainted with its various law enforcement representatives before an incident occurs. Procedures must be established that specify which incidents should be reported to them, how the reporting should be performed, what evidence should be collected, and how it should be collected. Members of the organization's public affairs office and legal department might need to participate in these discussions.

Law enforcement departments should be contacted through designated individuals in a manner consistent with the organization's procedures and legal restrictions. Many organizations appoint one incident response team member as the primary point-of-contact with law enforcement and the media. This contact must be familiar with the reporting procedures for all relevant law enforcement agencies and must understand which department is to be notified. There may be jurisdictional issues when the organizations and the incident span multiple states or countries.

Chapter Summary

White-collar crime involves criminal acts of fraud, bribery, insider trading, embezzlement, computer crime, and forgery. The types of crime committed are a function of the opportunities available to the potential offender. It is estimated that a great deal of white-collar crime is undetected or, if detected, it is not reported. Blue-collar crime will more often use physical force whereas white-collar crime will tend to be more technical in nature, such as the manipulation of accountancy or inventory records.

Different circumstances will require different types of response and investigation. Allegations of internal financial fraud or theft of trade secrets will require a different response than a violation of a security or computer-use policy. Illegal activities could include hacking the corporate databases, making illegal modifications to operating systems, copying unlicensed software, surfing pornography, etc. Suspicion of financial fraud might require a forensic accountant or computer forensic scientist to investigate the issue, whereas the security department or human resources could handle a policy violation.

The name of the game is documentation, documentation, and more documentation. Documentation of an incident or illegal activity creates a permanent historical record that must stand up to intense scrutiny and possibly litigation. Formal procedures and processes must be followed for each incident investigation. Documentation is an ongoing requirement throughout any incident scene investigation. There are numerous forms that have been developed to collect information relating to an incident.

Issues relating to electronic and computer evidence handling include documentation, labeling, packaging, transportation, and storage. Security and law enforcement personnel must be experienced in all phases of these evidence steps. Both criminal and civil action could result from a computer-related investigation. Computers and electronic devices such as cell phones can be used in the commission of a crime against a specific victim or can be used as a tool to commit some illegal activity.

E-mail abuse is an issue in many corporate organizations. Abuses can consist of inappropriate and offensive message content to various forms of harassment and threats. SPAM is also a major issue that is using up corporate resources. Investigating policy violations and crimes that include e-mail is similar to investigating other types of incidents relating to computer abuse. The objective of the investigator is to identify those individuals involved, collect evidence, and build a case.

Terms

Blue-collar crime — In criminology, is any crime committed by an individual from a lower social class.

Buffer — Area in computer memory used as a temporary storage location.

Checklist — A list in which items can be compared, scheduled, verified, and identified.

Cookie — Small text files stored on a computer while the user is browsing the Internet.

Disclaimer — A statement denying responsibility for a particular action.

Electronic evidence — Information and data of investigative value that is stored or transmitted by an electronic device.

Latent — Present, although not visible, but capable of becoming visible.

Printer spool files — Print jobs that are not printed directly and stored in spool files on disk.

Removable media — Items such as floppy disks, CDs, DVDs, cartridges, and tape that store data and can be easily removed.

Screen saver — A utility program that prevents a monitor from being etched by an unchanging image. It can provide access control to the device.

Seizure disk — A specially prepared floppy disk designed to protect the computer system from accidental alteration of data.

SPAM — Defined as unsolicited e-mail messages.

Temporary or swap files — Data stored temporarily on hard drives. These files, generally hidden and inaccessible, may contain investigative information.

Volatile memory — Memory that loses its content when power is turned off or lost.

White-collar crime — In criminology, is associated with crime committed by individuals of a higher social class.

Review Questions

1. In criminology, this type of crime is associated with illegal activities committed by individuals of a higher social class.
2. List five categories of corporate policy violations that can benefit from the introduction of forensic investigations.
3. List five examples of criminal activity where electronic evidence might assist the investigators.
4. During a corporate security fact-finding phase of an investigation, there are four considerations that might be viable. Describe them.
5. What is the most important form used in a computer forensic investigation to ensure evidence is viable in a court of law?
6. The two evidence forms most like completed by corporate security personnel include _____ and _____.
7. Why must a power source be available for electronic evidence that is kept in storage?
8. List four issues involving the transportation of electronic evidence.
9. What techniques can corporate security use to collect evidence concerning an ongoing computer investigation?
10. What special precautions must be taken with cell-phone evidence?

Chapter 9

Computer Systems Disk and File Structures

Chapter Objectives

- Identify the various components of a hard drive and the structure of disk media
- Learn the differences among the numerous disk drive interfaces and functions
- Become familiar with the Windows, Macintosh, and Linux file structures
- Learn the definitions of numerous terms relating to file and storage structures
- Identify forensic tools used to identify and retrieve evidence from Windows, Macintosh, and Linux systems

Introduction

This chapter provides an overview of computer disk drives and how data is stored and managed on Microsoft, Macintosh, and Linux systems. An understanding of the file systems and operating systems (OSs) are required in order to identify and recover latent evidence from these systems.

It is essential that the computer forensic examiner understand the operation of these OSs to avoid damaging or destroying valuable evidence. Start-up and shut-down processes of the file systems must also be understood.

Technical knowledge is required concerning the process of accessing and modifying system settings and options. A collection of OS manuals is required for each brand of computer system.

A thorough understanding of disk drive operations, components, and configurations are required to successfully identify and retrieve digital data evidence. A number of software and hardware tools are used in these recovery activities.

Forensic examination of disk drives and file systems requires a considerable amount of education and practical experience. This type of function would be part of a computer forensic lab environment, and would be in the domain of a digital forensic examiner.

A.   Disk Drive Overview

The hard disk drive is the primary storage location where data is permanently stored. Figure 9.1 provides a physical illustration of a hard disk drive. The four main components of a hard disk drive are the platters, head arm, chassis, and the head actuator.

Each platter on a hard drive contains a head for each side of the disk platter. The heads are devices that ride very close to the surface of the platter and allow information to be read from and written to the platter. The heads are physically attached to an arm, which is in turn attached to the head stack assembly. Usually all heads move together and are positioned together on the same track.

The capacity of a computer hard disk drive and the files it contains can be confusing. Table 9.1 provides a listing of the standards in different size values. It is important to realize that not all manufacturers and developers use these values. The capacity of the disk drive that is to be imaged will be a concern to the forensic examiner.

Most computer hard disk drives are permanently stored in an internal drive bay at the front of the computer and are connected with one ATA/SCSI cable and power cable. Unlike other drives, the hard disk drive is the only drive that is not physically accessed by the user like the floppy disk drive or the CD-ROM drive.

The forensic examiner must be familiar with disk drive operation and structure so data can be effectively located. Disk drives are constructed of one or more cylinders (platters) coated with magnetic material. There are particular organizations of the data stored on these cylinders (platters) and a number of elements that go to make up the physical hard disk drive. The geometry or configuration reflects the internal orga-

Figure 9.1   Hard disk drive.

Table 9.1   Disk Capacity Values.

Bit	Value of 0 or 1
Nibble	4 bits
Byte	8 bits
Kilobit	1,000 bits
Kilobyte	1,000 bytes
Kibibit	1,024 bits
Kibibyte	1,024 bytes
Mebibit	1,048,576 bits
Mebibyte	1,048,576 bytes
Megabit	1,000,000 bits
Megabyte	1,000,000 bytes
Gibibit	1,073,741,824 bits
Gibibyte	1,073,741,824 bytes
Gigabit	1,000,000,000 bits
Gigabyte	1,000,000,000 bytes
Tebibit	1,099,511,627,776 bits
Tebibyte	1,099,511,627,776 bytes
Terabit	1,000,000,000,000 bits
Terabyte	1,000,000,000,000 bytes

nization of the disk drive. The components that make up the physical disk platter include tracks, cylinders, and sectors.

A **cylinder** or **platter** contains a set of tracks on a multiheaded disk that may be accessed without head movement; in other words, the tracks that are the same distance from the spindle about which the disk platters rotate. **Tracks** are addressable concentric rings on magnetic, secondary storage disks used for storing data. These are the circular magnetic paths, onto which data is written and from which data is read. The tracks on a disk are divided into sectors and contain from 1 to 64 sectors.

Sectors are the smallest unit of storage on a disk. Diskettes or hard drive platters are divided into wedge-shaped sections that segment the circular tracks into small arcs like cutting a pie into a section, each section is one arc. Each arc is a sector that typically holds 512 bytes of data. Sectors are grouped together into clusters. The **boot sector** is the very first sector on a hard drive. It contains the codes necessary for the computer to start up. It also contains the partition table, also called the **master boot record (MBR)**, which describes how the hard drive is organized.

A computer hard drive is made up of a number of rapidly rotating cylinders that have a set of read/write heads on both sides of each cylinder. Each cylinder

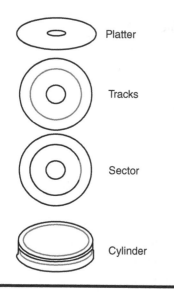

Platter

Tracks

Sector

Cylinder

Figure 9.2   Disk drive geometry.

is divided into a series of concentric rings (columns) called tracks. Each track is further divided into sections called sectors. Figure 9.2 provides a graphical representation of this configuration. **Drive geometry** refers to the number and positions of each of these structures. Digital images are written on the tracks as bytes, where each byte contains 8 bits. The relationship of cylinders, tracks, sectors, bytes, and bits is as follows:

A **byte** is a measurement unit of computer data that consists of a single character. A single byte usually consists of 8 bits. **Bit** is an abbreviation for binary digit and is the smallest unit of computer data. A bit consists of either 0 or 1. Appendix D provides additional information concerning the binary and hexadecimal numbering system.

The typical disk drive has a storage capacity of 512 bytes per sector. The disk manufacturer engineers the disk to have a specified number of sectors per track. The disk-byte capacity is determined by multiplying the number of cylinders (platters) by the number of read/write heads by the number of sectors. The hard disk drive industry calls this configuration CHS or cylinders, heads, and sectors. Table 9.2 shows a sample CHS capacity calculation.

B.   Computer Hard Drive Interfaces

Computer hard disk interfaces include various specifications of AT attachment (ATA) drives, and ATAPI, IDE, EIDE, RAID, SATA, and SCSI drives. The com-

Table 9.2   CHS Calculation.

1024 cylinders

× 32 read/write heads

× 63 sectors

2,064,384 sectors @ 512 bytes per sector = 1,056,964,608 bytes or 1.056 gigabytes

Tracks follow a numbering scheme starting at zero and increments until the maximum number of tracks are reached. If the specifications advise a configuration of 79 tracks, the actual count is 80 tracks, 0–79.

puter interfaces allow a computer to send and retrieve information for storage devices, such as computer hard disk drives and CD-ROM drives. A brief description of these categories of drives will be useful to the forensic examiner. Of particular interest is the configuration of the cable that will be used for the bit-imaging process. The forensic lab must possess a complement of cables for any type or brand of hard drive that is to be examined.

ATA interfaces are the most commonly used interfaces on IBM-compatible computers to connect to computer hard disk drives, CD-ROM drives, and other types of disk drives. The various ATA standards are compatible with each other, allowing a new ATA drive to be used in a computer using an older specification. Some ATA interfaces use the standard 40-pin ribbon or shielded cable; however, some require the 40-pin/80-wire cable for faster transfer rates. The interface cable types are dependent on the type of ATA drive. See Figure 9.3 for a collection of interface cables.

ATAPI (AT attachment packet interface) is an extension to ATA that allows support for devices such as CD-ROM drives, tape drives, and other computer peripherals and not just hard disk drives.

IDE (integrated drive electronics) is more commonly known as ATA and is a standard interface for IBM-compatible hard drives. IDE is different from the small computer systems interface (SCSI) and enhanced small device interface (ESDI) because its controllers are on each drive, meaning the drive can connect directly to the motherboard or controller in the computer chassis. IDE and its updated successor, enhanced IDE (EIDE), are the most common drive interfaces found in IBM-compatible computers today.

EIDE is the next generation of IDE interface that was developed by Western Digital and an interface commonly used on IBM compatible computers. EIDE

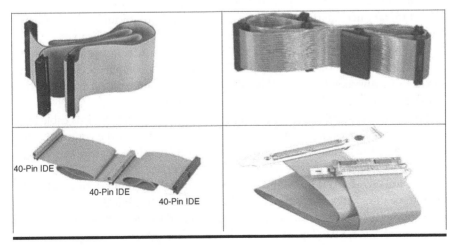

Figure 9.3   IDE/EIDE cables.

supports data rates from 4 and 16.6 MBps. In addition to being faster than IDE drives, EIDE supports drives up to 8.4 GB. Most forensic disk examinations involve EIDE disk drives. IDE and EIDE drives use a standard 40-pin ribbon or shielded interface cable.

There are several issues that must be noted when examining some disk drives. The **complementary metal oxide substrate (CMOS)** on some personal computers (PCs) uses logical block addressing and enhanced cylinder, head, and sector configurations. With newer computers, an automatic process is initiated that is an impediment to correctly configuring the hard drive. This problem can be solved by using a disk-imaging tool, such as EnCase, that allows for evidence to be copied correctly. The CMOS chip, located on the motherboard, holds information about the computer system and its peripherals, even while the system is turned off.

Another issue concerns the imaging of older hard drives, which might contain a limited storage capacity, such as 20–80 GB. Older forensic workstations cannot address storage on the newer high-capacity hard drives (80–500 GB). The solution is to use a forensic workstation that can access the greatest capacity storage device. The forensic lab must plan for this eventuality and recurring expense.

SCSI, pronounced as *Scuz-zee*, is a standard for parallel interfaces that transfers information at a rate of 8 bps and faster, which is faster than the average parallel interface. SCSI-2 and above supports up to seven peripheral devices, such as a hard drive, CD-ROM, tape drive, printer, and scanner, that can attach to a single SCSI port on a system's bus. Its original purpose was to provide a common bus communication device for all computer vendors. SCSI ports were designed for Apple Macintosh and Unix computers, and can also be used with PCs. It is necessary to determine if the computer has an internal or external SCSI drive. This will provide an indication of the types of SCSI cables, adapters, and terminators that will be required to examine the suspect device. Currently Windows XP and other systems have integrated software drivers; however, it may be necessary to use the Advanced SCSI Programmer Interface (ASPI) to allow for communication between the OS and the SCSI component. Figure 9.4 depicts several types of SCSI cables.

SATA (Serial ATA) was first released in August 2001 and is a replacement for the parallel ATA interface used in IBM compatible computers. Serial ATA is capable of delivering 1.5 Gbps (150 MBps) of performance to each drive within a disk array, offers backward compatibility for existing ATA and ATAPI devices, and offers a thin, small cable solution as seen in the below picture. This cable helps make a much easier cable routing and offers better airflow in the computer when compared to the earlier ribbon cables used with ATA drives. Figure 9.5 depicts a SATA cable assembly, a power cable, and SATA interface.

The **universal serial bus (USB)** is an external peripheral interface standard for communication between a computer and external peripherals over a cable using bi-serial transmission. The USB cables provide for interfaces to IDE, serial, and SCSI connections. Figure 9.6 depicts several USB interface cables.

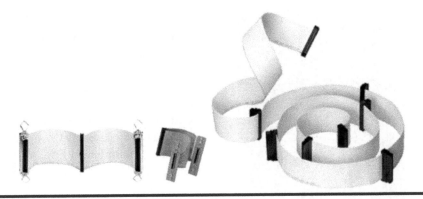

Figure 9.4   SCSI cables.

Figure 9.5   SATA cables.

Redundant array of inexpensive disks (RAID) is an assortment of hard disk drives connected and set up in ways to help protect and/or speed up the performance of a computer's disk storage. RAID is commonly used on servers and high-performance computers. RAID levels 1–5, 10, and 15 can be implemented through software or special hardware controllers. Copying or imagining RAID devices requires additional storage for the imaged data. It may be necessary to image the RAID drive in multiple small increments. With large RAID devices, it may not be possible to create a bitstream of the entire drive and will probably require a vendor's assistance. A RAID chassis is shown in Figure 9.7.

A **compact disk (CD)** is a flat round storage medium that is read by a laser in a CD-ROM drive. The standard CD is capable of holding 72 minutes of music or 650 MB of data. CDs that hold 80 minutes are also commonly used to store data and are capable of containing 700 MB of data. Figure 9.8 provides CD-Rom disk specifications.

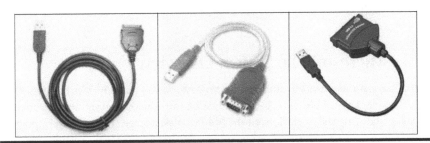

Figure 9.6   USB interface cables.

Figure 9.7   RAID storage device.

CD-ROM Disk Specifications

Figure 9.8   CD-ROM disk specifications.

Digital versatile disk (DVD) or digital video disk (DVD-ROM) is a type of disk drive that allows for large amounts of data on one disk the size of a standard CD. DVD drives were first sold in 1997 and today are widely used for storing and viewing movies and other data. To play a DVD on a computer, a user must have a DVD drive as well as a DVD player, which is a software program that is designed to play and control a DVD.

Many computer users use CD and DVD burners to transfer digital information from a hard disk to a CD or DVD. The computer forensics examiner might need to retrieve evidence from a CD or DVD. Optical media store information in a manner different from magnetic media. To create a CD, a laser burns flat areas, or lands, on the top side of the CD. Lower areas not burned by the laser are called pits. The transitions from lands to pits have the binary value of 1. Where there is no transition, the location has a value of 0.

On the surface of a CD, data is configured into three areas: lead-in, program, and lead-out. The lead-in area contains the table of contents. Up to 99 tracks are available for the table of contents.

Data is stored in the program area. The end-of-CD marker is stored in the lead-out area.

C.   Microsoft File System Overview

Forensic examiners need to understand how Windows and DOS computers store files. There are a number of terms that must be introduced to provide a foundation for understanding the operations of the file and disk storage system. Two important terms relate to the basic input/output system (BIOS) and CMOS. Settings must be accessed to avoid altering evidence on a Windows/DOS computer.

The **BIOS** runs at the computer start-up sequence where it configures devices and then boots the operating system. The function of the BIOS is so vital that the information on the BIOS is stored on a read-only memory (ROM) chip separate from the hard drive to protect it from potential crashes. BIOS information tells the computer how to read information contained on the computer's various drives, and includes the **bootstrap**, which is the first code executed when the computer is turned on. The computer stores system configuration and date and time information in the CMOS when the system is powered off.

New technology file system (NTFS) is Windows NT's replacement for the DOS FAT (file allocation table) and OS/2's HPFS (high-performance file system). NTFS offers many advantages over other file systems, including improved security and the ability to reconstruct files in the event of hardware failures. **FAT** is a file system table used by the FAT-file systems. It contains information about where on the disk the content of the files is stored. The method an OS uses to store data, NTFS or FAT, determines where data can be hidden. These hidden places need to be explored to determine whether they contain files or remnants of files that might contain evidence of a policy violation or criminal activity. There are three versions of FAT, namely FAT12, FAT16, and FAT32.

1.   Partitions

A **partition** is a segment of the hard drive that is separated from other portions of the hard disk drive. Partitions help enable users easily divide a computer hard disk drive into different drives and/or into different portions for multiple OSs to run on the same drive. There are various types of utilities used to create and manage partitions on hard disk drives, one of the most commonly used and known utilities is Microsoft Fdisk. Fdisk reformats a hard disk and can be destructive.

It is possible for users to hide data in voids between partitions on hard drives. This unused space between partitions is called the **partition gap**. If data is hidden in a partition gap, a disk editor utility could be used to alter information in the disk's partition table. This could remove all references to the hidden partition, effectively concealing it from the computer's OS. The forensics examiner can use a number of tools to examine a partition's physical level. These include Norton Disk Edit, WinHex, or Hex Workshop. These tools would also be used to analyze the key hexadecimal codes the OS uses to identify and maintain the file system.

2.   Master Book Record

The **master boot record (MBR)** is a small program that is executed when a computer boots up. Typically, the MBR resides on the first sector of the hard disk. The program begins the boot process by looking up the partition table to determine which partition to use for booting. It then transfers program control to the boot sector of that partition, which continues the boot process. The MBR stores information about the partitions on a disk and their locations, size, and other critical items.

3. Registry Data

The registry consists of a database that contains hardware and software configuration, setup information, and user preferences. The registry is used in Windows 2000, Me, 98, and XP operating systems. The forensic examiner might find useful information in the registry database. The **Regedit** program can also be used when examining Windows 9x computer systems. **Regedit32** can be used on Windows 2000 and XP systems. Various items of information might be recovered from the registry, such as the last person to log onto the computer. When reviewing the registry, ensure no settings are altered, as this could render the system inoperable.

The registry for Windows 9x is located in System.dat and User.dat, which are located in the Windows root directory. Registry information for Windows 2000 and XP is located in the \Winnt\Config and \Windows\System32\Regedt.exe. More technical details will be provided in Chapter 9.

4. Windows Forensic Tools

A number of computer forensic tools are described on vendor Web pages; however, care should be used to ensure they are credible and acceptable in the legal environment.

> Trinity Rescue Kit (TRK)
> The Farmer's Boot CD
> The SleuthKit
> Autopsy Browser

D. Macintosh Computer Systems

The **Macintosh (Mac)** is an alternative PC platform to DOS-based PCs developed by Apple in the 1980s. The Mac is a popular computer for schools and graphics professionals. Apple's innovations continue to make the Macintosh popular in the PC market. The current Mac OS is Mac OS-X v. 10.4.6, making the file and disk structures different from Microsoft systems. Computer forensic examiners must have a working knowledge in these computers, as they can become objects of forensic investigations.

The Mac uses a **hierarchical file system (HFS)** where files are stored in directories or folders. The file manager handles the reading, writing, and storage of data. It also collects data to manage the HFS. The **finder** is another Mac tool that interacts with the OS to keep track of files and maintain each user's desktop. A Mac OS file consists of a data fork and a resource fork. The **data fork** contains data that the user creates. When working with an application file, the **resource fork** contains the menu, icons, dialog boxes, controls, and executable code.

A volume is any storage media used to store files. A volume can be all or part of the storage for hard drives; however, in the Mac OS, a volume on a floppy disk is the entire floppy. With larger disks the user defines a volume that consists of allocation blocks and logical blocks. An **allocation block** consists of the number of blocks assembled in the Mac file system when a file is saved. A **logical block** is a collection not exceeding 512 bytes. The Mac file system provides for two end-of-file (EOF) descriptors: logical EOF and physical EOF. The **logical EOF** refers to the number of bytes that contain data. The **physical EOF** represents the number of the allocation block for that file. The Mac reduces fragmentation by using contiguous allocation blocks, called clumps.

Macintosh computers use **open firmware** instead of BIOS firmware. This is a platform-dependent boot firmware used on Mac computers to gather information, control devices, and load the OS. It is essential the examiner understand the open firmware process to be able to control boot device selection when booting a Mac system.

1.   Forensic Tools for Mac Systems

Most forensic tools are oriented toward the Windows environment; however, new packages have become available to assist in investigations involving Mac computers. **MacForensicsLab** is a complete suite of forensics and analysis tools available from SubRosaSoft. The **MacQuisition** Boot CD is a forensic acquisition tool used to safely and easily image Mac suspect drives using the suspect's own system. MacQuisition provides an intuitive user interface to traditional command line, providing both beginner and advanced forensic examiners with a valuable tool.

Open-source forensic tools such as SleuthKit, Autopsy, Foremost, and dcfldd are available to perform examinations on a Mac OS-X. There are a number of places to look for evidence on a Mac system. The Mac OS is a Unix-based system and most user files are created and saved in the user's home directory. A Mac OS-X system can have multiple users. Evidence might be located in the **Users/Userx/directories**. These include library, desktop, documents, pictures, and library/preferences directories. Other places to look include system logs, Mac OS-X mail, and Safari browser caches. A number of computer forensic tools are described in Chapter 10.

E.   UNIX/Linux Systems

UNIX is an OS that originated at Bell Labs in 1969 as an interactive time-sharing system. UNIX became the first OS written in the C programming language. UNIX has evolved as a kind of large freeware product, with many extensions and new ideas provided in a variety of versions of UNIX by different companies, universities, and individuals. UNIX is one of the most common OSs for servers on the Internet. UNIX is well known for its relative hardware independence and portable application interfaces. UNIX is designed to be used by many people at the same time and has built-in TCP/IP. Many companies are using UNIX servers for its reliability and scalability. Some of the popular flavors include Linux, Solaris, HP-UX, AIX, etc.

Linux is a version of UNIX that runs on a variety of hardware platforms. Linux is open-source software, which is freely available; however, the full distribution of Linux along with technical support and training are available for a fee from vendors such as Red Hat Software and Caldera. Due to its stability, Linux has gained popularity with ISPs as the OS for hosting Web servers. Linux, however, requires a higher level of skill from users.

Linux uses **inodes**, or information nodes, that contain descriptive information about each file or directory. The concept is particularly important to the recovery of damaged file systems.

The inode number is an integer unique to the device upon which it is stored. All files are hard links to inodes. Specifically, an inode is a pointer to other inodes or blocks. When the last pointer to a file is deleted, the file is effectively deleted. This allows Linux to store a file in one location and create pointers to it from other locations. Whenever a program refers to a file by name, the system conceptually uses the filename to look up the corresponding inode. Each inode keeps an internal link count, and when the number becomes 0, Linux deletes the file. To find deleted files, the forensics examiner would search for inodes that contain some data and have a link count of 0. The Linux file structure consists of metadata and data. Metadata includes items such as user ID, group ID, size, and permissions for each file.

Everything in UNIX and Linux is a file. This includes disk drives, workstation monitor, tape drives, network interface, memory, directories, and files. All UNIX files are defined as objects, which means that a file has properties and methods that can be performed on a file. UNIX consists of boot block, superblock, inode, and data block components that define the file system. A block is a disk allocation unit that ranges from 512 bytes and up.

A **partition** is a logical section of a disk. Each partition normally has its own file system. UNIX tends to treat partitions as though they were separate physical entities. In computer engineering, hard disk drive partitioning is the creation of logical divisions upon a hard disk that allows one to apply OS-specific logical formatting.

1.   Examining a UNIX or Linux System

The forensic personnel must first review the documentation of the UNIX system being examined for information concerning the boot process and other specifics to a particular system. UNIX systems, such as file servers or Web servers, probably cannot be powered down, which would lead to potential problems. There are also specific processes that occur when powering on a UNIX workstation. These processes load various instructions into the device's random access memory (RAM) and ROM. Users cannot log onto the UNIX workstation until all of these processes have been completed successfully.

2. *UNIX and Linux Forensic Tools*

UNIX and Linux tools are available from a number of sources including:

SMART Linux: Is a live CD and an installable distribution of Linux designed for Data Forensics and Incident Response from ASR Data. Every aspect of SMART Linux has been optimized for producing a clean, noninvasive, forensically sound OS environment.

ForensiX, Linux Forensic eXaminer: Collects and analyzes digital evidence; available from Fred Cohen and Associates.

Maresware: Catalogs, hashes and strings searching programs; available from Mares and Company.

Chapter Summary

Forensic examiners must understand the structure of computer disk drives and how data is stored and managed on Microsoft, Macintosh, and Linux systems in order to identify and recover latent evidence. Each OS is unique in structure and, therefore, requires different tools to identify and retrieve digital evidence.

The primary computer storage device that contains digital evidence is the hard disk. The four main components of a hard disk drive are the platters, head arm, chassis, and the head actuator. The forensic examiner must be familiar with disk drive operation and structure so data can be effectively located.

There are a number of computer hard disk interfaces. These include ATA, ATPI, IDE, EIDE, RAID, SATA, and SCSI drives. The interfaces allow a computer to send and retrieve information for storage devices such as computer hard disk drives and CD-ROM drives.

Forensic examiners need to understand how Windows, DOS, Mac, and Linux computers operate. Each if these systems employ different code and input/output structures and capabilities. Different forensic tools are required to identify and extract evidence from these systems.

Terms

Allocation block — A group of consecutive of logical blocks assembled in the Mac file system when a file is saved.

American Standard Code for Information Interchange (ASCII) — Consists of 128 standard ASCII codes, each of which can be represented by a 7-digit binary number: 0000000 through 1111111.

AT Attachment (ATA) — The most commonly used interface on IBM-compatible computers to connect to computer hard disk drives, CD-ROM drives, and other types of disk drives.

Autoexec.bat — In DOS- and Windows-based PCs, the file that contains a list of commands that are automatically executed on system start-up.

Bits — Short for binary digit, the smallest unit of information on a machine. A single bit can hold only one of two values: 0 or 1. More meaningful information is obtained by combining consecutive bits into larger units.

Boot sector — The very first sector on a hard drive.

Bootstrap — The bootstrap program can be used to start the computer, clear the memory, set up devices, and load the operating system from input/output internal or external memory.

Bytes — A unit of measurement for data storage equal to eight bits of information composed of ones and zeros.

Cache — Specialized random access memory (RAM) used specifically to optimize data transfers between system components with different performance capabilities.

Clump — A contiguous allocation block in the Macintosh file system.

CMOS — Complementary metal-oxide semiconductor.

Data fork — Part of the Mac file structure where data is stored.

Digital versatile disk or digital video disk (DVD) — A type of disk drive that allows for large amounts of data on one disk the size of a standard compact disk.

Disk operating system (DOS) — The name of the operating systems on most brands of personal computers contains the acronym DOS. Often when DOS is used without further description, the operating system being referred to is either PC DOS, the operating system used on IBM personal computers, or MS DOS, the variety of DOS that runs on IBM compatible computers.

File allocation table (FAT) — A file system table used by the FAT-file systems. It contains information about where on the disk the content of the files is stored.

Finder — A Mac tool that interacts with the operating system to keep track of files and maintains each user's desktop.

Heads — Devices that ride very closely to the surface of the platter and allow information to be read from and written to the platter.

Hierarchical file system (HFS) — The system where Mac files are stored in directories or folders.

Inodes (Information nodes) — Contain descriptive information about each Linux file or directory.

Integrated drive electronics (IDE) — More commonly known as ATA and is a standard interface for IBM-compatible hard drives.

Linux — Open-source version of UNIX that runs on a variety of hardware platforms.

Logical block — The Mac system assembles a collection of 512 kB of data into allocation blocks to store files.

Logical EOF — The number of bytes that contain data in the Mac file system.

Macintosh (Mac) — An alternative personal computer platform to DOS-based PCs developed by Apple in the 1980s.

Master boot record (MBR) — A small program that is executed when a computer boots up. Typically, the MBR resides on the first sector of the hard disk. The program begins the boot process by looking up the partition table to determine which partition to use for booting. It then transfers program control to the boot sector of that partition, which continues the boot process.

Metadata — Refers to small bits of information stored by some computer programs such as Microsoft Word. Metadata can contain the history of the document, including all users who have modified and/or saved it, the directory structure of all machines it was saved on, and names of printers it was printed on.

New technology file system (NTFS) — Windows NT's replacement for the DOS FAT (file allocation table) and OS/2's HPFS (high-performance file system). NTFS offers many advantages over other file systems, including improved security and the ability to reconstruct files in the event of hardware failures.

Open firmware — A platform-dependent boot firmware used on Mac computers to gather information, control devices, and load the operating system.

Partition — A segment of the hard drive that is separated from other portions of the hard disk drive. Partitions help enable users to easily divide a computer hard disk drive into different drives and/or into different portions for multiple operating systems to run on the same drive.

Partition gap — Unused space between partitions.

Physical EOF — The number of allocation blocks assigned to a file in a Mac system.

Random access memory (RAM) — The most common computer memory which can be used by programs to perform necessary tasks while the computer is on; an integrated circuit memory chip allows information to be stored or accessed in any order and all storage locations to be equally accessible.

Read-only memory (ROM) — Memory whose contents can be accessed and read but cannot be changed.

Registry — A database that contains information required for the operation of Windows NT and Windows 95, plus applications installed under Windows NT and Windows 95. The registry also includes user information, such as user IDs, encrypted passwords, and permissions. Windows NT and Windows 95 include RegEdit.exe for editing the registry.

Resource fork — Part of the Mac OS file system that contains the resources.

Small computer system interface (SCSI) — A standard interface for connecting external units such as disks, tape drives, CD players, scanners, etc. to a computer. It is usually pronounced "scuzzy."

SMART — An installable distribution of Linux designed for data forensics and incident response.

UNIX — An operating system cocreated by AT&T researchers Dennis Ritchie and Ken Thompson. UNIX is well known for its relative hardware independence and portable application interfaces. Many big companies are using UNIX servers for their reliability and scalability. Some of the popular UNIX flavors include Linux, Solaris, HP-UX, AIX, etc.

Volume — Consists of a single floppy disk, a hard drive partition, entire drive, or several drives. It refers to any storage media in the Mac file system.

Windows — Microsoft Windows is a range of closed source proprietary commercial operating environments for personal computers and servers. The range was first introduced by Microsoft in 1985 and eventually has come to dominate the world personal computer market. All recent versions of Windows are full-fledged operating systems.

Review Questions

1. A standard interface for connecting external units such as disks, tape drives, CD players, scanners, etc. to a computer is called _____.
2. The three major brands of small computer systems most likely objects of forensic investigations are _____, _____, and _____.
3. _____ is the most common type of computer memory that can be used by programs to perform necessary tasks while the computer is on.
4. This character code structure consists of 128 standard codes, each of which can be represented by a 7-digit binary number.
5. This disk drive component allows information to be read from and written to the platter.
6. NTFS and FAT are relevant for which operating system?
7. Inodes are used in which file system?
8. A contiguous allocation block in the Macintosh file system is called a _____.
9. What term refers to small bits of information stored by some computer programs that are useful in forensic investigations? This can contain the history of the document.
10. What is the function of an IDE and an EIDE?

Chapter 10

The Computer and Electronic Forensic Lab

Chapter Objectives

- Understand the functions of a computer and electronic forensic laboratory
- Identify the software, hardware, and personnel requirements for lab examinations
- Determine the infrastructure requirements of an electronic forensic laboratory
- Learn the training and certification requirements for lab examiners
- Look at the processes and tools required to identify and recover electronic evidence
- Understand the importance of documentation and chain-of-custody in the forensic process

Introduction

Computer and electronic forensic analysis is often useful in matters that, on the surface, seem unrelated to computers. In some cases, personal information containing evidence may have been stored on a laptop computer. In a divorce case, a husband hides joint funds in a secret bank account. In another, an employee pirates software developed by an employer to start another company. In still another, a male employee sends numerous suggestive e-mails to a female coworker. In all of these instances, the suspects use a cell phone and e-mail that provide evidence to support the charges.

Computer forensics is the use of specialized techniques for recovery, authentication, and analysis of electronic data in corporate, civil, and criminal cases. These processes involve issues relating to reconstruction of computer usage, examination of residual data, and authentication of data by technical analysis, or explanation of technical features of data and computer usage. The forensics lab is the facility that provides these examinations.

Specialized hardware and software products are utilized in investigations of computer systems, electronic devices, or any device that contains a processor and memory in order to determine the who, what, where, when, and how issues of usage. The use of these tools to identify and retrieve evidence will be explored.

With the proliferation of scams and identity theft over the Internet and e-mail systems, investigators are developing forensic techniques for tracking and identifying these criminals. Issues also relate to the enormous volume of SPAM clogging the Internet and e-mail transmissions that could contain destructive code such as worms and Trojan horses.

The categories of forensic examinations that can be conducted in the forensic laboratory include those involving e-mail, cell phones, hard drives, and any other electronic device that possesses a memory storage capacity. All forensic labs, however, do not possess the resources, hardware, software, or personnel to examine all devices. Examinations involving hard disk drives will be addressed in Chapter 11. Examinations involving e-mail are presented in Chapter 12 and those involving mobile devices are included in Chapter 13.

A.   Computer Forensic Issues

Computer forensics, also known as digital forensics, is concerned with preserving, recovering, and analyzing information stored within a digital medium. The purpose is to obtain information or evidence that can be used in a judicial review. Criminal prosecutors, civil litigations, insurance companies, corporations, law enforcement officials, and individuals can use computer forensic evidence. Forensic experts examine computer systems in order to determine if they have been utilized for any activities that may be illegal or otherwise unauthorized. Experts in computer forensics may examine data storage devices such as hard disks and compact disks (CDs). Their work is to identify, preserve, and analyze any evidence that may be used in a civil or criminal legal proceeding. They also have the responsibility of documenting and presenting these findings. All their work is conducted with certain standards of evidence that can be approved by a court of law. It is vital to take special care of handling those files belonging to a suspect because electronic devices are susceptible to viruses, and electromagnetic, and mechanical damage. In order to ensure evidence is not destroyed or compromised in any way, forensic experts are careful not to handle the evidence more than necessary, as overhandling can possibly change the data. The establishment and maintenance of the evidence's chain-of- custody requires that all latent evidence be clearly and comprehensively documented.

Suspects of crimes that were conducted with the aid of digital devices may very well have installed countermeasures against forensic practices. For this and other reasons, data gathered by a forensic specialist is rarely analyzed on the same machine from which it was obtained. Exact copies of all data storage devices (usually hard drives) are made. A thorough examination of a machine in question includes looking for concealed data containing passwords or security instructions and the collection of any recordable media. Examiners are also looking for any removable storage devices such as universal serial bus (USB) drives, MP3 players, or security tokens. If a machine is still running, all open applications are thoroughly examined and recorded. Some illegal communications such as terrorist traffic may not be stored on the hard drive. As such, it must be gathered while the machine is still powered on because when it is off, all the information stored only in random access memory (RAM) will be lost. Unique measures are also employed when shutting down a computer to not lose data. Experts are also on the lookout for traps such as intrusion detection devices and self-destruct mechanisms.

E-mail review is another technique to gather large amounts of digital evidence that could be in the body of the message or in attachments. Forensic experts check dedicated e-mail programs, Web browsers, and other e-mail reading and generating applications. Files for each of these applications can be stored on a local hard drive, network device, or a removable device of some sort. Looking for information through an e-mail review is not simple. The large volume of messages sent and received can be daunting. As such, more reviewers employ **keyword** search programs to find relevant data and information.

B.   Forensic Laboratories

Many corporations, educational institutions, and government departments are finding it necessary to establish an in-house electronic forensic laboratory. Violations of security and computer-use policies occur with increasing frequency. In large organizations, numerous personnel issues involving electronic devices and computer systems may arise daily. Issues relating to contractors, maintenance personnel, partners, visitors, sales personnel, and suppliers can occur that require some response from the security office. Many of these incidents can involve some type of electronic documentation or communication.

Internal electronic forensics laboratories can be an efficient and cost-effective way of handling routine incidents that are not likely to be referred to law enforcement for prosecution or that will require an expert witness testimony. Because an internal issue can easily become a legal issue, internal staffing, procedures, tools, and capabilities must hold up in a court situation. If an organization decides to establish an internal lab, the capabilities should be reviewed by an outside source to validate compliance to industry and federal standards. It is quite easy to have evidence discredited in civil and criminal litigation because of faulty or sloppy examinations.

A list of considerations and requirements that can assist in the decision-making process to develop an internal laboratory follows.

Personnel must qualify as expert witnesses in computer evidence processing
Staff must be properly trained in computer evidence processing procedures
Staff must be trained on multiple tool types
Examiners must be certified
Staff must have sufficient depth to handle multiple cases
Multiple sets of tools must be available for investigations
Internal forensics capabilities must meet potential legal challenges
Computer processing power and media storage must be state-of-the-art
Evidence must be protected and accessible to only authorized personnel
The chain-of-custody must be maintained and documented

It should be obvious that staffing is a critical component when developing and operating a forensic lab. Training and management will be an ongoing issue and process. A cost-benefit analysis might prove or disprove a need for an internal lab. There are a number of professional computer forensic laboratories that provide these lab services.

C.   Examining Computer Evidence

Physical computer evidence can be represented by physical items such as central processing units, chips, boards, storage media, monitors, and printers. Detailed plans describing acceptable methods for handling physical evidence exist for the logging, description, storage, and disposition of physical evidence. However, computer evidence, while stored in these physical items, is latent and exists only in an abstract electronic form. The result that is reported from an examination is the recovery of this latent information. Although forensic laboratories are adept at ensuring the integrity of the physical items in their control, computer forensics also requires methods to ensure the integrity of the data and information contained within those physical items. Computer forensic examiners must utilize methods and techniques that provide valid, repeatable, and reliable results while protecting the real evidence from destruction or modification.

The path an examiner takes in each case must be well documented and technologically sound for that particular case. It may not, however, be the same path the examiner takes with the next case. Traditional forensic examinations, such as the DNA examination of blood recovered from a crime scene, lend themselves to a routine and standardized series of steps that can be repeated in case after case. There is generally no such thing as generic computer evidence procedures. The evidence is likely to be significantly different every time the laboratory receives a submission and will likely require an examination plan tailored to that particular evidence. Although this situation may present a recurrent consideration of management checks and controls within the laboratory setting, it is a consideration that must be addressed and improved if this emerging forensic discipline is to remain an effective and reliable tool in the criminal justice system.

1. Procedures and Practices

Computer and electronic evidence almost never exists in isolation. It is a product of the data stored, the computer program used to create and store it, and the computer system that directed these activities. It can also be a product of the software tools used in the laboratory to extract it. There are a number of acceptable tools that have passed the scrutiny of the courts. There are also software tools available on the Web for searching and identifying data and information.

Computer forensic science issues must also be addressed in the context of an emerging and rapidly changing technology environment. State, national, and international law enforcement agencies recognize the need for common technical approaches. Because of this, a framework has been developed that includes a multilevel structure consisting of principles of examination, policies and practices, and procedures and techniques.

Principles of examination are large-scale concepts that almost always apply to the examination. They are the consensus approaches as to what is important among professionals and laboratories conducting these examinations. They represent the collective technical practice and experience of forensic computer examiners.

Organizational policy and practices are structural guidance that applies to forensic examinations. These are designed to ensure quality and efficiency in the workplace. In computer forensic science, these are the good laboratory practices by which examinations are planned, performed, monitored, recorded, and reported to ensure the quality and integrity of the work product.

Procedures and techniques employ software and hardware solutions to specific forensic problems. The procedures and techniques are detailed instructions for specific software packages as well as step-by-step instructions that describe the entire examination procedure.

As an overall example, a laboratory may require that examinations be conducted, if possible and practical, on copies of the original evidence. This logical approach taken by the computer forensic science community is based on the tenet of protecting the original evidence from accidental or unintentional damage or alteration. This principle is predicated on the fact that digital evidence can be duplicated exactly to create a copy that is true and accurate.

An examiner responsible for duplicating evidence must first decide on an appropriate level of verification to weigh time constraints against large file types. The mathematical precision and discriminating power of these algorithms are usually directly proportional to the amount of time necessary to calculate them. Circumstances could probably result in a decision to use a faster, but less precise and discriminating, data integrity algorithm. The common imaging algorithms are CRC, SHA1, and MD5.

Having decided how best to ensure the copying process will be complete and accurate, the next step is the actual task, which involves both procedures and techniques. These most closely represent the standard cookbook approach to protocol development. They are complete and contain required detailed steps that may be used to copy the data, verify that the operation was complete, and ensure that a true and accurate copy has been produced.

2.   *Documentation and Reporting*

A major function of the forensic lab consists of documentation and reporting. These are major activities that must be performed according to the rules of evidence, as these documents and reports will probably be the basis of some legal action. A number of forms have been developed to assist in these processes. There are so many steps required in these forensic examinations and investigations that it is very easy to overlook something important; therefore, forms and checklists are required. Samples of these forms are provided in Appendix A. These forms include:

Evidence Receipt	Macintosh Examination
Windows Examination	Macintosh Examination Checklist
Windows Examination Checklist	Disk Imaging Exam
Linux Examination	Imaging Checklist
Linux Examination Checklist	

D.   Data Recovery versus Forensic Recovery

Data frequently can be retrieved from a suspect computer, even if the user has deleted the information, defragged the drive, or even reformatted the drive. Computer forensics includes the specialized practice of investigating computer media for the purpose of discovering and analyzing available, deleted, or "hidden" information that may serve as useful evidence in a legal matter.

Computer forensics technicians employ sophisticated software to view and analyze information that cannot be accessed by the ordinary user. This information may have been deleted by the user months or even years prior to the investigation, or may never have been saved to storage media, but it may still exist in whole or in part somewhere on the computer or electronic device.

In order to determine whether a computer holds information that may serve as evidence, the examiner must first create an exact image of the drive. The examiner examines only this image drive to protect the original from inadvertent alterations. These images must be actual bit-by-bit or "mirror" images of the originals, not just simple copies of the data. Acquiring these kinds of exact copies requires the use of specialized forensics techniques. Both hardware and software products are available that can accomplish this task.

These mirror images are critical because each time someone powers up a computer, many changes are automatically made to the files. In a Windows system, for example, numerous modifications are made to the files during a power-on cycle. These changes are not visible to the user, but the changes that do occur can alter or even delete evidence, for example, critical dates related to criminal activity.

Each agency and examiner must ensure that a copy is true and accurate and must make a decision as to how to implement this principle on a case-by-case basis. Factors in that decision include the size of the data set, the method used to create it, and the media on which it resides. In some cases it may be sufficient to merely compare the size and creation dates of files listed in the copy to the original. In others the application of a more technically robust and mathematical rigorous technique of calculating a message digest (MD) may be required.

MD is a computer algorithm that produces unique mathematical representations of the data. The MD is calculated for both the original and the copy and then compared for identity. CRC, MD, and SHA algorithms have been discussed in Chapter 6. The selection of tools must be based on the character of the evidence rather than simply laboratory policy. It is likely that examiners will need several options available to them to perform this one function. Some examiners will use multiple tools to ensure a true copy has been made.

Ensuring chain-of-custody is as important to the specialist who oversees drive imaging and evaluation of the data for its evidentiary value as it is in medical forensics. The forensics specialist uses hash codes to ensure the digital image copies are identical.

Hash codes are large numbers, specific to each file and each drive, that are computed mathematically. These are the result of using the MD5, CRC32, or SHA1 algorithm process. If a file or drive is changed, even in the smallest way, the hash code will also change. These hash codes are recomputed on the original and images at various points during the investigation in order to ensure that the examination process itself does not modify the image being examined.

In many cases, even when the user has defragged or reformatted a drive, evidence can still be retrieved. Many segments of data are not altered by defragging a drive, because, as noted above, many documents contain internal information that describes dates, users, and other historical data that may be useful to the case. **Defragging** is a process (run by a defragging program) whereby parts of data files on all segments of a computer hard disk are taken from their fragmented state (with parts of files spread all over the disk), and grouped together in complete-file segments. And while **reformatting** a drive rebuilds the file system and reinitializes a disk, destroying the original contents, it does not remove the information that previously existed on the drive. A computer forensics specialist with the right software and experience can recover most of what was on the disk before the reformatting process took place. Simple recovery software available on the Web does not have the robust capabilities needed to recover most deleted files.

Particular programs, including Microsoft Word, retain facts about each document that they create, modify, or access within the documents themselves. These facts, known as **metadata**, chronicle the history of a document, including the identification of the users who have modified and/or saved it, the directory structure of the computer(s) it has been saved to, and any printer it has been printed on. Computer forensics professionals can retrieve metadata readily and learn all there is to know about a document's past life.

When a user accesses the Internet, the browser keeps records of the sites the user has visited. These are available by clicking on the "favorites" icon on the browser. Data stored also includes temporary files and cookies. **Cookies** are files that browsers use to track a user's Internet activity. They may furnish passwords and other information about the user's Internet practices. Cookies can be deleted if the user is aware of them, is conscientious about deleting them on a regular basis, and overwrites their locations. If not, forensics investigations can substantiate the Web sites the user has visited.

E.   Forensic Analysis

The **forensic analysis** of a computer or electronic system revolves around a cycle of data gathering and processing of the materials and evidence gathered. The more accurate and complete the effort, the probability of success increases and the quality of the result improves. The original evidence must be safeguarded in a pristine state and any analysis conducted must be performed on a copy rather than the original. This is somewhat analogous to taping off a murder scene to prevent physical evidence being destroyed, which is done to preserve evidence, allow others to verify conclusions, and minimize evidence tampering.

Ideally the investigator wants an exact copy of the entire system and all its data, but there are roadblocks that prevent this. The act of collecting data may cause other users or programs on the system to trigger changes in state or destroy valuable evidence. The computer user or owner could have set electronic mines or traps that might also damage data if agitated. The mere execution of a program will disturb the computer's state (date and time stamp) as it loads and runs.

These sorts of problems are the reasons that traditional forensic analysis has focused on data from systems that are not running at all. Operating system type dictates the correct process to power off the system and copy the data that has survived the transition—program logs, access times, the content of files, etc. Analysis is then done on a copy of the data, which eliminates or minimizes the danger to the original. This facilitates easy capturing of data and a reasonably nonrepudiated chain-of-logic when demonstrating results.

Reproducibility of results requires consistent mechanisms for gathering data and a good understanding of any side effects of the same. To obtain dependable results, automation is a necessity for gathering forensic data. The examiner must also show that the process can be repeated multiple times, using different tools.

Certainly care and planning should be used when gathering information from a running system. Isolating the computer from other users and the network is the first step. Given that some types of data are less prone to being disturbed by data collection than others it is a good idea to capture information in accordance to its expected life span. The life expectancy of data varies tremendously, going from picoseconds (one trillionth) to years. Table 10.1 can be used as a rough guide.

What is going on with all the bits stored on the computer system? In most cases, nothing is happening. A study showed that the vast majority of digital data on fairly typical Web servers had not been used during the last year. Even on an extraordinarily heavily used Usenet news system, less than 10 percent of the files were used within the last 30 days. Whether they are programs and configuration files that are never used, or archives of mail, news, and data, etc., there are many files that are seldom accessed. Similar patterns emerge from Windows PCs and other desktop systems. Often over 90 percent of files have not been touched in the past year.

Even a one MIPS (million instructions per second) computer could generate enough new data to fill a terabyte (trillion) drive in a short time. Computers are busy, but most activity accesses the same data, programs, and other resources over and over again. As a system keeps accessing the same files again and again, it is quite literally stepping upon its own "footprints." This is why footprints from unusual activity stand out, providing data for forensic evidence. These footprints are likely to stand out for a long time because most information on a system is rarely touched.

Table 10.1   Data Life Expectancy.

Registers, peripheral memory, caches, etc.	picoseconds
Main memory	nanoseconds
Network state	milliseconds
Running processes	seconds
Disk	minutes
Floppies, backup media, etc.	years
CD-ROMs, printouts, etc.	tens of years

F. Collecting Evidence Relating to Electronic Systems

Suspects often try to avoid prosecution by deleting files and data from their computers. Computer-forensic tools have solved this problem. A computer's operating system utilizes a directory that contains the name and placement of each file on the drive. When a file is deleted, several events take place on the computer. A file status marker is set to show that the file has been deleted. A disk status marker is set to show that the space is now available for another use. While the user can no longer see the file listed in any directory, nothing has been done to the file itself. This newly available space is called **free** or **unallocated space** and until the free space is overwritten by another file, the forensic specialist can retrieve the file in its entirety. Overwriting might be caused by a variety of user activities, such as adding a new program or creating new documents that happen to be written to the space where the "deleted" files exist. It is only when the data is overwritten by new data that part or all of the files are no longer retrievable through normal forensic techniques. New technologies now allow for new abilities to identify previously unrecoverable data.

The useable space on computer hard drives is divided into sectors of equal size. When a user needs to store information, the computer's operating system automatically determines which sectors will be used to perform the task. In many instances the information being stored will not use up all of the space available in the designated sector(s). When this happens, information that was previously stored on the hard drive remains in the unused part of the designated sector, in what is called **slack space**. This means that even if part of the drive has been overwritten with new data, chances are that some implicating evidence will remain in the slack space. Critical data contained in slack space is also recoverable using forensic techniques. Computer forensics specialists know how to access unallocated space and slack space as well as other hidden pockets of data and, with the proper tools, can recover their contents. This process, however, is time consuming and may not yield any relevant results. Review Chapter 9 for details concerning the various structures of the hard disk drive.

Computer system files contain valuable information that allows a forensic examiner to search for additional evidence. This hidden information contains details about computer processes and activities, such as Web sites visited, e-mail transmissions, financial-based Internet transactions, documents, letters, and photographs that have been created, modified, or accessed. In many instances transaction evidence is available even if data has not been saved on the computer's hard disk drive.

The operating system stores data in temporary locations on the computer. There are a number of storage buffers that might contain useful temporary data. When the computer is later turned off, the information continues to exist in the temporary location, even if the user does not save it as a file.

1. *Log Evidence*

Most computer and network devices, if programmed and configured properly, are capable of producing logs. Logs must have certain fundamental requisites for computer forensics purposes. These are integrity, time-stamping, normalization, and data reduction.

To possess integrity, the log must be unaltered and not admit any tampering or modification by unauthorized operators. Time-stamping is absolutely essential for making correlations after an incident. The log must guarantee reasonable certainty as to the date and hour a certain event was registered. Normalization is a technical term that means the ability of the correlation tool to extract data from the source format of the log file that can be correlated with others of a different type without having to violate the integrity of the source data. Data reduction, or filtering, is the data extraction procedure for identifying a series of pertinent events and correlating them according to selective criteria.

The log file can be used in all types of investigations to establish types of transactions and the all-valuable times stamp. These logs may contain important latent evidence for use in both civil and criminal cases and trials. The time stamp attached to the log file depends on the date/time that has been set on the computer. This data might not be correct, which means the examiner must check the date/time settings on the device to verify its validity.

G. **Forensic Lab Functions**

The cost to develop a forensic laboratory can be considerable. Requirements for physical work space and office areas, personnel, test equipment, supplies, and other supporting elements can lead to exorbitant costs. Most small law enforcement departments, consultants, and security departments cannot afford this expense; however, an entry-level system of forensic hardware and software can be purchased for less than $20,000. The Federal Bureau of Investigation (FBI) has published a document entitled Handbook of Forensic Services, which provides a comprehensive list of examinations that are possible at the Engineering Research Facility in Quantico, Virginia. Two categories of examinations relate specifically to computer and electronic forensic investigations. This document provides a list of functions that can be performed and also provides instructions for packing and shipping to the laboratory. This list of functions might provide a guide if there is a consideration to develop a local lab. Computer examinations could include the following activities:

Determine the type of data files in a computer
Compare data files to known documents and data files
Determine the time and sequence that data files were created

Extract data files from the computer or computer storage media
Recover deleted data files from the computer or computer storage media
Convert data files from one format to another
Search data files for a word or phrase and record all occurrences
Recover passwords and decrypt encoded files
Analyze and compare source computer code

Examinations can be conducted on commercial electronic devices, interception of communications devices, and miscellaneous electronic devices and circuits. It is often necessary to disassemble these devices during the examination. User- and owner-entered data and other information can be extracted from personal digital assistants (PDAs), cell phones, pagers, and global positioning system (GPS) devices. Operating characteristics can be determined from radio frequency transmitters and receivers. User- and owner-entered data, stored data, and other information can be obtained from fax machines, printers, scanners, and network devices. Any device that possesses magnetic storage has the potential of storing latent forensic evidence. Usually a computer forensic scientist will be required to identify and extract this evidence and special tools are often required.

1.   Cyber-Intelligence

There are new methodologies and goals relative to the new science of cyber-intelligence and how this discipline is being utilized to foster enhancements within the computer forensic community. As storage capability within computing systems increases and the proliferation of digital devices expands, it is commonly the responsibility of computer forensic examiners to perform the analysis of these instruments including, for example, cell phones and PDAs. Computer forensics is also increasingly being utilized to support not only traditional law enforcement functions, but also counter-intelligence, counter-terrorism programs as well. In order to keep pace with the growing caseloads and current technological trends related to computer crimes, traditional crimes supported by computing technology and counter-terrorism programs, the following procedures are necessary:

Establish common baselines and definitions
Identify sources and means, as well as, develop capabilities that perform intelligence analysis
Provide an increased capacity to conduct cyber-forensic examinations
Ensure the greatest amount of the most relevant information possible is discovered during that same forensic examination process

Hardware and software technology that is contained in the computer forensic lab can be used to provide cyber-intelligence support to law enforcement.

H. Lab Design and Components

Forensic laboratories can be designed for specific functions or can be generic in nature. Electronic forensic labs are usually built specifically for electronic and computer-related examinations. The infrastructure, hardware, software, supplies, storage, examination, and reporting requirements are unique. The capital investment is considerable and maintenance programs require annual expenditures. The organization might decide to contract the forensic lab functions to a third-party provider. There are a number of issues that relate to the overall design, physical construction, and security of the lab. Interior walls should reach from floor to ceiling, which provides not only security but also fire protection. Doors should be fire-rated and some type of fire suppression available. If visitors were allowed inside, monitoring of their movements would be required. If any evidence can be discredited, an attempt to do so will be made by opposing counsel. Lab personnel must limit the possibility of contaminating evidence or giving the impression that evidence could have been contaminated.

Whether an internal lab is developed or outsourced, there are a number of issues that need to be addressed. Negotiations with contractors can determine areas of responsibility. These include the following:

Environmental	Security
Lighting	Storage
Electrical and cabling	Work areas
Communications	Forensic workstations
Fire suppression	Hardware, software, and supplies

1. Environmental

Protection of any evidence present in the forensic laboratory must have a high priority. A number of natural and man-made impediments can have a negative impact on this evidence if attention is not focused on the physical environmental components. Adequate air conditioning and ventilation is required because of the heat generated by the various investigative devices. Humidity must be controlled to avoid arcing and static electricity. The safest method of ensuring adequate conditions is to employ an HVAC system specialist to analyze the laboratory space.

2. Lighting

Using forensic workstations can result in a considerable amount of eyestrain. It is essential that proper lighting be installed in the forensic lab. This includes both overhead lighting and that used for close examination of printed documents. The type of lighting is also an issue, as incandescent and fluorescent lights produce a different type of illumination. Shadows can make documents difficult to view. Specialists can use measurement devices to determine the level of light present in the various work areas of the lab.

3. *Electrical and Cabling*

Sufficient electrical power is required to run the forensic workstations and other equipment in the lab. Separate 30-ampere circuit breakers for these devices would be desirable. An uninterruptible power supply (UPS) and surge protector is required for each forensic device. The power company can provide a carbon block device to help isolate lightening strikes. Sufficient power must be supplied to the meter to avoid overloading and brownouts. An electrical contractor should look at the requirements and provide a recommendation. Consideration should be given to proving a generator to back up the entire lab.

The physical construction of the lab examination areas must be according to specifications that lend themselves to electronic devices. A critical issue concerns electrostatic discharges. An **electrostatic discharge** is the sudden and momentary electric current that flows when an excess of electric charge finds a path to an object at a different electrical potential (ground). Latent evidence stored on magnetic media, such as diskettes and hard disk drives, can be damaged or destroyed by a discharge, rendering it useless. Low humidity can cause arcing of static electricity and high humidity can cause shorts. Relative humidity should be kept around 50 percent. Electrical components can be damaged with an 80-volt spike. There are a number of solutions available to prevent these problems and all are expensive.

Examiners could become involved with electronic evidence that is based on a Tempest standard.

Tempest is a U.S. government code word for a set of standards for limiting electric or electromagnetic radiation emanations from electronic equipment, such as microchips, monitors, or printers. It is a counter-intelligence measure aimed at the prevention of electronic espionage. The term Tempest is often used more broadly for the entire field of compromising emanations or Emissions Security (EMSEC).

All cabling and wiring can be run under a raised computer floor. The raised floor consists of a number of panels supported eight inches above the floor by a series of pedestals. The grid is grounded to a common building ground. Both electrical power feeds and telephone circuits and network cabling can be run under the raised floor. Air conditioning and fire suppression pipes can also be fed through this area under the raised floor.

4. *Communications*

The lab must have both telephone and data communications capabilities. Small labs can get by with several private line terminations; however, large installations might require some type of telephone system. Dial-up service, private line service, or DSL could provide data communications capabilities. If large-volume transmissions are required, dial-up is not the answer; however, dial-up can be used as a backup. Consideration should be given to the security of these communication facilities. Firewalls and routers might be required to isolate the lab from the insecure Internet. Spyware and virus protection programs must also be utilized on the workstations.

5.   Fire Suppression

A fire in the lab would certainly be a disaster. Electrical devices can cause a fire. Most offices are equipped with sprinkler systems; however, these are not feasible where computers, test equipment, and other electrical devices are being used. Fire suppression systems using chemicals can be installed instead of sprinklers. Portable fire extinguishers for different types of fires would also be required in the lab.

6.   Security and Safety

Security policies must be in place for the lab and the personnel. A policy concerning access to the facility, storage rooms, computer systems, workstations, and evidence is a requirement. Risks are high because of the possibility of losing or damaging critical forensic evidence. Access control, logging, and monitoring must be a high priority to ensure integrity of the evidence. Physical security of the lab can be affected by guards, locks, biometric devices, or a combination of all three. Medeco and Mul-T-Lock carry a wide variety of locks and security systems ranging from standard security to very high security operations. Figure 10.1 depicts two entrance control devices.

A sign-in log must be maintained for all visitors, maintenance personnel, contractors, and law enforcement. An authorized member of the lab must escort all visitors. In large labs, badges would be required and a biometric or keypad entry device might control access to the area. Visitors must not be allowed to be in a position to observe or touch any forensic evidence. A security guard and perimeter intrusion system might be required for times when the lab is not occupied with staff.

7.   Storage

Storage areas must be provided for supplies, forms, evidence, and tools. Cabinets that can be locked are required for evidence. Open shelves for supplies, forms, and tools would be acceptable. A storage room that can be locked would also be required for computer and electronic evidence. It is essential that lab management determine the characteristics of a safe storage container, cabinet, or room. Legal counsel and prosecuting attorneys should be consulted on the proper methods of

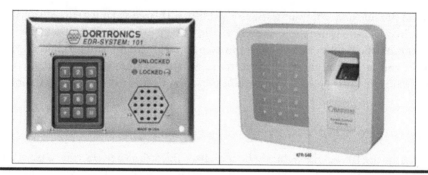

Figure 10.1   Entrance control devices.

preserving the chain-of-custody in the lab setting. Logs must be maintained on any movement or examination of evidence.

The common storage area is also a good place to maintain a supply of forms for the department. This would ensure that all personnel are using the correct version of documentation. Evidence collection and marking supplies could also be centrally located in this area. Any other crime-scene investigation materials and tools could also be stored here. This is a good place to store the flyaway kit. Still cameras and video cameras would be stored in locked cabinets.

All evidence must be secured in some type of cabinet, cage, or vault. A log entry must be made anytime the evidence is accessed. Many electronic devices require a battery source of power to maintain critical data. Sufficient electrical outlets would be required for the chargers that would be connected to the portable devices. A variety of storage containers and shelves might be utilized for evidence storage. Figure 10.2 depicts an evidence receipt that would be completed by the lab examiner and provided to the investigator handling the case. This form would be filed in a case binder.

8.   Work Areas

The configuration of the work area will depend upon the space available and the department's budget. Forensic workstations should have their own individual workspaces to avoid cross-contamination of evidence. Workstations for creating reports and accessing the Internet would require a separate workspace. Workbenches would be required for opening computer cases and other activities performed on evidence.

Workbenches must be sturdy enough to support desktop computers and server devices. The benches must have grounding straps to the raised floor. Sufficient electrical power receptacles must be available for the computer devices and test equipment. Network access jacks would be required at the workbench for connectivity to the Internet and other private networks. Additional measures include appropriate

Computer Evidence Receipt

Case Number:			Receipt Number:	
Items Relinquished By / Title:			Date / Time:	
Organization / Company:			Location / Address:	

Computer(s):

Desktop	Laptop	Server	Hard Drive	Serial Number
☐	☐	☐	☐	
☐	☐	☐	☐	
☐	☐	☐	☐	

Storage Media:

CD-ROM	USB Media	Floppy / Zip	Tape	Subject
☐	☐	☐	☐	
☐	☐	☐	☐	
☐	☐	☐	☐	

Other Materials:

Items Received By / Title:	Signature:
Organization / Company:	Location / Address:

Page ___ of ___

Figure 10.2 Evidence receipt.

packing materials, the use of conducting wrist straps and foot-straps to prevent high voltages from accumulating on workers' bodies, and antistatic mats to conduct harmful electric charges away from the work area.

I. Devices, Tools, and Supplies

The primary investigative components include forensic workstations, supplies, and tools.

1. Forensic Workstations

A decision must be made concerning the type(s) of forensic workstation(s) required in the lab. These computers can be obtained from a number of vendors. They can be configured and assembled by the internal personnel or procured as a production device, complete with operating system, hardware interfaces, and forensic software. Requirements vary; however, a generic configuration is possible. Three major types of computers could be the subjects of forensic examinations: Windows/DOS, Macintosh, and UNIX. It should be obvious that many different components are required to provide a computer forensic workstation that will operate in a designated environment. Usually the forensic departments do not have the expertise to select hardware and software components and successfully integrate them into a working forensic workstation. An easier approach is to purchase a "turnkey" solution. The digital intelligence **forensic recovery of evidence device (FRED)** provides an example solution.

2. Turnkey Forensic Workstation

FRED systems are optimized for stationary laboratory acquisition and analysis. Hard drives can be removed from the suspect system and plugged into FRED and acquire the digital evidence.

FRED will acquire data directly from IDE/EIDE/ATA/SATA/ATAPI/SCSI I/ SCSI II/SCSI III hard drives and storage devices and save forensic images to digital video disk (DVD), CD or hard drives. FRED systems also acquire data from floppies, 100/250/750 MB Zip cartridges, CD-ROM, DVD-ROM, Compact Flash, Micro Drives, Smart Media, Memory Stick, Memory Stick Pro, xD Cards, Secure Digital Media, and Multimedia Cards. With the RAID option FRED has 1.6 terrabytes (1600 gigabytes) of internal RAID storage.

The UltraBay option can be used to acquire a forensically sound image of IDE, SATA, and SCSI drives using a choice of forensic imaging software. Furthermore, IDE, SATA, and SCSI drives may be connected or removed from UltraBay without having to shut down the workstation or leave the graphical user interface (GUI).

FRED systems come with two high-capacity hard drives. One drive is used for forensic acquisition and processing tools and the other drive as a work drive for restoring and processing digital evidence. With multiple boot menu options, FRED can be booted into data acquisition mode and PDBlock loaded automatically, write protecting the suspect hard drive. Another boot option can be configured to place the FRED in data analysis mode with full access to forensic analysis tools. FRED systems also come with Suse Linux 9.1 Professional preconfigured. Both hard drives are supplied in removable trays with front panel switches for master/slave configuration.

All FRED systems can be connected directly to a network (10/100/1000 Mbps Ethernet) for use as a standard workstation or file server when not processing or acquiring data. Baseline FRED specifications can be obtained by visiting the digital intelligence Web site at www.digitalintelligence.com.

Software loaded on the FRED system includes the following:

MS-DOS 6.22 (preinstalled and configured)
Microsoft Windows 98SE Standalone DOS (preinstalled and configured)
Microsoft Windows XP Pro (preinstalled and configured)
Suse Linux 9.1 Professional (preconfigured)
SystemWorks Pro 2003 (GHOST 2003 and DiskEdit)
DVD/CD Authoring Software
DriveSpy, Image, PDWipe, PDBlock, PART

This list might make the reader decide to let someone else build the forensic workstation. This will be one of the most important pieces of investigative equipment in the lab and must operate properly and consistently. A list of generic specifications can be provided to a forensic-workstation provider if the design is to be outsourced. It is a good idea, and probably a requirement, to develop a competitive bid process for this equipment.

Computer equipment and its related operating system software will be a major expense item. Costs will depend on the number of investigators and forensic examiners that will be working in the lab. A model has been developed for a staff complement of four.

15 terrabytes of raw storage in a SAN, fiber, Ethernet environment
Ability to handle any forensic format and operating system
Imaging devices
Forensic workstations
Physical storage areas
Mobile imaging and analysis kit
External hard drive inventory
Ability to crack laptop hard drive passwords
Baseline password cracking ability
Ability to convert video home system (VHS)-formatted surveillance video to
    DVD format
Networked color printing

The total cost for a professional fully functional four-person lab that includes all hardware, racks, toolkits, software, and training is estimated at $150,000. This does not include the examiners, or any ongoing maintenance, supplies, utilities, and upgrade expenses.

A small start-up system consisting of hardware and forensic software can be obtained for around $22,500. This would include a forensic workstation costing

$2,500 and a set of forensic tools costing $20,000. Work space, supplies, and secure storage space would also be required. Obviously, the capabilities of this solution would be limited.

3. Supplies

A variety of forms, crime scene materials, and packaging supplies must be available for the forensic investigations. This stock could also be a central place for forensic investigators to obtain their crime scene supplies. An online supplier is located at evidentcrimescene.com.

Supply of forms
Tamper-resistant bags—multiple sizes
Evidence tape
Evidence tags
Evidence scales—6 inches, multiple colors
Storage containers—multiple sizes
Credit card scale
Photo macrographic scales
Photo evidence markers

4. Toolbox and Tools

The toolbox includes the components normally required when performing a forensic examination. The content of this toolbox is going to depend upon the type of computer systems being examined. A startup kit would include the following:

Adapters, terminators, and cables: All the necessary cables, adapters, and terminators to image and process internal/external SCSI drives, 2½ inch IDE (laptop) drives, and 3½ and 5¼ inch IDE drives. Examples of interface cables and devices are depicted in Figure 10.3. Figure 10.4 depicts several write blocker devices. Many interface cables are required for mobile phone and PDA investigations.

Custom imaging workshelf: This shelf provides a convenient drive-level surface for imaging IDE, SATA, or SCSI drives. The neoprene covered imaging shelf can be easily installed and removed from a standard removable drive bay.

128 Mb USB digital thumb camera: Useful to document your suspect's environment and hardware.

Security screwdriver set: A varied assortment of popular security bits for opening computer enclosures that may have been locked down in a corporate environment.

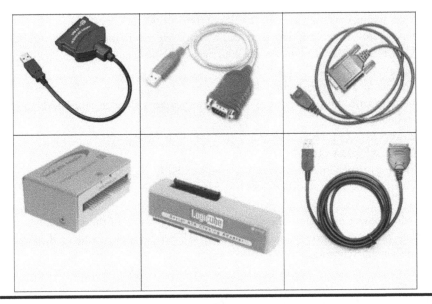

Figure 10.3   Interface cables and devices.

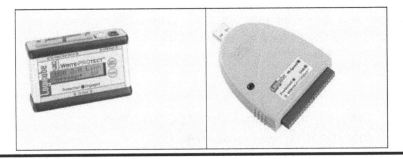

Figure 10.4   Write protection devices.

J.   Training Forensic Lab Examiners

Examiners must understand the chain-of-custody process and how their work might determine the outcome of a criminal proceeding. Specific training will be required for a number of devices manufactured by many different computer and electronic vendors. Training will also be required for the operating software that works with the hardware. Trial and error and on-the-job experience is the best trainer; however, time is expensive. When looking at prospective examiners, a short list has been developed to assist in that identification process.

Works with Microsoft Windows, DOS, and Apple devices
Has experience in Linux, UNIX, or Perl

Understands makeup and mechanics of hard-drive devices

Knows how to recover data from cell phones, pagers, digital cameras, and PDAs

Understands data streams, ASCII, binary, and hexadecimal

Knows how to handle media safely

Can make a bit-stream copy

Understands how to pattern match and carve evidence from hidden and deleted files

Knows how to prepare documentation for court cases

Can crack passwords

Has experience in a number of tools such as FTK, iLook, and Encase

Can use HTML and other tools for Internet investigations

Most novice examiners and wannabes will not possess all these skills. An individual training program would have to be developed for each examiner based upon his or her shortcomings.

1. Certification and Training

A number of organizations offer certifications and training in the area of computer forensics. This training is expensive and time-consuming, so those selected to be examiners must be serious about the career. Additional certifications in the area of security might be pursued by computer forensic investigators. Online courses are available; however, some certification organizations require students to attend hands-on classes.

2. International Association of Computer Investigative Specialists (IACIS)

The International Association for Computer Information Systems (IACIS) is a nonprofit organization providing a forum for interpersonal networking and the sharing of research, teaching, and technical information through an annual international conference and the quarterly scholarly publication, *Journal of Computer Information Systems*. The association encourages membership from the international community of computer professionals and educators.

3. High Technology Crime Investigation Association (HTCIA)

The **High Technology Crime Investigation Association (HTCIA)** is designed to encourage, promote, and facilitate the interchange of data, experience, ideas, and methodologies relating to investigations and security in advanced technologies. There are currently 37 chapters in the international HTCIA organization.

4.   SANS

SANS is the most trusted and by far the largest source of information security training and certification in the world. It also develops, maintains, and makes available, at no cost, the largest collection of research documents about various aspects of information security, and it operates the Internet's early warning system—Internet Storm Center. The SANS (SysAdmin, Audit, Network, Security) Institute was established in 1989 as a cooperative research and education organization. Its programs now reach more than 165,000 security professionals, auditors, system administrators, network administrators, chief information security officers, and chief information officers (CIOs) who share the lessons they are learning and jointly find solutions to the challenges they face. At the heart of SANS are the many security practitioners in government agencies, corporations, and universities around the world who invest hundreds of hours each year in research and teaching to help the entire information security community.

5.   Computer Technology Investigators Network (CTIN)

The Computer Technology Investigators Network (CTIN) has been providing high-tech crime fighting training since 1996 in the areas of high-tech security, investigation, and prosecution of high-tech crimes for both private and public sector security and investigative personnel and prosecutors. CTIN sponsors training from experts worldwide for the benefit of private organizations and law enforcement agencies.

6.   New Technologies, Inc. (NTI)

NTI supports more than 8,000 law enforcement, military, government and business clients. This information has been posted to provide a ready source of information on various topics that are related to computer evidence, computer forensics, document discovery, computer incident response, and computer security risk management issues.

7.   National White Collar Crime Center (NW3C)

The mission of NW3C is to provide a nationwide support system for agencies involved in the prevention, investigation, and prosecution of economic and high-tech crimes. Also to support and partner with other appropriate entities in addressing homeland security initiatives, as they relate to economic and high-tech crimes. They are a congressionally funded, nonprofit corporation whose membership primarily comprises law enforcement agencies, state regulatory bodies with criminal investigative authority, and state and local prosecution offices. While NW3C has no investigative authority itself, its job is to help law enforcement agencies better understand and utilize tools to combat economic and high-tech crime.

8. Certified Electronic Evidence Collection Specialist (CEECS)

The Certified Electronic Evidence Collection Specialist (CEECS) certification is granted to those who successfully complete the CEECS regional certification course. This level of certification is also granted to those students in the Certified Forensic Computer Examiner course who successfully pass the written test.

9. Certified Forensics Computer Examiners (CFCE)

The IACIS provides training for the external Certified Forensic Computer Examiner (CFCE). This process is open to active law enforcement officers and others who qualify for membership in IACIS. The external CFCE process can be particularly helpful to qualified examiners who cannot attend the annual IACIS training conference.

The process consists of the examination of six specially prepared examination diskettes and a specially prepared hard disk drive. Each problem disk must be examined, technical issues must be solved, and a thorough report must be prepared before continuing on to the next problem. There will be one retake of the six diskette problems, if the applicant does not resolve the technical issues in the problem. There will be no retake of the hard disk drive problem. The reports and evidence must be presented to IACIS in a manner that indicates that sound forensic procedures were used to conduct the examination and that the applicant understands the technical issues. There will be a thorough written examination at the conclusion of the process.

10. Certified Computer Forensic Technician (CCFT)—Basic and Advanced

The Certified Computer Forensic Technician (CCFT) is one of four computer forensic certifications aimed at law enforcement and private IT professionals seeking to specialize in the investigative side of the field. Basic requirements include three years of experience (or a college degree, plus one year of experience), 18 months of forensics experience, 40 hours of computer forensics training, and documented experience from at least 10 investigated cases. Advanced requirements entail three years of experience (or a college degree, plus two years of experience), four years of investigations, 80 hours of training and involvement as a lead investigator in 20 cases, with involvement in more than 60 cases overall.

11. Certified Computer Crime Investigator (CCCI)—Basic and Advanced

The Certified Computer Crime Investigator (CCCI) is one of four computer forensic certifications aimed at law enforcement and private IT professionals seeking to specialize in the investigative side of the field. Basic requirements include two years of experience (or a college degree, plus one year of experience), 18 months of investigative experience, 40 hours of computer crimes training and documented experience from at least 10 investigated cases. Advanced requirements entail three years of experience (or a college degree, plus two years of experience), four years of investigations, 80 hours of training and involvement as a lead investigator in 20 cases, with involvement in more than 60 cases overall.

12. EnCase Certified Examiner (EnCE)

The EnCase Certified Examiner (EnCE) program certifies both public- and private-sector professionals in the use of Guidance Software's EnCase computer forensic software. EnCE certification acknowledges that professionals have mastered computer investigation methodology as well as the use of EnCase during complex computer examinations. Recognized by both the law enforcement and corporate communities as a symbol of in-depth computer forensics knowledge, EnCE certification illustrates that an investigator is a skilled computer examiner.

K. Commercial Forensic Labs

A number of commercial forensic labs provide services for digital forensics and digital data recovery. These organizations work for attorneys, investigators, litigation support firms, law enforcement, government agencies, and corporate security/human resources in both civil and criminal proceedings. Costs for these services vary and can become expensive. Digital forensic techniques can be performed on the following:

Blackberries	Intrusion
Cell phones	Networks
Computers	PDAs
E-mails	

Digital data recovery techniques can be performed on the following:

Computers	Flash cards
Cell phones	Passwords
Deleted files	USB drives
iPods	E-mails

These companies provide information collection, extraction, and recovery functions that involve identifying critical information, protecting and preserving the integrity of electronic data during forensic examination from any possible alteration, damage or data corruption. Functions include analyzing information and data, which includes revealing the contents of hidden files as well as temporary swap files. The types of cases worked on in both the commercial and criminal arenas include:

Theft of intellectual property
Employment disputes
Destruction/misappropriation of data
Alteration of data, alteration/misuse of programs
Use of unlicensed software
Illegal duplication of software
Unauthorized access to a computer system
Unauthorized use of a company's computer for private gain
Unofficial access to confidential data
Downloading/distribution of pornographic material
Pedophilia
E-mail misuse
Insurance fraud
Blackmail
Money laundering
Murder
Rape
Terrorism

An important product of these commercial labs is the documentation and reports that can be used in legal proceedings. These organizations produce detailed and understandable reports of the forensics analysis and can also provide expert witness testimony. The lab forensic experts involved in the investigation can testify as to the methodologies used in the forensic investigation. Slide shows and charts can also be developed that explain the forensic evidence. Check the cost in advance of signing any contract for these services.

L. Forensic Lab Tools

The computer forensic lab should be equipped with imaging software, acquisition and seizure tools, hashing software, e-mail tracers, password recovery kits, and latent data recovery tools. A number of identification and recovery tools have been developed by technical computer analysts.

1. Software Tools

The Sleuth Kit — A collection of UNIX-based command line file and volume system forensic analysis tools. The file system tools allow the examiner to examine file systems of a suspect computer in a nonintrusive fashion. Because the tools do not rely on the operating system to process the file systems, deleted and hidden content is shown. It includes a collection of command line tools for the analysis of NTFS, FAT, FFS, and EXT2FS file systems and DOS, BSD, Sun, and Mac partitions. The tools allow for the recovery and analysis of deleted content, hash database lookups, sorting by file type, and timelines of file activity.

Autopsy — A graphical interface to the command line tools in the Sleuth Kit and allows one to view deleted NTFS, FAT, EXTxFS, and FFS files, perform keyword searches, and create timelines of file activity.

Netcat — Is dubbed the network Swiss Army knife. It is a simple UNIX utility that reads and writes data across network connections, using Transmission Control Protocol (TCP) or User Datagram Protocol (UDP). It can be used on a trusted server to save data from a suspect system and can be used on the suspect system to send the output of tools to the server instead of writing to the suspect disk.

dd — A common UNIX tool that copies data from one file to another. It can also be used with netcat to send data to a server over the network.

dcfl-dd — A modified version of the GNU binutils version of 'dd.' It calculates the MD5 hash value of the data while it copies the data.

Memdump — A memory dumper for UNIX-like systems.

Ethereal — Is used by network professionals around the world for troubleshooting, analysis, software and protocol development, and education. It has all of the standard features expected in a protocol analyzer, and several features not seen in any other product. Its open-source license allows talented experts in the networking community to add enhancements. It runs on all popular computing platforms, including UNIX, Linux, and Windows. Numerous open source forensic products are available at opensourceforensics.org/tools/windows.html and opensourceforensics.org/tools/unix.html.

The ILook Investigator Forensic Software — A comprehensive suite of computer forensics tools used to acquire and analyze digital media. ILook Investigator products include ILook v8 forensic application and the IXimager, which are both designed to follow forensics best practices. They meet the computer forensics needs of law enforcement and government. ILook Investigator is provided free of charge only to qualifying persons. Users must meet one of the criteria below:

1. Law enforcement agencies whose employees are sworn law enforcement officers
2. Government, state, or other regulatory agencies with law enforcement missions
3. Military agencies with authority in criminal and counter-intelligence investigations
4. Government intelligence agencies

Mac-Daddy — A Mac time collector for forensic incident response. This toolset is a modified version of the two programs tree.pl and Mactime from the Coroner's Toolkit by Dan Farmer and Venema Weiste. This program is portable and can be run directly from a floppy or a CD-ROM with a Perl interpreter that can also be on the floppy or CD-ROM.

2. CRCMd5 Data Validation Tool

This program mathematically creates a unique signature for the contents of one, multiple, or all files on a given storage device. Such signatures can be used to identify whether the contents of one or more computer files have changed. This forensics tool relies on 128-bit accuracy and can easily be run from a floppy diskette to benchmark the files on a specific storage device, e.g., floppy diskette, hard disk drive and/or Zip disk. CRCMd5 can be used as the first step in the implementation of a configuration management policy. Such a policy and related system benchmarking can help computer specialists isolate problems and deal with computer incidents after they occur. The program is also used to document that computer evidence has not been altered or modified during computer evidence processing.

3.   *Forensic Tool Testing*

The National Institute of Standards and Technology (NIST) has developed a computer forensic tool testing methodology directed at digital data acquisition tools. The latest version of this document can be found at www.cftt.nist.gov. The requirements were developed by individuals who have been trained and are experienced in the use of hardware write blocking tools and have performed investigations using these tools.

The two critical measurable attributes of the digital source acquisition process are accuracy and completeness. **Accuracy** is a qualitative measure to determine if each bit of the acquisition is equal to the corresponding bit of the source. **Completeness** is a quantitative measure to determine if each accessible bit of the source is acquired. The digital source may contain visible and hidden sectors. A clone of a digital source may contain benign fill-in place of source data that could not be acquired. An image file may contain other information in addition to a representation of the source data acquired. An image file may also be encrypted or compressed.

The accuracy and the completeness of an acquisition are influenced by several factors. To access the digital source, the physical device containing the digital source needs to be connected to the computer by a physical interface. Some interfaces have more than one version of the interface with differences that are significant to the acquisition process. The imaging tool must read the device by some protocol.

Another factor that influences the completeness of an acquisition is identifying the true size of the digital source. Hard drives built to the later ATA specifications may allow the creation of inaccessible or hidden areas, such as a host protected area.

The need for these procedures was predicated on the critical need of law enforcement to ensure the reliability of computer forensic tools. Use of computer tools in the evidence-gathering process must stand up in legal proceedings and, therefore, must provide reliable and repeatable results. The Computer Forensic Tool Testing (CFTT) is a joint project of the National Institute of Justice (NIJ) and other federal agencies.

4.   *Hardware Tools*

Imaging products for hard drives can be either hardware or software based, or both. Logicube and Intelligent Computer Solutions (ICS) offer hardware-/software-based solutions. Figure 10.5 depicts a security screwdriver set. Figure 10.6 illustrates forensic toolkits. Figure 10.7 provides a graphic of these portable-imaging devices.

Logicube provides a system for hard drive duplication and computer forensics systems. Their devices are used by IT departments, as well as by law enforcement agencies and the U.S. military. These hard-drive data capturing systems offer high-speed solutions for copying hard drives, drive formatting, data recovery, and disaster recovery. These products offer IDE, SATA and SCSI drive access, USB

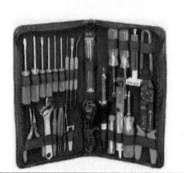

Figure 10.5   Security screwdriver set.

connectivity, and UDMA speeds. Features include software duplication, drive imaging, diagnostics, backup and recovery, file management, or computer forensic solutions.

ICS offers a number of products that perform hard disk duplication. Their primary product is the Image Masster Solo2 System series and a very large complement of interfaces and cables.

5.   Photography

A photo documentation kit is also available at www.evidentcrimescene.com. Evidence can be identified, photographed, sequenced, and oriented using photo evidence markers and scales. The cost of this kit is less than $200.

M.   Computer Forensic Lab Issues and Concerns

There are a number of common elements and items that should be part of a computer forensics lab environment. The following section enumerates issues and concerns that should be addressed when establishing the laboratory.

A major concern of the forensic lab is security and integrity of the facility. Personnel must have controlled access to the keys and/or combination locks to the facility. Access must be restricted to examination rooms and areas that are part of the overall lab facility. Evidence rooms or lockers within the lab must be physically secure with a separate key or combination lock different from those used to get into the main facility. Cleaning staff and others must not have access to the facility unless they are properly escorted or supervised.

Facility walls and ceiling must be constructed in such way that easy access is prevented (e.g., preventing someone from climbing over the wall and dropping through the ceiling). Protective mechanisms must be in place for disastrous events such as fire, flooding, lightning, and other events common to the environment.

Written policies and procedures for lab controls, evidence controls, forensic examinations, and validation of tools and equipment must be in place and available for personnel access. This includes a formal case management system. There are numerous requirements and formal steps that must be followed when conducting forensic examinations and investigations. Cases can be lost because of inattention to detail.

There should be a separate network connection for Internet access. Firewall and security software would be required in the computer systems that access the

Figure 10.6   Forensic toolkits.

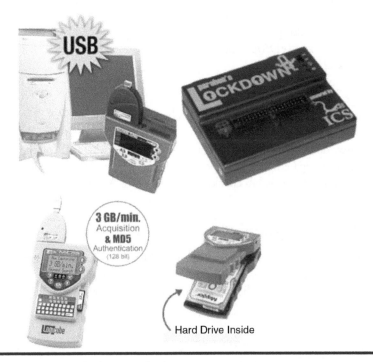

Figure 10.7   Portable forensic devices.

network. The forensic examination computer should be isolated from the network. Having evidence destroyed because of a virus or worm from the Internet would cause a "bad hair day."

There should be a central place to store documents. This could be in the evidence room or locker if it is large enough and fits your storage needs. Someone should be designated document librarian for centralized and consistent control of case data. Extra copies of forms, such as chain-of-custody forms and evidence receipts, should be available for departmental use.

Experience can provide information relative to hardware and storage that is consistent with the environment commonly investigated, including access to special equipment, extra drives, and other needed media. Contingency planning and disaster recovery planning (DRP) must also be considered when operating a laboratory. If something can go wrong, it will, and at the most inopportune moment. A backup facility that can perform similar types of examinations should be identified in the event of some catastrophe. Both the primary lab and the backup lab must ensure availability of hardware and/or software tools for:

> Write protection
> Acquisition
> Data recovery/discovery
> Internet history, images, e-mail
> Password cracking
> Mobile devices (PDA/cell phone)
> Malware/virus detection
> Binary analysis
> Large storage analysis
> Multifunction use (e.g., EnCase, Paraben Tools, FTK, SMART)

Also provided should be any other specialized tools helpful for the environment being investigated. Note the portable flyaway kit contains a subset of these tools. A computer forensic lab checklist is depicted in Appendix A.

1. Portable Flyaway Kit

A portable computer forensic flyaway kit would be an added enhancement to the lab if forensic investigations were to be conducted in the field. This kit would include a limited number of the items required in the laboratory. Items that might be included are as follows:

> Policy and procedure documentation
> Supplies of investigation forms
> Evidence bags and packaging

Manuals for tools utilized
Camera equipment with various lenses
Assorted hand tools
Storage media for capturing data
Hardware and software tools

Hardware and software tools need to provide the following functions:

Write protection
Acquisition
Data recovery/discovery
Internet history, images, e-mail
Password cracking
Mobile devices (PDA/cell phone) analysis
Malware/virus detection
Binary analysis
Large storage analysis
Multifunction use (e.g., EnCase, Paraben Tools, FTK, SMART)

Appendix A provides a sample checklist form identifying the tool complement that should be included in the kit. This kit contains a subset of the tools employed in the forensic lab. Also included should be any other specialized tools helpful for the environments investigated.

2. Lab Work Flow

The flow of forensic evidence examinations and investigations must proceed in a predictable and orderly manner. A number of steps and processes are required for each investigation to ensure the acceptability of the forensic report in legal proceedings. These steps include the following:

Case initiation
Evidence processing
Forensic imaging
Preprocessing analysis
Forensic analysis
Report writing/briefing
Peer review
Case archiving

3.   *Examinations*

Efforts have been made to collect a compendium of forms that are currently in use by a number of agencies in support of forensic investigations and examinations. There are undoubtedly numerous others currently being utilized. Information contained in this section includes items useful in maintaining the chain-of-custody, documenting evidence receipt, and evidence examination. All the forms are included in Appendix A. Descriptions of these forms and checklists for documenting forensic processes follow:

4.   *Chain-of-Custody Checklist*

Maintaining the chain-of-custody is one of the most important activities conducted in the investigation. The chain-of-custody form must be completed accurately for the potential use in legal proceedings. The chain-of-custody checklist is another tool to assist in this process. Tasks to be completed include:

Create unique case and evidence number
Document some asset tag or serial number that uniquely identifies the evidence
Document the make and model of system where the data was retrieved
Document basic input/output system (BIOS) time
Document location the evidence was found in (inside case, inside drawer of desk, inside briefcase)
Document physical description of evidence
Annotate notes for any accesses to the evidence before arriving
Annotate notes for any step that occurs outside of the normal process
Fill in history annotating when evidence was received and from whom
Update chain-of-custody for each action taken with the original evidence

5.   *Evidence Receipt*

An important document in the chain-of-custody process is the forensic evidence receipt form. This form must be completed for each case and filed where it can be retrieved later for case support. Items that can be inventoried include computers, storage media, and other materials relative to a particular case. Essential items that must be recorded include information concerning the receiving forensic lab agent and the provider of the latent evidence. Device serial numbers, if there are any present, must be recorded. Care must be made to ensure all information entered on this form is accurate.

6. Hard Drive Examination

One of the major activities in investigations involving computers is the imaging of the hard drive. It is essential that this task be performed according to acceptable rules. A number of hardware and software forensic tools are available to accomplish this task. The process must be documented in detail. Items of information concerning the hard drive that need to be identified and documented are as follows:

Make and model
Serial number
Capacity and size
Cylinders and heads
Sectors
Jumper settings
Volume label
Number of partitions and names

Imaging process information must also be identified. If multiple versions and techniques are employed, they must be identified. This includes the software versions for each image, the type of write-blocker used, and the hash results for each image. Information must be available as to the storage location of the image disks.

7. Imaging Checklist

When performing the imaging operation on a hard drive, it is essential that all steps be successfully completed. Steps required are as follows:

Computer is powered off
Drive is removed and serial number recorded
System is booted with drive removed and BIOS time recorded
Chain-of-custody form filled out
Drive is imaged with forensically sound method
Chain-of-custody updated
Drive either given back or taken with evidence receipt

8. Windows Examination Checklist

There are a number of steps to be employed when examining a computer with the windows operating system. Some of these steps also apply to all brands of computer devices, whether laptops or desktops. A sample checklist form is available in Appendix A. Those steps that apply include the following:

Document the Windows version
Document the last boot time and last shutdown time
Identify and resolve the delta of "local" versus "real" date and time
Search the drive for remnants of file system partitions
Recover and examine log files
Search the drive for mail spools and Internet mail
Recover INFO2 records and Internet history records
Carve documents from unallocated areas
Check the drive for wiping
Recover deleted files and printer spools
Recover XP-UserAssist records
Conduct keyword searches as appropriate
Decompress and examine archives

9. *Linux Examination Checklist*

Most of the steps for examining a Linux system are the same as those for the Windows system. A sample checklist is found in Appendix A. Steps that apply to the Linux system follows:

Document Linux distribution and version
Document the last boot time and last shutdown time
Identify and resolve the delta of "local" versus "real" date and time
Search the hard drive for remnants of file system partitions
Check user shell history files
Recover and examine log files
Search the drive for mail spools and Internet mail
Recover Internet history
Recover documents from unallocated areas
Check the drive for wiping
Recover deleted files
Recover printer spools
Conduct keyword searches as appropriate
Decompress and examine archives
Examine swap space

10. *Macintosh Examination Checklist*

Most of the steps employed examining the Mac are the same as those for the Windows machine. A sample checklist form is found in Appendix A. Steps that apply to the Mac follow:

Document the operating system version
Document the last boot time and last shutdown time
Identify and resolve the delta of "local" versus "real" date and time
Search the partition waste space for file system artifacts
Recover and examine log files
Search the drive for mail spools and Internet mail
Examine large files and image files
Recover Internet history
Carve documents from unallocated areas
Check the drive for wiping
Recover deleted files
Preprocess cache files and mbox files
Conduct keyword searches as appropriate
Decompress and examine archives

N.   Auditing the Forensic Lab

An audit function is required to ensure the forensic lab maintains a level of certification consistent with the court's requirements. Routine inspections should be conducted relating to the various policies and procedures of the lab. The audit should also include the following activities:

Check working order of locks and entry devices
Review visitor logs and evidence storage logs
Inspect doors to ensure they close properly
Check the facility perimeter
Look at the general cleanliness and order of the lab

Chapter Summary

A decision to develop a computer forensics laboratory can be a time-consuming and expensive endeavor. Decisions must be made concerning internal staffing, procedures, tools, and capabilities that must hold up in a court situation. The primary function of the lab concerns preserving, recovering, and analyzing information stored within some type of digital medium.

Staffing is a critical component when developing and operating a forensic lab. Technical training and evidence management will be an ongoing issue and process. Certifications will be required for the examiners, so that their testimony will hold up in legal proceedings.

Computer forensics requires methods to ensure the integrity of the data and information contained within those physical items. Computer forensic examiners must utilize methods and techniques that provide valid, repeatable, reproducible, and reliable results while protecting the real evidence from destruction or modification. The forensic analysis of a computer or electronic system revolves around a cycle of data gathering and processing of the materials and evidence gathered. The more accurate and complete the effort, the probability of success increases and the quality of the result improves.

A major function of the forensic lab consists of documentation and reporting. These are major activities that must be performed according to the rules of evidence, as these documents and reports will probably be the basis of some litigation. A number of forms and checklists have been developed to assist in these processes. There are so many steps required in these forensic examinations and investigations; it is very easy to overlook something important.

A major concern of the forensic lab is security and integrity of the facility. Personnel must have controlled access to the keys and/or combination locks to the facility. Access must be restricted to examination rooms and areas that are part of the overall lab facility. Cleaning staff and others must not have access to the facility unless they are properly escorted or supervised. It is essential that evidence not be contaminated.

Terms

Accuracy — A qualitative measure to determine if each bit of the acquisition is equal to the corresponding bit of the source.

Buffer — Memory allocated for temporary storage.

Completeness — A quantitative measure to determine if each accessible bit of the source is acquired.

Cookies — Files that browsers use to track a user's Internet activity.

Defrag — A process (run by a defragging program) whereby parts of data files on all segments of a computer hard disk are taken from their fragmented state (with parts of files spread all over the disk), and grouped together in complete-file segments. This makes it quicker for applications to find the files they need and frees up disk space, making the computer run more efficiently.

Electrostatic discharge — The sudden and momentary electric current that flows when an excess of electric charge finds a path to an object at a different electrical potential (ground).

File slack — The slack space created when a file is saved.

Forensic analysis — Revolves around a cycle of data gathering and processing of the materials and evidence gathered. Used in courts of law or public debate or argument.

FRED — The acronym for forensic recovery of evidence device.

Free space — Space on a disk drive that is not reserved for saved files.

Hash codes — Format in which data is stored in compressed form.

IDE — A hard drive interface system developed by a group of manufacturers whereby the controller system was integrated into the electronics for the rest of the drive; all of the components were within the hard drive unit removing the need to have a separate controller.

Keyword — A word or phrase used when searching for a Web site in the search engines or directories.

Metadata — Information about a particular data set that may describe, for example, how, when, and by whom it was received, created, accessed, and/or modified, and how it is formatted.

NISPOM (National Industrial Security Program Operating Manual) — The manual prescribes requirements, restrictions, and other safeguards that are necessary to prevent unauthorized disclosure of classified information and to control authorized disclosure of classified information released by U.S. government executive branch departments and agencies to their contractors.

SATA (Serial Advanced Technology Attachment) — An interface for connecting hard drives to a computer. Unlike IDE, which uses parallel signaling, SATA uses serial signaling technology. Because of this the SATA cables are thinner than the ribbon cables used by IDE hard drives. SATA cables can also be longer allowing connection to more distant devices without fear of signal interference. There is also more room to grow with data transfer speeds starting at 150 megabytes per second.

Slack space — Consists of space on a disk drive between the end of a file and the allocated space for a file.

Sleuth Kit — Previously called TASK, is a collection of UNIX-based command line file system and media management forensic analysis tools.

Tempest — U.S. government code word for a set of standards for limiting electric or electromagnetic radiation emanations from electronic equipment, such as microchips, monitors, or printers.

Unallocated space — The area of the disk drive where the deleted file resides.

Review Questions

1. A set of standards for limiting electric or electromagnetic radiation emanations from electronic equipment is called _____.
2. _____ revolves around a cycle of data gathering and processing of the materials and evidence gathered. Used in courts of law or public debate or argument.
3. _____ is an interface using serial signaling technology for connecting hard drives to a computer.
4. The sudden and momentary electric current that flows when an excess of electric charge finds a path to an object at a different electrical potential is called _____.

5. FRED is the acronym for _____ _____ _____
   _____.
6. Identify the steps of a forensic lab work flow.
7. Identify the items of information that must be obtained from a hard drive.
8. Identify software and hardware tools that must be part of a computer forensic lab.
9. Provide a list of items that would appear on a hard-drive examination checklist.
10. What items of information should appear on the chain-of-custody checklist?

Chapter 11

Extracting Computer and Electronic Evidence

Chapter Objectives

- Learn the functions that occur in a computer forensics lab
- Understand the techniques required to image a hard drive
- Identify a process for deciding what evidence to collect
- Look at the steps required to successfully process latent electronic evidence
- Understand the importance of the chain-of-custody and documentation

Introduction

The function of a computer forensics lab is to provide technical support in the detection, preservation, recovery, examination, and reporting of electronic and computer-related latent evidence.

Examination of a computer must be done thoroughly, carefully, and without changing anything on the computer. Procedures and techniques must be in place to preview the content of computer hard drives without risk of changing the data, capture an exact copy of the data held on computer hard drives and other media, and automatically produce a printable audit trail to identify the actions taken. At the preview stage, simple checks may be performed to determine the current status of the data files. This may provide useful information about ownership of the data and/or relevance to a particular investigation.

Capturing an exact copy of the data involves a process known as imaging. Here all the data is copied to create an image that includes data that is not normally visible. Often it is this hidden data that contains vital evidence to prove or disprove a case. The taking of an image is a vital step in a computer forensic investigation. It is accepted as the best method for capturing computer evidence that may be presented in a court of law.

Having captured the data from the suspect machine in a fashion that enables any information found to be used as evidence, the next step is to process the image. Data recovery and conversion expertise allow for virtually all file systems to be processed. An image can be processed in a variety of ways to suit the needs of the case and the customer.

Computer investigators can utilize highly sophisticated tools, many of which are not available for general release. These tools will quickly identify the required information in mere seconds. Word searching and text recognition technology, combined with the experience of an investigator, can provide quick access to evidence. With the right tools, an entire computer network can be searched for specific words or characters.

A. Forensic Laboratory Functions

Computer forensic consultant organizations and law enforcement organizations are usually the major players when it comes to operating an electronic evidence laboratory. Considerable resources and cost are associated with the operation and maintenance of these labs. The primary function of a computer forensics lab is to provide technical support in the detection, preservation, recovery, and examination of computer-related latent evidence. This is followed up with a report of findings that will be acceptable in the legal environment. As a note, it should be understood that all examiners must be trained and possess certifications in their areas of expertise.

Examiners will be utilizing nonevidentiary hardware and software to conduct forensic imaging or analysis of electronic and computer evidence. Equipment preparation and maintenance is an important lab operating procedure and equipment must be monitored and documented to ensure proper performance is maintained. It is essential that only suitable and properly operating equipment be employed in the forensic processes. Analysis and imaging software must be validated according to some industry standard. This validation process is essential to evidence being admissible in legal proceedings.

Documentation for each tool used is an important consideration. Manufacturing operation manuals is a must, as are software manuals. Standard operating procedures for the various examinations conducted in the lab are also required.

The main functions that occur in the lab will consist of forensic imaging, forensic analysis, forensic examination, and report generation. The first phases of the examination are evidence collection and documentation of the process and results.

B.   IACIS Guide for Forensic Examinations

The International Association of Computer Investigative Specialists (IACIS) has established a guide for forensic computer and digital evidence examinations. The IACIS is one of the oldest professional computing-forensic organizations.

Computer and digital media examinations are different and depend on the specific circumstances of the investigation. This means not all elements mentioned here are needed in every situation, and examiners may need to adjust to unusual or unexpected conditions in the field. Cases involving computers and other electronic devices cross multiple disciplines. Multiple jurisdictions and agencies may be involved in investigative and analytical activities, and each agency or jurisdiction may employ specific procedures. These jurisdictions may include organizations in the United States and foreign countries, as many investigations can involve Internet crimes and incidents. This document is not intended to supersede or conflict with jurisdictional or agency policies or procedures. Rather, it is a foundation document that outlines general principles.

Computer system components, other electronic devices, and digital and electronic media are items of evidence just like any other items of evidence. As such it is incumbent upon the examiner to follow agency procedures for documenting the receipt and handling of the items. The computer system and/or the media should be examined physically and an inventory of hardware components noted. Documentation should include a physical description and detailed notation of any irregularities, peculiarities, identifying markings, and numberings.

When examining a computer, the system, date, and time should be collected, preferably from the basic input/output system (BIOS) setup. The date and time should be compared to a reliable known time source, such as Greenwich Mean Time (GMT) or Universal Time Coordinated (UTC), and any differences noted. If the BIOS setup information is accessible, then drive parameters and boot order should be noted. Depending on the BIOS, other information such as system serial numbers, component serial numbers, hardware component hashes, etc. should be noted.

Examination of media should be conducted in a forensically sound examination environment. A forensically sound examination environment is one that is completely under the control of the examiner. No actions are taken without the examiner permitting them to happen; and when the examiner permits or causes an action, there is a reasonable certainty of the outcome. Examiners may choose to employ a forensically sound operating system. The use of physical write-blocking devices or software write-blocking devices may be used in operating system environments that are not forensically sound.

Conducting an examination on the original evidence media should be avoided. Rather, examinations should be conducted on a forensic copy of the original evidence, or via forensic evidence files. Properly prepared media should be used when making forensic copies to ensure no commingling of data from different cases. Properly prepared media consists of media that has been completely overwritten.

Regardless of whether the examiner performs a direct device-to-device copy of the media or creates forensic evidence copies for examination or restoration, the copy process should be forensically sound. Examination of the media should be completed logically and systematically by starting the search where the data of evidentiary value is most likely located. These locations will vary depending on the nature and scope of the case. Examples of items to be noted might include:

- The number and type of partitions for hard drives.
- The number of sessions for optical disks.
- File systems on the media.
- A full directory listing should be made that includes folder structure, filenames, date/time stamps, logical file sizes, etc.
- Installed operating systems.
- User-created files should be examined using native applications, file viewers, or hex viewers. This includes such files as text documents, spreadsheets, databases, financial data, electronic mail, digital photographs, sound and other multimedia files, etc.
- Operating system files and application created files should be examined, if present. This would include, but is not limited to boot files, registry files, swap files, temporary files, cache files, history files, and log files.
- Installed applications.
- File hash comparisons may be used to exclude or include files for examination.
- Unused and unallocated space on each volume should be examined for previously deleted data, deleted folders, slack space data, and intentionally placed data.
- Previously deleted filenames of apparent evidentiary value should be noted. Files may be automatically carved out of the unallocated portion of the unused space based upon known file headers.
- Keyword searches may be conducted to identify files or areas of the drive that might contain data of evidentiary value and to narrow the examination scope.
- The system area of the volume (i.e., FAT, MFT, etc.) should be examined and any irregularities or peculiarities noted.
- Examination of areas of the media that are not normally accessible, such as extra tracks or sectors on a floppy disk or a host-protected area on a hard drive, may be required.

To facilitate examination of data, user settings, device and software functionality, etc. the computer may be booted by using either a copy of the boot drive or a protected device on the original device to determine functionality of the hardware and/or software.

The forensic software used during the examination should be noted by its version and should be used in accordance with the vendor's licensing agreement. The software should also be properly tested and validated for its forensic use by the examiner or the examiner's agency.

At the conclusion of the examination process, sufficient notation of any discovered material of an apparent incriminating or exculpatory evidentiary nature should be made.

Sufficient documentation should be made of all standard procedures and processes initiated as well as detailed notation of any variations made to the standard procedures.

Any output of the recovered data should be properly marked with appropriate identifiers in accordance with policies from the examiner's agency.

C.   Managing the Imaging Process

The chain-of-custody must be maintained on devices received at the lab for examination. Receipts must also be completed for any device received and evidence logs maintained. A sample evidence receipt form is depicted in Appendix A. Precautions must be taken to prevent the exposure of evidence to damage or contamination. All items submitted for forensic examination should be examined for the integrity of the packaging. Any deficiency in the packaging may compromise the value of the examination and must be documented. The lab may refuse the items if damage is apparent. Any exceptions between the inventory documentation and the actual evidence must be documented.

Methods of acquiring evidence, as noted in the IACIS procedures, should be forensically sound and verifiable. The first step in the imaging process is to document the current condition of the evidence. The remaining steps would be conducted based on the standard procedures. Basically these include the following:

- Hardware or software write-blockers would be used to prevent modification of evidence.
- Forensic images would be captured using hardware and software that is capable of capturing a bit-stream image of the original media.
- Properly prepared media should be used when making forensic copies to ensure no commingling of data from different cases.
- Forensic images should be archived to media and maintained consistent with departmental policy and applicable laws.

Upon completion of the imaging process, the next step involves forensic examination and analysis.

D.   Evidence Collection and Archiving

The examiner should review the documentation that accompanies the evidence to determine the processes necessary to complete the examination and also ascertain legal authority to perform the request. Evidence management must be handled according to acceptable practices to stand up in a court of law. **RFC3227**, a document that provides guidelines for evidence collecting and archiving, provides "best practices" for accomplishing the evidence collection phase of an investigation. Basic guiding principles during evidence collection include the following:

- ■ Capture as accurate a picture of the system as possible.
- ■ Keep detailed notes. These should include dates and times. If possible, generate an automatic transcript. (On UNIX systems, the script program can be used; however, the output file it generates should not be appended to media that is part of the evidence.) Notes and printouts should be signed and dated.
- ■ Note the difference between the system clock and the UTC. For each timestamp provided, indicate whether UTC or local time is used.
- ■ Be prepared to testify (perhaps years later) outlining all actions taken and at what times. Detailed notes will be vital.
- ■ Minimize changes to user and system data as it is being captured. This is not limited to content changes; the examiner should avoid updating file or directory access times.
- ■ Remove external avenues for change.
- ■ When confronted with a choice between collection and analysis, conduct collection activities first and analyze later.
- ■ Proceed from the volatile to the less volatile.
- ■ Be methodical.

Procedures should be feasible, repeatable and reproducible. If possible, procedures should be automated for reasons of speed and accuracy. For each device, a methodical approach should be adopted that follows the guidelines laid down in the collection procedure. Additional types of examinations might need to be conducted on the same device. A decision might need to be made concerning the best choice of target data of evidentiary value. Speed will often be critical, so where there are a number of devices requiring examination it may be appropriate to spread the work among the forensic team to collect the evidence in parallel. However, on a single given system, collection should be done step by step.

Make two bit-level copies of the system's media. Forensics analysis would be conducted on the second bit-level copy of the evidence, as the analysis will almost certainly alter file access times. Avoid conducting forensic examinations on the primary evidence copy.

1. Order of Volatility

When collecting evidence, proceed from the volatile to the less volatile. Work on evidence first that can be easily destroyed. An example order of volatility for a typical system consists of the following:

Registers and cache
Routing table, Address Resolution Protocol (ARP) cache, process table, kernel statistics, memory
Temporary file systems
Disk
Remote logging and monitoring data that is relevant to the system in question
Physical configuration and network topology
Archival media

2. Things to Avoid

It is all too easy to destroy evidence, however inadvertently. Do not shut down the device until the evidence collection process is completed. Do not start the examination if there is not enough time to complete it. Much evidence may be lost and the attacker may have altered the start-up/shutdown scripts/services to destroy evidence. Experienced examiners have stated that some examinations have taken 12 continuous hours to complete. Several "don'ts" include the following:

- Do not trust the programs on the system. Run evidence-gathering programs from appropriately protected media.
- Do not run programs that modify the access time of all files on the system (e.g., "tar" or 'xcopy').
- When removing external avenues for change, note that simply disconnecting or filtering from the network may trigger "deadman switches" that detect when they are off the net and wipe evidence.
- Do not overlook the possibility of changes introduced via a wireless access.

Decision-making should be minimized during the collection process. This means that specific steps should be followed for each examination. This will become important if the evidence is presented in a court of law. Deviations in examination techniques can raise a "red flag" with opposing lawyers and juries.

3.   Privacy Considerations

Examiners must respect the privacy rules and guidelines of the organization and legal jurisdiction. In particular, make sure no information collected along with the evidence searched is available to anyone who would not normally have access to this information. This includes access to log files (which may reveal patterns of user behavior) as well as personal data files. Make sure examiners have the backing of the organization's established procedures in taking the steps to collect evidence from an incident.

Do not intrude on people's privacy without strong justification. In particular, do not collect information from areas where normally there is no reason to access (such as personal data files) unless there is sufficient indication of a real incident. The examiner must understand the implications of the various privacy laws. These were presented in Chapter 2.

4.   Legal Considerations

Computer evidence needs to be admissible, authentic, complete, reliable, and believable. It must conform to certain legal rules before it can be put before a court. It must be possible to positively tie evidentiary material to the incident. It must tell the whole story and not just a particular perspective. There must be nothing about how the evidence was collected and subsequently handled that casts doubt about its authenticity and veracity. It must be readily believable and understandable by a court. This issue raises the responsibility to conduct forensic examinations using strict procedures. Techniques and procedures must be objective. Examiners cannot work toward some expected outcome.

The methods used to collect evidence should be transparent and reproducible. Examiners should be prepared to reproduce precisely the methods used, and have those methods tested by independent experts. As previously stated, document all steps and processes used to identify and extract the evidence. The process of forensic testimony presentations in a court of law is discussed in Chapter 14.

E.   Residual Data

Proprietary information can be recovered from residual data that remains on hard drives. **Residual data** (or ambient data) refers to data that is not active on a computer system. Residual data includes data found on media free space; data found in file slack space; and data within files that have functionally been deleted. Delete, Format, and Fdisk commands do not remove data from a hard drive. During operation, operating systems and applications create files in the background that include the following:

Automatic backup files
Globally unique identifiers
Internet browser files
Internet history files
Metadata
Power saver features
Temporary files
Temporary Internet files
Spooler files
Virtual memory and swap files

These are the areas where the forensic examiner might find the best evidence.

F.   Examining the Digital Images

Examination of a computer must be done thoroughly, carefully, and without changing anything on the computer. Procedure and techniques must be in place to preview the content of computer hard drives without risk of changing the data, capture an exact copy of the data held on computer hard drives and other media, and automatically produce a printable audit trail to identify the actions taken. At the preview stage, simple checks may be performed to determine current status of the data files. This may provide useful information about ownership of the data and/or relevance to a particular investigation.

Capturing an exact copy of the data involves a process known as imaging. Here all the data is copied to create an image that includes data that is not normally accessible such as:

Data that may have been deleted
Information hidden outside the normal storage areas
Old data that has been partially overwritten

Often it is this hidden data that contains vital evidence to prove or disprove a case.

The image is an exact replica of the suspect computer hard drive or other media. It can be investigated instead of the original computer. Investigators can explore all areas of data to look for evidence or clues without changing or compromising the original data. The examiner can view the last accessed Internet site, read saved e-mail files, or navigate around the image as though it were part of the original computer. The taking of an image is a vital step in a computer forensic investigation. It is accepted as the best method for capturing computer evidence that may be presented in a court of law.

Having captured the data from the suspect machine in a fashion that enables any information found to be used as evidence, the next step is to process the image. Data recovery and data conversion expertise allows for virtually all file systems to be processed. An image can be processed in a variety of ways to suit the needs of the case and the customer. In some instances a file extraction may be appropriate, in others a data index may be created for search tools to be run against.

Looking for one or two words or an account number across gigabytes of data is a bit like looking for a needle in a haystack. Computer investigators can utilize highly sophisticated tools, many of which are not available for general release. These tools will quickly identify the required information in mere seconds. Word searching and text recognition technology, combined with the experience of an investigator, is used to locate evidence. With the right tools, an entire computer network can be searched for specific words or characters. This search will reveal every occurrence of these words or characters, even if the data was deleted to cover the criminal's tracks. Some forensic tools allow for keyword or pattern matching during the disk imaging process. A technique employed is called carving. **Carving** is the process of removing an item from a group of items.

G. Qualifying a Computer for Forensic Recovery

In practically every computer there is "deleted" data that can be recovered; however, the data recovered is not always relevant to the case. Typically, it is a judgment call which computers should be investigated when there is more than one computer involved. It helps to establish an order of priority for the computers to be recovered. Using this method, vital data would be revealed first, which would eliminate wasting resources on less credible computers. It is possible to predict and prioritize the best computers for recovery based on a series of questions, such as:

Q: Did any person involved use the computer? Note that this could include receiving e-mail or files from the party involved.

When a file or e-mail is deleted, it is not immediately removed from the hard drive. It still exists even though it cannot be easily accessed. There is a section of the hard drive that is similar to an index and when a file is deleted it is just removed from this index. The originally deleted file or e-mail is left as dead space on the hard drive. Since the file exists on the hard drive, special tools that bypass the index can search for files and potentially recover them. A file can be divided into several pieces and exist in various locations on a hard drive. Because of this, it is possible that only part of a file might be recovered. A vital component to a case might exist in one of those small pieces.

If the deleted item was an e-mail, a different set of rules apply. An e-mail, by its nature, exists in more than one place. There is always a "From:" (the sender);

a "To:" (the recipient); and at least one server (the machines that processed the e-mail). If there were "CC:" (carbon copy) or "BCC:" (blind carbon copy) addresses, then more copies exist. An e-mail has a greater potential to be recovered because an e-mail is stored in a file similar to a database. Consequently, when an e-mail is deleted, it is removed from the "Table of Contents" of the database and not the hard drive itself. It is possible for the e-mail to persist in a file or server for quite a long time after the e-mail is "deleted" by a user. This includes Outlook Express, Outlook 2002, AOL, Exchange Server and several other types of e-mail programs.

If e-mail is read via a Web browser (i.e., Hotmail) a copy of the e-mail will usually exist in the Internet cache or temporary files on the hard drive of the computer it was viewed from. There is an even greater probability that the e-mail might be recovered.

Q: How long has it been since files were deleted?

Because of the way files are left behind as dead space on the hard drive, as space is needed by different programs or Web pages, the file pieces are gradually over-written. The longer the time that has transpired since the files were deleted, the less probability that something can be recovered, although in some past instances data has been recovered dating back several years. If there had been limited writing of data to the disk, the possibility is greater that entire files can be recovered.

Q: How much has the computer been used since files were deleted?

Because files are overwritten gradually, the more the computer is used, the more likely new files have overwritten older files erasing your valuable information. A computer writes files every time a program is used (including Internet accesses). The Windows operating system will overwrite certain files every time the system is powered on. These standard files are not very large, but they account for a significant percentage of the destruction that occurs to recoverable files. This is an excellent reason to stop using a computer as soon as it is learned that it is involved in a case until a computer forensic specialist can examine it. If this computer is necessary for operations of the business, the specialist can safely and effectively "clone" or image the hard drive to preserve the information.

If there is someone who can answer these questions, there is a good chance of determining the usefulness of the computer in a case. This is not intended to be a final list of questions, but is a common set to help determine the possibility that something useful might exist. In some cases the client might not be able to answer any of these questions and it is also often that the answers given are incorrect.

Even when there is no one to answer questions, there is still a good possibility of recovering valuable evidence from the right computer, even when the files never existed on the computer.

Often a case will involve someone who believes they are a computer "guru." They consciously attempt to delete incriminating evidence, believing they know what they are doing. Their egos make them believe that they know how to delete a file, that it is permanently unrecoverable, and that they are safe. Many times they are mistaken.

H.   Forensic Tools

Tools should include programs needed to perform evidence collection and forensics on read-only media (e.g., a CD). A set of tools should be available for each of the operating systems being examined. The set of software tools should include the following features:

> Examine processes
> Examine system state
> Make bit-to-bit copies
> Generate checksums and signatures
> Generate core images and examine them
> Create scripts to automate evidence collection

The **Coroner's Toolkit** (TCT) is a suite of computer security programs by Dan Farmer and Wietse Venema. It is intended to assist in a forensic analysis of a UNIX system after a break-in. Parts of the TCT are also somewhat applicable to analysis of and data recovery from other computer disasters.

The programs in the set of tools should not require the use of any libraries other than those on the read-only media. Even then, since modern rootkits may be installed through loadable kernel modules, examiners must consider that the tools being utilized might not be providing a full picture of the system. Examiners must be prepared to testify to the authenticity and reliability of the tools being used. Forensic tools must not be compromised or even give the appearance of being compromised.

The **Ultimate Toolkit** available from AccessData includes the following modules:

> Forensic Toolkit (FTK)—Find, organize, and analyze computer evidence
> Password Recovery Toolkit (PRTK)—Recover lost or forgotten passwords
> Registry Viewer—Analyze and decrypt registry data
> FTK Imager—Capture the image, preserve the evidence

The Forensic Toolkit offers law enforcement and corporate security professionals the ability to perform complete and thorough computer forensic examinations.

EnCase Forensic, available from Guidance Software, provides investigators in law enforcement, government, small businesses, consulting firms, and corporations with the tools to authenticate, search, and recover computer evidence. EnCase Forensic software allows investigators to easily manage large volumes of computer evidence, viewing all relevant files, including deleted files, file slack, and unallocated space. Support includes acquisition solutions in Windows, DOS and Linux.

The **iLook Investigator** forensic software is a comprehensive suite of computer forensics tools used to acquire and analyze digital media. iLook Investigator products include iLook v8 forensic application and the IXimager, which are both designed to follow forensics' best practices. They meet the computer forensics needs of law enforcement and government. iLook Investigator forensic software will continue to be provided at no cost for qualifying users. The iLook Investigator forensic software is not granted to commercial and/or private companies.

The **Sleuth Kit** (previously known as TASK) is a collection of UNIX-based command line file and volume system forensic analysis tools. The file system tools allow the user to examine file systems of a suspect computer in a nonintrusive fashion. Because the tools do not rely on the operating system to process the file systems, deleted and hidden content is shown.

The volume system (media management) tools allow the user to examine the layout of disks and other media. The Sleuth Kit supports DOS partitions, BSD partitions (disk labels), Mac partitions, Sun slices (Volume Table of Contents), and GPT disks. With these tools, users can identify where partitions are located and extract them so that they can be analyzed with file system analysis tools.

When performing a complete analysis of a system, examiners know that command line tools can become tedious. The Autopsy Forensic Browser is a graphical interface to the tools in The Sleuth Kit, which allows users to more easily conduct an investigation. Autopsy provides case management, image integrity, keyword searching, and other automated operations.

The **Autopsy Forensic Browser** is a graphical interface to the command line digital investigation analysis tools in the Sleuth Kit. Together, they can analyze Windows and UNIX disks and file systems (NTFS, FAT, UFS1/2, Ext2/3).

The Sleuth Kit and Autopsy are both open source and run on UNIX platforms. As Autopsy is HTML-based, users can connect to the Autopsy server from any platform using an HTML browser. Autopsy provides a "File Manager"-like interface and shows details about deleted data and file system structures.

Foremost is a console program to recover files based on their headers, footers, and internal data structures. This process is commonly referred to as data carving. Foremost works on image files, such as those generated by dd, Safeback, Encase, etc., or can work directly on a drive. The headers and footers can be specified by a configuration file or may use command line switches to specify built-in file types. These built-in types look at the data structures of a given file format allowing for a more reliable and faster recovery.

Originally developed by the United States Air Force Office of Special Investigations and The Center for Information Systems Security Studies and Research, Foremost has been opened to the general public.

dcfldd is an enhanced version of GNU dd. It has some useful features for forensic investigators:

On-the-fly hashing of the transmitted data
Progress bar of how much data has already been sent
Wiping of disks with known patterns
Verification that the image is identical to the original drive, bit-for-bit
Simultaneous output to more than one file/disk is possible
The output can be split into multiple files
Logs and data can be piped into external applications

GNU (is Not Unix) is a set of programs written by the Free Software Foundation to provide a free UNIX framework. GNU is a large component of a Linux distribution.

SafeBack is used to create mirror-image (bit-stream) backup files of hard disks or to make a mirror-image copy of an entire hard disk drive or partition. SafeBack image files can detect attempts to alter the reproduction. SafeBack is a DOS-based industry standard self-authenticating computer forensics tool that is used to create evidence grade backups of hard drives. SafeBack does not write or otherwise modify the original system and can (and should) be started from a boot diskette.

The **MacQuisition Boot CD** is a forensic acquisition tool used to safely and easily image Mac suspect drives using the suspect's own system. MacQuisition provides an intuitive user interface to traditional command line, providing both beginner and advanced forensic examiners with a valuable tool to:

Easily identify the suspect device
Configure destination location
Image directly over the network
Use the command line (recommended for advanced users only)
Log case, exhibit and evidence tracking numbers and notes
Automatically generate MD5 hashes
Search extensions
Easily identify source and destination drives

I.   Disk Drive Examinations

Two techniques for disk drive examinations include the use of a hardware forensic imaging tool or a software forensic product. Various products have been identified in previous sections that provide descriptions and capabilities of these solutions. Some forensic labs might elect to use both techniques to verify the integrity and accuracy of the forensic evidence gathering process. The two techniques employed in this lab setting included the Logicube Forensic MD5 and AccessData Forensic Toolkit. Other vendors have products that provide similar capabilities. Some of these vendors provide online access to demonstration systems. Ensure a write-blocker is used in these imaging processes to avoid damaging or destroying evidence.

The primary function of the hardware solution is to produce a drive-to-drive image that is forensically sound. A suspect hard drive is copied bit-by-bit to a target drive that will be used later in a forensic investigation. The handling of the suspect drive is held to a minimum with zero alteration of its contents. A hash (MD5) is created to verify the integrity of the imaging process. Figure 11.1 shows several hardware tools involved in the imaging process. Hard drives can be imaged using an IDE-to-IDE cable or a USB-to-IDE cable.

1.   IDE-to-IDE Imaging

Bit-bit imaging is simple using the hardware device with an integrated drive electronics (IDE) and power cables. The first step is the most difficult as the case to the computer must be opened to reveal the internal hard drive. Be sure to wear the grounding strap to avoid static discharges that could alter or destroy the data on the disk drive. The remaining steps are straightforward:

■ After opening the case, the IDE cable and disk drive power cable must be disconnected from the internal hard disk.
■ Insert a blank hard drive into the imaging device. Connect to the IDE cable in the imaging device. This receiving hard drive must be completely erased and must have a capacity as a minimum of the drive being imaged. The system being tested provided this function as part of the imaging process. *Never place a hard disk into the imaging device that contains evidence.*
■ Connect the IDE cable from the imaging device to the internal hard drive.
■ Connect the power cable from the imaging device to the internal hard drive.
■ Connect the power cable from the imaging device to some acceptable power source. To be safe, this source should be filtered by a surge protector.

This completes the steps for the physical connectivity for an IDE image. The device being tested also provided interfaces for laptop drives, compact flash drives,

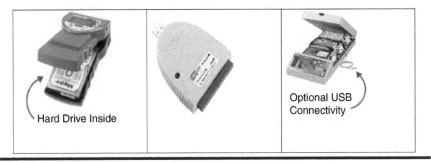

Figure 11.1   Hard drive IDE imager and USB imager tools.

and serial ATA drives. Examiners should review the particular lab requirements to ensure that all interfaces required can be imaged with the equipment selected. This unidirectional, forensically sound, cloning tool is known for its duplication accuracy and legal reliability.

The next step is to perform the actual imaging process. The image data capture is compatible, and may be analyzed with FTK, Encase, or iLook. There were numerous options available on the device tested, which allowed pattern-matching during the imaging process. Each imaging product will provide different levels of options that can take place during the imaging process.

2.   Software Acquisition

Software acquisition tools create a forensically sound image that makes no changes to the data and information on the suspect hard drive. The forensic image must be identical in every way to the original, including file slack and unallocated space. Software products allow for additional capabilities that hardware products often do not support. Such capabilities could include case management and sophisticated data searches. The software solutions also provide for a number of forensic reports that can be used in legal proceedings.

Forensic software products can examine hard drive images created by the bit-bit imaging process described in the previous section. The hardware bit-bit image allows the examiner to create a forensically sound image to be explored later in detail by forensic software in the lab. Figure 11.2 contains a screen shot of the AccessData FTK main screen. The file and memory contents selected could be displayed in text or hex mode.

J.   Review and Quality Assurance

The forensic lab should have a written policy establishing the protocols for technical, peer, and administrative review. Written policies should also exist if a re-examination is required because of a challenge. This challenge could originate from within the lab or from external sources. A statement should be provided that relates to the specific quality assurances of the forensic lab resources and personnel. Competency requirements are required for all roles in the forensic lab. These include qualifications, training, and maintenance of competence. Forensic lab personnel must possess those attributes that ensure a successful examination of evidence and completion of a formal report acceptable in a court of law. A number of observations are made concerning staffing:

■ An individual must have overall authority and responsibility for the management and quality of the work accomplished in the lab.

- Examiners must be responsible in a particular case for identifying, retrieving, interpreting, and reporting findings.
- Examiners must have achieved levels of competency for specific equipment and services. They must be able to write reports of factual information in their specific specialist areas and provide factual testimony in legal proceedings.

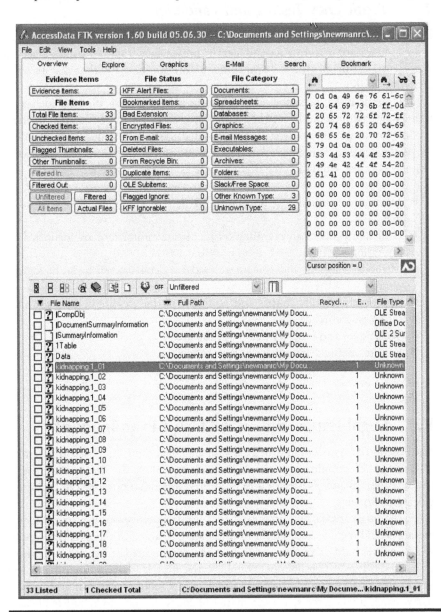

Figure 11.2   AccessData FTK main screen.

■ Technical specialists must be able to provide information concerning interpretations of various forensic tests.

1. Proficiency Testing and Validation

Proficiency testing is an integral part of an effective quality assurance program. It is used to monitor performance and identify areas where improvements are needed. Proficiency testing measures the capability of its examiners and the reliability of its analytical results.

It is essential that personnel involved in the field of forensic digital evidence and technology examinations be required to demonstrate competence at regular intervals.

It is important that only properly evaluated tools, techniques, and procedures are used when examining digital evidence. Audits for compliance are conducted in a timely manner. Validation requirements are as follows:

■ Minimum acceptable criteria for a particular technique or procedure are defined
■ Critical aspects of an examination procedure and/or tool are identified and limitations defined
■ Methods, material, and equipment used are demonstrated to be fit for their purpose
■ Appropriate quality control and assurance procedures are in place for monitoring performance
■ Techniques and procedures are documented
■ Results obtained are reliable and reproducible

K. Legal Issues with Hard Drive Examinations

The Federal Bar Association issued a document concerning "Civil Rules Regarding Discovery of Electronic Materials" on December 9, 2002. This document addressed issues (Rules 16 and 34) relating to hard drive examinations and the problem of deleted documents.

A thorough search for computer-based information responsive to a discovery request would include a search for information contained in the unallocated space of a computer hard drive. As previously stated, unallocated or free space is the portion of a hard drive that does not contain active files. It is where ostensibly deleted documents may be found. The imposition of any requirement that a responding party search unallocated space as a matter of course is likely to be resisted because of the expense involved. Few parties will have the ability to search unallocated space with in-house assets. Consequently, to search unallocated space on a single hard drive, a typical party will have to hire a computer forensic expert who can search the hard drive using special forensic software. The function to accomplish this task would probably exist in the computer forensic lab for both commercial and law enforcement organizations. Aside from the costs involved, there is no assurance that any information will be found or that information found will be complete enough to constitute admissible evidence.

In part, this is because the search process usually requires the use of keywords. A forensic expert uses keywords to search unallocated space for "hits." These hits may include parts of a document responsive to a discovery request or they may not. Determining what keywords will be used is likely to be a contested issue. As a note, there are five keywords that would be used when searching for pornography files. A requesting party would ordinarily seek a large number of keywords to increase the probability that responsive documents would be located. A responding party, on the other hand, would naturally be inclined to limit the number of keywords. In either case, the search will probably result in a substantial number of hits that have nothing to do with the issues in the case and may not result in the discovery of any relevant information. This becomes more probable in view of the fact that the deleted information remaining in unallocated space often comprises only part of a document. This is explained by the fact that documents are usually stored in small blocks of memory in noncontiguous "clusters" on a hard drive.

The Court in Rowe (205 F.R.D. at 429) examined eight factors:

Availability of the information from other sources
Likelihood of discovering critical information
Purpose for which the responding party maintains the data
Relative ability of each party to control costs and its incentive to do so
Relative benefit to the parties of obtaining the data
Resources available to each party
Specificity of the discovery requests
Total cost associated with the production

Practitioners report that a cost of $2,000 to $5,000 per hard drive examination is typical. As technology evolves, this cost may be reduced substantially; however, disk drive capacity is increasing, and the cost may remain static.

The document being searched may be stored in multiple clusters on the hard drive. These clusters are not always adjacent to one another. While the document is saved or is being viewed, the computer keeps track of those clusters comprising the document. After the document is deleted, however, the computer no longer keeps track of the specific clusters that comprise a document, and the clusters are subject to being overwritten with new data. The overwriting process is random; some clusters among those that formerly comprised a single document may be overwritten and some may not. A search of unallocated space may reveal individual clusters, which may or may not contain portions of a document, and often does not reveal entire documents, much less entire documents that are useful. Consequently, the utility of a forensic search of unallocated space on a computer hard drive is quite limited in most cases.

In other cases, however, a forensic examination of a hard drive and unallocated space may lead to the discovery of an important missing piece of evidence, such as a "smoking gun" document. It could reveal critical information regarding metadata, such as when a document was created, modified, or viewed, or whether it is genuine. For these legitimate reasons, the prospect of forensically examining the opposing party's hard drive and unallocated space can be very attractive. It is not surprising that requests to inspect computers pursuant to Rule 34 appear to be increasing. The invasiveness of hard drive examinations and the opportunity to eliminate the other party's ability to determine unilaterally which documents are relevant, however, can lead to abuse.

There are numerous legal implications of the various parties' responsibilities concerning preservation of electronic evidence, the need to meet-and-confer early in the case on electronic discovery issues, recovery of deleted electronic materials, management of electronic document production, privilege issues, and post-litigation electronic document return or destruction. Computer forensic examiners must stay current on the laws that impact electronic evidence investigations. Note that this brief is dated and probably has been superseded by some legislation or rules. Legal counsel will need to be involved in most cases that involve electronic forensic lab activities. Failure to abide by the various requirements can result in inadmissibility of the forensic evidence. Forensic examiners can waste hours and days of searching hard drives for relevant evidence. Most labs cannot afford this unproductive time.

1.   Redaction

The court may request redaction of evidence used in a trial. After litigation (Chapter 2), data may be redacted prior to returning media to the defendant. **Redaction** means cutting, rearranging, altering, or refining data off a hard drive. Items that may be included in such a request are:

E-mails   Free space
Files (*.doc, *.ppt, *.pdf, etc.)   Entire drive
Files and slack   Specific identified sectors
File slack only

After reviewing the following paragraphs, it should become obvious specialized forensic software is required to perform these actions. When procuring this type of software, make sure that it can perform these tasks. The following text describes how redaction is accomplished for e-mail, miscellaneous files, and free space.

Requests might be made to remove specific e-mails or the entire folder. Removing the entire folder is easier to perform. The process requires the removal of .pst, .ost, .mbx, and other style mailboxes. Specific mail programs may have to be identified to determine what type of mail container they use. Once specific e-mails have been identified, usually with a forensic program, an individual e-mail must be deleted. After deletion, the container might have to be cleansed to permanently delete the items.

Files to be deleted are based upon the analyst's report. The files can be deleted or overwritten by manual, automatic, or a combination of the two processes. Remember that deletion of the file does not wipe the data. Overwriting the file can take considerable time as numerous passes are required—usually seven. File slack might not be deleted when the file is deleted. This depends upon the operating system, the program used, or a combination of the two.

If free space is to be wiped, files may not have to be overwritten, as deleted files are located in drive free space. Some operating systems, when closing down a file, will overwrite any slack. This will eliminate any possibility of keeping the slack. If the object is to remove only the file slack, use a program to perform this task, based on the list provided. Note that the recycle bin must be cleared, otherwise those files held in the recycle bin will be recoverable. Specific sectors to be deleted would be identified by the analyst. It is necessary to use custom software to overwrite the list of sectors provided. Use caution here as the list of sectors to overwrite and the program that performs the overwrite must be on the same number sequence, otherwise data will be deleted.

Examination documentation should be case specific and contain sufficient details to allow another forensic examiner to perform an independent review of the facts and details. Documentation must be preserved according to the lab's policies. These policies must be consistent with those required by law. Examination reports issued by the examiner should address the requestor's needs and meet the requirements of the forensic laboratory. The report must provide the reader with all the relevant information in a clear and concise manner. This report has the potential of being entered as evidence in legal proceedings. Reexaminations are a possibility, so all reports and documentation should be stored in a safe location.

The chain-of-custody and investigative journal must be clearly documented. If possible, commonly used media (rather than some obscure storage media) should be used for archiving. Access to evidence should be extremely restricted and clearly documented. It should be possible to detect unauthorized access.

Chapter Summary

Computer forensic consultant organizations and law enforcement organizations are usually the major players when it comes to operating laboratories for processing computer and electronic evidence. The primary function of a computer forensics lab is to provide technical support in the identification, recovery, examination, and preservation of computer-related latent evidence.

The International Association of Computer Investigative Specialists (IACIS) has established a guide for forensic computer and digital evidence examinations.

Computer and digital media examinations are different and depend upon the specific circumstances of the investigation. The chain-of-custody is one of the most important components of the forensic examination and investigation. Examinations must be repeatable and reproducible to be admissible in litigation.

Forensic examiners must review the documentation that accompanies the evidence to determine the processes necessary to complete the examination and also ascertain legal authority to perform the request. Evidence management must be handled according to acceptable practices to stand up in a court of law. RFC3227 provides "best practices" for accomplishing the evidence collection phase of an investigation.

Examination of a computer must be done thoroughly, carefully, and without changing anything on the computer. Procedures and techniques must be in place to preview the content of computer hard drives without risk of changing the data, capture an exact copy of the data held on computer hard drives and other media, and automatically produce a printable audit trail to identify the actions taken. There are a number of forensic tools available that accomplish evidence collection and management.

Computer forensic labs must possess a wide range of tools to perform evidence collection and forensics on disk media. A set of tools should be available for each of the operating systems and computer platforms being examined. The tools selected must be acceptable for litigation and prosecution evidence examinations. The forensic lab should also have a written policy establishing the protocols for technical, peer, and administrative review of forensic tools and processes.

Terms

Autopsy Forensic Browser — A graphical interface to the command line digital investigation analysis tools in The Sleuth Kit.

Carving — The process of removing an item from a group of items.

Coroner's Toolkit (TCT) — Is intended to assist in a forensic analysis of a UNIX system after a break-in.

Foremost — A console program to recover files based on their headers, footers, and internal data structures.

IACIS — International Association of Computer Investigative Specialists.

Keyword — A keyword search is a technique for finding files or other information by providing characters, words, or phrases to a search tool.

Redaction — Includes cutting, rearranging, altering, or refining data off a hard drive.

Residual data — Refers to data that is not active on a computer system.

RFC3227 — Provides "best practices" for accomplishing the evidence collection phase of an investigation.

Rootkits — A set of software tools frequently used by a third party (usually an intruder) after gaining access to a computer system. These tools are intended to conceal running processes, files or system data, which helps an intruder maintain access to a system without the user's knowledge.

Sleuth Kit — A collection of UNIX-based command line file and volume system forensic analysis tools.

UTC — Universal Time Coordinated, the international time standard, also known as Greenwich Meridian Time (GMT).

Review Questions

1. The process of removing an item from a group of items is called _____.

2. The process of arranging, altering, or refining data off a hard drive is called _____.

3. What is meant by the "order of volatility"?

4. Three commercial software packages used in computer forensic labs are ____ _____, _____, and _____.

5. T/F. This computer forensic software package is only available to law enforcement personnel.

6. Capturing an exact copy of the data involves a process called _____.

7. What organization has established a guide for forensic computer and digital evidence examinations? It is one of the oldest professional computer forensic organizations.

8. _____ provides "best practices" for accomplishing the evidence collection phase of an investigation.

9. The current cost to examine a hard drive is approximately _____.

10. Describe residual data.

Chapter 12

E-Mail and Internet Investigations

Chapter Objectives

- Identify the Internet, Web, and network e-mail elements
- Become familiar with the basics concerning e-mail investigations
- Discover the various e-mail and Internet data that can provide forensic evidence
- Look at the tools used to track and identify e-mail evidence
- See how to identify and track SPAM and phishing attempts
- Develop testimonial evidence for scams and identity theft cases
- Learn how to prepare e-mail evidence for court proceedings

Introduction

Numerous computer system threats arrive daily via e-mail that is transmitted over the Internet and corporate networks. These transmissions are intrusive and can impact the safe operation of the user's information systems. These threats could involve SPAM, viruses, worms, Trojan horses, and phishing messages.

E-mail forensic investigations can be used for most civil and criminal legal proceedings. E-mail can be the vehicle of a threat or can contain the threat. E-mail forensic examiners use sophisticated software and hardware to track and identify evidence useful in cases involving misdemeanors and felonies.

Internet and e-mail investigations take on a worldwide scope because many scams involving identity theft originate in third-world countries. Evidence might be located in a number of Internet service provider (ISP) servers.

Warrants and subpoenas are probably required by the forensic examiners to obtain relevant e-mail evidence, when and where it is located. There are countries where these documents might not be honored.

Documentation is of major importance in the e-mail investigative process. The examiner's journal will be a major component in any civil or criminal action.

Forensic examiners and investigators will be required to become proficient in a number of software tools that have been designed for e-mail cases. There are a number of different e-mail systems that could be used to transport these messages, which makes the forensic effort more difficult for the examiners.

A. Internet Basics

The Internet is the publicly available worldwide system of interconnected computer networks that transmit data by packet switching using a standardized Internet Protocol (IP) and many other protocols. It is made up of thousands of smaller commercial, academic, domestic, and government networks. It carries various information and services, such as e-mail, online chat, remote login, file transfer, and newsgroups and the interlinked Web pages and other documents of the World Wide Web.

More than 100 countries are linked into exchanges of data, news, and opinions. Unlike online services, which are centrally controlled, the Internet is decentralized by design. Each Internet computer, called a host, is independent. Its operators can choose which Internet services to use and which local services to make available to the global Internet community.

Originally designed by the U.S. Defense Department so that a communication signal could withstand a nuclear war and serve military institutions worldwide, the Internet was first known as the ARPAnet. A network service provider (NSP) is a company that provides the national or international packet-switching networks that carry Internet traffic; also called a backbone operator. The NSP is usually transparent to the e-mail and Internet user.

An **Internet service provider (ISP)** is a company that provides individuals and other companies access to the Internet and other related services such as Web site building and virtual hosting. An ISP has the equipment and the telecommunication line access required to have a point-of-presence on the Internet for the geographic area served. Users connect to the Internet by dialing into its computers using a modem, cable, or a broadband link. ISPs typically charge a fee and provide in return the dial-up telephone number, an e-mail address, and some technical assistance (usually via e-mail), but no online content. This organization is an important resource for the forensic investigator and examiner. Archived e-mail messages might be resident on the ISP computer systems and servers.

The ISPs use various Internet software protocols to exchange messages; therefore, the examiner must be familiar with the network connection methods, technical rules, and particulars among e-mail applications. The primary Internet protocol is **Transmission Control Protocol/Internet Protocol (TCP/IP)**. TCP/IP refers to an entire suite of protocols used to provide communication on a variety of layers between widely distributed different types of computers. This protocol is the foundation of the Internet, an agreed upon set of rules directing computers on how to exchange information with each other. Other Internet protocols, such as File Transfer Protocol (FTP), Gopher and Hypertext Transfer Protocol (HTTP), sit on top of TCP/IP.

The **File Transfer Protocol (FTP)** is a common method of moving files between two Internet sites. FTP is a way to log in to another Internet site for the purposes of retrieving and/or sending files. FTP was invented and was in wide use long before the advent of the Web and originally was always used from a text-only interface.

The **Hypertext Transfer Protocol (HTTP)** is the set of rules for exchanging files (text, graphic images, sound, video, and other multimedia files) on the Web. It is relative to the TCP/IP suite of protocols that is the basis for information exchange on the Internet. It sets the rules for exchanges between browser and server and provides for the transfer of hypertext and hypermedia, recognition of file types, and other functions.

A **browser** is a client to a Web server that allows the user to read hypertext documents on the Web. Netscape Navigator and Microsoft Internet Explorer are examples of popular Web browsers. **Gopher** is an Internet server document browsing and searching system that lets a user search and retrieve texts on the Internet. Gopher has since been surpassed by the Web.

The Web is a collection of online documents stored on servers around the world, which are connected to the Internet. Researchers at CERN in Switzerland created the concept of the Web. Web documents are written in Hypertext Markup Language (HTML) and stored on a Web server. The documents can be accessed over the Internet using a Web browser, such as Internet Explorer or Netscape Navigator.

B.   E-Mail Basics

Electronic mail or **e-mail** is the transmission of messages over communications networks. The messages can be notes entered from the keyboard or electronic files stored on disk. Most mainframes, minicomputers, and computer networks have an e-mail system. Some e-mail systems are confined to a single computer system or network, but others have gateways to other computer systems, enabling users to send messages anywhere in the world.

Users can send and receive e-mail via the Internet or a local area network (LAN). A configuration called client/server is used to distribute data, such as e-mail, from a central server to many remotely located client computers. The central computer uses a server operating system such as UNIX, Novell Netware, or Windows, and runs an e-mail server program, such as Groupwise, Sendmail, or Exchange Server 2000. Client computers run Windows and Linux operating systems and contact the centrally located server to send and retrieve e-mail messages.

The computer user first accesses the Internet via an ISP using either a dial-up modem or some network service such as Digital Subscriber Line (DSL). The user then accesses the various Web sites or e-mail services through this network connectivity. E-mail programs use a standard such as **Multipurpose Internet Mail Extensions (MIME),** which encodes messages for transmission that contains information for sending messages from one point to another. UNIX, DOS, and Windows systems use another standard, called uuencode. Examiners should be familiar with the RFC 2045/2046 (MIME) standard when working with e-mail evidence.

Simple Mail Transfer Protocol (SMTP) is a core Internet protocol used to transfer e-mail messages between servers. An e-mail client or mail user agent is a computer program that is used to read and send e-mail. Protocols supported by e-mail clients include POP3 and IMAP. IMAP and the updated IMAP4 are optimized for storage of e-mail on the server, while the POP3 protocol generally assumes that the e-mail is downloaded to the client. The SMTP protocol is used by most e-mail clients to send e-mail.

An e-mail address is a place where someone can contact another person, typically in the format username@host.com. This address is good as a home address and provides the forensic examiner valuable information in e-mail investigations. The **Domain Naming System (DNS)** is the system that translates Internet domain names into IP numbers. A DNS server is a server that performs this kind of translation. Each computer that accesses the Internet is assigned a unique IP address that consists of 32 bits subdivided into four octets of 8 bits each. An IP address would look like this: 127.128.192.1. Information concerning IP addresses is presented in Appendix D.

E-mail is easily recognizable because a message header includes information such as IP addresses, date and time stamps, and attachments. Identifying and recovering e-mail attachments will be a major part of the forensic examiner's tasks. The IP address will be a valuable piece of data to research the origin of the e-mail transmission.

C.   E-Mail Systems

Windows/DOS, Macintosh, and UNIX computer systems all provide some type of e-mail transmission capability. E-mail systems include Novell Groupwise, Microsoft Outlook Express, Microsoft and Macintosh Eudora, UNIX Pine, and UNIX ELM. ISPs also offer AOL, Hotmail, Juno, and Yahoo e-mail messaging. Forensic examiners must understand many different e-mail formats, processes, and contents for each of these systems. An intense training program and experience will be required to become proficient in examining evidence on these systems. A variety of forensic techniques are required to identify, track, and recover forensic evidence from the network devices.

GroupWise is a workgroup application suite offering electronic mail and diary scheduling from Novell, Inc. It can operate on a number of server and workstation platforms. Server platforms include NetWare, Linux, and Windows, while the client software can run on Windows or Linux.

Microsoft **Outlook Express** is an e-mail and news client bundled with operating systems and the Internet Explorer Web browser by Microsoft, and also available as a no-charge download for the classic Apple Macintosh operating system (although not for the newer Mac OS-X, where it has been replaced by Microsoft Entourage, which costs as part of Microsoft Office).

Eudora is a popular e-mail software program. It works in conjunction with an ISP's mail server to allow reading and writing of mail offline. It is fully MIME-compliant, allowing a wide variety of attachments to be sent or received with e-mail messages. Eudora is available in both shareware and commercial versions for both Windows and Macintosh systems.

Pine is a popular mail and Usenet client for UNIX and Windows. Developed at the University of Washington, it offers an intuitive, easy-to-use menu interface and supports MIME, IMAP and PGP. Though it includes an extensive options list, in some cases, Pine sacrifices features for usability.

Elm is a text-based e-mail client that is commonly found on UNIX systems. It gained popularity because it was one of the first e-mail clients to use screen displays, and the source code was freely available.

D. Specialized Tools

After understanding the workings of the various e-mail systems, the examiner must now learn how to use the various tools to obtain evidence from the systems. Software companies offer a number of packages that provide forensic functions for e-mail investigations. Brief descriptions are provided for FINALeMAIL, Paraben, Sawmill-Groupwise, DBXtract, MailBag Assistant, and Coroner's Toolkit software products that are used for e-mail examinations.

FINALeMAIL can recover the e-mail database file and locates lost e-mails that do not have data location information associated with them. FINALeMAIL provides support for Outlook Express 4.0/5.0/6.0 and Eudora Mail.

Sawmill can read, analyze, and report on Groupwise Internet agent accounting logs and generate dynamic statistics from them, analyzing and reporting server traffic. Sawmill also supports almost 500 other log formats.

DBXtract extracts all mail and news messages from individual dbx files. After extracting the messages, one can drag them from a Windows Explorer folder into an Outlook Express mail folder.

MailBag Assistant provides tools to search, organize, analyze, and archive a large volume of messages. MailBag Assistant complements the mail program without interfering with it or modifying its message files. It reads and processes current and archived e-mails with ease, whether they are stored on the computer, on networked drives, or on removable media.

Paraben's **E-Mail Examiner** is a comprehensive forensically sound e-mail examination tool. E-mail Examiner recovers active and deleted mail messages. The tool recovers e-mail in the deleted folders and e-mail deleted from deleted items (deleted/deleted). It uses book-marking and advanced searching features, including multiple word and multiple phrase searching.

Access Data **FTK** provides for e-mail and Zip file analysis and supports Outlook, Outlook Express, AOL, Netscape, Yahoo, Earthlink, Eudora, Hotmail, and MSN e-mail. Functions include view, search, print, and export e-mail messages and attachments. It can recover deleted and partially deleted e-mail and can automatically extract data from PKZIP, WinZip, WinRAR, SZIP, and TAR compressed files.

EnCase software has a number of powerful features that facilitate efficient examinations, including recognition of the various files typically associated with Internet and e-mail artifacts. Two of the most critical areas of any investigation typically involve the analysis of artifacts related to the Internet and e-mail.

Coroner's Toolkit can be used to recover e-mail images from UNIX systems.

A number of the forensic packages allow the examiner to find e-mail database files, personal e-mail files, storage files, and log files. Some of the packages also include a viewer to look at e-mail messages and files, while others require another piece of software to accomplish this task. The objective of this examination is to locate date and time stamps, user names, e-mail account, IP addresses, domain names, message-ID, and actual contents of the e-mail. EnCase and Access Data also offer products for disk drive imaging and mining. It is important to remember that tools employed in the investigation must be acceptable in the legal environment. The use of freeware forensic software might constitute a valid objection raised by the opposing attorneys.

With a little luck, the examination will result in a match and there will be enough evidence for a warrant or subpoena. The warrant should include all possibilities in the areas of interest. All procedures and rules apply when identifying, collecting, documenting, and transporting any evidence related to the e-mail. Pay particular attention to the chain-of-custody for all evidence collected. It will be necessary to follow all the steps presented in previous chapters that relate to the reproducibility and repeatability of the process used to recover the e-mail evidence.

E.   Internet Search Tools

Several tools are available on the Web that allow for unique and specialized searches. These include ARIN WHOIS Database Search, Google, and Freeality.

The **American Registry for Internet Numbers (ARIN)** service provides a mechanism for finding contact and registration information for resources registered with ARIN. ARIN's database contains IP addresses, autonomous system (AS) numbers, organizations or customers that are associated with these resources, and related points of contact (POCs). Entering the IP address retrieved from the e-mail document will produce a considerable amount of information concerning the mail site, which could be useful in the investigation. The URL is http://www.arin.net/whois/. Figure 12.1 provides an image of the search page. ARIN's WHOIS will not locate any domain related information, nor any information relating to military networks. Use the Internic Web page located at http://www.Internic.com/ to locate domain information.

Do not overlook Google as a search tool. **Google** is a popular search engine and a tool for finding resources on the Web. Google scans Web pages to find instances of the keywords users have entered in the search box. Do not forget that the criminal can also have access to these search engines. Search engines are also tools used by identity thieves and child predators.

Freeality has a Web page that contains links to a number of search engines. The link to Reverse Lookup and E-mail Search at http://www.Freeality.com/ provides links to Reverse Call Phonebooks, Reverse E-mail, and Cell Phone Lookup Tools.

Query-by-record-type:

To limit a query to a specific record type, include one of the following flags:
    n - Network address space
    a - Autonomous systems
    p - Points of Contact
    o - Organizations
    c - End-user customers

Query-by-attribute:

To limit the query to a specific record attribute, include one of the following flags:
    @ <domain name> - Searches for matches by the domain-portion of an e-mail address
    ! <handle>   - Searches for matches by handle or id
    . <name>   - Searches for matches by name

Searches that retrieve a single record will display the full record. Searches that retrieve more than one record will be displayed in list output. The query response, if successful, will point to one of the following locations:

AfriNIC	www.afrinic.net/cgi-bin/whois
APNIC	www.apnic.net/search/index.html
LACNIC	lacnic.net/cgi-bin/lacnic/whois
RIPE	www.ripe.net/perl/whois/
InterNIC	www.internic.net/whois.htrh
DoDNIC	www.nic.mil/dodnic/

Figure 12.1   ARIN WHOIS search page.

Be sure to read the terms and conditions. Some of these functions incur a charge and this might be a cost of doing business for the forensic investigator.

F.   Crimes and Incidents Involving the Internet and E-Mail

Information concerning crimes that occur over the network and on computing and communication devices is presented in Chapters 3 and 4. These crimes can involve laptop and desktop computers, cell phones, personal digital assistants (PDAs), and a host of electronic devices. E-mail is transmitted and received on many of these devices and, therefore, they are candidates for a forensic investigation when an incident or crime occurs.

While all crimes have the potential of involving e-mail, those addressed in this chapter include those associated with identity theft, fraud, policy violations, and sex crimes. Identity theft can result from SPAM, Internet threats, and phishing attacks. The end result is fraudulent activities against Web and e-mail users. Another particularly disturbing criminal activity involves child exploitation, molestation, and abuse. The business community is not exempt from problems involving the network. Corporate e-mail can be the vehicle for sexual harassment, pornography, violations of company policies, corporate espionage, and the list is endless. E-mail is also an effective method of message transmission for terrorist organizations, which can also employ fraudulent techniques to obtain funds for their activities.

G.   E-Mail Investigations

E-mail forensic examinations conducted in the computer forensic lab will probably be criminal in nature since most e-mail incidents involving corporate policy issues will be conducted by security departments. This means that most criminal e-mail investigations will involve transmissions over the Internet and e-mail servers that are located at ISP computer sites.

Important considerations for incidents involving e-mail include:

What is the name of the ISP?
What are the offender's name and address?
Is there a copy of the e-mail and is it available?

The list of ISPs is too long to present here and could possibly change before this book is printed. The major players today are listed on several Web sites. Directory and Web listings and company profiles are posted at www.business.com/directory/.

Investigative departments and forensic labs should establish a working relationship with these ISPs in the event some evidence is located on one of their servers.

H.   Examining E-Mail Images

Categorizing some e-mail as a criminal activity depends upon the location of the sender. The examiner must determine the sending location during the early phases of the examination, in order to not waste resources on a nonissue. The examiner must also ascertain the type of crime that has been committed, where e-mail will be admissible and acceptable as evidence. Legal advice is required at this point of the investigation.

After it has been determined a crime has been committed using e-mail, it will be necessary to access the documents in question. The documents might be on an e-mail server, ISP server, or the suspect's computer. Different approaches will be required depending on the type of crime being investigated. For crimes where there is a victim, access to copies of the e-mail should be easily attained; however, where e-mail has been a tool in the commission of some crime, accessing the documents may be more difficult. Warrants and subpoenas must be issued if they have not been previously executed.

For many e-mail investigations, the forensic examiner can rely on e-mail message files, e-mail headers, and e-mail server log files to look for evidence. Often, server administrators are reluctant to cooperate, and the examiner must resort to using data recovery and computer forensic tools that are specially designed to recover e-mail data.

The investigator must secure a copy of the e-mail with header information and any attachments. The attachments may be the most important item of evidence, particularly those cases involving pornography.

E-mails can be copied with just several steps and the process is similar for most e-mail systems. With the message visible on the monitor, screen-scrape (copy) the contents and paste it into a notepad. The notepad should maintain the integrity of the format and probably will be saved as a "txt" file. Save it with a name relevant to the case. Next, click on the "view" or "view header" button of the original e-mail, which should display the header fields and information. Screen-scrape (copy) the header and save with an appropriate name. These text files (e-mail and header) can now be copied onto a floppy disk or universal serial bus (USB) drive for evidence collection. Make a copy of this media for any examinations, to avoid polluting the original evidence. Also make an entry in the journal concerning this activity and include in the evidence log. An explanation of the process should include all steps taken to identify, retrieve, and save this evidence.

Another piece of evidence that might be of value is the HTML code source. This component contains the programming language code that was used to collect data from the user. It could be used to show how the suspect was going to collect personal information from the victim and the data that was being requested. A right click on the e-mail text for some systems, such as Groupwise, will produce a pull-down menu, where "view source code" can be selected.

I.   E-Mail Headers

E-mail examiners must be familiar with memo header fields, received fields, and message-ID fields. The document providing details for e-mail headers is RFC 2076. Numerous fields are described in the **RFC 2076** standard and examiners should be familiar with this document. E-mail headers contain a subset of these fields. The e-mail header is basically a section of formatted text at the top of a message followed by a blank line. It is created by e-mail servers for delivery and is used for troubleshooting. The e-mail document consists of a message body, which contains the data intended for the recipient, and a header body, that is a record of the e-mail transmission.

Note the fields that are common and those that are different in these headers. There are only a few fields that are required in the message header. Originator, recipient, and date fields are listed in Figure 12.2.

The forensic examiner will use information attached to these fields in an attempt to develop case evidence. Critical evidence may also be present in attachments.

Samples of three e-mail headers are provided for header comparisons. Figure 12.3 depicts fields and respective information for a Microsoft Office Outlook e-mail transmission. Figure 12.4 consists of e-mail from an AOL transmission and Figure 12.5 is a Novell Groupwise header.

1.   SMTP Servers

SMTP is a protocol for sending e-mail messages between servers. Most e-mail systems that send mail over the Internet use SMTP to send messages from one server

```
Originator:

Authors or persons taking responsibility for the message        From:

Recipient:

Primary recipients                                              To:
Secondary, informational recipients (cc = Carbon Copy) cc:
Recipients not to be disclosed to                               bcc:

Date:

In Internet, the date when a message was written;
in X.400, the time a message was submitted. Some
Internet mail systems also use the date when the
message was submitted                                          Date:
```

Figure 12.2   Required header fields.

```
Content-Type:  multipart/signed; protocol="application/pgp-signature";
micalg="pgp-sha1"; boundary="PGP_Universal_14B027FB_FB9F813D_EEF9B760_F9FF91FC"
Date:  Tue, 20 Jun 2006 14:57:33 -0400 [06/20/2006 06:57:33 PM UTC]
Delivered-To:  student@frontiernet.net
From:  "(ISC)2 Management" <management@isc2.org>
List-Unsubscribe:  <mailto:leave-1473-1425167T@isc16.isc2.org>
MIME-Version:  1.0
Message-Id:  <LYRIS-1425167-1473-2006.06.20-15.01.24--
student#frontiernet.net@isc16.isc2.org>
Received:  from isc16.isc2.org (isc16.isc2.org [216.12.146.41]) by
mx04.roc.ny.frontiernet.net (Postfix) with SMTP id 29AAB3EE1 for
<student@frontiernet.net>; Tue, 20 Jun 2006 23:01:24 +0000 (UTC)
Return-Path:  <bounce-1473-1425167@isc16.isc2.org>
Subject:  OFFICIAL: Stay in Touch with (ISC)2
Thread-Index:  AcaUmYwMb/zNSYIyTheb2BUih48gpAAAWPVwAAAYyWA=
To:  student@frontiernet.net
X-Mailer:  Microsoft Office Outlook, Build 11.0.6353
X-MimeOLE:  Produced By Microsoft MimeOLE V6.00.2900.2869
X-PGP-Encoding-Version:  2.0.2
X-PGP-Universal:  processed; by mail-gw.isc2.org on Tue, 20 Jun 2006 15:33:15 -
0400
X-Spam-Checker-Version:  SpamAssassin 3.1.1 (2006-03-10) on
filter04.roc.ny.frontiernet.net
X-Spam-Level:  **
X-Spam-Status:  No, score=2.6 required=10.0 tests=HTML_MESSAGE,NO_DNS_FOR_FROM
autolearn=disabled version=3.1.1
X-Virus-Scanned:  by amavisd-new-2.3.2 (20050629) at
filter07.roc.ny.frontiernet.net
Part(s):  Download All Attachments (in .zip file)
Headers:  Show Limited Headers  |  Show Mailing List Information
```

Figure 12.3   E-mail header from Microsoft Office Outlook.

```
Content-Type:  multipart/alternative; boundary="-----------------------
----------1151008997"
Date:  Thu, 22 Jun 2006 16:43:17 EDT [06/22/2006 08:43:17 PM UTC]
Delivered-To:  student@frontiernet.net
From:  student@aol.com
MIME-Version:  1.0
Message-ID:  <26f.b64ca5b.31cc5ae5@aol.com>
Received:  from imo-m27.mx.aol.com (imo-m27.mx.aol.com [64.12.137.8])
by mx03.roc.ny.frontiernet.net (Postfix) with ESMTP id 6B7F78638E; Thu,
22 Jun 2006 20:44:01 +0000 (UTC)
from student@aol.com by imo-m27.mx.aol.com (mail_out_v38_r7.5.) id
n.26f.b64ca5b (29678); Thu, 22 Jun 2006 16:43:19 -0400 (EDT)

Return-Path:  <student@aol.com>
Subject:  party party party!!!!!!!
To:  student1@aol.com, student2@yahoo.com, student3@hotmail.com,
student4@alltel.net, student5@bellsouth.net, student6@bulloch.com,
student7@comcast.net, student8@frontiernet.net, student9@msn.com
X-Mailer:  9.0 for Windows sub 5057
X-Spam-Checker-Version:  SpamAssassin 3.1.1 (2006-03-10) on
filter03.roc.ny.frontiernet.net
X-Spam-Level:  *
X-Spam-Status:  No, score=2.0 required=10.0
tests=HTML_10_20,HTML_MESSAGE, NO_REAL_NAME,PLING_PLING
autolearn=disabled version=3.1.1
X-Virus-Scanned:  by amavisd-new-2.4.1 at
filter10.roc.ny.frontiernet.net
Part(s):  Download All Attachments (in .zip file)
Headers:  Show Limited Headers
```

Figure 12.4   E-mail header from AOL.

```
Content-Disposition:  inline
Content-Transfer-Encoding:  7bit
Content-Type:  text/plain; charset=US-ASCII
Date:  Tue, 20 Jun 2006 17:22:08 -0400 [06/20/2006 09:22:08 PM UTC]
Delivered-To:  student@frontiernet.net
From:  student <student@college.edu>
Message-Id:  <44982EC00020000A00040C42@groupwise.college.edu>
Mime-Version:  1.0
Received:  from mouse4.cc.College.edu (mouse4.cc.College.edu
[141.165.4.53]) by mx03.roc.ny.frontiernet.net (Postfix) with ESMTP id
48A3D8132B for <student@frontiernet.net>; Tue, 20 Jun 2006 21:22:44
+0000 (UTC)
from groupwise.college.edu (groupwise.College.edu [141.165.4.101]) by
mouse4.cc.College.edu (8.13.7/8.13.7) with ESMTP id k5KLMisY025137 for
<student@frontiernet.net>; Tue, 20 Jun 2006 17:22:44 -0400 (EDT)
from UNIV_GROUPWISE-MTA by groupwise.college.edu with Novell_GroupWise;
Tue, 20 Jun 2006 17:22:44 -0400

Return-Path:  <student@college.edu>
Subject:  test
To:  student@frontiernet.net
X-Mailer:  Novell GroupWise Internet Agent 7.0.1 Beta
X-Spam-Checker-Version:  SpamAssassin 3.1.1 (2006-03-10) on
filter11.roc.ny.frontiernet.net
X-Spam-Level:
X-Spam-Status:  No, score=0.0 required=10.0 tests=none
autolearn=disabled version=3.1.1
X-Virus-Scanned:  by amavisd-new-2.3.2 (20050629) at
filter05.roc.ny.frontiernet.net
Headers:  Show Limited Headers
```

Figure 12.5   E-mail header from Novell Groupwise.

to another. The messages can then be retrieved with an e-mail client using either POP or IMAP. In addition, SMTP is generally used to send messages from a mail client to a mail server; this is why both the POP (or IMAP) server and the SMTP server must be specified when configuring e-mail applications. Client/server systems were described in Chapter 5.

SMTP servers provide additional information in the e-mail transmission. The initial SMTP server adds the following to the e-mail message:

Memo header fields
Specifics about the mail message
Specifics about the client
Initial received field

Each additional SMTP server involved in the transmission adds a received field. This is added above the previous received field and must stay in order. These servers may add or rearrange other header fields. **RFC 822** provides the examiner with information concerning the format and some of the semantics of message contents. Figure 12.6 displays an Internet Mail Service e-mail transmission that contains a

```
Return-path: <salesman@BlackBox.com>
Received: from barracuda.email.college.edu (barracuda.cc.College.edu
[141.165.1.11])by groupwise.college.edu with ESMTP; Fri, 07 Jul 2006
14:06:44 -0400
X-ASG-Debug-ID: 1152295556-32092-46-0
X-Barracuda-URL: http://141.165.1.11:8000/cgi-bin/mark.cgi
Received: from mouse.cc.College.edu (mouse.cc.College.edu
[141.165.1.10])by barracuda.email.college.edu (Spam Firewall) with
ESMTP id 71C48D009B7Ffor <student@groupwise.College.edu>; Fri,  7 Jul
2006 14:05:56 -0400 (EDT)
Received: from mouse.cc.College.edu (localhost [127.0.0.1])by
mouse.cc.College.edu (8.13.7/8.13.7) with ESMTP id k67I5sd5010287for
<student@groupwise.College.edu>; Fri, 7 Jul 2006 14:05:56 -0400 (EDT)
Received: (from daemon@localhost)by mouse.cc.College.edu
(8.13.7/8.13.7/Submit) id k67I5P8C009207for
student@groupwise.College.edu; Fri, 7 Jul 2006 14:05:25 -0400 (EDT)
Received: from saturn.corp.bbns.com (saturn.blackbox.com
[12.4.234.78])by mouse.cc.College.edu (8.13.7/8.13.7) with SMTP id
k67I5JMs008838for <student@college.edu>; Fri, 7 Jul 2006 14:05:20 -0400
(EDT)
Received: by SATURN.corp.bbns.com with Internet Mail Service
(5.5.2658.3)id <3FK84AR6>; Fri, 7 Jul 2006 14:05:08 -0400
Message-ID:
<C070BEDCDF191F42A7BB08BF8C70631709C76FE1@SATURN.corp.bbns.com>
X-PH: V4.2@mouse
From: salesman <salesman@BlackBox.com>
To: "student" <student@college.edu>
X-ASG-Orig-Subj: RE: Permission
Subject: RE: Graphics
Received: Fri, 7 Jul 2006 14:05:07 -0400
MIME-Version: 1.0
X-Mailer: Internet Mail Service (5.5.2658.3)
Content-Type: multipart/mixed;boundary="----
_=_NextPart_000_01C6A1EF.E1860430"
X-Virus-Scanned: by Barracuda Spam Firewall at email.college.edu
X-Barracuda-Spam-Score: 0.00
X-Barracuda-Spam-Status: No, SCORE=0.00 using per-user scores of
TAG_LEVEL=3.5 QUARANTINE_LEVEL=1000.0 KILL_LEVEL=7.0 tests=
X-Barracuda-Spam-Report: Code version 3.02, rules version 3.0.16375Rule
breakdown below pts rule name            description---- -----------
--------- --------------------------------------------------
Content-Type: text/plain;charset="iso-8859-1"
Attachment Images.DOC
```

Figure 12.6   E-mail header from Internet Mail Service.

number of "received" fields, an attachment, and additional fields not contained in the other examples. Multiple SMTP received information fields in the header are ordered by clock time. Notice the differences in the UTC date time and the received time.

After the forensic examiner has a copy of the e-mail message, header, and attachments from the retrieval process, the examination can begin. Examiners must ensure the original copies have been preserved, as these e-mails will probably be entered as evidence in legal proceedings.

J.   E-Mail and Web Evidence

The following scenarios involve examinations of a Novell Groupwise message and MS Outlook message. One message is a SPAM message and the other is a phishing attempt. All e-mail systems have different formats and require different examination techniques. E-mail forensic examiners must be trained in the particulars of all systems.

The examiner can use ARIN's WHOIS service for finding contact and registration information for resources registered with ARIN. ARIN's database contains IP addresses, autonomous system numbers, organizations, or customers that are associated with these resources, and related points of contact. Entering the URL (www. arin.net/whois/) in a browser activates the Web site. Either record type or attribute can be entered as a query.

The phishing e-mail concerning eBay (Figure 12.7) is the first document to be examined. The software tool used for making these screen images was Snagit. This tool will allow the examiner to capture exactly what is visible on a computer screen—an image, an article, part of a Web page, or even the contents of a scrolling window. These images can be saved on various media for later use in court testimony. Note: the specific IP addresses and names have been changed; however, the steps and processes are accurate. *This is a specified eBay web page.*

The next step is to display the header information (Figure 12.8) associated with the e-mail. Use the technique associated with the e-mail system to view the header. Copy this header information to some storage device for examination. Remember to make two copies: one for the examination and one for any legal proceedings.

A preliminary check of the IP addresses found in the header might yield some information. Use the DOS PING command to validate the IP address.

Another step that can be taken is to use the DOS TELNET command. Screen snapshots for both the PING and TELNET commands are presented in Figures 12.9 and 12.10.

The results of the PING show that the IP address is viable. It is possible that the e-mail originator has disconnected the device from the network, and only connects it when transmitting messages.

The result of the TELNET does not reveal any new information, except there is a device at that IP address.

Note: the IP addresses, URLs, node names, and other names depicted in the various figures have been modified to protect any suspects.

Access http://ws.arin.net/cgi-bin/whois.pl.

Enter the IP address found in the e-mail. Figure 12.11 provides the results of this search.

Click on http://www.apnic.net/apnic-bin/whois.pl.

Enter the IP address in the "search for" block (Figure 12.12) and press "enter."

The search will display the following information (Figure 12.13).

Click on the OrgTechHandle: AWC12-ARIN field (Figure 12.14).

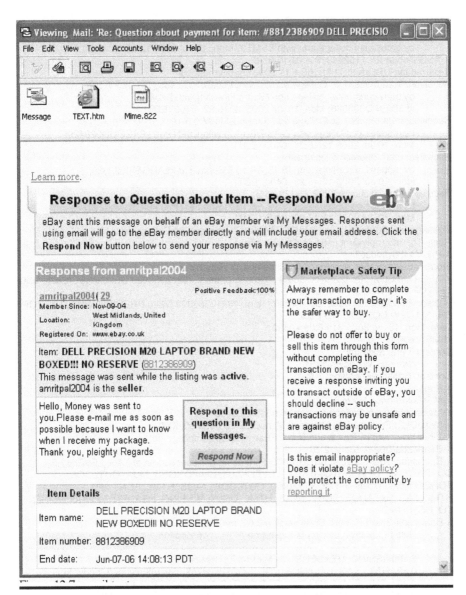

Figure 12.7   Specified eBay e-mail.

Return-path: <member@eBay.com>
Received: from barracuda.email.college.edu (barracuda.cc.College.edu [141.165.1.11])
    by groupwise.college.edu with ESMTP; Mon, 10 Jul 2006 12:16:33 -0400
X-ASG-Debug-ID: 1152548191-31810-67-0
X-Barracuda-URL: http://141.165.1.11:8000/cgi-bin/mark.cgi
Received: from mouse1.cc.College.edu (mouse1.cc.College.edu [141.165.1.10])
    by barracuda.email.college.edu (Spam Firewall) with ESMTP
    id 3D29AD000086; Mon, 10 Jul 2006 12:16:32 -0400 (EDT)
Received: from mouse1.cc.College.edu (localhost [127.0.0.1])
    by mouse1.cc.College.edu (8.13.7/8.13.7) with ESMTP id k6AGGU0j029429;
    Mon, 10 Jul 2006 12:16:31 -0400 (EDT)
Received: (from daemon@localhost)
    by mouse1.cc.College.edu (8.13.7/8.13.7/Submit) id k6AGGSiV029389;
    Mon, 10 Jul 2006 12:16:28 -0400 (EDT)
Received: from mail.com (**[202.71.136.235]**)
    by mouse1.cc.College.edu (8.13.7/8.13.7) with SMTP id k6AGGIvh029077;
    Mon, 10 Jul 2006 12:16:20 -0400 (EDT)
Message-Id: <200607101616.k6AGGIvh029077@mouse1.cc.College.edu>
Reply-To: <no.reply@mouse1.cc.College.edu>
X-PH: V4.2@mouse1
From: "eBay member: amritpal2004" <member@eBay.com>
X-ASG-Orig-Subj: Re: Question about payment for item: #8812386909 DELL PRECISION M20
LAPTOP BRAND NEW BOXED!!! NO RES
Subject: Re: Question about payment for item: #8812386909 DELL PRECISION M20 LAPTOP
BRAND NEW BOXED!!! NO RES
Date: Mon, 10 Jul 2006 21:46:29 +0530
MIME-Version: 1.0
Content-Type: text/html;
    charset="Windows-1251"
Content-Transfer-Encoding: 7bit
X-Priority: 3
X-MSMail-Priority: Normal
X-Mailer: Microsoft Outlook Express 6.00.2600.0000
X-MimeOLE: Produced By Microsoft MimeOLE V6.00.2600.0000
X-Virus-Scanned: by Barracuda Spam Firewall at email.college.edu
X-Barracuda-Spam-Score: 2.79
X-Barracuda-Spam-Status: No, SCORE=2.79 using per-user scores of TAG_LEVEL=3.5
QUARANTINE_LEVEL=1000.0 KILL_LEVEL=7.0 tests=FORGED_MUA_OUTLOOK,
FORGED_OUTLOOK_HTML, FORGED_OUTLOOK_TAGS, HTML_FONT_BIG,
HTML_TAG_BALANCE_BODY, MIME_HTML_ONLY, MISSING_HEADERS, PLING_PLING,
TO_CC_NONE
X-Barracuda-Spam-Report: Code version 3.02, rules version 3.0.16585
    Rule breakdown below pts rule name   description
    ---- ------------------- ---
    0.19 MISSING_HEADERS   Missing To: header
    0.39 HTML_TAG_BALANCE_BODY BODY: HTML has unbalanced "body" tags
    0.23 HTML_FONT_BIG   BODY: HTML tag for a big font size
    0.00 MIME_HTML_ONLY   BODY: Message only has text/html MIME parts
    0.00 FORGED_OUTLOOK_TAGS Outlook can't send HTML in this format
    0.13 TO_CC_NONE   No To: or Cc: header
    0.46 PLING_PLING   Subject has lots of exclamation marks
    0.02 FORGED_OUTLOOK_HTML Outlook can't send HTML message only
    1.36 FORGED_MUA_OUTLOOK   Forged mail pretending to be from MS Outlook

Figure 12.8   E-mail header.

```
Microsoft Windows XP [Version 5.1.2600]
(C) Copyright 1985-2001 Microsoft Corp.

C:\Documents and Settings\newmanrc>cd\

C:\>PING 202.71.136.235

Pinging 202.71.136.235 with 32 bytes of data:

Reply from 202.71.136.235: bytes=32 time=308ms TTL=114
Reply from 202.71.136.235: bytes=32 time=308ms TTL=114
Reply from 202.71.136.235: bytes=32 time=308ms TTL=114
Reply from 202.71.136.235: bytes=32 time=309ms TTL=114

Ping statistics for 202.71.136.235:
    Packets: Sent = 4, Received = 4, Lost = 0 (0% loss),
Approximate round trip times in milli-seconds:
    Minimum = 308ms, Maximum = 309ms, Average = 308ms

C:\>
```

Figure 12.9   Results for a PING command.

```
Microsoft Windows XP [Version 5.1.2600]
(C) Copyright 1985-2001 Microsoft Corp.

C:\Documents and Settings\newmanrc>cd\

C:\>telnet 202.71.136.235
Connecting To 202.71.136.235...Could not open connection to the host, on port 23:

C:\>
```

Figure 12.10   Results for a TELNET command.

A contact can be made with this administrator, who might possess some relevant information involving the investigation. Since these sites probably receive many complaints and requests daily, a correlation might identify the suspect.

K.   SPAM Investigations

The security officer received the following e-mail from a member of the corporate staff. It appears to be a common SPAM message; however, further investigation indicates there might be more to this than it appears on the surface. Of particular interest is the block that asks the e-mail receiver to select whether e-mails are to be discontinued. *Caution!* Clicking on this block can add the user's name to many mailing lists. The text part of the e-mail message is displayed in Figure 12.15. Note: the specific IP addresses and labels have been changed; however, the steps and processes are accurate.

Using the technique presented in the phishing e-mail, the header was retrieved using the view header function and is displayed in Figure 12.16. Figures 12.17

```
OrgName:     Asia Pacific Network Information Centre
OrgID:       APNIC
Address:     PO Box 2131
City:        Milton
StateProv:   QLD
PostalCode:  4064
Country:     AU

ReferralServer: whois://whois.apnic.net

NetRange:    202.0.0.0 - 203.255.255.255
CIDR:        202.0.0.0/7
NetName:     APNIC-CIDR-BLK
NetHandle:   NET-202-0-0-0-1
Parent:
NetType:     Allocated to APNIC
NameServer:  NS1.APNIC.NET
NameServer:  NS3.APNIC.NET
NameServer:  NS4.APNIC.NET
NameServer:  TINNIE.ARIN.NET
NameServer:  NS-SEC.RIPE.NET
NameServer:  DNS1.TELSTRA.NET
Comment:     This IP address range is not registered in the ARIN
database.
Comment:     For details, refer to the APNIC Whois Database via
Comment:     WHOIS.APNIC.NET or http://www.apnic.net/apnic-bin/whois2.pl
Comment:     ** IMPORTANT NOTE: APNIC is the Regional Internet Registry
Comment:     for the Asia Pacific region. APNIC does not operate
networks
Comment:     using this IP address range and is not able to investigate
Comment:     spam or abuse reports relating to these addresses. For more
Comment:     help, refer to http://www.apnic.net/info/faq/abuse
Comment:
RegDate:     1994-04-05
Updated:     2005-05-20

OrgTechHandle: AWC12-ARIN
OrgTechName:   APNIC Whois Contact
OrgTechPhone:  +61 7 3858 3100
OrgTechEmail:  search-apnic-not-arin@apnic.net
```

Figure 12.11   Search results for: 202.71.136.235.

Search for	202.71.136.235	Search

Figure 12.12   Entry screen on WHOIS.APNIC.NET Web page.

```
% [whois.apnic.net node-1]
% Whois data copyright terms
http://www.apnic.net/db/dbcopyright.html
inetnum:        202.71.128.0 - 202.71.159.255
netname:        NET4
descr:          Sterling Capital Pvt. Ltd.
descr:          Internet Service Provider
descr:          New Delhi
country:        IN
admin-c:        IG4-AP
tech-c:         IG4-AP
remarks:        ------------------------------------------------
remarks:        ------------------------------------------------
mnt-by:         APNIC-HM
mnt-lower:      MAINT-STERCAP-IN
mnt-routes:     MAINT-STERCAP-IN
changed:        qadeer.m@net4india.com 19990830
status:         ALLOCATED PORTABLE
changed:        hm-changed@apnic.net 20031008
source:         APNIC
route:          202.71.136.0/24
descr:          NET4 route object
country:        IN
origin:         AS17447
mnt-by:         MAINT-STERCAP-IN
changed:        suman.g@net4india.net 20060523
source:         APNIC
person:         Iqbal Gandham
nic-hdl:        IG4-AP
e-mail:         ipadmin@net4india.net
address:        D-25 , Sec 3 , Noida
address:        U.P , India
phone:          +91-120-4323500
fax-no:         +91-120-4323520
country:        IN
changed:        suman.g@net4india.net 20060307
mnt-by:         MAINT-STERCAP-IN
source:         APNIC
```

Figure 12.13   Results of search.

through 12.20 show the investigation steps to identify the originator and path of the e-mail transmission.

Use the DOS PING and TELNET commands to validate the IP address. Multiple tries might be required at different times of the day to successfully PING the IP address.

Neither PING nor TELNET was successful. Not any help here!
Access http://ws.arin.net/cgi-bin/whois.pl.
Enter the IP address found in the e-mail. **72.128.69.228**.
Click on RRWE and provide the IP address. **72.128.69.228**.
Click on IPTEC_ARIN and provide the IP address. **72.128.69.228**.
Note the comments from the searches at IPTEC-ARIN and RRWE.

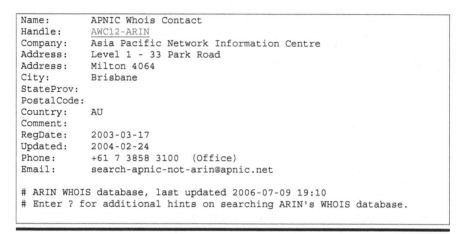

```
Name:         APNIC Whois Contact
Handle:       AWC12-ARIN
Company:      Asia Pacific Network Information Centre
Address:      Level 1 - 33 Park Road
Address:      Milton 4064
City:         Brisbane
StateProv:
PostalCode:
Country:      AU
Comment:
RegDate:      2003-03-17
Updated:      2004-02-24
Phone:        +61 7 3858 3100   (Office)
Email:        search-apnic-not-arin@apnic.net

# ARIN WHOIS database, last updated 2006-07-09 19:10
# Enter ? for additional hints on searching ARIN's WHOIS database.
```

Figure 12.14   Search results for: AWC12-ARIN.

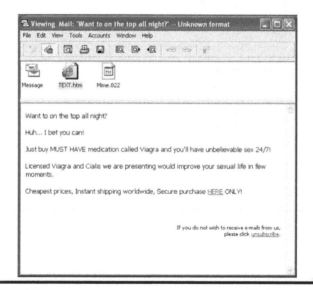

Figure 12.15   Original e-mail text.

Allocations for this OrgID serve Road Runner residential customers out of the Honolulu, Hawaii, Kansas City, Kansas, Orange, California and San Diego, California Regional Data Centers (RDCs). The information for this POC has been reported to be invalid. ARIN has attempted to obtain updated data, but has been unsuccessful. Not only is this a SPAM, it also is capturing unsuspecting users' addresses for a mail list.

```
Return path: <diatomic@letterbox.org>
Received: from barracuda.email.College.edu
(barracuda.cc.College.edu [141.165.1.11])
        by groupwise.College.edu with ESMTP; Mon, 10 Jul 2006
16:23:17 -0400
X-ASG-Debug-ID: 1152562992-2827-81-0
X-Barracuda-URL: http://141.165.1.11:8000/cgi-bin/mark.cgi
Received: from mouse.cc.College.edu
(mouse.cc.College.edu [141.165.1.10])
        by barracuda.email.College.edu (Spam Firewall) with ESMTP
        id 289A4D001FCB; Mon, 10 Jul 2006 16:23:12 -0400 (EDT)
Received: from mouse.cc.College.edu (localhost [127.0.0.1])
        by mouse.cc.College.edu (8.13.7/8.13.7) with ESMTP id
k6AKNAPj022921;
        Mon, 10 Jul 2006 16:23:11 -0400 (EDT)
Received: (from daemon@localhost)
        by mouse.cc.College.edu (8.13.7/8.13.7/Submit) id
k6AKN7w0022860;
        Mon, 10 Jul 2006 16:23:07 -0400 (EDT)
Received: from CPE-72-128-69-228.wi.res.rr.com (CPE-72-128-69-
228.wi.res.rr.com [72.128.69.228])
        by mouse.cc.College.edu (8.13.7/8.13.7) with SMTP id
k6AKMtF0022590;
        Mon, 10 Jul 2006 16:22:57 -0400 (EDT)
Date: Tue, 11 Jul 2006 01:18:00 +0400
X-PH: V4.2@mouse
From: "Online Shop" <diatomic@letterbox.org>
Message-ID: <10156.troubador@cormorant>
To: lhendrix@College.edu
X-ASG-Orig-Subj: Want to on the top all night?
Subject: Want to on the top all night?
MIME-Version: 1.0
Content-Type: text/html; charset=us-ascii
Content-Transfer-Encoding: 7bit
X-Virus-Scanned: by Barracuda Spam Firewall at
email.College.edu
X-Barracuda-Spam-Score: 1.10
X-Barracuda-Spam-Status: No, SCORE=1.10 using per-user scores of
TAG_LEVEL=3.5 QUARANTINE_LEVEL=1000.0 KILL_LEVEL=7.0
tests=DRUGS_ERECTILE, MIME_HTML_ONLY
X-Barracuda-Spam-Report: Code version 3.02, rules version 3.0.16598
        Rule breakdown below pts rule name                  description
        ---- --------------------- ------------------------------------
------------
        0.00 MIME_HTML_ONLY           BODY: Message only has text/html MIME
parts
        1.10 DRUGS_ERECTILE           Refers to an erectile drug
```

Figure 12.16   E-mail header.

If users receiving these e-mails and investigators working these cases send a complaint to the RDC, it might help track down and prosecute these people. The known information from this research includes various locations and the name "Road Runner." This information can be used in a search engine, such as Google, to attempt to gather additional intelligence. The investigator should use the services of various commercial and government organizations to assist in identifying the suspect in these identity-theft and fraud cases. These contacts, presented in Chapter 4, include the following:

```
Microsoft Windows XP [Version 5.1.2600]
(C) Copyright 1985-2001 Microsoft Corp.

C:\Documents and Settings\newmanrc>cd\

C:\>Ping 72.128.69.228

Pinging 72.128.69.228 with 32 bytes of data:

Request timed out.
Request timed out.

Ping statistics for 72.128.69.228:
    Packets: Sent = 2, Received = 0, Lost = 2 (100% loss),
Control-C
^C
C:\>
C:\>
C:\>telnet 72.128.69.228
Connecting To 72.128.69.228...Could not open connection to the host, on port 23:
C:\>
```

Figure 12.17   PING and TELNET attempt.

```
Search results for: 72.128.69.228


OrgName:    Road Runner HoldCo LLC
OrgID:      RRWE
Address:    13241 Woodland Park Road
City:       Herndon
StateProv:  VA
PostalCode: 20171
Country:    US

ReferralServer: rwhois://ipmt.rr.com:4321

NetRange:   72.128.0.0 - 72.135.95.255
CIDR:       72.128.0.0/14, 72.132.0.0/15, 72.134.0.0/16, 72.135.0.0/18,
72.135.64.0/19
NetName:    RRWE
NetHandle:  NET-72-128-0-0-1
Parent:     NET-72-0-0-0-0
NetType:    Direct Allocation
NameServer: DNS1.RR.COM
NameServer: DNS2.RR.COM
NameServer: DNS3.RR.COM
NameServer: DNS5.RR.COM
NameServer: DNS6.RR.COM
Comment:
RegDate:    2005-08-02
Updated:    2006-06-06

OrgAbuseHandle: ABUSE10-ARIN
OrgAbuseName:   Abuse
OrgAbusePhone:  +1-703-345-3416
OrgAbuseEmail:  abuse@rr.com

OrgTechHandle: IPTEC-ARIN
OrgTechName:   IP Tech
OrgTechPhone:  +1-703-345-3416
OrgTechEmail:  abuse@rr.com

# ARIN WHOIS database, last updated 2006-07-10 19:10
```

Figure 12.18   Search results.

```
Search results for: O ! RRWE


OrgName:     Road Runner HoldCo LLC
OrgID:       RRWE
Address:     13241 Woodland Park Road
City:        Herndon
StateProv:   VA
PostalCode:  20171
Country:     US
Comment:     Allocations for this OrgID serve Road Runner residential
customers out of the Honolulu, HI, Kansas City, KS, Orange, CA and San
Diego, CA RDCs.
RegDate:     2000-10-05
Updated:     2006-03-27

ReferralServer: rwhois://ipmt.rr.com:4321

AbuseHandle: ABUSE10-ARIN
AbuseName:   Abuse
AbusePhone:  +1-703-345-3416
AbuseEmail:  abuse@rr.com

AdminHandle: IPADD-ARIN
AdminName:   IP Addreg
AdminPhone:  +1-703-345-3416
AdminEmail:  ipaddreg@rr.com

TechHandle:  IPTEC-ARIN
TechName:    IP Tech
TechPhone:   +1-703-345-3416
TechEmail:   abuse@rr.com

# ARIN WHOIS database, last updated 2006-07-10 19:10
# Enter ? for additional hints on searching ARIN's WHOIS database.
```

Figure 12.19   Search results.

```
Search results for: P ! IPTEC-ARIN


Name:        IP Tech
Handle:      IPTEC-ARIN
Company:     Road Runner
Address:     13241 Woodland Park Road
City:        Herndon
StateProv:   VA
PostalCode:  20171
Country:     US
Comment:     The information for this POC has been reported to be
invalid. ARIN has attempted to obtain updated data, but has been
unsuccessful. To provide current contact information, please e-mail
hostmaster@arin.net.
RegDate:     2002-08-27
Updated:     2005-12-07
Phone:       +1-703-345-3416  (Office)
Email:       abuse@rr.com

# ARIN WHOIS database, last updated 2006-07-10 19:10
# Enter ? for additional hints on searching ARIN's WHOIS database.
```

Figure 12.20   Search results.

Credit reporting agencies
Federal Trade Commission
Federal Bureau of Investigation
Better Business Bureau
National Fraud Information Center
Chambers of commerce

L. Documenting Evidence

As mentioned previously, identifying and retrieving evidence is of little use if it has not been thoroughly and properly documented. The documentation for court testimony must meet with the requirements of the local jurisdiction. Of particular importance is the chain-of-custody, evidence documents, and investigative journals. Every step of the examination process can come under scrutiny of the court and the opposing attorneys. Chapter 14 provides guidance in the use of computer forensic evidence in the legal environment. Chapter 2 provides guidance concerning the legal environment, including the forensic testimony presentations. Copies of all forms used in forensic investigations and examinations are included in Appendix A.

Investigations concerning e-mail are a little different from those involving electronic devices and computers. Most evidence is obtained from the Internet or support organizations, such as credit bureaus and government operations and consists of printouts and screen captures. The investigative journal is important since it is very easy to forget how some piece of evidence was obtained.

Chapter Summary

E-mail examinations can comprise a large portion of the examiner's time. E-mail forensic examinations conducted in the computer forensic lab will probably be criminal in nature because most e-mail incidents involving corporate policy issues will be conducted by security departments. E-mail investigations can involve transmissions over the Internet and e-mail servers that are located at ISP computer sites.

A number of software companies are developing forensic packages for identifying and recovering e-mail evidence. EnCase and Access Data offer comprehensive solutions that include not only disk imaging and recovery, but also e-mail forensic functions. Screen-capture products such as Snagit are useful in developing presentations for court testimony.

E-mail investigations can be conducted on cases involving scams and various types of fraud. The primary tasks involve identifying the e-mail, retrieving it, and documenting the examination process. Various techniques are required for reviewing e-mail headers and tracking the transmission path and originator. The use of the ARIN WHOIS resource and search engines is critical in this endeavor.

Terms

American Registry for Internet Numbers (ARIN) — A service that provides a mechanism for finding contact and registration information for resources registered with ARIN.

Browser — Client to a Web server that allows the user to read hypertext documents on the World Wide Web. Netscape Navigator and Microsoft Internet Explorer are examples of popular Web browsers.

DNS (Domain Naming System) — The system that translates Internet domain names into IP numbers. A "DNS Server" is a server that performs this kind of translation.

E-Mail — The transmission of messages over communications networks.

Eudora — An e-mail program that uses the POP (Post Office Protocol).

Exchange — The Microsoft version of an e-mail server.

Freeality — A Web page that contains links to a number of search engines.

Google — A popular search engine and a tool for finding resources on the World Wide Web.

GroupWise — A workgroup application suite offering electronic mail and diary scheduling from Novell, Inc. It can operate on a number of server and workstation platforms. Server platforms include NetWare, Linux, and Windows, while the client software can run on Windows or Linux.

HTML (Hypertext Markup Language) — The authoring software language used on the Internet's World Wide Web. HTML is used for creating World Wide Web pages.

HTTP (Hypertext Transfer Protocol) — The Hypertext Transfer Protocol is the set of rules for exchanging files (text, graphic images, sound, video, and other multimedia files) on the World Wide Web.

Internet Protocol (IP) — A packet-based protocol for delivering data across networks.

Internet Service Provider (ISP) — A company that provides access to the Internet to individuals or companies. ISPs provide local dial-up and broadband access between a personal computer and the Internet.

IP Address — Internet Protocol addresses are the numerical codes that relate to a specific domain name. It is possible that a domain name may identify one or more IP addresses. The format of an IP address is a 32-bit numeric address written as four numbers separated by periods. Each number can be 0 to 255.

MIME (Multipurpose Internet Mail Extensions) — A protocol for Internet e-mail that enables the transmission of nontext data such as graphics, audio, video, and other binary types of files.

Outlook — An e-mail software that allows a user to send and receive e-mail, keep an address book, sort, organize and filter messages.

Outlook Express — An e-mail and news client bundled with operating systems and the Internet Explorer Web browser by Microsoft.

PINE — A program for Internet News and e-mail. A mail user agent used for reading, sending, and managing electronic messages. Online help is always available and it includes MIME and an address book.

POP (Post Office Protocol) — A protocol for retrieving e-mail. Also referred to as POP3 (version 3), it downloads all new e-mail messages from the server and stores them locally on a user's machine.

RFC 822 — Messages are viewed as having an envelope and contents. The envelope contains whatever information is needed to accomplish transmission and delivery. The contents compose the object to be delivered to the recipient. This standard applies only to the format and some of the semantics of message contents. It contains no specification of the information in the envelope.

RFC 2076 — Lists all Internet mail message headers in one document as an aid to people developing message systems or interested in Internet Mail standards.

RFC 2822 — An IETF Request for Comments document, released in April 2001 defining the format of SMTP e-mail. It makes obsolete the previous standard, RFC 822.

Sendmail — A UNIX based system for implementing the Simple Mail Transfer Protocol (SMTP) for transmitting e-mail.

SMTP (Simple Mail Transfer Protocol) — A core Internet protocol used to transfer e-mail messages between servers.

TCP — Transmission Control Protocol.

TCP/IP — Transmission Control Protocol/Internet Protocol.

uuencode (UNIX-to-UNIX Encoding) — A method for converting files from binary to ASCII (text) so that they can be sent across the Internet via e-mail.

WebMail — Users can access e-mail through a browser (such as Internet Explorer) from everywhere in the world, with advanced features (mailboxes, address book).

Review Questions

1. _____ is a core Internet protocol used to transfer e-mail messages between servers.
2. _____ is a protocol for Internet e-mail that enables the transmission of non-text data such as graphics, audio, video and other binary types of files.
3. _____ is the system that translates Internet domain names into IP numbers.
4. What service provides a mechanism for finding contact and registration information for Internet registered resources?
5. The document providing details for e-mail headers is _____.
6. What is the format of an IP address?

7. Which RFP defines the format of SMTP e-mail?
8. The five RDCs that are assessable to the general public for tracking e-mail are _____ ____, _____, _____, _____, and _____.
9. What protocol is the foundation of the Internet, an agreed upon set of rules directing computers on how to exchange information with each other?
10. Identify five tools that can be used to recover e-mail evidence.

Chapter 13

Mobile Phone and PDA Investigations

Chapter Objectives

- Become familiar with wireless networks, mobile phones, and personal digital assistants (PDAs)
- Identify the various wireless providers and communication devices currently in the wireless network
- Learn the definitions of terms associated with the wireless environment and infrastructure
- Look at the various forensic tools that can be utilized to obtain evidence
- Identify techniques and processes for identifying, retrieving, and managing wireless forensic evidence

Introduction

Mobile phones have come a long way since their inception. Once a tool for remote voice communications, the cell phone has evolved into a multifaceted personal communications device. The types and amount of data stored on the modern cellular phone increase every year, with cell phones possessing the capability and capacity of sending text messages, e-mail messages, and even sound files. It is not uncommon to see portable phones that can take and store photographs, as well as video. For many, these devices are personal organizers, storing important dates, events, address book information, and various other types of important data.

Unfortunately, there are times when either a catastrophic event has caused data loss, or the phone is used in a malicious manner and contains critical evidence. Either situation demands the expertise of a data recovery specialist or forensic examiners who specialize in recovering data from cell phones or performing mission critical forensic exams on these wireless devices. Mobile phone forensics is not to be compared with traditional bit-stream forensics used in disk imaging. Mobile phone data storage is proprietary, based on the manufacturer, model, and system.

Mobile phone forensics is the science of retrieving and examining data from a portable phone or personal digital assistant (PDA) under forensically sound conditions. This includes retrieval and examination of data found on the subscriber identity module or universal subscriber identity module (SIM/USIM), the phone body, and the optional memory cards. Data retrieved and examined can include images, videos, text, or short message service (SMS) messages, call times, and contact numbers. This information can then be used in litigation, for personal use, or even for committing a crime. Careful procedures must be followed in the retrieval and management of the data. Unlike with hard drives, data stored on mobile phones is proprietary; therefore, each phone needs to be analyzed with caution, as no two phones are guaranteed to be the same, and security mechanisms in mobile phones prevent a direct image of the data being taken.

The arduous task of data retrieval and examination from a mobile phone or PDA is not an easy one. Worldwide usage of these devices has increased dramatically in the past decade. With the ever-increasing daily use and convenience, the inevitable link from phone usage to clues about people's whereabouts, actions, and intentions, delivers the need for wireless-device forensics.

A.   Wireless Protocols and Components

The examiner must have a general understanding of the protocols used in the wireless network. This section will provide an overview and description of the major components and protocols that are part of the wireless infrastructure. The protocol standards and systems that operate in the wireless environment include global system for mobile communications (GSM), time division multiple access (TDMA), code division multiple access (CDMA), general packet radio service (GPRS), Wireless Application Protocol (WAP), and SMS. Network components and electronic devices include the SIM, handset, and mobile telephone switching office (MTSO). Figure 13.1 depicts the connectivity between the mobile device, local telco central office, and the MTSO. Access to the wireless device from a wired phone is through the MTSO.

GSM is the most widely used digital mobile phone system and the de facto wireless telephone standard in Europe. GSM was originally defined as a pan-European

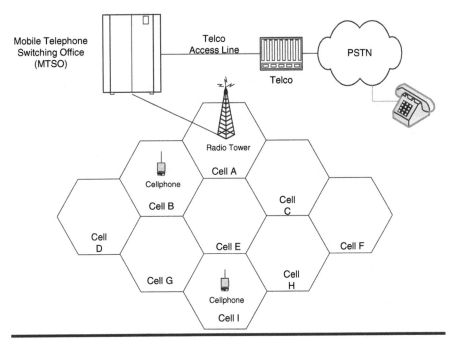

Figure 13.1   Cellular telephone system.

open standard for a digital cellular telephone network to support voice, data, text messaging, and cross-border roaming. GSM is now one of the world's main 2G digital wireless standards.

TDMA is a digital air interface technology used in cellular, personal communications service (PCS), and enhanced specialized mobile radio (ESMR) networks. TDMA is the type of digital cellular system most widely implemented in North America.

CDMA is a spread spectrum air interface technology used in some digital cellular, personal communication services, and other wireless networks. CDMA technology assigns a unique 10-bit code for each call known as the identifier. This identifier allows the base station to recognize the content of the packet and determine whether the message is voice or data.

GPRS is a packet-switched technology that allows Internet and other data communications over a GSM network. GPRS is considered a 2G technology and supports "always on" capability, which uses the network only when there is data to be sent.

The **WAP** is a secure specification that allows users to access information instantly via handheld wireless devices, such as mobile phones, pagers, two-way radios, smart phones, and communicators.

SMS is available on digital GSM networks allowing text messages of up to 160 characters to be sent and received via the network operator's message center to a mobile phone, or from the Internet, using a so-called "SMS gateway" Web site. If the phone is powered off or out of range, messages are stored in the network and are delivered at the next opportunity.

Multimedia messaging service (MMS) is a new standard that is being defined for use in advanced wireless terminals. The service concept is derived from SMS and allows for nonreal-time transmission of various kinds of multimedia contents such as images, audio, video clips, and as a further evolution of the current text mail. For example, electronic postcards, audio/video clips, etc. can be sent.

The **MTSO** is connected to a telephone central office and the public switched telephone network (PSTN). The MTSO coordinates all mobile calls between an area comprised of several cell sites and the local telephone central office. It contains a sophisticated computer that monitors all cellular calls, tracks the location of all cellular-equipped vehicles traveling in the system, arranges handoffs, and keeps track of billing information.

B. Mobile Telephone Service and Handset Providers

A **mobile phone** is a device that behaves as a normal telephone while being able to move over a wide area (compare cordless phone that acts as a telephone only within a limited range). Mobile phones allow connections to be made to the telephone network, through the MTSO, normally by directly dialing the other party's number on a keypad. The mobile phone consists of a handset, software, and memory. A **handset** is any handheld device used to transmit and receive calls from a wireless system. It is also known as a wireless phone, a cellular phone, a mobile phone, a PCS phone, among other terms.

Many different companies provide a variety of mobile communication devices and services. A short list of providers includes:

Verizon	BellSouth
Cingular	AT&T
Sprint	T-Mobile
Nextel	

Handsets with various features and options are available from a number of vendors. There are many different models and features offered by each of the phone manufacturers and providers. This is an issue with forensic examiners, as the number of different models, software, memory devices, and cables are almost infinite.

Nokia	SONY
Motorola	Samsung
Siemens	LG
Ericsson	PalmOne

1. Mobile Phone Features

Mobiles are designed to work on cellular networks and contain a standard set of services that allow phones of different types and in different countries to communicate with each other. Before the phone can be used, a subscription to a mobile phone operator (carrier) is required. For phones on GSM networks, the operator will issue a SIM card that contains the unique subscription and authentication parameters for that customer. Alternatively, the carrier will put the customer's handset identifier into its subscriber database so that the handset can make calls on the network. Once the SIM card is inserted into the phone, services can be accessed. Many mobile phones support auto-roaming, which permits the same phone to be used in multiple zones and countries. In order for this to work, the operators of the different carriers must have a roaming agreement.

Mobile phones not only support voice calls, but can also send and receive data and faxes (if a computer is attached), send short messages or text messages, and access WAP services. Support includes instant messaging, electronic mail, Web browsing, basic personal information manager (PIM) applications, and Internet access using technologies such as GPRS. Mobile phones usually have a clock and a calculator and often one can play games on them. Most current models also allow for sending and receiving pictures and have a built-in digital camera. Sound and video recording is often also possible. This feature is generally referred to as MMS. This gives rise to some concern about privacy, in view of possible voyeurism, for example in swimming pools. GPS receivers are also starting to appear integrated or connected to cell phones, using the Bluetooth technology.

There are also many additional features, such as user-defined and downloadable ring tones, phonebook, date book, encryption, walkie-talkie, and logos. A number of these features can provide the forensic examiner with possible sources of evidence. Special tools, however, are usually required to identify and extract this evidence.

A **smartphone** is generally considered any handheld device that integrates personal information management and mobile phone capabilities in the same device. Often, this includes adding phone functions to already capable PDAs or putting "smart" capabilities, such as PDA functions, into a mobile phone. In addition to network services and basic PIM applications, one can manage more extensive appointment and contact information, review electronic documents, give a presentation, and perform other tasks. PDAs will be discussed later in this chapter.

C. Subscriber Identity Module (SIM)

The **subscriber identity module (SIM)** is a smart card containing the telephone number of the subscriber, encoded network identification details, the personal identification number (PIN), and many other user data, such as the phone book. A user's SIM card can be moved from phone to phone and it contains key information required to activate the phone. The SIM card is the smart card inserted inside all GSM phones. It identifies the user account to the network, handles authentication, and provides data storage for basic user data and network information. It may also contain some applications that run on a compatible phone.

The terms SIM, smart card, and universal integrated circuit card (UICC) have an unfortunate tendency to be used interchangeably. The UICC is hardware. A SIM is a software application. Generally speaking, a smart card is a UICC running a SIM as well as possibly other applications.

The SIM is actually an application running on a smart card. A given card could contain multiple SIMs, allowing, for instance, a given phone to be used on multiple networks.

A typical SIM contains several categories of information. One is the actual identity of the card itself. The SIM needs to have a unique identity to the network. This allows the network to identify what sources the subscriber is entitled to, billing information, etc. A second category relates to the actual operation of the device. Information such as the last number called, or the length of the phone call, can be stored. A third category of information is personalized information. Phone books or calendars fall into this category.

A SIM has three major purposes:

Uniquely identifies the subscriber
Determines phone number
Contains algorithms for network authentication

A SIM (Figure 13.2) contains 16 to 64 kilobytes of memory, a processor, and an operating system. It should be noted that the 16 to 64 kilobytes memory limit can be thought of as a rule of thumb; however, the recent trend has been to produce SIM cards with larger storage capacities, ranging from 512 megabytes up to 1 gigabyte.

The **UICC** is the chip card used in mobile terminals in 3G telecom networks and systems. The UICC is an essential component for UMTS, just as the SIM is for GSM. Extending the concept of the SIM card, the UICC contains the USIM application and also provides a platform for other IC card applications. It ensures the integrity and security of all kinds of personal data, enabling secure support for all kinds of multi-application schemes.

The **UMTS** is the upcoming globally standardized system for mobile telephony and data communication. Contrary to the current GSM systems, UMTS will allow for broadband data communication to mobile units.

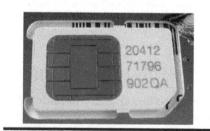

Figure 13.2   Sample SIM.

1. SIM Implementations

SIM cards can be used in any kind of device or situation where there is a need to authenticate the identity of a user. They are particularly useful when there is a need or desire to provide different types or levels of service to many users who have different configurations.

The primary use of SIM cards in the United States is in cell phones. There are other uses as well. The U.S. military issues smart cards as identification to its personnel. These cards are used to allow users to log into computers.

Europe has seen a wider use of these cards. The credit and debit card industry has integrated this technology in their cards for years. Similarly, a number of European phone companies have used these as phone cards to use in public telephones. The card companies in the United States have evidently not seen enough fraud to have a business justification to switch to this technology. There is some speculation that American credit cards will use a future generation of the technology when the added robustness and security of the system will make more economic sense.

The SIM uses a hierarchically organized file system that stores names, phone numbers, and received and sent text messages. It also contains the network configuration information. The SIM also allows for easy transporting of all information from one phone to another.

One downside to the use of SIM cards is the amount of thefts that occur. A person could steal a SIM card and use it for personal calls, which would still be on the original owner's information log. This is becoming a problem in European countries with the theft of SIM cards.

2. SIM Security

The personal identification number (PIN) and the card holder verification (CHV) help secure the information located on the SIM. The **PIN** is a number entered into computer and/or telephone systems to authenticate the user.

Unblocking CHV1 and CHV2 is a secret code made up of 8 to 10 digits that is used to reactivate a SIM card that has been blocked, and to define a new PIN.

When PIN protection is enabled, every time the phone is turned on, the PIN must be entered. The information on the SIM is locked until the correct code is entered. The PIN by default is at a standard default number and can be changed on the handset.

If the PIN is incorrectly entered three times in a row, the phone is locked, making the phone unable to make or receive any calls or SMS messages. This situation is known as PIN-locked. The personal unlock key (PUK), which is an 8-digit code, is needed from the network provider to unlock the phone. If the PIN is entered 10 times incorrectly, the SIM is permanently disabled and the SIM must be exchanged.

D.   Memory Cards

Removable media extends the storage capability of the mobile phone, which allows for the storage of additional information beyond the device's built-in capacity. It also provides another avenue for sharing information between wireless users that have compatible devices. Removable media is nonvolatile storage that allows for the retention of recorded data when removed from the device. The primary type of removable media for a wireless phone is a **memory card**, which is similar to a SIM in size, but has a different set of specifications and characteristics. Some of these card specifications allow for extended functions and standards, such as Bluetooth and Wi-Fi (wireless fidelity).

A wide variety of memory cards exist on the market for mobile phones and other mobile devices. The storage capacity of these cards range from megabytes to gigabytes and are available in various sizes. This media is normally formatted with conventional file systems and can be treated as a disk drive. This allows for the cards to be imaged and analyzed using a conventional forensic tool with a compatible media adapter, such as integrated drive electronics (IDE), which is the most common disk interface for hard drives. These adapters can be used with a write-blocker, ensuring the contents remain unaltered. Several types of memory cards currently available include the following devices:

Multi-media cards (MMC)
Secure digital (SD) cards
Memory sticks
microSD (TransFlash)
Compact flash (CF) card

E.   Mobile Phone Investigations

Forensic examination of wireless communication and computing devices is a growing subject area in computer forensics. Consequentially, mobile phone forensic tools are a relatively recent development and in the early stages of maturity. Forensic examination tools translate data to a format and structure that is understandable by the examiner and can be effectively used to identify and recover evidence for civil and criminal litigation. It is possible that some forensic tools may contain a degree of inaccuracies, requiring the examiner to employ several tools to verify the accuracy of the examination. For example, the tool may contain a software programming error or the protocol structure generated by the mobile device as input may be incorrect, causing the tool to function improperly. In addition, a suspect may tamper with device information to foil the workings of a tool or apply a wiping tool to remove or eliminate data. Over time, experience with a tool provides an understanding of its limitations, allowing an examiner to compensate where possible for any shortcomings or to turn to other means of recovery. New versions of these forensic tools are expected to improve and provide a higher quality result for investigative requirements. A National Institute of Standards and Technology (NIST) publication concerning mobile forensic examinations, tools, and techniques is available at http://csrc.nist.gov/publications/nistir/nistir-7250.pdf.

1. SIM Forensics

The data that a SIM card can provide the forensics examiner can be invaluable to an investigation. Acquiring a SIM card allows a large amount of information that the suspect has dealt with over the phone to be investigated. In general, some of this data can help an investigator determine:

Phone numbers of calls made/received
Contacts
SMS details (time/date, recipient, etc.)
SMS text (the message itself)

There are many software solutions that can help the examiner to acquire the information from the SIM card.

2. SIM Data Acquisition

Data that can be extracted from the SIM card includes:

International mobile subscriber identity (IMSI): A unique identifying number that identifies the phone/subscription to the GSM network
Mobile country code (MCC): A three-digit code that represents the SIM card's country of origin
Mobile network code (MNC): A two-digit code that represents the SIM card's home network
Mobile subscriber identification number (MSIN): A unique ten-digit identifying number that identifies the specific subscriber to the GSM network
Mobile subscriber international ISDN number (MSISDN): A number that identifies the phone number used by the headset
Abbreviated dialing number (ADN): Basic phone book entries
Last dialed numbers (LDN)
Short message service (SMS): Text messages
Public land mobile network (PLMN) selector
Location information (LOCI)
General packet radio service (GPRS) location
Integrated circuit card identifier (ICCID)
Service provider name (SPN)

Phase identification
SIM service table (SST)
Language preference (LP)
Card holder verification (CHV1 and CHV2)
Broadcast control channel (BCCH)
Ciphering key (Kc)
Ciphering key sequence number
Emergency call code
Fixed dialing number (FDN)
Forbidden PLMN
Local area identity (LAI)
Own dialing number
Temporary mobile subscriber identity (TMSI)
Routing area identifier (RIA) network code
Service dialing number (SDN)
Depersonalization keys

This information can be used to contact the service provider to obtain even more information than is stored on the SIM card. Some additional information the service provider might store include:

A customer database
Call detail records (CDRs)
Home location register (HLR)

3. SIM Card Text Encoding

Originally the middle-European GSM network used only a 7-bit code derived from the basic ASCII code. However, as GSM spread worldwide it was concluded that more characters, such as the major characters of all living languages, should be able to be represented on GSM phones. Thus, there was a movement toward a 16-bit code, known as UCS-2, which is now the standard in GSM text encoding. This change in encoding can make it more difficult to accurately obtain data from SIM cards of the older generation, which use the 7-bit encoding. This encoding is used to compress the hexadecimal size of certain elements of the SIMs data, particularly in SMS and ADNs.

F. Wireless Device Forensics

When a cell phone is found, proper forensic protocol says to leave it in the current state. The phone should be placed in a Faraday bag, which prevents stray signals from going in or out. The bag is made of metallic Mylar with a small metal grid on the surface. A phone boosts its output power when it is placed in a Faraday bag; therefore, an external battery should be attached. Another valuable tool, called the Faraday cage, is employed in the forensic lab for wireless examinations. A Faraday cage is an enclosure, used in a forensic lab, designed to exclude electromagnetic fields.

Wireless device forensics is a new and emerging subject area within the electronic forensics field that traditionally emphasized individual workstations, hard drive, and network servers. Differences between mobile device forensics and computer forensics exist due to the following factors:

- Devices are compact in size, portable, battery powered
- Devices require specialized interfaces, media, and hardware
- File systems can reside in volatile memory versus nonvolatile memory
- Devices can remain active, but in hibernation state, when powered off or idle
- Devices contain a diverse variety of embedded operating systems
- Mobile devices have a short product cycle

Most mobile phones offer a set of basic capabilities that are comparable. However, the various families of devices on the marketplace differ in such areas as the hardware technology, advanced feature set, and physical format.

Most mobile phones provide users with some ability to load additional applications, and store and process personal and sensitive information independently of a desktop or notebook computer. As digital technology evolves, the capabilities of these devices continue to improve rapidly. When mobile phones or other wireless devices are involved in a crime or other incident, forensic examiners require tools that allow the proper retrieval and speedy examination of information present on the device. This section provides an overview of current forensic software and hardware, designed for acquisition, examination, and reporting of evidence discovered on mobile wireless devices, and an understanding of their capabilities and limitations.

1.   Acquisitions and Device Seizures

There are a number of issues that must be addressed when acquiring evidence from electronic devices such as mobile phones and PDAs. These include:

Reporting acquired data
    Review of seizure techniques
    Faraday technology
    Power issues
    Order of acquisition

Protection of device
SIM processing
Device processing without SIM
Network tracing and systems

Interpreting provider data
How to get it?
What to do with it?
How do you write protect a phone?
Registry modifications
USB write protection
Software drivers
Other techniques for phones

Project-a-phone
Hardware and software tools

2.   To Prevent a Phone from Becoming PIN-Locked

A radio screened foil bag is used to protect an active exhibit from the ingress of new data, such as phone calls or text messages. The exhibit is protected while in transit between the scene of crime and laboratories where localized blockers protect the exhibit during the forensic examination. Figure 13.3 depicts a Paraben tool bag, stronghold bag, and a first-responder kit. The process is as follows:

- Place the phone into the Faraday bag. Avoid pressing the phone keys.
- Tightly fold the open edge of the bag. Make at least five folds, smoothing between folds.
- Fold over the excess bag and place inside the tamper-proof container. Take care not to puncture the bag.
- Exhibit must be placed inside an evidence bag and then sealed.
- Be aware of a phone's limited battery life.

Figure 13.3   Paraben first-responder tools.

Figure 13.4 depicts the basic cellular device seizure procedures. This procedure applies to mobile communication devices utilizing TDMA, CDMA, and GSM, operating on a variety of frequencies.

G. Forensic Tools

The variety of forensic toolkits for mobile phones and other handheld devices is considerable. A number of software tools and toolkits exist, but the range of devices over which they operate is typically narrowed to platforms for a manufacturer's product line, a family of operating systems, or a type of hardware architecture. The tools usually require the examiner have full access to the device and is, therefore, not protected by some authentication mechanism. The following criteria highlight some items to consider when choosing among available tools:

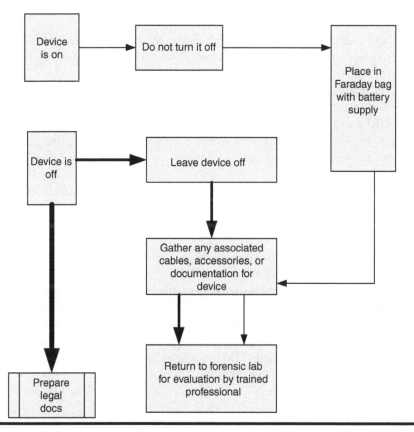

Figure 13.4   Cellular device seizure procedures.

- Accuracy — The quality that the output of the tool has been verified and a margin of error ascertained.
- Acceptance — The degree of peer review and agreement about the methodology or technique used by the tool.
- Affordability — The cost versus the associated benefits in productivity.
- Capability — The supported devices, feature set, performance, and richness of features with regard to flexibility and customization.
- Comprehensiveness — The ability to present all data to an investigator so evidence pertaining to an investigation can be identified.
- Determinism — The ability for the tool to produce the same output when given the same set of instructions and input data.
- Quality — The technical support, reliability, and maintenance provided by the manufacturer.
- Usability — The ability to present data in a form that is useful to an investigator.
- Verifiability — The ability to ensure accuracy of the output by having access to intermediate translation and presentation results.

While most toolkits support a full range of acquisition, examination, and reporting functions, some tools are limited. Different tools may be capable of using different interfaces, such as infrared data association (IrDA), Bluetooth, or serial cable, to acquire device contents. The types of information a tool can acquire can range widely and include PIM data, logs of phone calls, messages, e-mail, IM content, URLs and content of visited Web sites, audio, video, and image and SIM content. Information present on a mobile phone can vary depending on several factors, including the following:

- Inherent capabilities of the phone implemented by the manufacturer
- Network services subscribed to and used by the user
- Modifications made to the phone by the service provider or network operator
- Modifications made to the phone by the user

Acquisition through a cable interface generally yields superior acquisition results than other device interfaces. Note many different cable configurations are required for the multitude of different wireless devices. Regardless of the interface used, one must be vigilant about any forensic issues associated. Note too that the ability to acquire the contents of a resident SIM may not be supported by some tools, particularly those strongly oriented toward PDAs.

H.   Forensic Software Tools

There are a number of mobile phone forensic tools available in the commercial market. All of these tools provide some level of evidence identification and retrieval from the mobile device. Note that GSM mobile phones are logically and physically partitioned into a handset and SIM, resulting in some forensic tools that deal exclusively with SIM. The forensic laboratory management will probably want to compare features, capabilities, and costs when selecting a product. A short overview of some forensic products follows:

Device Seizure, provided by Paraben, takes the SIM card acquisition and analysis components from Paraben's Device Seizure and puts it into a specialized SIM card forensic acquisition and analysis tool. SIM card seizure includes the software as well as a **forensic SIM card reader**. The tool targets certain models of GSM, TDMA, and CDMA mobile phones.

ForensicSIM, provided by Evidence Talks, allows trained operators to easily clone a SIM card and examine it without any chance of damaging the evidence. It also allows the examination of phone memory without any possibility of accidental connection to the phone network, a possible breach of the Interception of Communications Act.

USIMdetective, provided by Quantaq Solutions, can read both 2G SIM and 3G USIM cards and automatically performs the correct acquisition for each type. Quantaq has designed the software to acquire data from any SIM or USIM card within the minimum number of key strokes, which is an absolute requirement when processing a large number of SIM cards.

SIMCON, provided by Inside Out Forensics, is a program that allows the user to securely image all files on a GSM SIM card to a computer file with a standard smart card reader. The user can subsequently analyze the contents of the card including stored numbers and text messages. The software is offered free of charge to law enforcement agencies.

.XRY, provided by Micro Systemation, retrieves information stored on a mobile telephone quickly and securely. Examples of information that can be retrieved include telephone books, SMS messages, pictures, calendar information, and sound files. The tool targets certain GSM models and supports internal and external SIM access.

MOBILedit! Forensic, provided by Compelson Laboratories, provides reports with tamper-proof and indisputable evidence in a court of law. This report details out every piece of information in the phone such as call history, list of contacts, messages, photos, voice recordings, video, files, calendars, tasks, and notes. This tool targets certain GSM phones and provides both internal and external SIM support.

Oxygen PM—Forensic edition lets the user extract all information and settings from mobile phones and smartphones. Forensic version has a unique difference from Oxygen Phone Manager II. It prohibits any data change in the program or the phone itself. The program allows reading data from the phone, saving it to a file, or exporting into any of supported formats. Software support is available for forensic investigations on Nokia, Samsung, Mobiado, and Symbian OS smartphones. The tool supports only internal SIM acquisition.

BitPim is an open source program that allows a user to view and manipulate data on many CDMA phones from LG, Samsung, Sanyo, and other manufacturers. This includes the phone book, calendar, wall papers, ring tones and the file system for most Qualcomm CDMA chipset-based phones. The matrix of supported phones and features is in the online help. There is no support for recovering SIM information.

TULP2G is a .NET 2.0-based open source forensic software framework for extracting and decoding data stored in electronic devices. Along with the framework, this version includes several plug-ins in the area of retrieving data from mobile phones and generating the accompanying reports. This tool targets GSM and CDMA phones that use the supported protocols to establish connectivity.

I.   Forensic Card Reader (FCR)

The **forensic card reader (FCR)** consists of a smart card reader with a USB connection and the software that provides the examiners with the ability to acquire data from SIM cards without modification. The examiner has the ability to select specific data elements that can be later stored and displayed in a finalized report. SIM cards for GSM mobiles and 3G SIM cards can be used with a FCR.

The FCR provided by BKForensics allows a forensically clean method of extracting data from a SIM card. It was developed in cooperation with the German Federal Police Agency (BKA). The FCR accesses areas beyond the capability of standard SIM readers. FCR will not alter any data it analyses, including data and time stamps of SMS read/unread tags.

The UltraBlock forensic card readers are available as a set: one read-only and one read-write. The read-only unit should be used for forensic acquisition of information found on multimedia and memory cards. The read-write unit is included to provide the ability to write to memory cards for testing or validation. These card readers are the same units integrated into the FRED systems and are exclusively available from Digital Intelligence.

J.   The International Mobile Station Identity (IMSI)

The **international mobile station identity (IMSI)** is a unique 15-digit number assigned to a mobile station at the time of service subscription. It contains a mobile country code, a mobile network code, mobile subscriber identification number, and a national mobile subscriber identity.

An **IMSI catcher** is a device for intercepting GSM mobile phones. It subjects the phones in its vicinity to a man-in-the-middle attack, acting to them as a preferred base station in terms of signal strength.

The IMSI catcher logs the IMSI numbers of all the mobile phones in the area, as they attempt to attach to the base station, and can determine the phone number of each individual phone. It also allows forcing the mobile phone connected to it to revert to A5/0 for call encryption (in other words, no encryption at all), making the call data easy to intercept and convert to audio. It can also tap and record the phone calls on its own.

The GSM specification requires the handset to authenticate to the network, but does not require the network to authenticate to the handset, which is a glaring and reportedly intentional security hole.

IMSI catchers are used by law enforcement and intelligence agencies. Several countermeasures against IMSI catchers exist. A directional antenna can be used to lock the telephone to a distant base station, making it not see the nearby IMSI catcher, or the phone can be forced to a specific base station ID (if the firmware supports it), sacrificing mobility for security. To avoid being wiretapped, even if the phone is still seen and recognized, a GSM compatible secure telephone or cipher unit for end-to-end voice encryption is required.

K.   PDA Investigations

A **PDA** is a handheld device that combines computing, telephone/fax, and networking features. A typical PDA can function as a cellular phone, fax sender, and personal organizer. Many PDAs incorporate handwriting and/or voice recognition features. PDAs also are called palmtops, handheld computers, and pocket computers.

The PDA could be a handheld device such as a Palm Pilot, next-generation cell phone, or Research in Motion (RIM) BlackBerry. Many of these devices now provide the ability to access Web content remotely, over wireless networks. Depending on the device, these tools can either display native HTML Web content, or repurpose Web content into the WAP markup language, stripping the "Web pages" of all imagery, but transmitting the text portion.

The many uses and tasks of a basic PDA include many features: calculating, using as a clock and calendar, playing computer games, accessing the Internet, sending and receiving e-mails, using as a radio or stereo, video recording, recording notes, using as an address book, and using as a spreadsheet. Newer PDAs also have both color screens and audio capabilities, enabling them to be used as mobile phones (PDA phones), Web browsers, or media players. Many PDAs can access the Internet, intranets or extranets via Wi-Fi, or Wireless Wide-Area Networks (WWANs).

1.   PDA Devices

PDA devices are available in many configurations, with various features. The list of available devices and models changes frequently as the technology improves.

Psion	Sharp Wizard
Apple Newton	Zaurus
BlackBerry	Sony CLIÉ
hp iPAQ Pocket PC	Tapwave Zodiac
hp Jornada Pocket PC	AlphaSmart Dana
Palm Pilot	Dell Axim
Tungsten	GMate Yopy
LifeDrive	Fujitsu Siemens Loox
Treo	PocketMail
Zire	

2. Hardware Characteristics

Most types of PDAs employ an operating system and application software and possess hardware features and capabilities. They house a microprocessor, read-only memory (ROM), random access memory (RAM), a variety of hardware keys and interfaces, and a touch-sensitive, liquid crystal display. The operating system (OS) of the device is held in ROM. Several varieties of ROM are used, including Flash ROM, which can be erased and reprogrammed electronically with OS updates or an entirely different OS. RAM, which normally contains user data, is kept active by batteries whose failure or exhaustion causes that information to be lost.

The latest PDAs include considerable memory capacity and contain slots that support memory cards and peripherals, such as a digital camera or wireless communications card. Wireless communications such as infrared, IrDA, Bluetooth, and Wi-Fi may also be built-in. PDA devices have different technical and physical characteristics, such as size, weight, processor speed, and memory capacity. Devices may also use different types of expansion capabilities, such as input/output (I/O) and memory card slots, device expansion sleeves, and external hardware interfaces, to provide additional functionality. Additionally, PDA capabilities are sometimes combined with those of other devices such as cell phones, Global Positioning Systems (GPSs), and cameras to form new types of hybrid devices. Characteristics for a wide range of PDAs can be found on manufacturer and vendor Web sites, as well as product review sites.

A wide array of memory cards also exists on the PDA market. Their storage capacity is substantial, ranging from 8 megabytes to beyond 2 gigabytes, though their size is diminutive, no larger than a matchbook, and easy to overlook. Memory cards allow individuals to store additional files beyond the device's built-in capacity and provide another avenue for sharing data between compatible devices. Unlike the RAM of a PDA, removable media is nonvolatile storage, normally flash memory, and does not require battery power to retain data. Fortunately, if a PDA forensic tool cannot handle such media, the memory card can be treated similarly to a removable disk drive, and imaged and analyzed with the aid of an external media adaptor using conventional forensic tools. Memory card adapters exist that support an integrated development environment (IDE) interface, allowing removable media to be treated as a hard disk and used with a write blocker to ensure that the contents of the removable media remain unaltered during acquisition.

L.   PDA OS

The currently major PDA operating systems include Symbian, Research in Motion (RIM), Palm OS, Pocket PC, and Linux. Symbian OS (formerly EPOC) is owned by Ericsson, Motorola, Panasonic, Nokia, Samsung, Siemens, and Sony Ericsson. Palm OS is owned by PalmSource, Windows Mobile (Pocket PC), based on the Windows CE kernel, is owned by Microsoft, and the BlackBerry is owned by RIM. Many operating systems are based on the Linux kernel and are free.

Palm OS is a compact operating system developed and licensed by PalmSource, Inc. for PDAs manufactured by various licensees. It is designed to be easy to use and similar compared with desktop operating systems such as Microsoft Windows. Palm OS is combined with a suite of basic applications including an address book, clock, note pad, sync, and security software. Palm OS was originally released in 1996.

Windows **Mobile 5.0** marks the convergence of the Phone Edition and Professional Edition operating systems into one system that contains both phone and PDA capabilities. A phone application is now included in the OS, and all PIM applications have been updated to interface with it. Windows Mobile 5.0 is compatible with Microsoft's Smartphone operating system and is capable of running Smartphone applications.

The first **BlackBerry** integrating a cell phone, as well as the first BlackBerry sold outside of North America was released in 2001, using the European GSM/GPRS standard. Since then, RIM has released a variety of devices running on GSM, CDMA, and Motorola iDEN networks. RIM develops its own software for its devices, using C++ and Java technology. RIM also develops and sells embedded wireless data components.

Symbian OS is an operating system, designed for mobile devices, with associated libraries, user interface frameworks, and reference implementations of common tools, produced by Symbian Ltd. It is a descendant of Psion's EPOC and runs exclusively on ARM processors. Symbian OS's major advantage is the fact that it was built for handheld devices, with limited resources, that may be running for months or years. There is a strong emphasis on conserving memory, using Symbian-specific programming idioms, such as descriptors and a cleanup stack. Together with other techniques, these keep memory usage low and memory leaks rare. There are similar techniques for conserving disk space. Furthermore, all Symbian OS programming is event-based, and the CPU is switched off when applications are not directly dealing with an event.

M. PDA Forensics

As with digital computers in general, both the functionality and information capacity of handheld devices are improving rapidly. Present-day memory capacities can hold megabytes of information, easily extendable into the gigabyte range. Though an investigator can browse the contents of the device through its user interface to obtain evidence, the approach is highly impractical and problematic, and should be used only as a last resort. Instead, applying forensic tools is the preferred alternative. Forensic software tools facilitate the proper acquisition of data from a device and the examination, organization, and reporting of the evidence recovered. A number of specialized tools are available for PDA forensic examinations. These include Device Seizure, Palm dd, Pilot-Link, **Palm OS Emulator (POSE)**, and **Duplicate Disk (dd)**.

Device Seizure — A Paraben product that supports forensic acquisition, examination, and analysis of PDA devices for the Palm, Windows CE, and BlackBerry operating systems. It provides for capture and report on data from PDAs by a two-step acquisition of PDA device: (1) all files in original structure and (2) full memory card acquisition. The product includes an easy-to-use interface with built-in searching and book-marking, text and Hex view, and HTML reporting. Device Seizure uses the MD5 hash function. Law enforcement, consultants, and corporate security examiners can use this tool.

Palm dd (pdd) — A Windows-based tool for memory imaging and forensic acquisition of data from the Palm OS family of PDAs. pdd will preserve the crime scene by obtaining a bit-for-bit image or "snapshot" of the Palm device's memory contents. Such data can be used by forensic investigators, incident response teams, and criminal and civil prosecutors. Files created from pdd can be imported into a forensic tool, such as EnCase, to aid analysis; otherwise, the default tool is a hex editor. pdd does not provide hash values for the information acquired. Paraben has integrated elements of the pdd engine into Device Seizure.

Pilot-Link — A suite of tools used to connect a Palm or Palm OS compatible handheld with Unix, Linux, and any other POSIX-compatible machine. Pilot-link works with all Palm OS handhelds, including those made by Handspring, Sony, and Palm, as well as others. Pilot-link includes user space "conduits" that allow the user to synchronize information to and from a Palm device, as well as libraries of Palm-compatible functions that allow other applications to take advantage of the code included in pilot-link. The two programs of interest to forensic specialists are pi-getram and pi-getrom, which respectively retrieve the contents of RAM and ROM from a device, similar to the physical acquisition done by pdd.

Palm OS Emulator (POSE) — Palm OS powers 40 million handhelds and smartphones. More than 20,000 software programs run on Palm OS. The Palm OS Emulator is a software that emulates the hardware of various models of Palm powered handhelds. Since it allows a user to create "virtual" handhelds on Windows, Mac OS, or Unix computers, the Palm OS Emulator is extremely valuable for writing, testing, and debugging applications. In particular, it emulates 68 K devices and runs ROM images of the Palm OS through Palm OS 4.x. Built-in PIM applications, such as Datebook, Address Book, To Do, etc., run properly and the hardware buttons and display react accurately. ROM images can be obtained from the PalmSource Web site or by copying the contents of ROM from an actual device, using pdd, Pilot-Link, or a companion tool provided with the emulator.

Duplicate Disk (dd) — A common UNIX program whose primary purpose is the low-level copying and conversion of files. Unlike the other tools described above, dd executes directly on the PDA. An image of the device can be obtained by connecting to the PDA, issuing the dd command, and dumping the contents elsewhere, for example, to auxiliary media such as a memory card or across a network session to a forensic workstation. Caution should be exercised because dd may destroy parts of the file system, such as overwriting data, if used incorrectly. As with pdd, dd produces binary data output, some of which contains ASCII character information. Images created from dd may be imported for examination into a forensic tool, such as EnCase, if the file system is supported.

A number of forensic examinations are relevant to PDA devices. The activities of the examiner could involve PDA evidence in the following categories:

Device content acquisition	Deleted files
PIM applications	Misnamed files
Web and e-mail applications	Peripheral memory cards
Graphics file formats	Cleared devices
Compressed file archive formats	Password protected devices

Tests conducted on DPA devices using the tools discussed above resulted in mixed successes. The examiner must understand the functionality and scope of the tools being used. It might be necessary and desirable to use several different tools in the forensic examination process. This can be time consuming; however, the effort might be well spent.

1.   A Caution when Using Forensic Tools

Unlike the situation with desktop computers and workstations, the number and variety of toolkits for PDAs and other handheld devices are limited. Not only do fewer specialized tools and toolkits exist, but also the range of devices over which they operate is typically narrowed to only the most popular families of PDA devices—those based on the Pocket PC and Palm OS. Linux-based devices can be imaged with the dd utility, somewhat analogously to a Linux desktop, and analyzed with the use of a compatible tool, such as EnCase. Since Palm OS devices have been around the longest, more forensic tools are available for them than for other device families. Most tools require the examiner have unobstructed access to acquire contents, which means no authentication technique needs to be satisfied to gain access.

Forensic tools acquire data from a device in one of two ways: physical acquisition or logical acquisition. Physical acquisition implies a bit-by-bit copy of an entire physical store, such as a disk drive or RAM chip, while logical acquisition implies a bit-by-bit copy of logical storage objects, such as directories and files that reside on a logical store, such as a file system partition. The difference lies in the distinction between memory as seen by a process through the operating system facilities, as in a logical view, versus memory as seen in raw form by the processor and other related hardware components, as in a physical view.

Physical acquisition has advantages over logical acquisition, since it allows deleted files and any data remnants present, such as unallocated RAM or unused file system space, to be examined, which otherwise would go unaccounted. Physical device images are generally more easily imported into another tool for examination and reporting. However, a logical structure has the advantage that it is a more natural organization to understand and use during examination. Thus, if possible, doing both types of acquisition on PDAs is preferable and desirable, if time allows.

Tools not designed specifically for forensic purposes are questionable and should be thoroughly evaluated before use. Nonforensic software tools generally focus on logical acquisition, using an available protocol for device synchronization and management to communicate with the device, as opposed to a debugging or testing protocol that could be used to acquire a memory image. Such tools support two-way flow of information, unconcerned with blocking changes, and avoid taking hashes of acquired content for integrity purposes. Documentation also may be limited and source code unavailable for examination, respectively increasing the likelihood of error and decreasing confidence in the results.

As with any tool, forensic issues might be associated with the usage of a nonforensic tool. For example, a tool may inadvertently alter a time stamp on the device, such as the date and time of last synchronization, incorrectly decode and display information, or alter the state of the device. On one hand, nonforensic tools might be the only means to retrieve information that could be relevant as evidence. On the other, they might overwrite, append, or otherwise cause information to be lost, through a reset, during use. This situation could lead to the evidence being ruled inadmissible in a court of law.

2.   Data Retrieval

In forensics, data retrieval is a most sensitive issue. Some of the simplest things can corrupt the data and so the retrieval must be done in a manner that is tamper- proof and indisputable in court. Removing the battery from some phones causes vital information, such as time stamps, to be lost. Because we are surrounded by mobile network cells, RFID tags, two-way pagers, and EZ-passes, interference with mobile phones is difficult to prevent. When a phone has been seized for forensic analysis, it is vital that this interference is prevented. Some mobile phones automatically download data such as updates and this immediately compromises the data as evidence. In forensics, a Faraday bag and Faraday cage is used to avoid this problem.

Figure 13.5   Paraben first responder kit and Faraday tent.

To avoid a mobile phone from becoming PIN-locked, the radioscreened Faraday bag can be used to protect active exhibits from the ingress of new data, such as phone calls or text messages. It is still necessary to provide a localized signal blocker, such as a Faraday cage, at the laboratory when conducting the forensic investigation on the mobile device. Figure 13.5 depicts a Paraben first-responder kit and a Faraday tent.

N.   Forensic Examination Protocol

There are a number of specific steps the investigator must follow to successfully identify, retrieve, and preserve mobile phone and PDA evidence. These include those documentation and chain-of-custody actions that must be followed in all forensic investigations. These include:

Identify the specific make and model of the device.
Preserve the device as much as possible.
Do not under any circumstances access the device.
Do not turn the device on/off.
Photograph the screen if it is on.
Try to obtain the PIN number for the phone.
Store the device in a Faraday bag where possible or another suitable storage media.
Time is an issue. If the battery dies, evidence can be lost.
Check the device for fingerprints and DNA.
Check the crime scene for any related items, such as SIM cards, memory cards, batteries, charger, cables, manuals, etc.

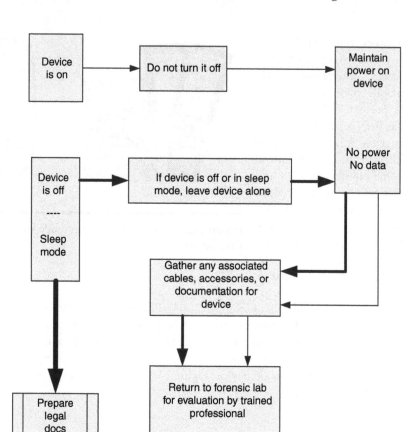

Figure 13.6   PDA device seizure on/off rule.

Remember the PDA devices require power be maintained in order for the potential evidence to remain intact. The PDA typically uses active memory as the main method of data storage. Figure 13.6 depicts the rule for seizing a PDA device.

The evidence recovered will be transported to the forensics lab. The chain-of-custody form must be completed, as does the other documentation required in any electronic forensic investigation. Copies of all forms are contained in Appendix A. It is also important to complete the evidence receipt for all devices and paraphernalia when the evidence is provided to any commercial or law enforcement lab for examination. Ensure the forensic reports from the lab will be acceptable for the action that is expected to occur as a result of the examination. This could include civil litigation and/or criminal charges.

Chapter Summary

The examiner must have a general understanding of the protocols used in the wireless network. The wireless communication network contains a number of components, interfaces, and software. There are also many standards associated with the mobile and PDA network. The protocol standards and systems that operate in the wireless environment include GSM, TDMA, CDMA, GPRS, WAP, and SMS. Network components and electronic devices include the SIM, handset, and MTSO.

Many different companies provide a variety of mobile communication devices and services. Handsets with various features and options are available from a number of vendors. There are many different models and features offered by each of the phone and PDA manufacturers and providers. This is an issue with forensic examiners as the number of different models, software, memory devices, and cables are almost infinite.

The subscriber identity module (SIM) is a smart card containing the telephone number of the subscriber, encoded network identification details, the personal identification number (PIN), and many other user data that can be useful to the forensic examiner. A SIM has three major purposes including uniquely identifying the subscriber, determining a phone number, and network authentication.

Removable memory card extends the storage capability of the mobile phone, which allows for the storage of additional information beyond the device's built-in capacity. A wide variety of memory cards exist on the market for mobile phones and other mobile devices. The storage capacity of these cards ranges from megabytes to gigabytes and is available in various sizes. This storage can contain a wealth of forensic information.

Wireless forensic examination tools translate data to a format and structure that is understandable by the examiner and can be effectively used to identify and recover evidence for civil and criminal litigation. The variety of forensic toolkits for mobile phones and other handheld devices is considerable.

PDA devices are available in many configurations, with numerous features and options. The list of available devices and models change frequently as the technology improves. The latest PDAs include considerable memory capacity and contain slots that support memory cards and peripherals, such as a digital camera or wireless communications card.

Forensic examinations involving PDAs are more difficult due to the multitude of models, software, storage, and interfaces.

Forensic data retrieval from mobile phones and PDAs is a most sensitive issue. Some of the simplest things can corrupt the data and so the retrieval must be done in a manner that is tamper-proof and protects the integrity of the evidence. Devices such as Faraday bags and Faraday tents must be used to protect against spurious radio signals.

Terms

2G — Second generation of GSM is the technology currently used in the operation of mobile phones.

3G — Third generation wireless is digital and includes, but is not limited to, such enhanced features as high-speed transmission, global roaming, and advanced multimedia access. This generation will become more and more visible within the next few years.

4G — Fourth generation is short for the fourth-generation successor of 3G and is a wireless access technology. It describes two different but overlapping ideas.

Bluetooth — A computing and telecommunications industry specification that describes how mobile phones, computers, and PDAs can easily interconnect with each other and with home and business phones and computers using a short wireless connection.

CDMA (code division multiple access) — A spread spectrum air interface technology used in some digital cellular, personal communications services and other wireless networks.

Cellular — A mobile telephone service provided by a network of base stations, each of which covers one geographic cell within the total cellular system service area.

CHV (card holder verification) — Access condition used by the SIM for the verification of the identity of the user.

ESMR (enhanced specialized mobile radio) — A Motorola-developed mobile communications implementation that integrates radio services with TDM mobile telephony to provide digital mobile communications service using primarily the 800 megahertz frequency band. This facilitates applications such as paging, data transmission, dispatch, and interoperability with the wire-line PSTN.

Faraday bag — Used to protect active wireless exhibits from the ingress of new data such as phone calls or text messages.

Faraday cage — An enclosure designed to exclude electromagnetic fields.

FCR (forensic card reader) — Consists of a smart card reader with a USB connection and the software that provides the examiners with the ability to acquire data from SIM cards without modification.

Flash card — A type of memory that retains data after power is removed. It operates both like memory and like a storage device. Examples include Compact Flash, SmartMedia, and PCMCIA, among others. It is used in devices such as digital cameras, audio players, handheld computers, cell phones, USB drives, and printers.

GPRS (general packet radio service) — A packet-switched technology that allows Internet and other data communications over a GSM network.

GSM (global system for mobile) — The most widely used digital mobile phone system and the de facto wireless telephone standard in Europe.

Handset — Any handheld device used to transmit and receive calls from a wireless system.

IrDA (infrared data association) — The standard for infrared communication. Infrared interfaces exist on most laptops, PDAs, and some mobile phones, though not all of them implement the full IrDA standard.

Memory card — Or flash memory card refers to solid-state electronic flash memory data storage devices used with digital cameras, handheld and laptop computers, telephones, music players, video game consoles, and other electronics.

Memory stick — Used as storage media for a portable device, in a form that can easily be removed for access by a PC or Mac.

Mobile phone — A device that behaves as a normal telephone while being able to move over a wide area.

MSISDN (mobile station integrated services digital network) — The mobile equivalent of ISDN. Used as a value, MSISDN refers to the MSISDN subscriber ID, which is a max 15-digit number.

PCS (personal communications service) — An American generic term for a mass-market mobile phone service, emphasizing personal communication, independent of the technology used to provide it. PCS includes such digital cellular technologies as GSM 1900, CDMA, and TDMA IS-136.

PIM (personal information management) — Includes calendar, scheduling, and calculator programs.

PIN (personal identification number) — An alphanumeric or numeric code used to verify the identity of an individual attempting to use a credit card, debit card, or other account.

PIN-locked — An incorrect PIN will cause the device to become "PIN-locked" and cannot be used until it is reset.

Serial cable — A cable that can be used to transfer information between two devices. The universal serial bus (USB) is a serial bus standard to interface devices.

Smartphone — Is generally considered any handheld device that integrates personal information management and mobile phone capabilities in the same device.

Symbian — A company created by Psion, Nokia, Ericsson, and Motorola in 1998 with the aim of developing and standardizing an operating system that enables mobile phones from different manufacturers to exchange information.

TMDA (time division multiple access) — A digital air interface technology used in cellular, PCS, and ESMR networks.

USIM (universal subscriber identity module) — Subscriber identity modules for 3G mobile telephony. They are the same physical size as normal 2G GSM SIM cards.

WAP (Wireless Application Protocol) — A secure specification that allows users to access information instantly via handheld wireless devices such as mobile phones, pagers, two-way radios, smart phones and communicators.

Wi-Fi (wireless fidelity) — A wireless feature that is available on Palm Pilots and Pocket PCs and that allows wireless communication between the device and a network.

Review Questions

1. The wireless network infrastructure component that provides connectivity between mobile phone users and the wired network is called a _____.

2. The _____ is a smart card containing the telephone number of the subscriber, encoded network identification details, the personal identification number (PIN), and many other user data.

3. The three purposes of a SIM include _____, _____ _____, and _____.

4. The primary type of removable media for a wireless phone is the _____.

5. Describe the situation called "PIN-locked."

6. List five criteria for choosing a wireless forensic tool.

7. Information available on a wireless device can depend on several factors. They include _____.

8. Provide a list of forensic software tools for mobile devices.

9. What device consists of a smart card reader with a USB connection and the software that provides the examiners with the ability to acquire data from SIM cards without modification?

10. List the forensic tools that can be used to recover evidence from PDA devices.

Chapter 14

Court Preparation, Presentations, and Testimony

Chapter Objectives

- Identify testimony requirements for electronic evidence presentations
- Learn how to be effective in technical courtroom presentations
- Understand why examiners and investigators must be technically proficient
- Learn the various legal terms associated with forensic testimony
- Become familiar with direct examination and cross-examination processes

Introduction

Forensic investigators and examiners can be expected to provide expert testimony in civil and criminal litigation. Obviously, training, expertise, and courtroom experience will be an advantage when testifying concerning electronic forensic cases. This chapter will provide guidance in the area of courtroom decorum.

Electronic evidence might be used in both civil and criminal litigation. Technical testimony might involve cases relating to civil cases involving domestic investigations, theft of trade secrets, extortion, embezzlement, and interference with commerce. Computer forensic experts could provide supporting evidence to prosecute criminal cases relating to all categories of serious crimes.

The forensic team must know how the various state and federal laws apply to the case and evidence. The legal team members must be in step with the technical members. The legal team must avoid conflicts by being prepared to offer convincing forensic evidence and testimony.

Forensic examiners must know how all the computer and electronic devices work. The opposing team will try to discredit all testimony possible. Detailed explanations concerning forensic examinations may be required.

Forensic investigators and first responders must understand the forensic process and how to identify, collect, log, protect, and transport evidence. Documentation will be required to support all allegations presented.

A.   Computer and Electronic Evidence

Forensics, as it relates to computers and data, is the collection and preservation of data to investigate or establish facts for any type of legal purpose. For each case, computer forensics can contain many different types of material and can be gathered from many sources. Information can be limited to what exists on a hard drive and may also include data from the Internet, e-mail, cell phones, disks, or printouts made by a specific computer.

Computer and electronic forensics is an emerging specialty that has no defined criteria. This makes it difficult to find a person with the knowledge, experience, and skills needed to be an expert in this area. Colleges and technical schools are beginning to recognize this as a growing field and are adding degrees and certification programs to their curriculum.

With the speed at which the computer industry changes, it is often a struggle for the legal profession to keep up with all the new laws established to convict criminals or business insiders who use technology as a weapon. It is equally challenging to locate a knowledgeable computer specialist that has the interest, expertise, and skills in fields other than computer science. Consequently, a computer forensic specialist who has skills in other disciplines, such as accounting and/or law, will produce a higher quality result.

Methodologies are a set of processes that can be applied to any situation. While the tools or items used to lay the groundwork for the discovery phase may vary, the methodology remains the same. Some of these methods are still being developed in the area of computer forensics. Changes are frequent because of new laws that dictate the way processes are completed. Other changes are due to an ever-evolving technology and the ability to completely remove two or three processes with new software or hardware.

Civil testimony might involve cases relating to domestic investigations, theft of trade secrets, extortion, embezzlement, interference with commerce, and the list goes on. Electronic evidence might be used to prosecute criminal cases relating to drug trafficking, murder, kidnapping, terrorism, and another endless list. Those giving testimony must know their field of expertise. Qualified computer forensic specialists spend considerable time staying in front of the new technology curve. It takes an extreme amount of work to keep up with the changes in the computing industry, as well as issues involving the law.

Most attorneys have little knowledge about computers and will need guidance as a case develops. They will continually need to discuss the case with a computer forensic specialist and review new material even when it seems unnecessary. When dealing with computers and data, the process of understanding what is achievable and what is not requires an advanced understanding of technology generally not found outside the professional computer security community. Not only must the computer forensic specialist assist the attorney with what can be done, but he or she must also stand as a credible witness under the pressure and scrutiny of cross-examination.

The majority of work is often discovering how to look at the information and display it so that it makes sense to laymen. This also includes educating the attorney about the technical details so they can decide how to approach the case. It is of no value if the information is so complex that it cannot be explained clearly.

During the discovery phase of a case, being a forensic computer specialist can be compared to being a private investigator, only the subject matter is mainly dealing with computers and electronic data. Discovery often involves several passes at the data. As new facts are revealed about the case, the old data will need to be reviewed to see what has been discovered and how it is applicable to the case. In some cases, knowing what happened is more important than the actual data itself.

Chapter 2 provides considerable background information reference the legal environment and the various processes that might occur in a court case. The forensic witness must be well versed on the court standards and protocols when presenting as either a technical or expert specialist.

1.   When Is Forensic Evidence Relevant?

The legal team is interested in determining what evidence can possibly be recovered that might have some influence on the case. Like other types of investigations, the answer will not be fully determined until after the data has been recovered and the findings are meticulously researched. The process involved to investigate a computer can be exceptionally time intensive. An average of seven hours is required before a basic assessment can be created. The assessment will help establish if the computer contains valuable information that would justify additional resources. Because it is initially uncertain what evidence a computer contains, it is essential to qualify a particular computer before investing additional resources. Qualification of computer evidence is included in Chapter 11.

B.   Technical and Expert Testimony

Either technical or expert witnesses might provide forensic testimony. A **technical witness** provides facts that have been uncovered in the investigation that might contribute to the resolution of the crime or incident. The technical witness presents evidence, explains it, and describes how it was obtained. Only facts are offered, not conclusions.

The **expert witness**, however, can present opinions and observations. These can be based on experience, using deductive reasoning with facts found during an investigation. The ability to form an opinion based on an examination of electronic evidence makes for an expert witness. The expert should be able to present highly technical matters in language that can be easily understood by nonexperts. The expert must be able to justify a professional opinion under cross-examination. A computer forensics examiner who serves as an expert witness provides an opinion that contributes to the legal process.

There are a number of different roles of the witness that possesses technical knowledge. The different capacities in which the expert technical witness may serve in the legal system include:

Consulting expert — A consultant or advisor to a legal team. This usually involves training attorneys, reviewing existing technology, and advising on strategy.

Court's expert — A consultant or advisor to a court; especially valuable to judges presiding over cases involving complex technical issues in which the parties present wildly divergent views.

Testifying expert — The role that most technologists think of when asked to serve as an expert witness. This requires an additional ethical responsibility for the expert to be impartial and objective.

Expert as witness to fact — Here an expert is asked to testify as a "normal" nonexpert witness to something personally witnessed. The expert's mastery of a certain area is not the central feature of this role.

C.   The Financial Forensic Expert

The financial forensic expert is concerned with fact-finding and interpretation of business documents and records. The knowledge, skills, and experience of a good forensic accountant are extremely useful as a consultant to litigation counsel or judges. The expert must understand and interpret the integrity of an organization's day-to-day operations, and whether its people, processes, and systems have functioned, or are functioning, according to practices. The financial expert also looks at matters related to how an organization reports its performance, controls activities and transactions, protects its resources from theft and misuse. Functions include understanding of its sources and uses of funds, minimization of the risk of fraud, and investigations of alleged misconduct.

There is a difference between a financial forensic expert and a traditional certified public accountant (CPA) or auditor.

The forensic accountant employs a much higher degree of professional skepticism when conducting examinations. Explanations and documents are not necessarily accepted at face value. A forensic accountant burrows much deeper into the facts and issues than a traditional auditor.

A forensic accountant is more familiar with how employees can abuse and misuse controls and processes and with the various types of fraud, schemes, and the methods used to circumvent internal controls. In gathering facts and evidence, a forensic accountant is more experienced in activities that involve:

Knowing where to look
Identifying the types of evidence
Describing how to extract the evidence
Knowing what constitutes relevant and valid support

The forensic accountant is more adept at interviewing and eliciting information from company personnel, witnesses, and subjects. A forensic accountant is more experienced at interpreting facts and evidence, as well as presenting findings in a manner that is meaningful and can be used to support the civil, criminal, administrative, and political processes. But most importantly, a forensic accountant has a keen understanding and sixth sense for the facts and evidence that are not obvious, but that indirectly may verify, support, or refute a given explanation, transaction, or activity.

D.   Forensic Accounting Testimony

Recent court cases have involved crimes involving financial wrongdoing. The expertise of forensic accountants who have an in-depth knowledge of financial systems has become a hot commodity. Forensic accounting and investigation requires a background and expertise that encompasses the following areas:

Generally accepted accounting principles (GAAPs) and generally accepted auditing standards (GAASs) issues
Accounting and auditing malpractice
Securitization analysis and fraud
Financial consulting
Forensic actuarial services
Expert witness testimony

Securities fraud
Business fraud
Business valuations
Actuarial services and testimony

Forensic accounting experts must possess experience and knowledge in the following areas of financial management:

Business valuation
Primary market identification and the effect of new entrants on sales, costs, and profits
Franchise disputes involving auto dealers, beer distributors, and other businesses given exclusive trade areas
Restraint of trade and other issues involving the Commerce Clause
Tax cases involving sales tax, property tax, income tax, and city income tax
State, federal, and local government regulation
Fiscal and economic impact assessments
Lost profit calculations
Antitrust issues
Damage claim calculations

A forensic accountant is often retained to analyze, interpret, summarize, and present complex financial and business related issues in a manner that is both understandable and properly supported. Forensic accountants can be engaged in public practice or employed by insurance companies, banks, police forces, government agencies, and other organizations. A forensic accountant is often involved in the following:

Investigating and analyzing financial evidence
Developing computerized applications to assist in the analysis and presentation of financial evidence
Communicating findings in the form of reports, exhibits, and collections of documents
Assisting in legal proceedings, including testifying in court as an expert witness
Preparing visual aids to support trial evidence

In order to properly perform these services, a forensic accountant must be familiar with legal concepts and procedures. In addition, a forensic accountant must be able to identify substance over form when dealing with an issue. Another level of financial forensic expertise is the certified fraud examiner.

A **certified fraud examiner** (CFE) is a designation awarded by the Association of Certified Fraud Examiners (ACFE). The ACFE is a 35,000 member-based global association dedicated to providing antifraud education and training. When certified, individuals must have at least two years of professional experience in a field either directly or indirectly related to the detection or deterrence of fraud. The ACFE recognizes the following areas as qualified professional experience:

Accounting and auditing
Criminology
Fraud investigation
Loss prevention
Law — fraud related
Sociology — fraud related

If computer systems have been a part of the alleged wrongdoing—and most are—then an additional expertise must also include the introduction of electronic or computer forensics. Most financial specialists will probably not possess sufficient skills in computer forensics, which means an additional expert must be added to the team. The computer forensic expert, who has data processing and database experience, particularly in financial computing, will provide additional depth to the team.

E.   Court Appearances

This is the venue where all the investigations, examinations, and long hours researching an incident pay off. If the court appearance is ineffective, then all this work is for naught. The investigative team must determine if the court will allow live demonstrations and if visual aids can be displayed in the area. The types of connections for laptops, video projectors, and audio equipment must be determined.

All litigants must be aware of their actions and activities when in a public area. It is essential that all members of the incident team behave in a professional manner. This applies to both on and off the stand. Witnesses need to know that someone might be gathering intelligence for the trial. There are a number of guidelines and preparations that the expert witness can observe to present a professional appearance.

Before a trial starts, walk into the courtroom and become familiar with the location of the witness chair and the path to get there. Wandering around looking for the witness chair is not a good start. This small detail enables the witness to walk directly to the stand in a forthright manner and be sworn in.

It is essential to dress professionally; most law enforcement officers will be wearing an official uniform. Studies have shown that blue for men and black for women are the most appropriate colors for "looking believable." Both men and women should dress in a conservative fashion and avoid flashy colors, jewelry, and ties.

The court must hear your testimony. When sworn in, look at the jury and respond to the questions in a clear, loud voice. This also follows when answering questions from the judge or attorneys. Once seated, posture counts; sit up straight and look at the questioning attorney. When answering, make eye contact with the jurors or judge in the absence of a jury. It is important to remember that witnesses are not talking to the attorneys; rather they are talking to the jurors.

Witnesses must have a copy of the investigative report on the stand and should not be afraid to refer to it. Permission must be granted to refer to documentation. Visual evidence will probably be offered during the trial. This might include posters, evidence, and slide shows. When showing demonstrations, be sure to verbalize everything that is occurring.

The witness must answer all questions clearly and avoid nodding as an answer. Nodding will cause the court reporter and the judge to tell the witness to answer audibly, making the witness look incompetent. Keep hands in your lap and away from your mouth.

The witness must listen very carefully to every question asked, and make sure the question is understood before responding. The witness can ask the attorney to rephrase the question. If any attorney enters an objection, stop talking immediately and let the judge rule on the objection before continuing.

Attorneys may try to make witnesses lose their cool. Do not fall for this "baiting" approach. Avoid being combative—this is the attorney's job. Witnesses must stay cool and answer all questions in a professional manner. Witnesses can ask the judge a question. The proper approach is to look at the judge and say "your honor" and wait for the judge to acknowledge. Wait until the judge gives permission before asking the question.

Witnesses can make a mistake and respond incorrectly to questions. Do not try to cover up a mistake—admit it. However, numerous mistakes will show incompetence and the courts might assume that your testimony is not truthful. If the opposing side asks a question that might be objectionable, pause before answering and allow for an objection. If either attorney objects, stop the answer and wait for the judge to advise to continue.

Witnesses must avoid looking at their counselors when answering questions. This appears to the court that the witness is asking for help and might be construed by the jury as a damaging question. It is important to tell the truth, the whole truth, and nothing but the truth. Avoid the temptation to embellish the truth just a bit. This is not necessary, and if challenged, makes the whole testimony suspect.

1.   Preparing for Testimony

The protocol and decorum rules have been established; now is the time to start to thoroughly prepare for the task of presenting the computer forensic evidence to the court. Remember that the orientations are different for technical and expert witnesses! Also keep in mind the differences between civil and criminal litigation needs. This means the forensic specialist must communicate effectively with the legal staff and attorneys for specific guidelines. Expert witnesses work with attorneys and not defendants and plaintiffs. This is the attorney's responsibility. Any negative findings must be promptly transmitted to the case attorney.

Before testifying in court, be prepared to provide definitions of electronic and computer terms. Most attorneys and jurors will not know technical terms or understand the field of computer forensics. It is not the witness's job to teach the opposing legal team or jury; however, the witness does need to explain how a tool works or an examination is completed. An overview of electronic and computer forensics can be provided. A brief description of how data is stored on media and how it can be retrieved with various forensic tools should be sufficient. These tools can be described generically. Describe the locations where forensic evidence might be located on the devices in question. A graphic might be useful as these concepts could be difficult to grasp.

Witnesses must substantiate findings with documentation and collaboration from supporting sources. Use notes that have been developed in the investigation. These can be handwritten notes or a formal journal, and might be located on a laptop computer. In the analysis and report-generating phase of the investigation, develop and maintain a standard method of processing documentation in expectation of testifying. This will eliminate confusion and provide the specialist with a predefined process for testifying. The various investigators and examiners should have a preponderance of evidence at this time. If not, it is probably too late.

Witnesses must be aware of a practice called **conflicting out**. This is an attempt to prevent a witness from being used by another attorney on an important case. This situation is more common in the private sector when the specialist is working as an independent forensic consultant. A tactical move by opposing attorneys is to call and discuss the case, only to have the specialist excluded from the case. This creates a conflict of interest for the specialist and the other attorney trying the case. A good rule is to avoid conversations with opposing attorneys. Remember that there is no such time as an "off the record' conversation with opposing attorneys.

Most of the preceding chapters have provided information and guidance concerning all the phases of the forensic investigation and examination. All steps must have been documented and all examinations must be repeatable and verifiable. All the forms that have been completed by the investigative team should have been reviewed for completeness and accuracy. Testimony will lose credibility if the witness cannot certify the findings.

It is also essential that documentation show how the evidence was preserved. Forensic tools must be validated with multiple products. Hash checks must be performed and can include MD5, SHA-1, or CRC algorithms.

An important note—do not create a formal checklist of investigative or examination procedures or integrate a checklist into the final report. This is because opposing counsel can easily challenge a checklist. Checklists are tools used by the investigative team to ensure all work-related tasks have been successfully completed and should not be presented in a trial.

Maintaining the chain-of-custody has been emphasized throughout the previous chapters. The opposing attorneys will attempt to discredit evidence based on contamination and gaps in custody. If there are any gaps or lapses in the chain-of-custody, document them. It will not look good if the opposing legal team exposes a custody gap.

F.   Testifying in Court

Chapter 2 provides considerable information concerning various laws and legal processes. Before appearing in court, be sure to become familiar with the procedures followed during a trial or legal process. The legal team will demonstrate the competence of the expert and technical witnesses. The opposing legal team will try to discredit them. A document that will be helpful in this process is called **curriculum vitae** (CV). This document is a professional history used to qualify a witness's testimony. The CV emphasizes an individual's skills, training, and professional experience. A testimony log should be maintained in the CV that records expert testimony provided. Information contained in the CV should be kept up to date. During the qualification phase, called **voir dire**, the witness's expert qualifications are demonstrated. The process is used to determine competency, interest, or bias that may affect a decision. Voir dire is also used to show the expert's superiority over the competition.

What does all this say to the novice forensic investigator or examiner? It appears a priority is to embark on a comprehensive training program and become associated with a forensic laboratory. Participating in the identification and analysis of electronic evidence will establish a foundation in becoming an expert. Working with a mentor is an excellent method of accumulating forensic experience. This is called paying your dues!

G.   Presenting Evidence

A technique employed is to tell the court what evidence is going to be presented, present the evidence, and then tell what evidence was presented. When providing testimony, cite the source of the evidence and methodology employed to retrieve it. Expert witnesses must keep the audience in mind, particularly the jury and sometimes the court. Jurors typically average just over twelve years of education with an eighth-grade reading level. Graphics and PowerPoint slides could improve the effectiveness of the expert witness. Make sure that the courtroom can accommodate electronic presentations and the court will allow them.

When preparing the forensic testimony, consider the following items that could enhance the quality of the presentation:

Provide the scope of the case
Describe the forensic overview and components of the case
Identify the most powerful elements of evidence
Tie the forensic evidence to the devices and media
State how the evidence supports the conclusions
Support the allegations of the legal team

Now comes the hard part! The expert witness must be ready to explain MD5, SHA-1, and CRC. If disk imaging has been performed, an explanation of the process will be required, as will the tools that were utilized in the process. Learn how to describe various practices and procedures used in the forensic process. These descriptions must be presented so that a nontechnical person can understand them. Limit the extent of the technical explanations unless the legal team advises otherwise. Learning how to read the jury is an advantage—if everyone's eyes are glazed over, take another approach. There are specific questions that might be asked during the evidence testimony. The witness should prepare to answer the following questions:

How is data or evidence stored on the media in question?
What is a bit-stream image or digital copy?
How is deleted data recovered from the media in question?
What is the importance of temporary files and where are they located?
What data is contained on system, Internet, e-mail, or network log files?

It is important to be an impartial expert witness and not be an advocate. It is also essential to create a case outline and develop a document similar to a business case. The outline and case documentation should support the content of any graphics or aids used in the testimony. The technical testimony must correlate with other evidence that has been presented. It is also essential to coordinate forensic testimony with other experts that might be testifying in the trial.

H.   Direct Examination Testifying

Direct examination is the most important part of testimony at a trial. Direct testimony is provided when the technical or expert witness testifies at a trial. There are several direct testimony techniques that are effective. These include the following:

State background and qualifications to testify as a computer forensic expert
Provide a clear overview of the examination findings
Describe evidence collection methods and processes
Describe complex details at the layman's level
Gauge speech at the juror's education level

Preparation is the key to a successful testimony.

Use the case documentation from the actual written records created during the examinations of evidence.

Provide testimony concerning facts that are known about a case without being prompted.

Know the customary practice that has occurred in similar cases.

When questioned, provide the answers needed to bring attention to the actual findings and opinions that are part of the investigation.

Remember to engage the jury, making sure to project your voice. If the jury cannot hear the testimony, the effort is fruitless.

The use of graphics, such as PowerPoint slides and flipcharts, can enhance the expert testimony. There are, however, considerations when using graphics in the presentation. Graphics and artwork can illustrate and clarify the findings. It is essential that the jury can see the graphics and read them. Graphics must not be "busy." They must be clear and easy to understand, with bold lettering. Hard copies of the graphics can be provided to the opposing team as well as the jury, if allowed by the court. When describing the graphics, take the role of a teacher; face the jury; talk to the jury; and stay out of the graphic. A pointer is very helpful when using a graphic presentation. Always conduct a trial run-through of any graphic presentation to avoid any miscues.

A final note on direct testimony: do not volunteer information or be overly friendly (or hostile) to the opposing attorney. Use a sales concept: after the client has been convinced to buy—shut up!

I. Cross-Examination Testifying

In law, cross-examination is the interrogation of a witness called by one's opponent. It is preceded by direct examination and may be followed by a redirect. A redirect is a trial process by which the party who offered the witness has a chance to explain or otherwise qualify damaging testimony brought out by the opponent during cross-examination. Redirect examination may question only those areas brought out on cross-examination and may not stray beyond that boundary.

When answering questions from the opposing attorney; witnesses should rephrase the answer using their own words. Certain words have additional meanings that an opposing attorney can easily exploit (suspicious versus concerned). One trick an attorney uses during cross-examination is to interrupt the witness answering a question. Usually the judge will not allow this tactic. Sample questions the opposing attorney might ask are as follows:

How many tools were used to verify the evidence?
What tools were used?
What are the known problems and weak features of these tools?
Are the tools reliable?
Are the tools consistent in producing results?
Is the witness a consultant?
Are computer forensic manuals being reviewed?
Is the witness a member of a cyber-forensic organization?

Questions might be posed to require conflicting answers. In many instances, opposing counsel uses rapid-fire questions to confuse the witness. Remember that the jury is the witness's focal point. Slow down and consider the proper answer to counsel's questions. Do not lose control, everyone will make mistakes. In summary, maintain a vigorous demeanor and use energetic speech to make the jury listen to the testimony. Be fluent, use unrehearsed speech, do not memorize the testimony, stay cool, and keep going.

J.   The Deposition

A **deposition** is a formal meeting where an individual is questioned in which only the opposing attorneys, opposing parties, defendant, and plaintiff are present. This is considered part of discovery. A deposition differs from a trial because a judge and jury do not participate. The purpose of a deposition is to allow the opposing attorney the opportunity to review testimony that has been developed. The two types of depositions include discovery and testimony preservation.

The **discovery deposition** is part of the discovery process. It is a hostile but open examination under oath before trial. The attorney who requested the deposition frequently conducts the equivalent of a direct and cross-examination. The testimony preservation deposition is usually requested to preserve testimony because of health issues or schedule conflicts.

There are several rules to follow during the deposition. These include the following:

Act professionally
Use facts when describing an opinion
Understand this episode is a discovery function
Avoid making mistakes or providing incorrect information

The witness should take time in answering questions, ensuring that answers are correct and understood.

Chapter Summary

Computer and electronic forensics is the collection and preservation of data used to investigate or establish facts for civil and criminal litigation. For each case, computer forensics can contain many different types of material and evidence.

Technical and/or expert witnesses might provide forensic testimony. The technical witness presents evidence, explains it, and describes how it was obtained. Only facts are offered—not conclusions. The expert witness, however, can present opinions and observations. These can be based on experience, using deductive reasoning with facts found during an investigation.

Forensic accounting and investigation activities require a background and expertise that encompass many areas, including financial malpractice and fraud. Forensic accounting experts must possess experience and knowledge in many areas of financial management that use computer technologies.

Forensic witnesses must prepare for the courtroom environment. All litigants must be aware of their actions and activities when in a public area. It is essential that all members of the incident team behave in a professional manner. Rules and decorum must be followed. Witnesses must be sure to become familiar with the procedures followed during a trial or legal process before appearing in court. The legal team must demonstrate the competence of the expert and technical witnesses. Be prepared for the opposing legal team to try to discredit the witnesses.

A common technique employed in court is to tell what evidence is going to be presented, present the evidence, and then tell what evidence was presented. When providing technical testimony, witnesses must cite the source of the evidence and methodology employed to retrieve it. Expert witnesses must keep the audience in mind, particularly the expertise level of the jury and sometimes the court.

Forensic testimony will be presented during direct examination and cross-examination. Direct examination is the most important part of testimony at a trial. Direct examination is usually performed to elicit evidence in support of facts that will satisfy a required element of a party's claim or defense. Cross-examination allows opposing attorneys the opportunity to ask questions concerning testimony and evidence.

A deposition is a formal meeting where an individual is questioned where only the opposing attorneys, opposing parties, defendant, and plaintiff are present. This activity is considered part of discovery. The purpose of a deposition is to allow the opposing attorney the opportunity to review testimony that has been developed.

Terms

Conflicting out — An attempt to prevent the witness from being used by another attorney on an important case.

Cross-examination — Opposing attorneys have the opportunity to ask questions concerning testimony and evidence.

Curriculum vitae — An extensive resume of professional history that includes work history, cases, testimony, and training, along with details of other skills.

Deposed — The process of being called on to testify in a deposition.

Deposition — A formal meeting where an individual is questioned in which only the opposing attorneys, opposing parties, defendant, and plaintiff are present. This is considered part of discovery.

Deposition banks — Examples of previous expert witnesses' testimony.

Direct examination — (Also called examination in chief) is the questioning of a witness by the calling party at a trial in a court of law. Direct examination is usually performed to elicit evidence in support of facts that will satisfy a required element of a party's claim or defense.

Discovery — The pretrial phase in a lawsuit in which each party can request documents and other evidence from other parties or can compel the production of evidence by using a subpoena or other discovery devices.

Discovery deposition — The opposing attorney sets the deposition and frequently conducts the equivalent of both direct and cross-examination.

Expert witness — A person who has knowledge in a field and can offer an opinion in addition to the facts being presented.

Forensic accountant — Utilizes accounting, auditing, and investigative skills when conducting an investigation. The individual possesses the ability to respond immediately and to communicate financial information clearly and concisely in a courtroom setting.

Lay witness — Person, with knowledge based on firsthand observations, whose testimony is helpful to determine the facts at issue.

Technical witness — A person who has performed the actual fieldwork, but does not offer an opinion in court, only the results of their findings.

Voir dire — A preliminary examination usually of a juror, to determine competency, interest, or bias that may affect a decision.

Review Questions

1. A _____ witness is a person who has performed the actual fieldwork in a case.
2. The _____ is a person who has knowledge in a field and can offer an opinion in addition to the facts being presented.
3. T/F. Conflicting out is the action taken by a witness when there is a conflict of interest.
4. What information is contained in the forensic witness's curriculum vitae?
5. The process to determine competency, interest, or bias is called _____.
6. T/F. A deposition includes all members of the litigation including the judge.

7. _____ is the pretrial phase where each party can request documentation and other evidence.
8. T/F. This individual utilizes, accounting, auditing, and investigative skills when conducting an investigation.
9. What is the difference between an expert witness and a lay witness?
10. What should be considered when presenting forensic evidence?

Glossary

2G — Second generation of GSM is the technology currently used in the operation of mobile phones.

3G — Third generation wireless is digital and includes, but is not limited to, such enhanced features as high-speed transmission, global roaming, and advanced multimedia access. This generation will become more and more visible within the next few years.

4G — Fourth generation is short for the fourth-generation successor of 3G and is a wireless access technology. It describes two different but overlapping ideas.

Accuracy — A qualitative measure to determine if each bit of the acquisition is equal to the corresponding bit of the source.

Administrative audit worksheet — Provides for documentation of major events, times, and movements relating to the search efforts.

Affidavit — Written declaration made under oath; a written statement sworn to be true before someone who is legally authorized to administer an oath.

Allegation — An assertion, declaration, or statement of a party to an action made in a pleading, stating what the party expects to prove.

Allocated data — Data on a hard drive that has not been deleted or overwritten.

Allocation blocks — A group of consecutive, logical blocks assembled in the Mac file system when a file is saved.

Application software — A set of electronic instructions, also known as a program, that instructs a computer to perform a specific set of processes.

Archive — A copy of data on a computer drive, or on a portion of a drive, maintained for historical reference.

ASCII (American Standard Code for Information Interchange) — Consists of 128 standard ASCII codes, each of which can be represented by a 7-digit binary number: 0000000 through 1111111.

Assault — The crime of violence against another person.

ATA (advanced technology attachment) — Disk drive implementation that integrates the controller on the disk drive itself.

Auction fraud — Fraud that occurs on Internet sites offering consumer items for sale to the general public.

Autoexec.bat — In DOS and Windows-based PCs, the file that contains a list of commands that are automatically executed on system start-up.

Automatic call distributor (ACD) — A telephone facility that manages incoming calls and handles them based on the number called and an associated database of handling instructions.

Autopsy forensic browser — A graphical interface to the command line digital investigation analysis tools in the Sleuth Kit.

Backdrop — A computer desktop background that could be a sprite (small icon) or just a pattern.

Backup — A copy of active data, intended for use in restoration of data.

Bitmap image — A representation of a graphics image in a grid-type format.

Bits — Short for binary digit, the smallest unit of information on a machine. A single bit can hold only one of two values: 0 or 1. More meaningful information is obtained by combining consecutive bits into larger units.

Bit-stream copy — A bit-by-bit copy of data located on the original storage medium.

Bit-stream image — The file used to store the bit-stream copy.

BlackBerry — A handheld device made by RIM (Research In Motion) that competes with another popular handheld, the Palm, and is marketed primarily for its wireless e-mail handling capability.

Blue-collar crime — Any crime committed by an individual from a lower social class.

Bluetooth — A computing and telecommunications industry specification that describes how mobile phones, computers, and PDAs can easily interconnect with each other and with home and business phones and computers using a short wireless connection.

Boot sector — The very first sector on a hard drive.

Bootstrap — The bootstrap program can be used to start the computer, clear the memory, set up devices, and load the operating system from input/output internal or external memory.

Browser — Client to a Web server that allows the user to read hypertext documents on the World Wide Web. Netscape Navigator and Microsoft Internet Explorer are examples of popular Web browsers.

Buffer — Area in computer memory used as a temporary storage location.

Bytes — A unit of measurement for data storage equal to eight bits of information composed of ones and zeros.

Cache — Specialized random access memory (RAM) used specifically to optimize data transfers between system components with different performance capabilities.

Carving — The process of removing an item of data from a group of items. This could involve pattern matching.

Case file — The official record of actions taken and evidence collected at the scene.

CCPA — Cable Communications Privacy Act.

CD-R (compact disk-recordable) — A disk to which data can be written but not erased.

CD-RW (compact disk-rewritable) — A disk to which data can be written and erased.

Cellular — A mobile telephone service provided by a network of base stations, each of which covers one geographic cell within the total cellular system service area.

Chain letter — A typical chain letter consists of a message that attempts to induce the recipient to make a number of copies of the letter and then pass them on to two or more new recipients.

Chain-of-custody — The route the evidence takes from initial possession until final disposition. It is also called the chain-of-evidence.

Child exploitation — Includes child pornography, trafficking, obscenity, and child prostitution.

Circumstantial evidence — Indirect evidence, usually a theory, that is supported by a significant quantity of corroborating evidence.

Civil laws — Concerned with wrongs inflicted upon an organization or individual that result in some damage or loss.

Client/server — Describes the relationship between two computer programs in which one program, the client, makes a service request from another program, the server, which fulfills the request.

Clik! — A portable disk drive.

Clump — A contiguous allocation block in the Macintosh file system.

Cluster — Windows allocates space to files in units called clusters. Each cluster contains from 1 to 64 sectors, depending on the type and size of the disk. A cluster is the smallest unit of disk space that can be allocated for use by files.

CMOS (complemetary metal-oxide semiconductor) — A chip on the motherboard, which holds information about the system and its peripherals, even while the system is turned off.

Code division multiple access (CDMA) — A spread spectrum air interface technology used in some digital cellular, personal communications services, and other wireless networks.

Command.com — Provides a prompt when booting to the MS-DOS mode.

Completeness — A quantitative measure to determine if each accessible bit of the source is acquired.

Computer forensic science — The science of acquiring, preserving, retrieving, and presenting data that has been processed electronically and stored on computer media.

Computer forensics — Those activities associated with the identification and preservation of computer or electronic evidence in support of some official or legal action.

Config.sys — A text file containing commands typically run only at system start-up to enhance the computer's DOS configuration.

Conflicting out — An attempt to prevent the witness from being used by another attorney on an important case.

Controlled substances — Drugs and certain other chemicals, both narcotic and non-narcotic, that come under the jurisdiction of federal and state laws regulating their manufacture, sale, distribution, use, and disposal.

Cookie — Small text files stored on a computer while the user is browsing the Internet. It is used to track a user's Internet activity.

COPPA — A U.S. law that took effect on April 21, 2000, and requires parental consent for certain Web sites to knowingly collect personally identifiable information on children under the age of 13.

Coroner's Toolkit (TCT) — Is intended to assist in a forensic analysis of a UNIX system after a break-in.

Court order — A document prepared and signed by a court, to give effect to a decision of a judge of that court.

Criminal law — Concerned with individual conduct that violates governmental laws that were enacted for public protection.

Cross-examination — Opposing attorneys have the opportunity to ask questions concerning testimony and evidence.

Curriculum vitae — An extensive resume of professional history that includes work history, cases, testimony, and training, along with details of other skills.

Cyberspace — Defined as the global network of interconnected computers and communication systems.

Cyber-terrorism — Includes the convergence of terrorism and cyberspace.

Cylinders — A hard disk consisting of two or more platters, each with two sides. Each side is further divided into concentric circles known as tracks; and all the tracks at the same concentric position on a disk are known collectively as a cylinder.

Data — Raw facts that can be processed by some computing device into accurate and relevant information.

Data block — A cluster of hard disk sectors in the Linux file system.

Data compression — A complex algorithm that is used to reduce a file size.

Data fork — The part of the Macintosh file structure that contains a file's actual data.

Database management system (DBMS) — Manages the data files in the database and may provide independence of programs and data.

Defrag — A process (run by a defragging program) whereby parts of data files on all segments of a computer hard disk are taken from their fragmented state (with parts of files spread all over the disk), and grouped together in complete file segments. This makes it quicker for applications to find the files needed and frees up disk space, making the computer run more efficiently.

Deposed — The process of being called on to testify in a deposition.

Deposition — A formal meeting where an individual is questioned in which only the opposing attorneys, opposing parties, defendant, and plaintiff are present. This is considered part of discovery.

Deposition banks — Examples of previous expert witness's testimony.

Digital intelligence — Has created several forensic software tools in-house specifically for forensic use.

Direct examination (also called examination in chief) — The questioning of a witness by the calling party in a trial in a court of law. Direct examination is usually performed to elicit evidence in support of facts that will satisfy a required element of a party's claim or defense.

Direct testimony — Includes statements made under oath by a party or the party's witness.

Disaster recovery plan — Outlines the procedures for an organization to return to normal operations following a disaster or incident.

Disclaimer — A statement that denies responsibility for a particular action.

Discovery — The process whereby civil litigants seek to obtain information both from other parties and from nonparties or third parties.

Discovery deposition — The opposing attorney sets the deposition and frequently conducts the equivalent of both direct and cross-examination.

DNS (domain naming system) — The system that translates Internet domain names into IP numbers. A "DNS Server" is a server that performs this kind of translation.

Document — Includes but is not limited to any electronically stored data on magnetic or optical storage media as an "active" file or files (readily readable by one or more computer applications or forensics software); any "deleted" but recoverable electronic files on said media; any electronic file fragments (files that have been deleted and partially overwritten with new data); and slack (data fragments stored randomly from random access memory on a hard drive during the normal operation of a computer [RAM slack] or residual data left on the hard drive after new data has overwritten some but not all of previously stored data).

Documentation — Includes written notes, printed forms, sketches, photographs, evidence recovered, and actions taken during an investigation.

Domestic violence — Physical and/or emotional harm suffered by a person who is a family member of, or residing in the same home as, the offender who caused the harm or injury.

Dongle — A hardware key.

DOS (disk operating system) — The name of the operating systems on most brands of personal computer contains the acronym DOS. Often when DOS is used without further description, the operating system being referred to is either PC DOS, the operating system used on IBM personal computers, or MS DOS, the variety of DOS that runs on IBM compatible computers.

Drive slack — Any data that had been on the storage device previously.

DriveSpy — A Digital Intelligence product, DriveSpy is designed to emulate and extend the capabilities of DOS to meet forensic needs. DriveSpy processes large hard drives, FAT12/16/16x/32/32x partitions, hidden DOS partitions, non-DOS partitions, long file names, file creation/modification/access dates, erased files, slack space, and unallocated space.

Dumpster diving — The practice of rummaging through trash, whether commercial or residential, to find items of use that have been discarded.

DVD (digital versatile disk, digital video disk) — A type of disk drive that allows for large amounts of data on one disk the size of a standard compact disk.

ECPA — Electronic Communications Privacy Act.

EIDE (Enhanced Integrated Drive Electronics) — A hardware interface that is faster than IDE, allows more memory, and can connect up to four devices (such as hard drives, tape drives, and CD-ROM drives) to the computer.

Electronic business (E-business) — The use of Internet and digital technology to execute all the business processes in the enterprise.

Electronic commerce (E-commerce) — Consists of the process of buying and selling goods and services electronically, involving the Internet and other networks.

Electronic discovery (E-discovery) — Refers to any process in which electronic data is sought, located, secured, and searched with the intent of using it as evidence in a civil or criminal legal case.

Electronic evidence — Data and information of some investigative value that is stored on or transmitted by an electronic device.

Electrostatic discharge — The sudden and momentary electric current that flows when an excess of electric charge finds a path to an object at a different electrical potential (ground).

Encase — By Guidance Software, offers an industry standard in computer forensic investigation technology.

End-of-file marker — The code 0x0FFFFFFF that shows where a file ends.

E-SIGN — Congress enacted the Electronic Signatures in Global and National Commerce Act, which establishes the validity of electronic records and signatures.

ESMR (enhanced specialized mobile radio) — A Motorola-developed mobile communications implementation that integrates radio services with TDM mobile telephony to provide digital mobile communications service using primarily the 800 megahertz frequency band. This facilitates applications such as paging, data transmission, dispatch, and interoperability with the wire-line PSTN.

Eudora — An e-mail program that uses the POP (Post Office Protocol).

Evidence — Provides the means by which disputed facts are proved to be true or untrue in any trial before a court of law or an agency that functions like a court. Evidence includes testimony, records, documents, material objects, or other things presented at a trial to prove the existence or nonexistence of a fact.

Evidence custodian — A collector, recorder, and custodian who is responsible for the evidence integrity and chain-of-custody.

Exchange — The Microsoft version of an e-mail server.

Expert witness — A person who has knowledge in a field and can offer an opinion in addition to the facts being presented.

Extortion — Obtaining property or money by the use of violence, threats, or intimidation.

Faraday bag — Used to protect active wireless exhibits from the ingress of new data such as phone calls or text messages.

Faraday cage — An enclosure designed to exclude electromagnetic fields.

Felony — A crime of a graver or more atrocious nature than those designated as misdemeanors.

File allocation table (FAT) — A table that an operating system maintains on a hard disk that provides a map of the clusters (the basic units of logical storage on a hard disk) that a file has been stored in.

File slack — The slack space created when a file is saved.

Finder — A Mac tool that interacts with the operating system to keep track of files and maintains each user's desktop.

Firewire — A high-speed serial-bus standard that offers enhanced connectivity and data transfer for video, audio, and storage peripheral applications through a universal input/output (I/O) interface.

First Amendment — The First Amendment to the United States Constitution contained in the Bill of Rights. It provides for freedom of speech, press, religion, peaceable assembly, and to petition the government.

First responder — The initial person arriving at an incident scene, prior to the arrival of the investigator in charge.

Flash card — A type of memory that retains data after power is removed. It operates both like memory and like a storage device. Examples include Compact Flash, SmartMedia, and PCMCIA, among others. It is used in devices such as digital cameras, audio players, handheld computers, cell phones, USB drives, and printers.

Foremost — A console program to recover files based on their headers, footers, and internal data structures.

Forensic accountant — Utilizes accounting, auditing, and investigative skills when conducting an investigation. The individual possesses the ability to respond immediately and to communicate financial information clearly and concisely in a courtroom setting.

Forensic accounting — Accounting that is suitable for legal review by including data that has been arrived at in a scientific fashion.

Forensic analysis — Consists of a cycle of data gathering and processing of the materials and evidence gathered. Used in courts of law, public debate, or argument.

Forensic Toolkit (FTK) — By Access Data, provides a tool for complete and thorough forensic examination.

Forensic workstation — The computer where the forensic software tools are located.

Forensics — A study or practice relating to legal proceedings or augmentation.

Fourth Amendment — The Fourth Amendment to the United States Constitution contained in the Bill of Rights. It dictates probable cause for search and seizure.

Fraud — Intentional perversion of truth; deceitful practice or device resorted to with intent to deprive another of property or other right; a deception deliberately practiced in order to secure unfair or unlawful gain.

FRED — Forensic recovery of evidence device.

Free space — Space on a disk drive that is not reserved for saved files.

FTP (File Transfer Protocol) — The language used for file transfer from computer to computer across the Web. An anonymous FTP is a file transfer between locations that does not require users to identify themselves with a password or log-in. An anonymous FTP is not secure because it can be accessed by any other user of the Web.

GAAP (generally accepted accounting principles) — The accounting rules used to prepare financial statements for publicly traded companies and many private companies in the United States.

Gambling — The unlawful engaging in playing, operating, or assisting in operating a game of chance for money or some other stake.

General packet radio service (GPRS) — A packet-switched technology that allows Internet and other data communications over a GSM network.

Ghost imaging — The copying of the contents of a computer's hard disk into single compressed files or set of files.

Global system for mobile (GSM) — The most widely used digital mobile phone system and the de facto wireless telephone standard in Europe.

GroupWise — A workgroup application suite offering electronic mail and diary scheduling from Novell, Inc. It can operate on a number of server and workstation platforms. Server platforms include NetWare, Linux, and Windows, while the client software can run on Windows or Linux.

Handset — Any handheld device used to transmit and receive calls from a wireless system.

Hardware — The physical equipment, media, and attached devices used in a computer system. This includes the computer, printers, and communication devices.

Hash codes — Format in which data is stored in compressed form.

Head — The electromagnetic device used to read and write to and from magnetic media such as hard and floppy disks, tape drives, and compact disks. The head converts the information read into electrical pulses sent to the computer for processing.

Hearsay evidence — Consists of statements made out of court by someone who is not present to testify under oath at a trial.

Help features/documentation — Instructions that assist a user on how to set up and use a product including but not limited to software, manuals, and instruction files.

Hierarchical file system (HFS) — The system where Mac files are stored in directories or folders.

HTML (hypertext markup language) — A standardized hypertext language used to create World Wide Web pages and other hypertext documents.

HTTP (Hypertext Transfer Protocol) — The set of rules for exchanging files (text, graphic images, sound, video, and other multimedia files) on the World Wide Web.

IDE (integrated drive electronics) — In 1986, Compaq started work to integrate Western Digital controller technology with Control Data Corporation hard drives, IDE is the result of this work. IDE had several advantages. Besides a power cable, only a single cable was required.

Identity theft — The act of impersonating another, by means of using the person's information, such as birth date, Social Security number, address, name, and bank account information, usually to gain access to the person's finances or frame him or her for a crime.

ILook — An all-in-one computer forensics suite currently maintained by the Internal Revenue Service (IRS).

Indirect testimony — Providing only a basis for inference about the fact in dispute.

Information — Processed data that enhance the recipient's knowledge. Raw facts, called data, are transformed into something meaningful and useful.

Information warfare — A new kind of warfare where information and attacks on information and its system are used as a tool of warfare.

Inodes (information nodes) — Contain descriptive information about each Linux file or directory.

Internet service provider (ISP) — A company that provides access to the Internet to individuals or companies. ISPs provide local dial-up and broadband access between a personal computer and the Internet.

Interrogatory — A written question, as to a witness, usually answered under oath.

Intrusion — Any set of actions that attempt to compromise the integrity, confidentiality or availability of a resource.

Intrusion prevention — Any device that exercises access control to protect computers from exploitation.

IP address — Internet Protocol addresses are the numerical codes that relate to a specific domain name. It is possible that a domain name may identify one or more IP addresses. The format of an IP address is a 32-bit numeric address written as four numbers separated by periods. Each number can be 0 to 255.

IrDa (infrared data association) — The standard for infrared communication. Infrared interfaces exist on most laptops, PDAs, and some mobile phones, though not all of them implement the full IrDa standard.

ISO 17799 — The Code of Practice for Security Management.

ITRC — Identity Theft Resource Center.

Jaz — A high-capacity removable hard disk system.

Journal — A notebook that is used by first responders and investigators when working a crime scene. All investigative activities that take place are recorded in the journal.

Keyword — A word or phrase used when searching for a Web site in the search engines or directories.

Latent — Is present or has potential, but is not evident or active.

Lay witness — Person, with knowledge based on firsthand observations, whose testimony is helpful to determine the facts at issue.

Linux — Open-source version of UNIX that runs on a variety of hardware platforms.

Logical address — When files are saved on hard disks. They are assigned to clusters. The OS numbers these clusters starting at 2. The cluster number defines the logical address.

Logical block — The Mac system assembles a collection of 512 kilobytes of data into allocation blocks to store files.

Logical EOF — The number of bytes that contain data in the Mac file system.

LS-120 (Laser Servo-120) — A floppy disk technology that holds 120 megabytes of data.

Macintosh (Mac) — An alternative personal computer platform to DOS-based PCs developed by Apple in the 1980s.

Magnetic media — Disk, tape, cartridge, diskette, or cassette device used to store data magnetically.

Mainframe — An industry term for a large computer, typically manufactured by a large company such as IBM for the commercial applications of Fortune 1000 businesses and other large-scale computing purposes.

MBR (master boot record) — A small program that is executed when a computer boots up. Typically, the MBR resides on the first sector of the hard disk. The program begins the boot process by looking up the partition table to determine which partition to use for booting. It then transfers program control to the boot sector of that partition, which continues the boot process.

Megan's Law — Enacted in 1996, this federal law requires local law enforcement agencies in all 50 states to notify schools, day care centers, and parents about the presence of certain sex offenders in their area.

Memory card — Or Flash Memory Card refers to solid-state electronic flash memory data storage devices used with digital cameras, handheld and laptop computers, telephones, music players, video game consoles, and other electronics.

Memory stick — Used as storage media for a portable device, in a form that can easily be removed for access by a PC or Mac.

Message digest-5 (MD5) — A hashing algorithm that is used to verify data integrity through the creation of a 128-bit message digest from data input.

Metadata — Information about a particular data set, which may describe, for example, how, when, and by whom it was received, created, accessed, and/or modified and how it is formatted. Metadata can contain the history of the document, including all users who have modified and/or saved it, the directory structure of all machines it was saved on, and names of printers it was printed on. Metadata is data about data. It includes information describing aspects of actual data items, such as name, format, content, and the control of or over data.

Metafiles — A file that contains information about other files, particularly those used for data interchange.

MFT (master file table) — Is used by the NTFS to track files. It contains information about access rights, data and time stamps, and system attributes.

MIME (Multipurpose Internet Mail Extensions) — Protocol for Internet e-mail that enables the transmission of nontext data such as graphics, audio, video and other binary types of files.

Miranda warning — Based on a U.S. Supreme Court decision, is a person's legal rights under U.S. law (the right to remain silent, etc.), and, except on Indian Reservations, is supposed to be read to persons being arrested.

Misdemeanor — Any crime that is not a felony. Punishment for a misdemeanor is typically a fine or possibly jail time of less than one year. These are sometimes called "simple" misdemeanors.

Mobile phone — A device that behaves as a normal telephone while being able to move over a wide area.

MSISDN (mobile station integrated services digital network) — The mobile equivalent of ISDN. Used as a value, MSISDN refers to the MSISDN subscriber ID, which is a maximum 15-digit number.

NCMEC — National Center for Missing & Exploited Children.

NetView — Functions provided by NetView allow the user to quickly identify the root cause of network failures.

NISPOM (National Industrial Security Program Operating Manual) — The manual prescribes requirements, restrictions, and other safeguards that are necessary to prevent unauthorized disclosure of classified information and to control authorized disclosure of classified information released by U.S. government executive branch departments and agencies to their contractors.

NTFS (new technology file system) — Windows NT's replacement for the DOS FAT (file allocation table) and OS/2's HPFS (high performance file system). NTFS offers many advantages over other file systems, including improved security and the ability to reconstruct files in the event of hardware failures.

Open firmware — A platform-dependent boot firmware used on Mac computers to gather information, control devices, and load the operating system.

OpenView — Manages applications, device availability, network conditions and status, system performance, service and program maintenance, and storage resources.

ORB — High-capacity removable hard disk drive.

Outlook — An e-mail software that allows a user to send and receive e-mail, keep an address book, and sort, organize, and filter messages.

Outlook Express — An e-mail and news client bundled with operating systems and the Internet Explorer Web browser by Microsoft.

Partition — A segment of the hard drive that is separated from other portions of the hard disk drive. Partitions help enable users easily divide a computer hard disk drive into different drives and/or into different portions for multiple operating systems to run on the same drive.

Partition gap — Unused space between partitions.

PCS (personal communications service) — An American generic term for a mass-market mobile phone service, emphasizing personal communication, independent of the technology used to provide it. PCS includes such digital cellular technologies as GSM 1900, CDMA and TDMA IS-136.

Pedophile — An adult whose primary sexual interest is in children.

Personal computer (PC) — A computer designed for use by one person at a time.

Petit jury — A lesser, minor jury.

Phreaking — The art of exploiting bugs and glitches in the telephone system.

Physical address — The actual sector in which a file is located.

Physical EOF — The number of allocation blocks assigned to a file in a Mac system.

Physical evidence — Evidence that does not forget and is not confused by the excitement of the moment. This refers to any material items that would be present on the crime scene.

Physical drive — A real device in the computer that you can see or touch, rather than a logical drive, which is a part of the hard disk that functions as if it were a separate disk drive but is not. One physical drive may be divided into several logical drives.

PIM (personal information management) — Includes calendar, scheduling, and calculator programs.

PIN (personal identification number) — An alphanumeric or numeric code used to verify the identity of an individual attempting to use a credit card, debit card, or other account.

Pin-locked — An incorrect PIN will cause the device to become "PIN-locked" and cannot be used until it is reset.

PINE — Program for Internet news and e-mail. A mail user agent used for reading, sending, and managing electronic messages. Online help is always available and it includes MIME and an address book.

Piracy — The unauthorized duplication of goods protected by intellectual property law (e.g., copying software unlawfully).

Pixel — Contraction of picture element. The smallest element display software can use to create text or graphics.

Platter — The actual disk inside a hard disk enclosure that carries the magnetic recording material. Many hard disks have multiple platters, most of which have two sides that can be used for recording data.

Policies — Plans or courses of actions designed by organizations, both governmental and private, to influence and determine decisions and actions for a particular situation.

Policy — An established course of action that must be followed.

POP (Post Office Protocol) — Protocol for retrieving e-mail. Also referred to as POP3 (version 3), it downloads all new e-mail messages from the server and stores them locally on a user's machine.

Printer spool files — Print jobs that are not printed directly and stored in spool files on disk.

Privacy — Being secluded from the sight, presence, or intrusion of others.

Privacy Protection Act — Designed to protect people involved in First Amendment activities from searches when they themselves are not involved in criminal activity.

Private branch exchange (PBX) — A telephone system within an enterprise that switches calls between enterprise users on local lines while allowing all users to share a certain number of external phone lines.

Private key — One of the two keys used in an asymmetric encryption system.

Proactive policies — Establish expected behavior in anticipation of an incident.

Probe — An action taken or an object used for the purpose of learning something about the state of the network.

Prostitution — Includes sex offenses, including attempts, of a commercialized nature.

Public key — One of the two keys used in an asymmetric encryption system; a digital code used to encrypt information and verify digital signatures. It is used in conjunction with a corresponding private key.

Pyramid scheme — A fraudulent scheme in which people are recruited to make payments to the person who recruited them while expecting to receive payments from the persons they recruit.

RAID (redundant array of independent disks) — A collection of disk drives that offers increased performance and fault tolerance.

RAM (random access memory) — The most common computer memory that can be used by programs to perform necessary tasks while the computer is on; an integrated circuit memory chip allows information to be stored or accessed in any order and all storage locations to be equally accessible.

RAM slack — The slack space in the last sector of a file. Any data currently residing in RAM at the time the file is saved can appear in this area.

Reactive policies — A response after an incident occurs, and is therefore too late to impact a situation.

Redaction — Consists of the process of altering, adapting, or refining a result to suit a particular purpose.

Registry — A database that contains information required for the operation of Windows NT and Windows 95, plus applications installed under Windows NT and Windows 95. The registry also includes user information, such as user IDs, encrypted passwords, and permissions. Windows NT and Windows 95 include RegEdit.exe for editing the registry.

Regulatory law — A law that sets standards of performance and conduct expected by various entities.

Removable media — Items such as floppy disks, CDs, DVDs, cartridges, and tape that store data and can be easily removed.

Repeatability — Conditions where independent test results are obtained with the same method on identical test items in the same laboratory by the same operator using the same equipment within short intervals of time.

Reproducibility — Conditions where test results are obtained with the same method on identical test items in different laboratories with different operators using different equipment.

Residual data — Data that is not active on a computer system.

Resource fork — Part of the Mac OS file system that contains the resources.

RFC3227 — Defines guidelines for evidence collection and archiving.

RMON (remote network monitoring) — Provides standard information that a network administrator can use to monitor, analyze, and troubleshoot a group of distributed local area networks (LANs) and interconnecting network circuits from a central site.

ROM (read-only memory) — Memory whose contents can be accessed and read, but cannot be changed.

Rootkits — A set of software tools frequently used by a third party (usually an intruder) after gaining access to a computer system. These tools are intended to conceal running processes, files or system data, which helps an intruder maintain access to a system without the user's knowledge.

Router — An intelligent connecting device that can send packets to the correct local area network (LAN) segment to take them to their destination. Routers link LAN segments at the network layer of the ISO/OSI model.

SATA (serial advanced technology attachment) — An interface for connecting hard drives to a computer. Unlike IDE, which uses parallel signaling, SATA uses serial signaling technology. Because of this the SATA cables are thinner than the ribbon cables used by IDE hard drives. SATA cables can also be longer, allowing you to connect to more distant devices without fear of signal interference. There is also more room to grow with data transfer speeds starting at 150 megabytes per second.

Scam — A confidence trick, confidence game, or con is an attempt to intentionally mislead a person usually with the goal of financial or other gain. The confidence trickster, con man, scam artist, or con artist often works with an accomplice, called the shill, who tries to encourage the mark by pretending to believe the trickster.

Scam baiting — The practice of eliciting attention from the perpetrator of a scam by feigning interest in whatever bogus deal is offered.

Screen saver — A utility program that prevents a monitor from being etched by an unchanging image. It can provide access control to the device.

Script kiddies — Younger and less sophisticated users who break into a network or computer system with malicious intent.

SCSI (small computer system interface) — A standard interface for connecting external units such as disks, tape drives, CD players, scanners, etc. to a computer. It is usually pronounced "scuzzy."

Search — The organized and legal examination of the crime scene to locate items of evidence to the incident or crime under investigation.

Search warrant — In criminal law, is an order of a court, usually of a magistrate, issued to an officer of the law.

Sectors — The smallest unit of storage on a disk, usually 512 bytes. Sectors are grouped together into clusters.

Secure hash algorithm (SHA) — A set of related cryptographic hash functions. SHA-1 creates a 256-bit message digest.

Security — Freedom from risk or danger, and freedom from doubt, anxiety, or fear.

Security incident — Any act or circumstance that involves classified information that deviates from the requirements of governing security publications.

Security policy — A generic document that outlines rules for computer network access, determines how policies are enforced, and sets forth the basic architecture of the organization's security environment.

Security violation — An instance in which a user or other person circumvents or defeats the controls of a system to obtain unauthorized access to information contained therein or to system resources.

Seizure disk — A specially prepared floppy disk designed to protect the computer system from accidental alteration of data.

Sendmail — A UNIX-based system for implementing the Simple Mail Transfer Protocol (SMTP) for transmitting e-mail.

Serial cable — A cable that can be used to transfer information between two devices. The universal serial bus (USB) is a serial bus standard to interface devices.

Sketch — Establishes a permanent record of items, conditions, and distance/size relationships. They also supplement the photograph record.

Slack space — Consists of space on a disk drive between the end of a file and the allocated space for a file.

Sleuth Kit — Previously called TASK, is a collection of UNIX-based command line file system and media management forensic analysis tools.

SMART — An installable distribution of Linux designed for Data Forensics and Incident Response.

Smartphone — Generally considered any handheld device that integrates personal information management and mobile phone capabilities in the same device.

SMTP (Simple Mail Transfer Protocol) — The most common protocol used for transferring e-mail across the Internet.

sniffer (with a lowercase "s") — A program that monitors and analyzes network traffic, detecting bottlenecks and problems. *Note: Sniffer with uppercase S is a registered product name.*

Snooping — In a security context, is unauthorized access to another person's data or company's data.

Social engineering — Includes the practice of obtaining confidential information by manipulation of legitimate users. A social engineer will commonly use the telephone or Internet to trick people into revealing sensitive information.

Software — Instructional coding that manipulates the hardware in a computer system.

SPAM — The practice of sending massive amounts of unsolicited, unwanted, irrelevant, or inappropriate messages, especially commercial advertising in mass quantities.

Spoliation — The deliberate or inadvertent modification, loss, or destruction of evidence by a party who has been put on notice of litigation, but has failed to take appropriate steps to preserve potentially relevant data.

Steganalysis — The practice of detecting and decoding steganography.

Steganography — A cryptographic technique for embedding information in something else.

Stored electronic communications — E-mail while it resides on the e-mail server.

Subject matter expert (SME) — Individual possessing expertise and experience in some topic.

Subpoena — A process to cause a witness to appear and give testimony, commanding him or her to appear before a court therein named at a time therein mentioned to testify for the party named under a penalty therein mentioned.

SunNet Manager — A comprehensive set of tools and services used to perform fundamental tasks in managing a network.

Symbian — A company created by Psion, Nokia, Ericsson, and Motorola in 1998 with the aim of developing and standardizing an operating system that enables mobile phones from different manufacturers to exchange information.

TCP — Transmission Control Protocol.

TCP/IP — Transmission Control Protocol/Internet Protocol.

Technical witness — A person who has performed the actual fieldwork, but does not offer an opinion in court, only the results of his or her findings.

Tempest — A U.S. government code word for a set of standards for limiting electric or electromagnetic radiation emanations from electronic equipment, such as microchips, monitors, or printers.

Temporary or swap files — Data stored temporarily on hard drives. These files, generally hidden and inaccessible, may contain investigative information.

Testimonial evidence — Any witnessed accounts of an incident.

Time division multiple access (TDMA) — A digital air interface technology used in cellular, PCS, and ESMR networks.

Track density — The space between tracks on a disk.

Tracks — A concentric collection of sectors on a hard disk or floppy disk.

UCITA — Uniform Computer Information Transactions Act.

UETA — Uniform Electronic Transactions Act.

Unallocated space — The area of the disk drive where the deleted file resides.

Universal serial bus (USB) — Hardware interface.

UNIX — An operating system cocreated by AT&T researchers Dennis Ritchie and Ken Thompson. UNIX is well known for its relative hardware independence and portable application interfaces. Many big companies are using UNIX servers for their reliability and scalability. Some of the popular UNIX flavors include Linux, Solaris, HP-UX, AIX, etc.

USIM (universal subscriber identity module) — Subscriber identity modules for 3G mobile telephony. They are the same physical size as normal 2G GSM SIM cards.

UTC — Universal Time Coordinated, the international time standard, also known as Greenwich Meridian Time (GMT).

Voir dire — A preliminary examination usually of a juror, to determine competency, interest, or bias that may affect a decision.

Volatile memory — Memory that loses its content when power is turned off or lost.

Volume — Consists of a single floppy disk, a hard drive partition, entire drive, or several drives. It refers to any storage media in the Mac file system.

Walk-through — An initial assessment conducted by carefully walking through an incident scene to evaluate the situation, recognize potential evidence, and determine resources.

WAP (Wireless Application Protocol) — A secure specification that allows users to access information instantly via handheld wireless devices such as mobile phones, pagers, two-way radios, smartphones and communicators.

Web browser — A software application that enables a user to display and interact with text, images, and other information typically located on a Web page at a Web site on the World Wide Web.

WebMail — Users can access e-mail through a browser (such as Internet Explorer) from anywhere in the world, with advanced features (mailboxes, address book).

White-collar crime — Is associated with crime committed by individuals of a higher social class.

Wi-Fi (wireless fidelity) — A wireless feature that is available on Palm Pilots and Pocket PCs that allows wireless communication between the device and a network.

Windows — Microsoft Windows is a range of closed source proprietary commercial operating environments for personal computers and servers. The range was first introduced by Microsoft in 1985 and eventually has come to dominate the world personal computer market. All recent versions of Windows are full-fledged operating systems.

Wiretapping — The monitoring of telephone conversations by a third party, often by covert means.

Witness — Someone who testifies to what he or she has seen, heard, or otherwise observed and who is not a party to the action.

X-Ways Forensics — An advanced computer-examination and data recovery software product.

Zip — A 3.5-inch removable disk drive.

Appendix A

This appendix includes sample forms that were presented throughout the book. They are divided into two categories, namely forms that are used in the forensic investigations and those that are used in a forensic laboratory. Forms include a number of checklists and forms for entering investigative information. Forms for computer system and disk examinations are not included as intense training is required for computer forensics examiners before attempting these tasks.

Investigation Forms

Computer and Electronic Investigation Journal
First Responder Seizure Record
Computer and Electronic Photographic Log
Computer Evidence Receipt
Electronics Evidence Receipt
Computer Forensic Evidence Receipt Checklist
Chain-of-Custody Record
Chain-of-Custody Checklist
Computer Forensic Investigation Checklist

Examination Forms

Computer Forensic Lab Checklist
Computer Forensic Fly-Away Kit
Windows Computer Examination Checklist
Linux Computer Examination Checklist
Macintosh Computer Examination Checklist
Computer Hard Drive Details
Computer Disk Imaging Checklist

Computer and Electronic Investigation Journal

Investigator		Agency	Case
Date/time	Journal entry		

Page ___ of ___

First Responder Seizure Record

Case No.	Case Name	First Responder	
Location of seizure- Complete address			
Details of evidence seized		Where located	
Type: Computer, cell phone, disk, paper, etc.			
Make and model		Serial No. and evidence bag No.	
Acquisition details and comments		Comments	
Provide any login and passwords obtained			
Was equipment connected to a telephone line or LAN?			
Equipment on/off status when seized			
Was equipment switched on or off after seizure?			
Photographs taken?			
Sketch completed?			
Other			
Witness information			
	Witness 1	Witness 2	Witness 3
Name Title Address Phone Dept. Date/time Signature			

Note: One form required for each item seized

Computer and Electronic Photographic Log

Investigator-	Agency -	Case # -
Camera brand-	Camera lens -	
Film type/brand-	Film speed-	Film/digital -

Photo #	Date/Time	Photo Description/Location

Computer and Electronics Chain-of-Custody Record

Case No.:		Evidence No.:	
Client:		Date/Time Received:	
BIOS Time:		Location Found:	
Evidence Description:			
Manufacturer:		Model:	SN:
History/Chain-of-Custody			
Date/Time	By	Action	
Notes:			

Page ___ of ___

Computer and Electronics Chain-of-Custody Checklist

☐	Created unique case and evidence number
☐	Documented an asset tag or serial number that uniquely identifies the evidence
☐	Documented make and model of system the data was taken from
☐	Documented BIOS time
☐	Documented location the evidence was found in (inside case, inside drawer of desk, inside briefcase)
☐	Documented physical description of evidence
☐	Annotated notes for any accesses to the evidence before arrival
☐	Annotated notes for any step that occurs outside of your normal process
☐	Filled in history annotating when you received the drive and from whom
☐	Updated chain-of-custody for each action taken with the original evidence

Computer Evidence Receipt

Case No.:		Receipt No.:		
Items Relinquished by/Title:		Date/Time:		
Organization/Company:		Location/Address:		

Computer(s):

Desktop	Laptop	Server	Hard Drive	Serial No.
☐	☐	☐	☐	
☐	☐	☐	☐	
☐	☐	☐	☐	

Storage Media:

CD-ROM	USB Media	Floppy/Zip	Tape	Subject
☐	☐	☐	☐	
☐	☐	☐	☐	
☐	☐	☐	☐	

Other Materials:

Items Received by/Title:		Signature:	
Organization/Company:		Location/Address:	

Page ____ of ____

Electronics Evidence Receipt

Case No.:		Receipt No.:		

Items Relinquished by/Title:		Date/Time:		

Organization/Company:		Location/Address:		

Electronics:

Cell Phone	PDA	BlackBerry	Other	Serial No.
☐	☐	☐	☐	
☐	☐	☐	☐	
☐	☐	☐	☐	

Storage Media:

USB	Flash	Disk	Other	Subject
☐	☐	☐	☐	
☐	☐	☐	☐	
☐	☐	☐	☐	

Other Materials:

Items Received By/Title:		Signature:		

Organization/Company:		Location/Address:		

Page ___ of ___

Computer and Electronics Evidence Receipt Checklist

☐	Took evidence with authorization
☐	Created unique case and evidence number
☐	Documented an asset tag or serial number that uniquely identifies the evidence
☐	Received signature from owner or manager
☐	Noted date and time of seizure
☐	Completed receipt for all evidence taken
☐	Provided copies to owner or manager

Computer Forensic Investigation Checklist

Task	Date	Signature	Task	Date	Signature
Case No.			Case Name		
Case assigned			Preliminary report		
Secure and protect scene			Hard disks imaged (2)		
Initiate preliminary survey			Disks carved and pattern match		
Evaluate physical evidence options					
Photograph scene			Cell phone evidence retrieved		
Prepare diagram and sketch			Electronic media searched		
Prepare narrative description					
Record and collect physical evidence			Final walk-through		
Retrieve hard drives			Release crime scene		
Retrieve media					
Take inventory of evidence					
Packed evidence					
Transported evidence					
Evidence to forensic lab					

Computer Disk Imaging Checklist

☐	Computer is powered off
☐	Drive is removed and serial number recorded
☐	System is booted with drive removed and BIOS time recorded
☐	Chain-of-custody form filled out
☐	Drive is imaged with forensically sound method
☐	Chain-of-custody updated
☐	Drive either given back or taken with evidence receipt

Hard Drive Details

Case No.: _____   Date: _____

Exhibit Reference No.: _____   Examiner: _____

_____

Make		Model	
Serial No.		Size	
Cylinders		Heads	
Sectors		Tracks	
Jumper settings		Volume label	
No. of partitions			
Partition name 1		Partition name 3	
Partition name 2		Partition name 4	
Software name and version Image 1		Write blocker used	
Software name and version Image 2		Write blocker used	
Time corrected		Time source	
Hash match image 1		Hash match image 2	
Hash verified?			
Original disk location		Reference tag	
Image 1 disk location		Reference tag	
Image 2 disk location		Reference tag	

Computer Forensic
Fly-Away Kit

The computer forensic fly-away kit should contain the following items:

☐   Assorted hand tools including screwdrivers, nut drivers, pliers, snips, flashlight, magnifying glass, and other common tools

☐   Digital camera with date/time stamp and various camera lenses

☐   Digital and hard copies of forms utilized in investigations

☐   Digital or hard copies of policies and procedures

☐   Evidence bag for storing and locking evidence during travel

☐   Manuals for tools utilized

☐   Storage media for capturing hard drive data

☐   Hardware and software tools for the following:

         Write protection

         Acquisition

         Data recovery/discovery

         Pass cracking

         Large storage analysis

         Tools such as FTK, EnCase, Paraben

         Binary/hex analysis

         Malware/virus detection

         Mobile devices (PDA/cell phones)

         Internet history, images, e-mail

         Other specialized tools

Windows Computer Examination Checklist

☐	Windows version documented
☐	Last boot time documented
☐	Last shutdown time documented
☐	"Local" vs. "real" date/time delta identified and resolved
☐	Drive searched for remnants of file system partitions
☐	Log files recovered and examined
☐	Drive searched for mail spools and Internet mail
☐	INFO2 records recovered
☐	Internet history recovered
☐	Documents carved from unallocated (Microsoft Office, PDF, etc.)
☐	Drive checked for wiping
☐	Deleted files recovered
☐	Printer spools recovered
☐	XP–UserAssist records recovered
☐	Archives decompressed and examined
☐	Keyword searches conducted as appropriate
☐	Summary of findings/report/conclusions/opinion written

Linux Computer Examination Checklist

☐	Linux distribution and version documented
☐	Last boot time documented
☐	Last shutdown time documented
☐	"Local" vs. "real" date/time delta identified and resolved
☐	Drive searched for remnants of file system partitions
☐	Swap space examined
☐	Log files recovered and examined
☐	User shell history files checked
☐	Drive searched for mail spools and Internet mail
☐	Internet history recovered
☐	Documents recovered from unallocated (Microsoft Office, PDF, etc.)
☐	Drive checked for wiping
☐	Deleted files recovered
☐	Printer spools recovered
☐	Archives decompressed and examined
☐	Keyword searches conducted as appropriate
☐	Summary of findings/report/conclusions/opinion written

Macintosh Computer Examination Checklist

☐	OS version documented
☐	Last boot time documented
☐	Last shutdown time documented
☐	"Local" vs. "real" date/time delta identified and resolved
☐	Partition waste space searched for file system artifacts
☐	Large files and image files examined
☐	Log files recovered and examined
☐	User shell history files checked
☐	Drive searched for mail spools
☐	Internet history recovered
☐	Documents carved from unallocated (Microsoft Office, PDF, etc.)
☐	Drive checked for wiping
☐	Deleted files recovered
☐	Cache files and mbox files preprocessed
☐	Archives decompressed and examined
☐	Keyword searches conducted as appropriate
☐	Summary of findings/report/conclusions/opinion written

Computer and Electronic Forensic Lab Checklist

☐	Ensure lab door locks and personnel have controlled access to the keys and/or combination
☐	Ensure the cleaning staff and others do not have access to the facility unless they are properly escorted
☐	Ensure the walls and ceiling are constructed in such a way that easy access is prevented (e.g., preventing someone from climbing over the wall and dropping through the ceiling)
☐	Ensure protective mechanisms are in place for disastrous events such as fire, flooding, lightning, and other events common to the environment
☐	Ensure there is a physically secure evidence room or locker within the lab with a separate key or combination lock than what's used to get into the lab
☐	Ensure there are written policies and procedures for lab controls, evidence controls, forensic examinations, and validation of tools and equipment
☐	Ensure a formal case management system is in place
☐	Ensure there is a separate network connection for Internet access that is separate from the forensic examination computer
☐	Ensure the forensic examination computer is isolated from the network
☐	Make certain there is a central place to store documents (could be in the evidence room or locker if it is large enough and fits your storage needs)
☐	Ensure there is a designated document librarian for centralized and consistent control of case data
☐	Ensure there is a standard validated field kit including the hardware and software tools used in most investigations
☐	Ensure availability of extra copies of forms, such as Chain-of-Custody Forms and Evidence Receipts
☐	Ensure hardware and storage are consistent with the environment commonly investigated, including access to special equipment, extra drives and other needed media

☐	Ensure availability of hardware and/or software tools for:
	■ Write protection
	■ Acquisition
	■ Data recovery/discovery
	■ Internet history, images, e-mail
	■ Password cracking
	■ Mobile devices (PDA/cell phone)
	■ Malware/virus detection
	■ Binary analysis
	■ Large storage analysis
	■ Multifunction use (e.g., EnCase, Paraben Tools, FTK, SMART)
	■ Other specialized tools helpful for the investigated environments

Appendix B

Forensic Cases and Exercises

This appendix contains a number of exercises that can be worked to reinforce information presented in this book. Access to the Internet is required for many of these exercises. Do not forget to practice safe Internet surfing! Make sure your computer files are backed up. Your workstation should have the latest operating system (OS) updates, virus protection, and antispyware installed. Many of these exercises require access to the Internet.

1. Two sample cases are presented that involve computer-related evidence: one criminal in nature and one that involves a policy violation.

Case 1

John Q. has reported to the local police that his ten-year-old son is missing. John Q. is a wealthy businessman located in a small suburb of a major city. John Q. has received an e-mail asking for a large ransom. How can computer forensics be used to help solve this potential crime?

Action

A report must be made to the appropriate authorities. A determination must be made if a criminal situation exists. A forensic department can use the e-mail transmission in its investigation. If a suspect is located, information may be gleaned from the transmitting computer and from the Internet service provider and used as evidence. If a telephone or cell phone was used, evidence might be obtained from the telephone carriers.

Exercise

Develop an alternative scenario to the one above. Describe the types of forensic evidence that might be identified and retrieved.

Case 2

Mary J. has been using the corporate Internet connection to surf for personal items. What are the issues?

Action

Several questions must be answered. Who filed the complaint? Are there any corporate policies regarding the personal use of the Internet? Must employees sign a document that specifies the use of the Internet? Does the organization use resources to track employee usage of the Internet? Is Mary a quality employee or a goof-off? Who is Mary's boss?

Exercises

1. Provide a comparison of outcomes where corporate computer-use policies exist and where they do not. Describe how a case can be made if there are computer-use policies.

2. Develop a list of terms and definitions presented in Section 2510 of Title 18, Crimes and Criminal Procedure. Use a search engine and look for "Crimes and Criminal Procedure." Look at the categories of crimes.

3. Identify sample computer and Internet-use policies and procedures that are currently implemented in government and educational sectors. Searching for "computer use policies" will produce a large list of Web sites.

4. Develop an overview of the various laws that apply to electronic communications. A good search parameter is "Electronic Communications Privacy Act."

5. Provide a matrix of features available on the various forensic software tools. A good place to start is the Web site of Digital Intelligence.

6. Identify training organizations that provide educational programs in the field of computer forensic investigations. InfoSec Institute and SANS Institute are good places to start.

7. Decode a hexadecimal stream of data into readable ASCII text. The user must locate a complete ASCII table to accomplish this task. There are also a number of hexadecimal conversion utilities on the Web; just surf for "hex conversion." Note that some of these routines only convert one character at a time, whereas others will convert the entire string. Hex values are preceded by a percent sign (%).

%53%65%6e%64%20%6f%6e%65%20%74%68%6f%75%73%61%6e%64%2
0%6f%72%20%53%61%6d%20%69%73%20%68%69%73%74%6f%72%79

After converting this hex string, provide a short statement that describes the type of incident and potential evidence that might be gathered.

8. A number of employees have received e-mails asking for personal account information. A number of these e-mails were sent from organizations where the recipients did not have an account. Some of the personnel forwarded the suspect e-mails to the security office. A preliminary investigation by the security department reveals a similarity between the e-mails. An investigation is initiated. Document the steps taken on a journal form.

What is this e-mail effort called? Why is it a problem for the organization and the employees? What should be the security department's response to this activity?

9. Log into CERT (www.cert.org/) and provide a summary of the currently active technology threats. How can the security department use these alerts? What tools might be used in investigating these incidents?

10. Provide an analysis of Encase (www.guidancesoftware.com/) and FTK (www.accessdata.com/) forensic tools. Show the features of each tool, cost of the packages, advantages and disadvantages, and any other relevant details.

11. Obtain a configuration and cost of a computer forensic workstation for a small corporate laboratory. Include all hardware and software components required when performing simple forensic examinations. Use a search engine with "forensic workstation" as the search parameter.

12. Download a review copy of Encase (www.guidancesoftware.com/) and FTK (www.accessdata.com/) and provide an analysis of its usefulness and utility. Describe the process that these packages use for managing an investigation.

13. Price out a portable forensic evidence kit for corporate security investigations. Include items such as packaging, labels, and anything else an examiner might need to investigate a computer incident. Use a search engine with "forensic kit" as the search parameter. You will need to scan for computer forensic supplies as many kits are related to DNA, fingerprint, and other personal evidence.

14. Log onto the ARIN WHOIS Web site (http://www.arin.net/whois/) and look at the options available for tracking IP addresses. Try several different known IP addresses and several at random. Provide an explanation of the results.

15. This exercise involves the use of Web tools to investigate e-mail scams and phishing attacks. The investigator must have a copy of the suspect e-mail and have access to the Internet. It is necessary to look at the e-mail header information. Most e-mail systems have a "view" function. The domain name or IP addresses can be gleaned using this feature. The sending IP address is usually the Internet work organization; however, the fake URL may or may not be the suspect phisher. Use the Web site to identify the IP address. Use this information to identify the domain. Send a transmission to this organization reporting the phishing scam.

16. DOS commands can be used in e-mail investigations. Use the CMD or COMMAND instruction in the RUN block to get a DOS prompt. Look up DOS commands on the Web. Use CD\ and DIR/P to get started.

Type in the TRACERT (trace route) command followed by any of the IP addresses. What is the result?

Type in TELNET followed by an IP address. What is the result? Did you get an error message or a login prompt? What should you do next?

Typing in PING and the IP address will let you know if the address can be reached. Typing EXIT will get you out of DOS.

17. This exercise involves the use of MS Outlook. Select a SPAM message or a phishing e-mail. If you do not get any, look in the Trash folder. Select the header option on the e-mail screen. Decode the domain name of the sender using the internic.com/whois.html Web tool. Use the arin.net/whois Web tool to identify the Internetwork organization. Use the same DOS commands in number 16. What did you learn that was useful? What causes the differences between the times and dates? What is the UTC?

18. Use a search engine such as Google to locate some personal information. See if you can find your home address, a mapquest entry, telephone numbers, cell phone numbers, financial information, education, property transactions, etc.

19. Search the www.familywatchdog.us Web site provided by the National Sex Offender Registry. Search for sex offender lists in the various states. How would these Web sites assist in e-mail investigations?

20. Search for sites with the following domain name suffixes: .aero, .arpa, .biz, .cat, .com, .coop, .edu, .info, .int, .jobs, .mobi, .museum, .name, .net, .org, .pro, or .travel. What are the identities of these site domains? What would these suffixes tell the investigator about the suspect?

21. This exercise involves the use of RFC 2076. Select an e-mail message and access the header information. Provide a definition for all field names displayed in the e-mail header. Describe which headers are the most useful in e-mail examinations.

22. The use of file transport protocol (FTP) can be used to move digital files across the network, between computers. The technique can be used to move illegal documents. Use the DOS FTP command to access a computer. Look up the options of the FTP command. The format is FTP [IP Address]. What is the response from the remote device? What is anonymous FTP?

23. Identify the various cell phone models currently available. Identify the different interface cables required for cell phone investigations. This is a large endeavor, so you might limit the search to one vendor.

24. Identify all the fields associated with the SIM. Provide a short description of each field.

25. Research the password cracker market and provide a report on features and cost for each product.

26. The investigator of an incident scene is looking for physical and testimonial evidence. There are six activities that must be addressed in this endeavor. Describe each and provide a comment referencing its relevance. Look in Chapter 7 for assistance.

27. There are a number of basic steps involved in a computer incident scene search. List all and give a brief description of each. Think about managing the incident/ crime scene.

28. Describe the differences in investigating an incident involving a single, stand-alone computer device and one that involves a local area network (LAN). The networked computer will usually be located in a computer center or commercial office area.

29. Identify the various interface cables that will be required to image a computer hard drive. A good place to start is BlackBox.com.

30. The development of a forensic lab for computers and mobile phones involves numerous specialized tools. Describe both hardware and software tools that might be utilized in such a lab.

Appendix C

Answers to Review Questions

Chapter 1

1. Acquisition, identification, evaluation, and presentation.
2. False.
3. True.
4. False.
5. Circumstantial, physical, and hearsay.
6. True.
7. True.
8. Murder, kidnapping, theft, assault, stalking, burglary, espionage, forgery, drugs, organized crime, prostitution, robbery.
9. Proactive.
10. Electronic evidence is data and information of some investigative value that is stored on or transmitted by an electronic device. Latent evidence is present or has potential, but is not evident or active.

Chapter 2

1. GAAP.
2. A subpoena is a process to cause a witness to appear and give testimony, commanding him to appear before a court therein named at a time therein mentioned to testify for the party named under a penalty therein mentioned. A warrant authorizes the officer

to seize particularly described items and to bring them before the court that issued the warrant.

3. A felony is described as a crime of a graver or more atrocious nature than those designated as a misdemeanor. A misdemeanor is described as any crime that is not a felony.

4. Sniffer.

5. Wiretapping.

6. FBI, SEARCH, HTCIA, FACT, NC3, USPS.

7. Stored electronic communications refers to e-mail while it resides on the e-mail server.

8. Ascertaining whether the device(s) in question may contain information relevant to the subject of concern. Assisting in preparing and responding to interrogatories (written questions). Planning and providing expert testimony. Retrieving and examining information that is accessible only through the use of forensics techniques, software, hardware, and methods. Developing court reports.

9. Modifying system facilities, operating systems, or disk partitions, attempting to crash or tie up a computer, damaging or vandalizing computing facilities, equipment, software, or computer files.

10. Privacy Protection Act.

Chapter 3

1. Civil law is concerned with wrongs inflicted upon an organization or individual that result in some damage or loss. Criminal law is concerned with individual conduct that violates governmental laws that were enacted for public protection. Regulatory law sets standards of performance and conduct expected by various entities.

2. Fraud, cyber-terrorism, child molestation, network intrusions, destruction of data and information, modification of data or data-diddling, denial-of-service (DoS) and distributed DoS (DDoS), eavesdropping, software piracy, music piracy, theft of logins and passwords, malicious code and programs.

3. Customer information, credit card data, e-mail transmissions, image files and printouts, Internet activity logs, Internet browser history, online financial institution records, telephone records, databases, testimonial documents, chat logs.

4. Identity theft can involve social engineering activities, dumpster diving, mail theft, ATM ID theft, and numerous scams.

5. Address books, configuration files, e-mail transmissions, executable programs, Internet activity logs, system logs, IP addresses and usernames.

6. Forensic accounting is accounting that is suitable for legal review by including data that has been arrived at in a scientific fashion.

7. Software downloading, spam control, inappropriate material, intellectual property, viruses, worms and Trojan horses, malicious intruders, DoS and DDoS.

8. A policy designates a required process or procedure within an organization.

9. Cyber-terrorism includes the convergence of terrorism and cyberspace. Cyber-terrorism is any premeditated, politically motivated attack against information, computer systems, computer programs, and data, which results in violence against noncomba-

tant targets by subnational groups or clandestine agents.
10. "SPAM" mail is the practice of sending massive amounts of e-mail promotions or advertisements (and scams) to people that have not asked for it.

Chapter 4

1. Information is gathered by overhearing conversations made on cell phones, from faxes and e-mails, by hacking into computers, from telephone and e-mail scams, and even from careless online shopping and banking.
2. Scam baiting.
3. Credit information requests, check cashing, charities, free prizes, job advertisements, free credit reports, pyramid schemes and chain letters, questionnaires, work-at-home.
4. Equifax, Experian, and TransUnion.
5. Identity theft.
6. Fraud.
7. Online auctions (51 percent) and general merchandise (19 percent).
8. Dumpster diving.
9. Social engineering.
10. SPAM.

Chapter 5

1. Electronic business.
2. Intrusion detection is a type of security management for computers and networks. Intrusion prevention is any device that exercises access control to protect computers from exploitation.
3. Mainframes.
4. Client/server describes the relationship between two computer programs in which one program, the client, makes a service request from another program, the server, which fulfills the request.
5. The DBMS manages the data files in the database and may provide independence of programs and data. Data are the raw elements that make up the files, image graphics.
6. E-mail files, documents/text files, address books, mailing lists, calendars, Internet bookmarks/favorites, spreadsheet files, database files, audio/video files.
7. History files, system logs, temporary files, hidden files, configuration files, print spool files, cookies.
8. Deleted files, free space, unallocated space, bad clusters, hidden partitions, lost clusters, reserved areas, slack space, metadata, software registration information, system areas, computer date/time.
9. RAID, IDE, SCSI, serial ATA, USB/Fire Wire drives, CDs/DVDs, 4 mm, 8 mm tapes, zip disk, floppies, flash drive, USB, computer hard disk drives, laptop hard disk drives, server hard disk drives, external hard disk drives, mobile phone SIM cards, tape.

10. Appointment calendars, caller ID, electronic serial number, e-mail, memos, PIN numbers, password, phone book, text messages, voice mail, instant messages, voice mail password, Web browsers, calling card numbers, debit card numbers.

Chapter 6

1. Flat blade and Phillips screwdrivers, torque drivers, hex-nut drivers, needle-nose pliers, secure-bit drivers, small tweezers, specialized computer case screwdrivers, standard pliers, star nut drivers, wire cutters, bolt cutters, hammer.
2. Antistatic bags, Faraday bags, antistatic bubble wrap, evidence bags, evidence boxes, evidence tape/seals, crime-scene tape, packaging material, such as styrofoam and styrofoam peanuts, packing tape, sturdy boxes of various sizes.
3. Antistatic gloves, large rubber bands, magnifying glass, seizure disks of various capacities, flashlight, floppy disks, printer paper, hand truck, power strip, extension cord.
4. Using an imaging product, you can clone (copy) the entire contents of a hard disk to a portable medium such as a writeable CD. Examinations must not be conducted on original disk media, because the data could be compromised and therefore is not useful in legal proceedings.
5. A sniffer (with a lowercase "s") is a program and/or hardware that monitors and analyzes network traffic, detecting bottlenecks and problems. A sniffer is used to collect evidence of network intrusions.
6. Probe.
7. Message digest-5 (MD5) is a hashing algorithm that is used to verify data integrity through the creation of a 128-bit message digest from data input. Secure hash algorithm (SHA) is a set of related cryptographic hash functions. SHA-1 creates a 256-bit message digest.
8. Hardware, software, and procedural.
9. True.
10. NetView, OpenView, SunNet Manager, and RMON.

Chapter 7

1. Testimonial evidence is any witnessed accounts of an incident. Physical evidence refers to any material items that would be present on the crime scene.
2. A case file is the official record of actions taken and evidence collected at the scene.
3. A sketch establishes a permanent record of items, conditions, and distance/size relationships. They also supplement the photograph record.
4. Narrative description, photographic log, diagram/sketch, evidence recovery log, latent print log.
5. Law enforcement and security personnel identify, seize, and protect such devices in accordance with applicable statutes, policies and best practices and guidelines, because any and all computer and electronic evidence might be useful in future civil and criminal actions.
6. Scene recognition, scene documentation, and evidence collection.
7. Methods, techniques, and procedures.

8. Secure and protect scene. Initiate preliminary survey. Evaluate physical evidence possibilities. Prepare narrative description. Photograph scene. Prepare diagram/sketch of scene. Conduct detailed search/record and collect physical evidence. Conduct final survey. Release crime scene.

9. Determine all the locations that might need to be searched. Look for any specifics relating to hardware and software that must be addressed. Identify possible personnel and equipment needs for the investigation. Determine which devices can be physically removed from the site. Identify all individuals who had access to the computer or electronic resources.

10. Team leader. Photographer and photographic log recorder. Sketch preparer. Evidence recorder/evidence recovery personnel. Specialists.

Chapter 8

1. White collar crime.

2. Corporate espionage. Discrimination issues. Employee Internet or e-mail abuse. Improper accounting practices. Misuse of company resources. Pornography. Security and computer policy violations. Sexual harassment. Theft of company property. Unauthorized disclosure of corporate information and data.

3. Capital crimes where information and data is stored electronically. Crimes against the state. Criminal fraud and deception. Cyber-crimes. Cyber-terrorism. Industrial and governmental espionage. Damage assessment following an incident. Information warfare. Petty crimes where information and data is stored electronically. Unauthorized disclosure of government data or information.

4. Has a crime been committed? Explain the incident and the depth of the situation. Preserve any evidence. Keep the incident from reoccurring.

5. Chain-of-custody.

6. Journal and chain-of-custody.

7. Date, time, and configurations are preserved on computer systems via an internal battery.

8. Keep electronic evidence from electromagnetic sources. Avoid storing evidence in vehicles for prolonged time periods because circuit boards and storage media could warp. Ensure that any computers or other devices too large or bulky to box are secured in the vehicle against shock or excessive vibrations. Maintain the chain-of-custody on all evidence transported.

9. Investigate data and settings from installed applications and programs. Look at the general system structures. Identify factors relating to the user's activities. Identify and recover all files including those deleted. Access and copy hidden and protected files. Access and copy temporary files. Use forensic techniques to recover residue from previously deleted files.

10. Cell phones and other handheld wireless devices collected at the scene must be immediately placed in Faraday bags to avoid corruption of evidence contained in the device.

Chapter 9

1. SCSI (small computer system interface).
2. Windows, UNIX, Macintosh.
3. RAM (random access memory).
4. ASCII (American standard code for information interchange).
5. Heads.
6. Windows NT.
7. Linux.
8. Clump.
9. Metadata.
10. A standard interface for IBM-compatible hard drives.

Chapter 10

1. Tempest.
2. Forensic analysis.
3. SATA (serial advanced technology attachment).
4. Electrostatic discharge.
5. Forensic recovery of evidence device.
6. Case initiation. Evidence processing. Forensic imaging. Preprocessing analysis. Forensic analysis. Report writing/briefing. Peer review. Case archiving.
7. Make and model. Serial number. Capacity and size. Cylinders and heads. Sectors. Jumper settings. Volume label. Number of partitions and names.
8. The computer forensic lab should be equipped with imaging software, acquisition and seizure tools, hashing software, e-mail tracers, password recovery kit, and latent data recovery tools. Imaging products for hard drives can be either hardware or software based, or both.
9. Computer is powered off. Drive is removed and serial number recorded. System is booted with drive removed and BIOS time recorded. Chain-of-custody form filled out. Drive is imaged with forensically sound method. Chain-of-custody updated. Drive is either given back or taken with evidence receipt given.
10. Create unique case and evidence number. Document an asset tag or serial number that uniquely identifies the evidence. Document the make and model of system where the data was retrieved. Document BIOS time. Document location the evidence was found in (inside case, inside drawer of desk, inside briefcase). Document physical description of evidence. Annotate notes for any accesses to the evidence before arrival. Annotate notes for any step that occurs outside of the normal process. Fill in history annotating when evidence was received and from whom. Update chain-of-custody for each action taken with the original evidence.

Chapter 11

1. Carving.
2. Redaction.

3. When collecting evidence, proceed from the volatile to the less volatile. Work on evidence first that can be easily destroyed.
4. Ultimate Toolkit, EnCase Forensic, Autopsy Forensic Browser.
5. iLook Investigator.
6. Imaging.
7. International Association of Computer Investigative Specialists (IACIS).
8. Request for Comments (RFC) 3227.
9. $2,000 to $5,000.
10. Residual data refers to data that is not active on a computer system.

Chapter 12

1. SMTP (Simple Mail Transfer Protocol).
2. MIME (multipurpose Internet mail extensions).
3. DNS (domain naming system).
4. ARIN WHOIS.
5. RFC 2076.
6. A total of 32 bits in 4–8 bit segments, called dotted decimal notation. Each 8 bits represents one number, i.e., 128.127.254.1 or 10000000.01111111.11111110.00000001.
7. RFC 2822 (replaces RFC 822).
8. AfriNIC, APNIC, LACNIC, RIPE, InternIC.
9. TCP/IP.
10. Encase, FTK, FINALeMAIL, Sawmill, DBXtract, Mailbag Assistant, E-mail Examiner.

Chapter 13

1. MTSO.
2. Subscriber identity module (SIM).
3. Uniquely identifies the subscriber, determines phone number, contains algorithms for network authentication.
4. Memory card.
5. An incorrect PIN will cause the device to become "PIN-locked" and cannot be used until it is reset.
6. Accuracy, acceptance, affordability, capability, comprehensiveness, determinism, quality, usability, verifiability.
7. Inherent capabilities of the phone implemented by the manufacturer. Network services subscribed to and used by the user. Modifications made to the phone by the service provider or network operator. Modifications made to the phone by the user.
8. Cell Seizure, ForensicSIM, USIMdetective, SIMCON, MOBILedit!, BitPim, TULP2G.
9. Forensic card reader.
10. PDA Seizure, pdd, Pilot-Link, POSE, dd.

Chapter 14

1. Technical witness.
2. Expert witness.
3. False.
4. It contains an extensive resumé of professional history that includes work history, cases, testimony, and training, along with details of other skills.
5. Voir dire.
6. False.
7. Discovery.
8. Forensic accountant.
9. A lay witness is a person, with knowledge based on firsthand observations, whose testimony is helpful to determine the facts at issue. An expert witness is a person who has knowledge in a field and can offer an opinion in addition to the facts being presented.
10. Keep the audience in mind, particularly the jury and sometimes the court.

APPENDIX D

Binary and Hexadecimal Number Systems

This appendix includes information that will assist the reader in understanding the process for converting decimal numbers to both a binary representation and hexadecimal representation. Also included in this appendix are the binary representations that are used in the ASCII system. An understanding of these processes is required for the computer forensic examiner to successfully identify and retrieve latent data from suspect systems. A general overview will be provided in addition to a step-by-step process for accomplishing these conversions.

Overview

A number of network and data-processing applications require a conversion to binary or hexadecimal in order for the individual programs to successfully produce the desired results. Binary digits are used to form the ASCII characters that make up words. It is also necessary to understand IP addressing schemes and the concept of netmasks. These network addresses are programmed in the network devices' routing tables. Network surveillance programs often display their information in a hexadecimal format. Network monitors such as sniffers and protocol analyzers display information in both binary and hexadecimal.

Decimal to Binary Conversion

Decimal numbers are in a base 10 format and binary numbers are in a base 2 format. There are ten different digits in decimal and two different digits in binary. To start this process, it is necessary to create a table of binary representations. Binary can be represented as 2^n, where n is a number from 0 to N. When converting IP addresses, n can vary from 0 to 7, because an IP address is 8 bits. This produces the following table for converting an IP address.

Decimal	7	6	5	4	3	2	1	0
Binary	128	64	32	16	8	4	2	1

The decimal digits of 0 through 10, therefore, can be represented in binary as follows:

Decimal	Binary
0	00000000
1	00000001
2	00000010
3	00000011
4	00000100
5	00000101
6	00000110
7	00000111
8	00001000
9	00001001
10	00001010

Additionally, when converting IP addresses, it is useful to know the binary representation of the various netmasks. The following table shows these values.

Decimal	Binary
128	10000000
192	11000000
224	11100000
240	11110000
248	11111000
252	11111100

254	11111110
255	11111111

A simple conversion of an IP address from decimal is as follows:

IP address in decimal: 10.10.10.1
IP address in binary: 00001010.00001010.00001010.00000001

The same process applied to a netmask is as follows:

Netmask in decimal: 255.240.0.0
Netmask in binary: 11111111.11110000.00000000.00000000

The first step in the conversion process is to create the 2^n heading. The next step is to identify which of these numbers is larger than the number to be converted to binary, and then use the next smallest number as the base for the conversion. For example, use the decimal number 97 to convert to binary.

The options that are available are 1, 2, 4, 8, 16, 32, 64, 128, etc. Select 64 as it is the next smallest number from 97.

Binary base 2 scale   128 64 32 16 8 4 2 1
                          0 1 1 0 0 0 0 1

Is there a 64 in 97? Yes. Is there a 32 in 64? Yes. Is there a 16 in 1? No. Is there an 8 in 1? No. Is there a 4 in 1? No. Is there a 2 in 1? No. Is there a 1 in 1? Yes.

97
64
=   33
32
=   1
1
=   0

To check the binary answer, add the elements of the binary scale that have 1s: $64 + 32 + 1 = 97$.

Binary to Hexadecimal Conversion

Hexadecimal characters include the digits 0 through 9 and the alpha characters A through F.

A table that provides a conversion between decimal, binary, and hexadecimal for the digits 0 through 15 follows:

Decimal	Binary	Hexadecimal
0	00000000	0
1	00000001	1
2	00000010	2
3	00000011	3
4	00000100	4
5	00000101	5
6	00000110	6
7	00000111	7
8	00001000	8
9	00001001	9
10	00001010	A
11	00001011	B
12	00001100	C
13	00001101	D
14	00001110	E
15	00001111	F

One method to convert decimal numbers to hexadecimal is to first use the previous process of converting decimal numbers to binary and then convert the binary digits to hexadecimal.

Using the previous example of a decimal 97 and a binary equivalent of 01100001, proceed as follows:

Binary 0 1 1 0 0 0 0 1 divide the binary string into bits of four digits: 0 1 1 0 | 0 0 0 1

Create a new scale of "8 4 2 1" for each four digits.

8 4 2 1 | 8 4 2 1
0 1 1 0 | 0 0 0 1

Multiply the scale by the binary digits and add.

0 4 2 0 0 0 0 1
  6 | 1

The hexadecimal representation of decimal 97 is 61.

Binary Complement (Logical AND)

The process required to identify the network addresses that must be programmed in routers and other layer 3 devices is called "bitwise AND." Basically, the IP address and the netmask are converted to binary and the complement is taken between the two binary strings. The resulting binary string is converted back to decimal for optioning the router. When performing AND operations, each of the pairs of binary 1s and 0s is multiplied together. An example of this operation is as follows:

Binary string A 1 0 1 0 1 0 1 0
Binary string B 0 1 1 1 0 0 1 0
AND result 0 0 1 0 0 0 1 0

This process can be applied to a IPv4 32 bit address. First, convert the IP address to a binary representation. Next, convert the netmask to a binary representation. It is important that all three dots, eight 1s and 0s be properly aligned for this process to work correctly. A bit-wise AND using the IP address and the netmask produces the network address. This binary representation is then converted back into a decimal address. An example of an IP address and a netmask complement operation is as follows:

IP address	192.10.249.5	11000000.00001010.11111001.00000101
Netmask	255.255.254.0	11111111.11111111.11111110.00000000
Network address	192.10.248.0	11000000.00001010.11111000.00000000

ASCII

The American Standard Code for Information Interchange (ASCII) provides for a representation of 128 different characters, including uppercase and lowercase, numerals, punctuation, and symbols. ASCII uses a series of seven bits to form each character. This extract represents the uppercase letters A through Z. There are numerous ASCII tables that contain all 128 characters located on the Web.

Decimal	Hex	Binary	Value
065	041	01000001	A
066	042	01000010	B
067	043	01000011	C
068	044	01000100	D
069	045	01000101	E
070	046	01000110	F
071	047	01000111	G
072	048	01001000	H

073	049	01001001	I
074	04A	01001010	J
075	04B	01001011	K
076	04C	01001100	L
077	04D	01001101	M
078	04E	01001110	N
079	04F	01001111	O
080	050	01010000	P
081	051	01010001	Q
082	052	01010010	R
083	053	01010011	S
084	054	01010100	T
085	055	01010101	U
086	056	01010110	V
087	057	01010111	W
088	058	01011000	X
089	059	01011001	Y
090	05A	01011010	Z

The computer forensic examiner would use the ASCII table hex and binary values to search disk files for pattern-matching of specific character strings. The hex pattern "053045058" would translate to "SEX." Many of the current forensic tools will provide the conversion from hex to ASCII automatically.

Bibliography

"Child Predators on the Internet." World Wide Web. http://us.geocities.com/Capitol-Hill/7836/predator.html. Accessed on June 30, 2006.

Electronic Discovery Resources. "Sample Electronic Discovery Interrogatories and Requests for Production". World Wide Web. http://www.discoveryresources.org/docs/eddrequest.doc. Accessed on June 20, 2006.

Federal Bar Association Federal Litigation Section. "Comment of the Federal Litigation Section, Federal Bar Association in Response to the Inquiry from the Discovery Subcommittee Advisory Committee on Civil Rules Regarding Discovery of Electronic Materials." December 9, 2002. World Wide Web. http://www.kenwithers.com/rulemaking/civilrules/ed06.pdf. Accessed on June 5, 2006.

IACIS. "Forensic Examination of Computers and Digital and Electronic Evidence." World Wide Web. http://www.iacis.info/iacisv2/pages/forensicprocedures.php. Accessed on June 3, 2006.

IETF. RFC 3227. "Guidelines for Evidence Collection and Archiving." World Wide Web. http://www.faqs.org/rfcs/rfc3227.html. Accessed in February 2002.

IOCE. "Guidelines for Best Practice in the Forensic Examination of Digital Technology." May 2002.

Jansen, W. and R. Ayers. "An Overview and Analysis of PDA Forensic Tools." (NIST). World Wide Web. http://csrc.nist.gov/mobilesecurity/Publications/ForensicArticle-DI-fin.pdf. Accessed in 2006.

Netsmartz. "Keeping Kids and Teens Safer on the Internet." World Wide Web. http://www.netsmartz.org/. Accessed on June 30, 2006.

National Institute of Standards and Technology (NIST). NISTIR 7250. "Cell Phone Forensic Tools: An Overview and Analysis." World Wide Web. http://csrc.nist.gov/publications/nistir/nistir-7250.pdf. Accessed in October 2005.

National Institute of Standards and Technology (NIST). NISTIR 7100. "An Overview and Analysis of PDA Forensic Tools." World Wide Web. http://csrc.nist.gov/publications/nistir/nistir-7100-PDAForensics.pdf. Accessed in August 2004.

OhioCopsOnLine. "Computer Forensics —Stopping the Internet Criminal." World Wide Web. http://www.acopsview.net/computer/. Accessed on June 5, 2006.

Phillips, A., B. Nelson, F. Enfinger, and C. Steuart. Guide to Computer Forensics and Investigations. 1st Ed., Thomson/Course Technology: Boston. 2004.

Steen, S. and J. Hassell, Computer Forensics 101. Ph.D. thesis. October 2004.

SWGDE. "Best Practices for Computer Forensics." World Wide Web. http://ncfs.org/swgde/documents/swgde2006/Best_Practices_for_Computer_ Forensics%20July06.pdf. Accessed on April 12, 2006.

USDOJ. Computer Crime and Intellectual Property Section (CCIPS)—Criminal Division.

"Searching and Seizing Computers and Obtaining Electronic Evidence in Criminal Investigations." World Wide Web. http://www.cybercrime.gov/s&smanual2002.htm. Accessed in July 2002.

USDOJ. Office of Justice Programs. "Electronic Crime Scene Investigation: A Guide for First Responders." World Wide Web. http://www.ncjrs.gov/txtfiles1/nij/187736.txt. Accessed in July 2001.

USDOJ. Office of Justice Programs: NIJ. "Crime Scene Investigation —A Guide for Law Enforcement." World Wide Web. http://www.ncjrs.gov/txtfiles1/nij/178280.txt. Accessed in January 2000.

USDOJ. Office of Justice Programs: NIJ. "Forensic Examination of Digital Evidence: A Guide for Law Enforcement." World Wide Web. http://www.ncjrs.gov/pdffiles1/ nij/199408.pdf. Accessed in April 2004.

U.S. Secret Service. "Best Practices for Seizing Electronic Evidence." World Wide Web. http://www.ustreas.gov/usss/electronic_evidence.shtml. Accessed in 2006.

Whitman, M. E., "Computer Forensics in the Academic Environment." October 21, 2004.

Index

Milton Keynes UK
Ingram Content Group UK Ltd.
UKHW021834071024
449327UK00021B/1494